CLASSIC READINGS IN OPERATIONS MANAGEMENT

CLASSIC READINGS IN OPERATIONS MANAGEMENT

VICTOR E. SOWER
Sam Houston State University

JAIDEEP MOTWANI
Grand Valley State University

MICHAEL J. SAVOIE
Integrated Resources Group, Inc.
University of New Orleans

THE DRYDEN PRESS
Harcourt Brace College Publishers

Fort Worth   Philadelphia   San Diego   New York   Orlando   Austin   San Antonio
Toronto   Montreal   London   Sydney   Tokyo

Acquisitions Editor:	**Scott Isenberg**
Developmental Editor:	**Tracy Morse**
Project Editor:	**Sheila M. Spahn**
Art Director:	**Brian Salisbury**
Production Manager:	**Erin Gregg**
Electronic Publishing Coordinator:	**Ellie McKenzie**
Product Manager:	**Scott Timian**
Marketing Assistant:	**Kathleen Sharp**
Permissions Editor:	**Elizabeth Banks**
Copy Editor:	**Pamela Whiting**
Indexer:	**Leoni McVey**
Compositor:	**Electronic Publishing**
Text Type:	**10/13 Times Roman and Galliard**
Cover:	**The Detroit Institute of Art, Diego Rivera *Detroit Industry***

Requests for permission to make copies of any part of the work should be mailed to: Permissions Department, Harcourt Brace & Company, 6277 Sea Harbor Drive, Orlando, Florida 32887-6777.

Address for orders:
The Dryden Press, 6277 Sea Harbor Drive, Orlando, FL 32887-6777
1-800-782-4479 or 1-800-433-0001 (in Florida)

Address for editorial correspondence:
The Dryden Press, 301 Commerce Street, Suite 3700, Fort Worth, TX 76102

ISBN: 0-03-098054-2

Library of Congress Catalog Card Number: 94-69133

Printed in the United States of America.

4 5 6 7 8 9 1 2 3 067 9 8 7 6 5 4 3 2 1

The Dryden Press
Harcourt Brace College Publishers

Credits Page 326, Appeared in *Harvard Business Review,* November/December 1987 with article by David A. Garvin, "Competing on the Eight Dimensions of Quality." © Leo Cullum. Page 464, Appeared in *Harvard Business Review* July/August 1986 in an article by Wickham Skinner, "The Productivity Paradox," 57. © Ed Fisher.

THE DRYDEN PRESS SERIES IN MANAGERIAL SCIENCE AND QUANTITATIVE METHODS

COSTIN
Readings in Total Quality Management

ETIENNE-HAMILTON
Operations Strategies for Competitive Advantage: Text and Cases

FINCH AND LUEBBE
Operations Management: Competitive Decision-Making for a Changing Environment

FORGIONNE
Quantitative Management

FREED
Basic Business Statistics

GAITHER
Production and Operations Management
Sixth Edition

GLASKOWSKY, HUDSON, AND IVIE
Business Logistics
Third Edition

HAMBURG AND YOUNG
Statistical Analysis For Decision Making
Sixth Edition

INGRAM AND MONKS
Statistics for Business and Economics
Second Edition

LAPIN
Statistics for Modern Business Decisions
Sixth Edition

LAPIN
Statistics for Modern Business Decisions
Sixth Edition Alternate Version

LAPIN
Quantitative Methods for Business Decisions with Cases
Sixth Edition

LEE
Introduction to Management Science
Second Edition

LENGNICK-HALL
Experiencing Quality

MILLER AND WICHERN
Intermediate Business Statistics

SHIPLEY AND RUTHSTROM
Cases in Operations Management

SOWER, MOTWANI, AND SAVOIE
Classic Readings in Operations Management

VAN MATRE
Foundations of TQM: A Readings Book

WEIERS
Introduction to Business Statistics
Second Edition

ZIKMUND
Business Research Methods
Fourth Edition

PREFACE

Central to the establishment of a formal discipline is the identification of the fundamental body of knowledge underlying the discipline. Each discipline within the business "supradiscipline" boasts a collection of renowned researchers and classic works that have structured and defined that particular field of knowledge. For example, Shafritz and Whitbeck's *Classics of Organization Theory* (1978), Merrill's *Classics in Management* (1970), Thompson's *The Great Writings in Marketing* (1981), and the Fall 1990 *Journal of the Academy of Marketing Science, The History of Marketing Thought: Special Issue* all identify classic theorists and works in their respective disciplines. These works provide valuable insight into the early development of the respective bodies of knowledge and are valuable in understanding the basis for the current theoretical underpinnings of the discipline. To our knowledge, no such compilation has been attempted in the field of production and operations management (POM).

This book of readings contains a collection of some of the seminal works that led to the establishment of the field of production and operations management. In addition, the development of the ideas and theories presented in these works is followed by the inclusion of chapter bibliographies—Selected Readings—of other works significantly contributing to this body of knowledge.

The textbook is divided into five chapters. Chapter One discusses the criteria used to determine which works to include in the book. This chapter is based upon a survey of the membership of the Production and Operations Management Society conducted by the authors during 1991–1992, and a second survey of POM academicians conducted during 1992–1993.

Chapters Two through Five are similar to the major divisions in many POM textbooks. These chapters are respectively titled Operations Strategy, Quality, Productivity, and Service Operations Management. Development of the global perspective in POM is included where appropriate. Each of these chapters contains an introductory section outlining the relationships between the works included in the chapter and the significance of those works and their authors to the field of POM.

Designed for use as a supplementary textbook in undergraduate, graduate, and doctoral courses in POM, it could also serve as a supplementary textbook in graduate courses in the history of management thought, as well as a reference book for theorists, practitioners, and consultants.

The authors hope you enjoy reading this book and welcome your comments regarding its contents and suggestions for other works which have helped define the POM discipline. Please send your comments and suggestions to: The Dryden Press, c/o Editorial Assistant, Management Science and Quantitative Methods, 301 Commerce St., Fort Worth, TX 76102.

ACKNOWLEDGMENTS

Producing a book like this one requires the input of literally hundreds of people. While we would very much like to thank all of them by name, for the sake of brevity we have forced ourselves to recognize just a few.

First, we would like to thank Dr. Don Powell, Ph.D., for inspiring our interest in management classics. It was this interest that led to the idea of this book.

Second, we would like to thank all of the survey participants who took the time and effort to provide us with their insights into the classics in the field. Their responses are what makes this book truly unique.

Third, we would like to thank the staff at The Dryden Press for recognizing the importance of this book, and for putting up with our changes, revisions, and other attempts to make the book the best it could be. Special recognition goes to Scott Isenberg, Tracy Morse, Sheila Spahn, Brian Salisbury, Ellie McKenzie, Erin Gregg, Scott Timian, and Deidre Lynch.

Fourth, we would like to thank Sam Houston State University, Grand Valley State University, The University of New Orleans, and Integrated Resources Group, Inc. for their support, both in personnel and resources.

Finally, we would like to thank our families for their support and understanding, without which this book would not be possible. It is your guidance and inspiration that has allowed us the opportunities to make this work a reality.

V. E. S.
J. G. M.
M. J. S.

CONTENTS

Preface   vii

CHAPTER 1   **SELECTING THE CLASSICS**   **1**
Exploratory Research   1
Follow-Up Research   3
Use of Survey Data   5

CHAPTER 2   **OPERATIONS STRATEGY**   **6**
Introduction   7
Henry L. Gantt "Training Workmen in Habits of Industry and Cooperation" (1908)   11
Frederick W. Taylor "The Principles of Scientific Management" (1911)   23
Frank B. Gilbreth "Science in Management for the One Best Way to do Work" (1923)   47
Wickham Skinner "Manufacturing—Missing Link in Corporate Strategy" (1969)   85
Wickham Skinner "The Focused Factory" (1974)   101
Steven C. Wheelwright "Reflecting Corporate Strategy in Manufacturing Decisions" (1978)   115
Robert H. Hayes and William J. Abernathy "Managing Our Way to Economic Decline" (1980)   129
Elwood S. Buffa "Research in Operations Management" (1980)   151
Martin K. Starr "Global Production and Operations Strategy" (1984)   165
Richard J. Schonberger "The Vital Elements of World-Class Manufacturing" (1986)   177
Selected Readings   185

CHAPTER 3   **QUALITY**   **186**
Introduction   187
Walter A. Shewhart "Excerpts from *Economic Control of Manufactured Product*" (1931)   191
Walter A. Shewhart "Excerpts from *Statistical Method from the*

Viewpoint of Quality Control" (1939)   215

W. Edwards Deming "Improvement of Quality and Productivity through Action by Management" (1981–1982)   231

Joseph M. Juran "Consumerism and Product Quality" (1970)   249

Joseph M. Juran "The Quality Trilogy" (1986)   277

Armand V. Feigenbaum "Excerpts from *Quality Control Principles, Practice, and Administration"* (1951)   289

Armand V. Feigenbaum "Total Quality Control" (1956)   307

David A. Garvin "Competing on the Eight Dimensions of Quality" (1987)   323

Selected Readings   339

CHAPTER 4   PRODUCTIVITY   340

Introduction   341

Frederick W. Taylor "A Piece-Rate System, Being a Step Toward Partial Solution of the Labor Problem" (1895)   345

Ray Stannard Baker "Frederick W. Taylor—Scientist in Business Management" (1911)   369

Frederick W. Taylor "The Gospel of Efficiency: The Principles of Scientific Management" (1911)   377

Frederick W. Taylor "The Gospel of Efficiency II: The Principles of Scientific Management" (1911)   395

Frederick W. Taylor "The Gospel of Efficiency III: The Principles of Scientific Management" (1911)   405

"The Principles of Scientific Management"—a criticism by Upton Sinclair and an answer by Frederick W. Taylor (1911)   423

Joseph A. Orlicky, George W. Plossl, and Oliver W. Wight "Structuring the Bill of Material for MRP" (1972)   429

Oliver W. Wight "Effective Company Operation as Never Before!" (1979)   455

Wickham Skinner "The Productivity Paradox" (1986)   461

Robert H. Hayes and Kim B. Clark "Why Some Factories Are More Productive Than Others" (1986)   471

Selected Readings   487

CHAPTER 5   SERVICE OPERATIONS MANAGEMENT   488

Introduction   489

Richard B. Chase "Where Does the Customer Fit in a Service Operation?" (1978)   491

Selected Readings   **500**

Index   **501**

CHAPTER ONE

SELECTING THE CLASSICS

ost collections of classic works are the result of primarily subjective criteria applied by one editor or a small group of editors. This project applies more objective criteria and draws upon the collective wisdom of the academic POM community to determine the classic contributors and works within the field of POM. The results of the exploratory and follow-up surveys serve to define the historical underpinnings of the POM discipline.

EXPLORATORY RESEARCH

Selecting the classics in one's chosen field is an awesome responsibility—one which the editors of this book felt they could not shoulder alone. Consequently, a project was initiated in 1991 to survey the membership of the Production and Operations Society to obtain input as to which scholars and works they considered to be classic. The survey also endeavored to determine an appropriate set of criteria to be used in determining whether an individual or work is a "classic."

While the response rate to that survey was low (probably because of the time and thought necessary to complete the questionnaire), valuable insight into two research questions was obtained.

Research Question 1: What are the criteria which should be used for judging a person or work to be a classic in that field of production/operations management?

Eight criteria were presented to the survey respondents to rate on a scale of 1 (not important) to 4 (very important). The eight criteria and their mean respondent ratings are shown in Table 1–1.

Ten other criteria were mentioned by at least one respondent. While these criteria were not mentioned frequently enough to allow an assessment of their strength, they were incorporated into a follow-up survey.

TABLE 1–1	RESPONDENT RATINGS FOR CRITERIA	
CRITERIA	**MEAN RATING**	**% RATING IMPORTANT OR VERY IMPORTANT**
1. Vitality	3.492	95.385%
2. Historic Significance	3.323	78.462%
3. Seminal	3.323	84.615%
4. Readability of Work	3.031	72.308%
5. Degree of Interest	2.953	66.154%
6. Recognition by Serious Students in Field	2.862	66.154%
7. Time	2.815	66.153%
8. Frequency of Quotation	2.553	56.923%

Research Question 2: Which works or person can be judged as classics within the framework established in question 1?

Each respondent was asked to identify classic contributors to the field of POM. Sixty names were proposed by at least one respondent. Of these, thirty-two were mentioned only once. Twelve, which were mentioned by seven or more respondents, are listed in Table 1–2.

The respondents were asked to list the criteria they used to judge these contributors as classics. Table 1–3 shows the criteria used by the respondents who listed these 12 contributors as classics.

TABLE 1–2   CLASSIC CONTRIBUTORS TO POM

CONTRIBUTOR	FREQUENCY
Skinner, W.	23
Taylor, F.	20
Deming, W. E.	17
Hayes, R.	15
Schonberger, R. J.	13
Orlicky, J.	12
Wheelwright, S.	10
Clark, K.	8
Shewhart, W.	7
Gilbreth, F. & L.	7
Wight, O.	7
Buffa, E.	7

TABLE 1–3   CLASSIC CONTRIBUTORS VERSUS SELECTION CRITERIA

CONTRIBUTOR	CRITERIA NUMBER							
	1	2	3	4	5	6	7	8
Skinner, W.	X	X	X				X	X
Taylor, F.	X	X	X		X	X	X	X
Deming, W. E.	X	X			X			
Hayes, R.	X		X					X
Schonberger, R.	X	X	X	X	X			
Orlicky, J.		X	X		X	X	X	X
Wheelwright, S.	X		X				X	X
Clark, K.			X	X	X	X		
Shewhart, W.		X	X		X	X	X	
Gilbreth, F. & L.	X	X	X	X	X			X
Wight, O.		X	X	X				
Buffa, E.			X			X		

Each respondent was asked to identify classic works in the field of POM. Sixty works were proposed by at least one respondent. Of these, 33 were mentioned by six or more respondents, and are listed in Table 1–4.

The absence from this list of works by Taylor, who ranked second in frequency of listing as a classic contributor, Schonberger, who ranked fifth, and the Gilbreths, who ranked tenth, is unexpected. Given that "Time" was rated as being an important criteria for judging a work a classic, it is also surprising that no work published prior to 1970 was listed.

FOLLOW-UP RESEARCH

In 1992 a follow-up survey, based upon the results of the exploratory survey, was conducted of a sample of the Production and Operations Management Society membership and POM participants at a national conference. All the survey respondents were terminally qualified, and all but two currently taught POM classes.

Rather than the open ended format of the exploratory questionnaire, the follow-up questionnaire presented the respondent with a list of names of potential "classic contributors." The names were those listed by respondents to the exploratory survey.

Respondents to this follow-up survey rated on a scale of 1 (disagree) to 5 (agree) their agreement with the statement, "This person in a classic contributor to the field of POM." The results are shown in Table 1–5.

TABLE 1–4	**CLASSIC WORKS IN POM**

WORK	FREQUENCY
"Manufacturing—Missing Link in Corporate Strategy." Skinner	14
"Link Manufacturing Process & Product Life Cycles." Hayes & Wheelwright	10
Material Requirements Planning. Orlicky	10
"The Focused Factory." Skinner	8
"Why Some Factories are More Productive Than Others." Hayes & Clark	8
"Out of Crisis." Deming	7
"Restoring Our Competitive Edge." Hayes & Wheelwright	7
"Dynamic Manufacturing: Creating the Learning Organization." Hayes, Wheelwright, & Clark	6
"Competing Through Manufacturing." Wheelwright & Hayes	6
"Zero Inventory." Hall	6
"Managing Our Way to Economic Decline." Hayes & Abernathy	6
"Quality on the Line." Garvin	6

The follow-up survey respondents also rated on a scale of 1 (Not Important) to 4 (Very Important) the same list of criteria for judging a person or work a "classic" as in the exploratory survey. These results are in Table 1–6.

While there are some differences between the ranking from the two surveys, one can infer that there is agreement that criteria 1, 2, and 3 are most important,

---

TABLE 1–5   **CLASSIC CONTRIBUTOR RATINGS**

CONTRIBUTOR	RATING	RANK
Deming	4.50	1
Taylor	4.45	2
Skinner	4.24	3
Juran	4.15	4
Buffa	4.06	5
Gantt	4.06	6
Gilbreths	3.98	7
Wheelwright	3.94	8
Hayes	3.93	9
Shewart	3.87	10
Danzing	3.81	11
Orlicky	3.79	12
Schonberger	3.68	13
Feigenbaum	3.67	14
Shingo	3.67	15
Chase	3.65	16
Abernathy	3.64	17
Wight	3.52	18
Wybark	3.52	19
Babbage	3.43	20
Brown	3.41	21
Crosby	3.38	22
Clark	3.27	23
Garvin	3.26	24
Hall	3.25	25
Hill	3.24	26
Modigl	3.23	27
Starr	3.21	28
Goldratt	3.20	29
Mayo	3.20	30
Hax	3.16	31
Woolsey	3.05	32
Schroeder	3.02	33
Swamidas	2.82	34
Martin	2.70	35
Wild	2.69	36
Mood	2.57	37

		F-UP	**EXPLORATORY**
TABLE 1–6 FOLLOW-UP SURVEY RESPONDENT RATINGS FOR CRITERIA			
CRITERIA	**MEAN**	**RATING RANK**	**RANK**
1. Vitality	3.48	1	1
2. Historic Significance	3.44	2	2
3. Seminal	3.37	3	3
4. Readability of Work	2.88	5	4
5. Degree of Interest	2.68	8	5
6. Recognition by Serious Students in Field	3.20	4	6
7. Time	2.73	7	7
8. Frequency of Quotation	2.86	6	8

and criteria 7 and 8 are among the least important. Both samples agreed that criteria 4 was more important than criteria 7 and 8, but less than criteria 1, 2, and 3. There was significant disagreement only over criteria 5.

USE OF THE SURVEY DATA

The potential classic contributors who scored above 3.0 on the follow-up survey were divided among the topics to be covered in this book: Productivity, Quality, Operations Strategy, and Service Operations. This was done on the basis of key word searches using computerized databases. Those names on the list which clearly fit into one or more of the four topic areas were selected for inclusion in this book.

Simply appearing on the follow-up survey list is indicative of a recognized contribution to the POM field. Selection for inclusion in this book indicates a recognized contribution of highly significant proportions which fits into one or more of the topic areas. Other highly significant contributions may go unrecognized simply because they were made in a topic area not included in this book.

We encourage the reader to not only read the articles in this book, but the ones on the readings lists as well. As with all things, time will add to our understanding of the field and its classic contributors. We encourage the reader to become part of this classification program by writing the editors with recommendations of classic authors and articles in the field of Production and Operations Management.

CHAPTER TWO

OPERATIONS
STRATEGY

Operations strategy has gained tremendous attention since the 1970s from both practitioners and researchers. Several factors that have contributed to the growing interest in this area are: the increasing strength of our global competitors; a new emphasis on manufacturing excellence by top management; increasing labor productivity abroad, especially in Germany and Japan; and the need to accelerate new product and process development in order to remain competitive.

This chapter focuses on the classical authors in the area of operations strategy. Contributors to this field include: Frederick W. Taylor, Henry L. Gantt, Frank Gilbreth, Elwood Buffa, Wickham Skinner, Steven Wheelwright, Robert Hayes, Richard Schonberger, William Abernathy, and Martin Starr.

Strategic operations management began with Taylor's pioneering work in the early 1900s. Taylor proposed the "Principles of Scientific Management" and the concept of "bottom-up" manufacturing. The "bottom-up" manufacturing approach consists of these steps:

1. selecting an operation for review,
2. breaking it down into individual process elements,
3. analyzing and improving each individual element, and
4. putting the process back together as a whole.

Henry Gantt, a disciple of Taylor's, later expanded upon the importance of certain elements of Taylor's Principles in his own writings. In a presentation before the American Society of Mechanical Engineers, Gantt stressed his philosophy concerning the management strategy of the future: "to teach and to lead." Gantt characterized the prevailing management philosophy as "management driving the worker." He suggested that it was more important to pay attention to the man who was doing the work, rather than the analysis and organization of the work itself in solving operational problems.

In early 1922 Frank Gilbreth presented a paper at a management conference in Milan, Italy, addressing several operations management issues. Gilbreth offered micro-motion study, the "one best way to do work" discussion, the three position plan of promotion, and a study on the effect of fatigue on productivity. Gilbreth worked with his wife Lillian in this area. He and his wife stressed the psychology of scientific management.

The concept of the "manufacturing task" and "top-down" manufacturing was promoted by Wickham Skinner in his 1969 article, "Manufacturing—Missing Link in Corporate Strategy." In this article, Skinner discusses how "top down" management differs from Taylor's and other industrial engineers. The "top-down" approach focuses first on the company and its competitive strategy. The goal is to define manufacturing policy.

In a 1974 article, Skinner introduced the concept of focused manufacturing. Skinner defines the focused factory as "a factory which focuses on a narrow product mix for a particular market niche." Skinner claims that the focused factory will outperform a conventional plant.

Wheelwright expanded on Skinner's 1969 paper in 1978, suggesting that management methods could be employed to mesh corporate and manufacturing decisions. He also promoted an effort to conceptualize strategic process variables.

Since the 1980s, operations strategy literature has focused on the importance of international operations as a strategic necessity for global survival. Suggested readings include Buffa (1984), Hayes and Wheelwright (1984), Schonberger (1986), and Starr (1988).

The survey data discussed in Chapter 1 suggests that the respondents differentiate among the classic contributors (see Table 2–1). For the sake of simplicity, we will refer to three levels of classic contributors: Type I, Type II, and Type III. Assignment to a specific type does not represent a hierarchy of relative merit of the contributions made by the individual, instead, it represents the current classification of that individual's contribution relative to other classic contributors in the minds of today's POM professionals. Figure 2–1 depicts the relationship between these types.

FIGURE 2–1 CLASSIC CONTRIBUTORS IN OPERATIONS STRATEGY

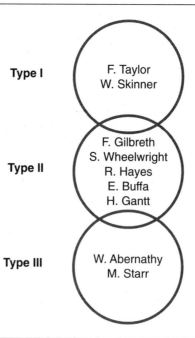

Type I — F. Taylor, W. Skinner

Type II — F. Gilbreth, S. Wheelwright, R. Hayes, E. Buffa, H. Gantt

Type III — W. Abernathy, M. Starr

TABLE 2–1	SURVEY SCORES FOR CLASSIC CONTRIBUTORS	
CONTRIBUTOR	**MEAN SCORE***	**STANDARD DEVIATION**
F. Taylor	4.45	0.985
W. Skinner	4.24	0.995
E. Buffa	4.06	0.942
H. Gantt	4.06	1.071
F. Gilbreth	3.98	1.105
S. Wheelwright	3.94	0.990
R. Hayes	3.93	1.063
J. Abernathy	3.64	1.075
M. Starr	3.21	1.089

*The survey scores denote the degree of agreement with the following statement: "This person is a classic contributor in the field of POM." A score of 1 indicates "Disagree"; a score of 2 indicates "Somewhat Disagree"; a score of 3 indicates "No Opinion"; a score of 4 indicates "Agree Somewhat"; and a score of 5 indicates "Agree."

TRAINING WORKMEN IN HABITS OF INDUSTRY AND COOPERATION

HENRY L. GANTT

The widespread interest in the training of workmen which has been so marked for several years is due to the evident need for better methods of training than those now generally in vogue.

The one point in which these methods as a class seem to be lacking is that they do not lay enough stress on the fact that workmen must have industry as well as knowledge and skill.

Habits of industry are far more valuable than any kind of knowledge or skill, for with such habits as a basis, the problem of acquiring knowledge and skill is much simplified. Without industry, knowledge and skill are of little value, and sometimes a great detriment.

If workmen are systematically trained in habits of industry, it has been found possible, not only to train many of them to be efficient in whatever capacity they are needed, but to develop an effective system of cooperation between workmen and foreman.

This is not a theory, but the record of a fact.

It is too much to hope, however, that the methods about to be described will be adopted extensively in the near future, for the great majority of managers, whose success is based mainly on their personal ability, will hesitate before adopting what seems to them the slower and less forceful policy of studying problems and training workmen; but should they do so they will have absolutely no desire to return to their former methods.

The general policy of the past has been to drive, but the era of force must give way to that of knowledge, and the policy of the future will be to teach and to lead, to the advantage of all concerned. The vision of workmen in general eager to cooperate in carrying out the results of scientific

Reprinted from *Transactions of The American Society of Mechanical Engineers,* Volume 30, 1037–48. Paper presented at December 1908 meeting of the Society, New York. Reprinted with permission from the American Society of Mechanical Engineers.

investigations must be dismissed as a dream of the millennium, but results so far accomplished indicate that nothing will do more to bring about that millennium than training workmen in habits of industry and cooperation. A study of the principles on which such training has been successfully established will convince the most skeptical that if they are carried out good results must follow. An outline of these principles has already been submitted to the Society in a paper entitled "A Bonus System of Rewarding Labor."[1]

Under this system each man has his work assigned to him in the form of a task to be done by a prescribed method with definite appliances and to be completed within a certain time. The task is based on a detailed investigation by a trained expert of the best methods of doing the work; and the task setter, or his assistant, acts as an instructor to teach the workmen to do the work in the manner and time specified. If the work is done within the time allowed by the expert, and is up to the standard for quality, the workman receives extra compensation in addition to his day's pay. If it is not done in the time set, or is not up to the standard for quality, the workman receives his day's pay only.

This system, in connection with the other work of Mr. F. W. Taylor, so greatly increased the output and reduced the cost of the work in the large machine shop of the Bethlehem Steel Company that for the past seven years the writer has given a large portion of his time to the development of its possibilities. The results have far exceeded his expectations.

In his closing remarks on the above paper, the writer emphasized the value of the system as a means of training workmen, and the late Dr. Robert H. Thurston[2] in his discussion of it was so optimistic as to the results it would produce on "workmen and foremen and employer alike" that the writer felt that his enthusiasm over a new and promising method had carried him, perhaps, a little too far. Results have fully justified Dr. Thurston's predictions, however, for today the method has been developed as a practical system of education and training for all, from the highest to the lowest. The fact, so repeatedly emphasized by Mr. Taylor, *that tasks should be set only as the result of a scientific investigation,* has proved of an educational value hardly to be over-estimated, for the scientific investigation of a process

---

[1]"A Bonus System of Rewarding Labor," December 1901, a system of task work with a bonus which had recently been introduced by the writer into the large machine shop of the Bethlehem-Steel Company, as a part of the system of management being introduced into their works by Mr. F. W. Taylor.

[2]Robert Henry Thurston, 1839–1903. American engineer and educator. Founder and first president of ASME.

that has been developed without the assistance of science almost always reveals inconsistencies which it is possible to eliminate, thus perfecting the process and at the same time reducing its cost.

It is this scientific investigation that points to improvement in methods and educates owners and managers; but the average workman is interested only in his daily wage and has no special desire to learn improved methods. The results of our investigations are of little practical value, therefore, unless we can first teach our workmen how to use them, and then can induce them to do as they are taught.

PRACTICAL APPLICATION

For this purpose *an instructor, a task and a bonus* have been found most useful. People as a rule prefer to work at the speed and in the manner to which they have been accustomed, but are usually willing to work at any reasonable speed and in any reasonable manner, if sufficient inducement is offered for so doing, and if they are so trained as to be able to earn the reward. In carrying out this plan we try to find men who are already skilled and able to perform the task set. It frequently happens, however, that the number of such men is insufficient and it takes time to train the unskilled to a proper degree of efficiency; but with a bonus as an incentive, and a proper instructor, a very fair proportion of the unskilled finally succeed in performing a task that was at first entirely beyond them.

Unskilled workmen, who under these conditions have become skilled in one kind of work, readily learn another, and soon begin to realize that they can, in a measure at least, make up for their loss in not having learned a trade.

As they become more skilled, they form better habits of work, lose less time and become more reliable. Their health improves, and the improvement in their general appearance is very marked. This improvement in health seems to be due to a more regular and active life, combined with a greater interest in their work, for it is a well known fact that *work in which we are interested and which holds our attention without any effort on our part, tires us much less than that we have to force ourselves to do*. The task with a reward for its accomplishment produces this interest and holds the attention, with the invariable results of more work, better work, and better satisfied workers.

The Task and Bonus method of training not only furnishes the workman with the required knowledge, but by offering an inducement to utilize that knowledge properly, trains him in proper habits of work.

HABITS OF WORK

In all work both *quantity* and *quality* must be considered, and our task method demands a maximum quantity, all of which must be up to the standard for quality. Workmen trained under this method acquire the habit of doing a large amount of work well, and disprove the oft-repeated fallacy that good work must be done slowly. As a matter of fact, our quickest workers almost always do the best work when following instructions. We set great store by the habit of working quickly, for no matter how much skill a workman may have, he will not attain the best success without quickness as well.

Habits of work in a mechanic are comparable with *habits of thought* in an engineer, and our industrial schools should make proper habits of work the basis on which to build their training in manual dexterity. The engineering school does not make engineers, but tries to furnish its graduates with an equipment that will enable them to utilize readily and rapidly their own experience and that of others. In the same manner, industrial training schools should equip their graduates with habits of industry that will make them as mechanics capable, and willing to do a large amount of good work.

As the writer sees it, one of the most valuable assets that the graduate of a technical college or an industrial school can have *is the habit of doing promptly and to the best of his ability the work set before him.* With this habit and reasonable intelligence he can make good progress. This habit is one of the first results of the Task and Bonus system, for it is a noticeable fact that task workers form habits of industry which they maintain when on day's work with no bonus in sight.

In all schemes for technical or industrial education or training that the writer has seen, emphasis has been laid on the importance of knowing how. The writer wishes to add that ability and willingness to do are of at least equal importance. Many skilled workmen make their skill an excuse for slow work. Those that have not been trained to utilize efficiently what they have learned never attain the success that should be theirs.

Under our task system the workman is *taught how* and *trained to do* at the same time. *Knowing* and *doing* are thus closely associated in his mind, and it is our experience that the habit of doing efficiently what is laid out for him becomes so fixed that he performs without hesitation tasks at which a man not trained to follow instructions would absolutely fail. This is exactly what should be expected and means nothing more than that in our industrial army the workman who has gained confidence in his superior follows his orders without hesitation, just as the private soldier follows the orders of his officer even though he does not see where they lead.

This is not a fanciful comparison, for I have known more than one case in which a workman expressed his doubts as to the possibility of doing a task, and on getting the reply that the task was all right, said, "If you say it can be done, I will do it."

Workers who have been unable to perform their tasks in the time set have frequently asked to have an instructor stand by them with a stopwatch to time the detail operations and show them just wherein they failed, with the result that they soon learned to earn their bonus regularly.

The first essential for a workman to become successful under our task system is to obey *orders,* and having acquired this habit he soon finds out that a skilled investigator can learn more about doing a piece of work than he knows "off hand." Having satisfied himself on this point, he goes to work at the tasks set him with the determination to earn his bonus, with the result, if he has the natural ability, that he soon becomes a rapid and skillful workman.

Learning to obey orders is often the hardest part of the workman's task, for a large percentage of men seem so constituted as to be apparently unable to do as they are told. As a rule, however, this is a feature of a certain stage of their development only, which under proper conditions they overcome at a later date. For instance, many very capable men who were impatient of restraint when they should have learned a trade, find themselves at the age of twenty-five or less in the class of unskilled workmen, although their ability would have enabled them to do well at almost any trade. It is this class of men, when they have come to realize the difference between a skilled workman and one not skilled, that furnishes us with many of our best task workers. Such men often see in our *instructor, task,* and *bonus* a chance to redeem some of their earlier errors, and by learning thoroughly how to do, and doing one thing after another, in the best way that can be devised, get a training, in a short time, that does much to make up for the previous neglect of their opportunities.

Bosses as Servants and Teachers

In a shop operated on this system, where each workman has his task, one man whom we term a *gang boss* usually tends a group of workmen, supplying them with work and appliances and removing the work when finished. Such a man is paid a bonus for each workman who earns a bonus, and an extra bonus if all of his group earn their bonuses. The result is that so long as the workmen perform their tasks, though nominally their boss, he is really their servant, and becomes the boss only when a workman fails to perform his task. The loss of money to the gang boss in case a workman fails to earn his bonus is such that he constantly has his eye on the poor workman and helps him all he can. If, however, he finds the workman is incapable of being taught, he uses his influence to have a better man put in his place.

In starting a shop on task work, an instructor who is capable of teaching each workman how to perform his task must be constantly on hand, and must as a rule teach one workman at a time. This instructor may be the man who has investigated the work and set the task, or he may simply be an instructor capable of following out the work of such an investigator, but he must be readily available as long as any of the workmen need his services, for we make it a rule not to ask a man to do anything in a certain manner and time unless we are prepared to show him how to do it as we specify.

TASK SETTING

A task must always be set for performing a definite operation in a specific manner, a minimum time being set for its accomplishment. As compensation, the workman is paid for the time set plus a percentage (usually 20 to 50) of that time, provided the work is done in the time allowed or less. If the time taken is more than time allowed, the workman gets his day's pay only. The fact that in setting the task the manner of performing the operation is specified enables us to set another task for the same operation if we develop a better or quicker method.

If after having performed his task a workman wishes to suggest a quicker or better method for doing the same work, he is given an opportunity if possible to demonstrate his method. If the suggested method really proves to be quicker or better, it is adopted as the standard, and the workman is given a suitable reward. *No workman, however, is allowed to make suggestions until he has first done the work in the manner and time specified.*

It is the duty of the investigator to develop methods and set tasks, and unless the methods developed by him are pretty generally a great deal better than those suggested by the workmen, he is not retained in the position. Working at tasks is pretty good training for task setting, and the writer has gotten more than one task setter from the ranks of task doers.

Inasmuch as, after a satisfactory method has been established, a large proportion of the work of the task setter is the study of the time in which operations can be performed, he is popularly known as the *Time Study* man. This term has led to a misconception of his duties and has caused many honest people to claim that they were putting in our methods when they have put a stop watch in the hands of a bright clerk and told him to find out how quickly the best men were doing certain work. Unquestionably they have in many cases been able to set more accurate piece rates by this method than they had been able to set by the older methods, but they are still far from our ideal, in which the best expert available investigates the work, standardizes the appliances and methods and sets a task that involves utilizing them to their very best efficiency. While the stopwatch is often used to establish a method, it is used to determine the time needed to do the work only when the standard methods and appliances are used efficiently. Stopwatch observation on work done inefficiently or with ill-adapted appliances, or by poor methods, is absurd and serves only to bring into disrepute all work in which the stop watch is used. Moreover, such use of the stopwatch justly excites the contempt and opposition of the workman.

To make real and permanent progress, the expert must be able to standardize appliances and methods and write up such instructions as will enable an intelligent workman to follow them. Such standards become permanent, and if the workman is paid a proper bonus for doing the work in the manner and time set, he not only helps maintain the standards, but soon begins to exert his influence to help the progress of standardization.

STANDARDIZATION

All work, and all knowledge, for that matter, may be divided into two classes: *expert* and *standard*. Expert knowledge may be described as that which has not been reduced to writing in such a manner as to be generally available, or exists only in the minds of a few. By analogy, expert work is work, the methods of doing which either are known only to a few or have not been so clearly described as to enable a man familiar with that class of work to understand them.

On the other hand, standard methods are those that are generally used, or have been so clearly described and proved that a man familiar with that class of work can understand them and safely employ them.

The largest problem of our expert is to standardize expert methods and knowledge. When a method has been standardized, a task may be set, and by means of *an instructor and a bonus* a method of maintaining that standard permanently may be established. With increasing efficiency on the part of the workman the standard always has a tendency to become higher.

We have here the workman and the foreman using their efforts to maintain standards, for both fail to obtain a bonus if the standard is not maintained. This is so different from the case in which the standard is maintained only by the man in authority with a club that there can be no comparison.

From workmen trained under these methods, we get a good supply of instructors and foremen, and occasionally an investigator. From our investigators, who standardize our methods and appliances, we get our superintendents, and our system of management thus becomes self-perpetuating.

The superintendent who believes that the sovereign cure for all troubles is to go into the shop and raise a row, has no place under our methods, for when the task and bonus has been established, errors are far more frequent in the office than in the shop, and the man who is given to bluffing soon finds that his methods produce no effect on men that are following written instructions.

OBSTACLES

Among the obstacles to the introduction of this system is the fact that it forces everybody to do his duty. Many people in authority want a system that will force everybody else to do his duty, but will allow them to do as they please.

The Task and Bonus system when carried out properly is no respecter of persons, and the man who wishes to force the workman to do his task properly must see that the task is properly set and that proper means are available for doing it. It is not only the workman's privilege, but his duty, to report whatever interferes with his earning his bonus, and the loss of time educates him to perform this duty no matter how disagreeable it is at first. We investigate every loss of bonus, and place the blame where it belongs. Sometimes we find it belongs pretty high up, for the man who has neglected his duty under one system of management is pretty apt to neglect it at first under another. He must either learn to perform his duty or yield his place, for the pressure from those who lose money by his neglect or incompetence is continuous and insistent.

This becomes evident as soon as the task and bonus gets fairly started, and the effect is that opposition to its extension develops on the part of all who are not sure of making good under it, or whose expert knowledge is such that they fear it will all soon be standardized. The opposition of such people, however, is bound to give way sooner or later, for the really capable man and the true expert welcome these methods as soon as they understand them.

HELPS

The fact that the task and the bonus enable us to utilize our knowledge and maintain our standards, and that the setting of tasks after a scientific investigation must necessarily not only increase our knowledge but standardize it, brings to our assistance the clearest thinkers and hardest workers in any organization. Our greatest help, however, comes from the workmen themselves. The most intelligent realize that we really mean to help them advance themselves, and the ambitious ones welcome the aid of our instructor to remove obstacles that have been in their way for perhaps years. As soon as one such man has earned his bonus for several days, there is usually another man ready to try the task, and unless there is a great lack of confidence on the part of the men in the management, the sentiment rapidly grows in favor of our task work.

DAY WORK AND PIECEWORK

As used by the writer, the Task and Bonus system of pay is really a combination of the best features of both day work and piecework. The workman is assured his day rate while being taught to perform his task, and as the bonus for its accomplishment is a percentage of the time allowed, the compensation when the task has been performed is a fixed quantity, and is thus really the equivalent of a piece rate. Our method of payment then is piecework for the skilled, and day work for the unskilled, it being remembered that if there is only work enough for a few, it will always be given to the skilled. This acts as a powerful stimulus to the unskilled, and all who have any ambition try to get into the bonus class. This cannot be to clearly borne in mind, *for we have here all the advantages of day work combined with those of piecework without the disadvantage of either,* for the day worker who has no ambition to become a bonus worker usually of his own accord seeks work elsewhere, and our working force soon becomes composed of Bonus Workers, and day workers who are trying to become Bonus Workers.

COOPERATION

When 25 percent of the workers in a plant are Bonus Workers, they, with those who are striving to get into their class, control the sentiment, and a strong spirit of cooperation develops. This spirit of cooperation in living up to the standards set by the experts, which is the only way a bonus can be earned, benefits the employer by the production of

> More work,
> Better Work,
> Cheaper work.

It benefits the workmen by giving them

> Better wages,
> Increased skill,
> Better habits of work,
> More pleasure and pride in their work.

Not the least important of these results is the fact that the workmen take more pride in their work, for this of itself insures good work. As an instance of this pride, the writer has known girls working under the task system to form a society, admission to which was confined to those that could earn bonus on their work; the workers themselves thus putting a premium on industry and efficiency.

The fact that we get better work as well as quicker work seems inconceivable to some. The reasons are:

a. Careful inspection, for no bonus is paid unless the work is up to the standard.
b. Work done by a prescribed method, and always in the same way.
c. Attention needed to do high-speed work, which keeps the mind of the worker on what he is doing and soon results in exceptional skill.

The development of skilled workmen by this method is sure and rapid, and wherever the method has been properly established, *the problem of securing satisfactory help has been solved*. During the past few years while there has been so much talk about the "growing inefficiency of labor," the writer has repeatedly proved the value of this method in increasing its efficiency, and the fact that the system works automatically, when once thoroughly established, puts the *possibility of training their own workmen within the reach of all manufacturers*.

TRAINING HELP A FUNCTION OF MANAGEMENT

Any system of management that did not make provision for obtaining proper materials to work with would be thought very lax. The day is not far distant when any management that does not make provision for training the workmen it needs will not be regarded as much better, for it is by this means only that a system of management can be made permanent.

To be satisfied to draw skilled workmen from the surplus of other plants means as a rule that second rate men only are wanted, and indicates a lack of appreciation of the value of well-trained, capable men. The fact that few plants only have established methods of training workmen does not necessarily mean that the managers are satisfied with that condition, but rather that they know of no training system that can be satisfactorily operated in their plants; and as questions are sure to be asked about the method of introducing this system, a few words on that subject may not be amiss, it being borne in mind that *the changing of a system of management is a very serious matter, and cannot be done by a busy superintendent in his spare time*.

METHOD OF INTRODUCTION

In order to set tasks we must know beforehand what work is to be done and who is to do it. In order to pay a bonus, we must know after the work is done whether it was done exactly as specified. Hence our first care in starting to introduce this method is to provide means for assigning tasks to the workmen, and means for obtaining such a complete set of returns as will show just what each man has done. When this much has been introduced, the output of a plant is always increased and the cost of manufacture reduced.

The next step is to separate such of the work as is standard, or can be readily made standard, from the more miscellaneous work and set tasks for the standard work. Then we begin to standardize, and as fast as possible reduce the expert and increase the routine work. The effort to classify and standardize expert knowledge is most helpful to the experts themselves, and in a short time they begin to realize that they can use their knowledge far more efficiently than they ever dreamed.

As soon as work has been standardized, it can be intelligently planned and scheduled, each workman being given his specific task, for which he is paid a bonus when it is done in the manner and time specified. As bonus is paid only on the written statement of the inspector that the whole task has been properly done, failure to earn a bonus indicates that our plans have not been carried out.

An investigation of every case of lost bonus keeps the management closely in touch with the progress of the work, and as the workmen are ever ready to help disclose and remove the obstacles that prevent their earning their bonus, the managing problem is greatly simplified; for, as one of my co-workers has very aptly put it, *"the frictional lag due to the inertia of the workman is changed by the bonus into an acceleration."*

With increase in the number of bonus workers, this force of acceleration increases, and not only does the careless worker, who by his bad work prevents some other from earning his bonus, fall into disfavor, but the foreman or superintendent who is lax in his duty finds his short-comings constantly brought before him by the man whose duty it is to investigate all cases of lost bonus.

MORAL TRAINING

The fact that under this system, everybody, high and low, is forced by his co-workers to do his duty, for someone else always suffers when he fails, acts as a strong moral tonic to the community and many whose ideas of truth and honesty are vague find habits of truth and honesty forced upon them. This is the case with those in high authority as well as those in humble positions, and the man highest in authority finds that he also must conform to laws, if he wishes the proper cooperation of those under him.

THE PRINCIPLES OF SCIENTIFIC MANAGEMENT

FREDERICK W. TAYLOR

On behalf of several of my colleagues who are here tonight, and more particularly on my own behalf, I wish to express the appreciation which we feel for the honor which is being conferred on us by the presence of this platform of the present governor of this state and of one of its most distinguished past governors. I think that I can say that it is the most distinguished honor which has yet been conferred on any meeting at which Scientific Management has been discussed, and we are deeply grateful that these gentlemen, busy as they are, should have taken the time and the trouble to come here.

There is one fact which has been impressed on me more than any other during the past six months. I knew it to be a fact before, but it had never been brought home to me in the same way as during the past six months. It is the fundamental and the very sad fact that almost every workman who is engaged in the mechanic arts, who is engaged in anything like cooperative work, looks upon it as his duty to go slow instead of to go fast. This is the most unfortunate fact in any way connected with Scientific Management, and the causes which lead to it should therefore be very carefully considered.

I may say at the start, that if any one is to blame for this attitude, we are, and not the laborers. It is our fault more than the laborers', that almost every workman looks upon it as his duty to do as small a day's work as he can instead of as large a day's work as he can. Now do not misunderstand me on this point; I am referring only to those workmen who are engaged in what may be called organized industry. I am not referring to the isolated men who work perhaps for themselves, perhaps for an employer with one or two employees, but I am speaking chiefly of the great mass of men who are doing the industrial work of this country. This going slow, instead of

---

Reprinted from the book, *Scientific Management*, 22–55. Published by Dartmouth College, Hanover, N. H., 1912. Paper presented at First Conference on Scientific Management, The Amos Tuck School, Dartmouth College, October 1911. Used by permission of The Amos Tuck School.

going fast, to my mind is the most serious fact that we have to face in this country. It is certainly the most serious fact that is being faced by the English people at this time.

If any of you will get close to the average workman in this country—close enough to him so that he will talk to you as an intimate friend—he will tell you that in his particular trade if, we will say, each man were to turn out twice as much work he is now doing, there could but one result follow: namely, that one-half the men in his trade would be thrown out of work. Now this fallacy is firmly believed by nineteen men out of twenty of all the workmen throughout the country, and, strange to say, I have found that perhaps three-quarters of the people in this country who have spent the larger proportion of their life in getting an education doubt very much if it would be of any great advantage to the working people to turn out more work than they are doing. The average man then, in all classes in this country, doubts if it would really be of any great benefit to the working people to turn out a larger output than they are now doing. Every labor union in this country, so far as I know, has taken steps, or is taking steps, to restrict output.

In this these men are strictly honest; they are doing just what you and I would do if we were in their position and held their views. If any of us thought that by increasing our work we should throw one-half of our friends out of employment, we should take the same view that they do.

This doctrine is preached by almost every labor leader in the country, and is taught by every workman to his children as they are growing up; and I repeat, as I said in the beginning, that it is our fault more than theirs that this fallacy prevails.

What men here—not more than two or three—have ever spoken to an audience of workmen and attempted to counteract that fallacy? Not more than two or three in this audience have ever gone before an audience of working men and tried to point out the truth, that the greatest blessing that working men can confer on their brothers and themselves is to increase their output.

While the labor leaders and the workmen themselves in season and out of season are pointing out the necessity of restriction of output, not one step are we taking to counteract that fallacy; therefore, I say, the fault is ours and not theirs.

All that it is necessary to do, for any one who questions the fact whether it is a good thing for working people to increase their output or not, is to look into the history of any trade in this country. Look into the history of any trade in this country, and you will see that directly the opposite is true; that an increased output invariably gives more work to more men, and never in the history of the world has it more than temporarily, and then for only a very short time, diminished the number of men at work in any trade. That is the truth! Just look into any trade and you will see it.

I shall take the time to give one illustration only. Take the great cotton industry, one of the greatest industries of your state; one of the greatest, if not the greatest industry of New England. In Manchester, England, in 1840 or thereabouts, there were 5,000 cotton operatives. Power machinery began to be introduced in the cotton mills about that time, and the moment those 5,000 men saw the new machinery coming they *knew* that there would not be work for more than 1,000 out of the 5,000 in their trade. There was no question about it whatever. So what did they do? They did just what you or I would have done under similar circumstances. They broke into the mills where the machinery was being installed and smashed it up; they burned down the mills and beat up the "scabs" who were employed to run the new machinery; and they did it for self-protection, just as you or I would have done it, believing what they did as firmly as they did.

Now power machinery came in the cotton industry, just as all labor-saving machinery is sure to come in any industry, in spite of any opposition from any source. It always has come, and it always will come. And what was the result? I am told that the average yardage of cloth now turned out per man in the cotton industry is about eight or ten times the yardage turned out under the old hand conditions.

In 1840, in Manchester, England, there were 5,000 cotton operatives; in Manchester, England, now there are 265,000 cotton operatives. Multiply that ratio by eight to ten and you will see that between 400 and 500 times the yardage of cloth is now being turned out from Manchester, England, that was turned out in 1840. Has the increase in production thrown people out of work? No. It is merely typical of what has taken place and is taking place in every trade. The increase of output merely means bringing more wealth into this world. That is the meaning of it; that now 450 times as much wealth in cotton goods is brought into this world as was brought in 1840, and that is the real wealth of the world. And the workmen, the trades union, the philanthropist, or the mill owner who restrict output as a permanent policy (I do not mean to say it is not necessary both for workmen and manufacturers at times to temporarily restrict output) are about the worst enemies to their fellow men there are. There is hardly any worse crime to my mind than that of deliberately restricting output; of failing to bring the only things into the world which are of real use to the world, the products of men and the soil. The world's history shows that just as fast as you bring the good things that are needed by man into the world, man takes and uses them. That one fact, the immense increase in the productivity of man, marks the difference between civilized and uncivilized countries, marks the one great advance we have made on 100 to 200 years ago; it is due to that increase of productivity that the working people of today, with all the talk about their misery and their horrible treatment, live almost as well as kings did 250 years ago. They have better food, better clothing, and on the whole more comforts than kings had 250 years ago. And that is due to just one thing, *increase of output.*

Take this matter of cotton goods. Tell the average workman of today that when he has a cotton shirt on he has a luxury. Will he not laugh at you? In 1840 a cotton shirt worn by a workman was a luxury; now every man, woman, and child in every workman's family wears cotton goods as an absolute necessity. Just so with a hundred other things that we have come to look upon as necessities, which a hundred years ago were luxuries. And to what is that due? To the increased productivity of man.

I am talking so long on this subject because it lies at the very root of Scientific Management, for Scientific Management has for its object just what labor-saving machinery has for its object, *increased output per unit of human effort.*

The second cause for going slow is *entirely* due to us. I think we are more to blame than they for the first cause, the fallacy that the increase of output will throw men out of work, but we are entirely to blame for the second cause. *It lies in our own inefficient systems of management.*

The piecework system has been introduced in the industries of this country to such an extent that hardly a workman can be found in any industry who does not know something about its working. All of you gentlemen doubtless understand all about the piecework system. If you do, then I will remind you that when you put a workman on piecework and ask him to make, we will say, ten implements like this slide rule in a day, and offer to pay him twenty-five cents for making each of them, you count on his using his ingenuity and on his making a careful study of the methods by which he is going to make them, and so increase his daily output. You hope that later instead of making ten pieces per day, he will make twelve, fourteen, fifteen, or even twenty pieces a day. This is the hope of the manufacturer.

We will assume that that workman knows nothing about the piecework system. With the opportunity before him to have his ingenuity and his harder work rewarded by getting more pay per day, he would very likely, after six months or a year, learn how to make fifteen of these instead of ten, or, let us say, twenty instead of ten. If he made twenty he would be earning $5.00 per day in place of $2.50 which he earned before he was put on piecework.

The foreman over those men, we will say, is a straight, square man, and in all honesty he encourages them to turn out more than ten pieces; we will say he encourages them to get out twenty pieces. Now in almost all boards of directors of our companies there are a number of very wise gentlemen who are perhaps members of other boards of directors, and at certain intervals these wise and philanthropic men are very apt to ask for an analysis of the payroll of their company. And when they see that a certain workman in their employ is earning $5.00 a day, they are naturally horror stricken. "Why," they say, "our orders to that superintendent were that he was to pay the ruling wages which prevail around here; $2.50 a day is all any machinist ought to earn; it is horrible to think of a mere machinist with no education earning $5.00 a day; Mr. President, I move that our superintendent be instructed to see that the men in this establishment are paid no more than other machinists in other establishments. Why should we be spoiling the labor of this part of the country?" So Mr. Foreman, although he may be an honest man, and although he has encouraged those men to turn out that work, in many cases perhaps has actually made promises to them that if they increased their output their wages would not be cut, that man is forced by the board of directors to go back on his word, to cut down the piecework price; he has to force those men to make twenty pieces for $2.50 a day where before they made ten pieces for $2.50 a day. Now the working people of this country are not fools; generally one cut of that sort is enough; two always are enough; and from that time forward a workman is nothing but a fool if he does not soldier to "beat the band," if he does not deliberately try to make the people around him believe that he is working as fast fast as he can, while he is really doing a very ordinary day's work. And, gentlemen, that is our fault, not his, and not a thing are we doing as a whole to remedy that state of affairs.

It was precisely this condition which forced us to take the first step which led towards Scientific Management. I had had a war lasting some two or three years with the workmen who were my friends, over whom I was finally placed, a constant running fight for two or three years, in which I was trying to drive them in spite of their resistance to do a larger amount of work. Having worked with them, I knew they were soldiering to the extent of about two-thirds, and I hoped to be able to get them to at least double their work, and finally I did, and then they were one-third short of what they could have done. After three years of that fight, three years of never looking a man in the face from morning till night except as a tactical enemy, three years of wondering what that fellow was going to do to me next and wondering what I could do to him next, I made up my mind that some remedy would have to be devised for that state of things or I would cease to be a foreman and go into some other business. It was in an endeavor to remedy such a state of things that the first step was taken leading towards Scientific Management.

In taking account of stock, after I had definitely made up my mind either to try to remedy that state of things or get out of industrial management, I found that the chief lack was the lack of knowledge. I had no illusions as to my own knowledge; I knew that those workmen knew ten times as much collectively as I knew. And we started to take measures which should enable the foreman of that shop to know approximately what his men knew. We started then along various lines of study with the purpose of educating the owners and managers of the shops of the Midvale Steel Works so that they also should know approximately what their men knew. That was the first step leading towards Scientific Management.

I want to tell you as briefly as I can what Scientific Management is. It certainly is not what most people think it to be. It is not a lot of efficiency expedients. It is not the printing and ruling of a lot of pieces of blank paper and spreading them by the ton about the country. It is not any particular system of paying men. It is not a system of figuring costs of manufacture. It is none of the ordinary devices which unfortunately are going by the name of Scientific Management. It may in its essence be said in the present state of industry to involve a complete mental revolution, both on the part of the management and of the men. It is a complete change in the mental attitude of both sides towards their respective duties and towards their opponents. That is what constitutes Scientific Management.

There are now, I don't know exactly how many, but at a fair estimate I should say 50,000 men working under Scientific Management. These men are on the average turning out twice as much work per day as they formerly did.

As a result of this increase in output, their employers are profiting by a very material reduction of the cost of whatever they are making. This diminution of cost has enabled them, on the one hand, to earn a larger profit and, on the other hand, in most cases to somewhat reduce the selling price of the goods which they make. And let me tell you, gentlemen, that in all cases of Scientific Management, in all cases of increase in efficiency, the general public takes almost the whole of the increase in the end. We consumers are the beneficiaries of the increase in output. The history of the matter shows that neither the manufacturer nor the workman through any long period gets very much benefit from increased output except as the whole world takes it. The world takes that benefit and is perfectly entitled to it. Now the workman: what have these 50,000 men who are working under Scientific Management got out of it. On an average those men are earning from 30 percent to 100 percent higher wages than they did, and I look upon that as perhaps the smallest part of their gain. Those workmen, to my mind, have gained something far greater than that; in place of looking at their employers with suspicion, in place of looking upon them as at least tactical enemies, although they may be personal friends, they look upon their employers as the very best friends they have in the world. I look at that as the greatest gain that can come under Scientific Management, far greater than any increase in wages. The harmony that exists between employer and employee under Scientific Management is the greatest gain that can come to both.

That is mere assertion, but in proof of the fact that this harmony does exist between the workman and the employers under Scientific Management, I wish to make the statement that until perhaps three months ago there never had been a single strike of men employed under Scientific Management. Even during the difficult period of changing from the old management to the new, that difficult and dangerous period when a mental revolution was taking place and causing readjustment of attitude towards their own duties and towards the duties of the management, there had never been a strike until this year. This system has been applied to a great number and variety of industries, and the fact that until recently there had never been a single strike is ample proof that these friendly relations actually exist between both sides. That, perhaps, is the most important characteristic of Scientific Management.

In order to explain what Scientific Management is, I want to present first what I believe all of you gentlemen will recognize as the best of the older types of management and to contrast with that type the principles of Scientific Management. If you have an establishment with 500 or 1,000 men, there will be, perhaps, twenty different trades represented. Each of the workmen in those trades has learned practically all he knows from watching other workmen. When he was a young apprentice he would watch a journeyman, imitate his motions, and finally perhaps the journeyman would get interested and turn around and give the boy a little friendly advice; and thus the boy, merely by personal observation and a very small amount of incidental teaching, learned the trade. In just this way every operative in every one of those 20 different trades in your establishment has learned his trade; it has come to him just as it did in the Middle Ages, from mouth to mouth, or rather from hand to eye, not through teaching. Nevertheless, in spite of the old traditional way of learning a trade, this knowledge is the greatest asset that a workman possesses. It is his capital.

The manufacturer who has any intelligence must realize that his first duty should be to obtain the initiative of all these tradesmen who are working under him, to obtain their hard work, their goodwill, their ingenuity, their determination to treat their employer's business as if it were their own. And in this connection I wish to strain the meaning of the word "initiative" to indicate all of those good qualities. It should be the first object of a good employer to obtain the real initiative of his workmen.

There is an occasional employer, possibly one in a hundred, who deliberately sets out to give his employees something better in the way of wages and opportunities than his competitors give their men. These very few rare employers who are farther sighted than the average, deliberately set out to give their men a special incentive, and in return they expect, and they frequently get, from their men an initiative which other employers do not dream of getting. However, this initiative is generally spasmodic. Workmen come to have confidence in their superintendent, or in their foreman, and in the honor of their company; and when the superintendent tells them that he intends to have them earn more money than other employers are paying their workmen, they believe it and respond in a generous way. But I want to tell what happens almost always, even in such a case: some new workman comes in for whom they have respect; he tells the men the usual story; that the same promise had been made to him or to friends of his in some other shop by a foreman, a square man, but it happened that that foreman died, or was replaced, or the board of directors did just what I outlined at the beginning, and then those promises went to the winds, and the men found themselves working harder than before at the old wages. When a man comes in among them and tells them that story the men think, "Perhaps that is so—it is likely to happen in our shop; I guess we had better not work too hard," and they slow down. Finally, as they think it over and realize that their foreman can be relied on, they say, "This fellow is all right, he can't treat us like that, we have got to be square," and eventually they will work hard again. But under the old system the initiative of the workmen is obtained spasmodically at best; it is rarely obtained to the fullest extent.

The first advantage which Scientific Management has over the older type is that under Scientific Management the initiative of the workmen is obtained with absolute regularity; their hard work, good will and ingenuity are obtained with absolute regularity. I refer of course only to those cases in which Scientific Management is actually introduced and in operation, not where it has just been started; but in practically all cases where Scientific Management has been once established the initiative of the workmen is obtained with absolute regularity. That alone is a marked advantage of Scientific Management over the best of the other types.

This is not, however, the greatest advantage of Scientific Management. This is the lesser of two advantages. The greater advantage comes from the new and unheard-of burdens and duties which are assumed by the men in the management, duties which have never been performed before by the men on the management side. These new duties are divided into four large classes which have been, properly or improperly, called "The Four Principles of Scientific Management."

The first of these four great duties which are undertaken by the management is to deliberately gather in all the rule-of-thumb knowledge which is possessed by all the twenty different kinds of tradesmen who are at work in the establishment—knowledge which has never been recorded, which is in the heads, hands, and bodies, in the knack, skill, dexterity which these men possess—to gather that knowledge, classify it, tabulate it, and in most cases reduce it to laws and rules; in many cases, work out mathematical formula which, when applied with the cooperation of the management to the work of the men, will lead to an enormous increase of the output of the workmen. That is the first of the four great principles of Scientific Management, the development of a science to replace the old rule-of-thumb knowledge of the workmen.

The second of the new duties assumed by the management is the scientific selection and then the progressive development of the workmen. The workmen are studied; it may seem preposterous, but they are studied just as machines have been studied in the past and are being more than ever studied. In the past we have given a great deal of study to machines and little to workmen, but under Scientific Management the workman becomes the subject of far more careful and accurate study than was ever given to machines. After we have studied the workman, so that we know his possibilities, we then proceed, as one friend to another, to try to develop every workman in our employ, so as to bring duties best faculties and to train him to do a higher, more interesting and more profitable class of work than he has done in the past. This is the second of the principles of Scientific Management.

The third duty is to bring the scientifically selected workman and the science together. They must be *brought* together; they will not come together without it. I do not wish for an instant to have any one think I have a poor opinion of a workman; far from it. I am merely stating a fact when I say that you may put your scientific methods before a workman all you are of a mind to, and nine times out of ten he will do the same old way. Unless some one brings the science and the workman together, the workman will slip back as sure as fate into the same old ways, and will not practice the better, the scientific, method. When I say, make the workman do his work in accordance with the laws of science, I do not say *make* in an arbitrary sense. If I did it would apply far more to the employing than to the working class, because in the work of changing from the old to the new system, nine-tenths of our troubles are concerned with those on the management side, and only one-tenth with the workmen. Those in the management are infinitely more stubborn, infinitely harder to make change their ways than are the workmen. So I want to qualify the word make; it has rather a hard sound. Someone must *inspire* the men to make the change, for it will not occur naturally. If you allow things to wait, it will not occur in ten years when it should occur in two months. Someone must take it in hand.

The fourth principle of Scientific Management is a little more difficult than the others to make clear. It is almost impossible to explain to the average man what I mean by it, until he sees one of our companies organized under Scientific Management.

The fourth principle is a deliberate division of the work which was formerly done by the workmen into two sections, one of which is handed over to the management. An immense mass of new duties is thrown on the management which formerly belonged to the workmen. And it is this handing of duties which they never dreamed of assuming before over to those on the management side, requiring cooperation between the management and the workmen, which accounts more than anything else for the fact that there has never been a strike under Scientific Management. If you and I are doing a piece of work together, and realize that we are mutually dependent upon one another, it is impossible for us to quarrel. We may quarrel, perhaps, during the first few days. Some men find it difficult to cooperate. But when they once get to going and see that the prosperity of both sides depends on each man doing his share of the work, what is there to strike about? They realize they cannot strike against the friend who is helping them. That is what it is, a case of helpfulness. I think I can say truthfully that under Scientific Management the managers are more the servants of the men than the men are the servants of the managers. I think I can say that the sense of obligation is greater on the part of the management than on the part of the men. They have to do their share and be always ready. That is the feeling of those on the management side under Scientific Management.

In order to make that equal division a little clearer, I will say that in one of our machine shops, for instance where we do miscellaneous work, not work that is repeated over and over again, there will be at least one man on the management side for every three workmen throughout the whole establishment. That indicates a real division of work between the two sides. And those men on the management side are busy, just as busy as the workmen, and far more profitably busy than they were before.

Let me repeat briefly these four principles of Scientific Management. I want you to see these four principles plainly as the essence of the illustration I am going to give you of Scientific Management. They are the development of a science to replace the old rule-of-thumb methods; the scientific selection and then the progressive teaching and development of the workmen; the bringing of the scientifically selected workmen and the science together; and then this almost equal division of the work between the management and the men.

I wish to convince you of the importance of these principles. So far what I have said has been mere assertion. The only means that I have of convincing you of the value of these principles is to give illustrations of their application. But I fear my time is too short to give more than two or three.

I usually begin with the most elementary kind of labor that I know, and try to show the immense power of those four principles when applied even to that extraordinarily elementary form of labor. The simplest kind of work that I know is handling pig iron. A man stoops down to the ground or a pile, picks up with his hands a piece of pig iron weighing usually about ninety pounds, walks a certain number of steps and drops it on a pile or on the ground. I dare say that it seems preposterous to you to say that there is any such thing as the science of handling pig iron, that there is any such thing as the training of a workman and the cooperation and the equal division of the work between the two sides in handling pig iron. It seems absolutely preposterous. But I assure you that had I the time I could convince every one of you that there is a great science in handling pig iron. It takes a little too long to give that particular illustration, and I very much regret that I must begin with a form of labor which is far more scientific than handling pig iron, namely, shoveling dirt.

I dare say that you think there is no science in shoveling dirt, that anyone can shovel dirt. "Why," you say, "to shovel it you just shovel, that is all there is to it." Those who have had anything to do with Scientific Management realize, however, that *there's a best way in doing everything,* and that that best way can always be formulated into certain rules; that you can get your knowledge away from the old chaotic rule-of-thumb knowledge into organized knowledge. And if anyone of you should start to find the most important element in the science of shoveling, everyone of you with a day's or two days' thought would be on the track of finding it. You would not find it in a day, but you would know what to look for. We found it after we started to think on the subject of shoveling. And what is it? There are very many elements, but I want to call your attention to this important one. At what shovel load will a man do his biggest day's work? There must be some best shovel load; what is it?

The workers of the Bethlehem Steel Company, for instance, almost all owned their own shovels, and I have seen them go day after day to the same shovel for every kind of work, from shoveling rice coal, three and a half pounds to a shovel-load, to shoveling heavy wet ore, about thirty-eight pounds to the shovel-load. Is three and a half pounds right or is thirty-eight pounds right? Now the moment the question "What is the proper shovel-load?" is asked under Scientific Management, it does not become the duty of the manager to ask someone, to ask any shoveler, what is the best. The old style was, "John, how much ought you to take on your shovel?" Under Scientific Management it is the duty of the management to *know* what is the best, not to take what someone thinks. We selected two first-class shovelers. Never examine anyone but a first-class man. By first class I do not mean something impossible to get, or even difficult to get. Very few people know what you mean when you say first class. I think I can explain it to you better by talking about something with which we are all familiar. We know mighty little about men, but there is hardly one of us here who does not know a good deal about horses, because we are in the habit of studying horses. Now if you have a stable full of horses containing large dray horses, carriage horses, saddle horses, and so on, and want to pick a first-class horse for hauling a coal wagon, I know every one of you here would take the dray horse. I do not believe any of you would take the trotting horse and call him first class at all. That is what I mean when I say *first-class man.* If you have a very small stable, when you have a good deal of coal to haul you may have to hitch your trotting horse to a light grocery wagon or even to your buggy to haul coal. But that is not a first-class horse for the purpose, and no one would think of studying a trotting horse hauling a buggy of coal to find what a first-class horse should do in hauling coal. There are many people who say, "You are looking for impossible people; you are setting a pace that nobody can live up to." Not at all. We are taking the man adapted to the work we wish done.

So when we wanted to study the science of shoveling we took two men and said, "You are good shovelers; we want you to work squarely. We are going to ask you to do a lot of fool things, and we are going to pay you double wages while this investigation is going on. It will probably last two or three months. This man will be over you all day long with a stopwatch. He will time you; he will count the shovel-loads and tell you what to do. He does not want you to hurry; just go at your ordinary fair pace. But if either of you fellows tries to soldier on us, that will be the end of it; we will find you out as sure as you are born, and we will fire you out of this place. All we want is a square day's work; no soldiering. If you don't want to take that job, don't, but if you do we are very glad to pay you double wages while you are doing it." These men said they would be very glad to do it, and they were perfectly square; they were ready to do a fair day's work. That was all we asked of them, not something that would tire them out or exhaust them, but something they could live under forty years and be all right.

We began by taking the maximum load on the shovel and counting the shovelfuls all day long and weighing the tonnage at the end of the day. I think it was about thirty-eight pounds to the shovel. We found how much those men could do when they were shoveling at thirty-eight pounds to the shovel on an average. And then we got shorter shovels holding about thirty-four pounds, and measured the tonnage per day, and it was greater than when they were using the thirty-eight pound shovel. They shoveled more with the thirty-four pound shovel-loads than with the thirty-eight pound shovel-loads. Again we reduced the load to thirty pounds and they did a still greater tonnage; again to twenty-eight pounds, and another increase; and the load kept on increasing as we diminished the shovel-load until we reached about twenty-one pounds; at twenty-one pounds the man did his biggest day's work. With twenty pounds, with eighteen pounds, with seventeen, and with fourteen, they did again a smaller day's work. Starting with a thirty-eight pound shovel, they went higher and higher until the biggest day's work was done with a twenty-one pound shovel; but when they got the lighter shovel the load went down as the shovel load diminished.

The foundation of that part of the science of shoveling, then, lies in always giving a shoveler a shovel which will hold twenty-one pounds, whatever the material he is using.

What were the consequences of that? In the Bethlehem Steel Works we had to build a shovel room for our common laborers. Up to that time the men had owned their own shovels. We had to equip this room with eight or ten different kinds of shovels, so that whatever the man went at, whether rice coal on the one hand, or very heavy ore on the other, he would have just a twenty-one pound load. That meant organization in place of no organization.

It meant also arranging that each one of the laborers in that yard had the right shovel every day for the kind of material he was going to work on. That required more organization. In place of the old-fashioned foreman who walked around with his men to work with them, telling them what to do, it meant the building of a large, elaborate labor office where three college men worked, besides their clerks and assistants, planning the work for each of these workmen at least one day in advance. That yard was about two miles long and half a mile wide; you cannot scatter 500 to 600 men over a space of that size, doing all kinds of miscellaneous work, and get the man, the shovel, and the other implements, and the work together at the right time unless you have an organization. It meant, then, building a big labor office and playing a game of chess one day in advance with these 500 men, locating them just as you would locate chessmen on your board. It required a timetable and a knowledge of how long it took them to do each kind of work.

It meant also informing the men each day just what they had done the day before and just what they were to do that day. In order to do that, as each man came in the morning he had to reach his hand up to a pigeonhole (most of them could not read and write, but they could all find their pigeonholes) and take out two slips of paper. One was a yellow slip and one was a white slip. If they found the yellow slip, those men who could not read and write knew perfectly well what it meant; it was just the general information: "Yesterday you did not earn the money that a first-class man ought to earn. We want you to earn at least 60 percent beyond what other laborers are paid around Bethlehem. You failed to earn that much yesterday; there is something wrong." It is merely a notice to the man that there is something wrong. The other piece of paper told him what implement to use. He went to the tool-room, presented it, received the proper implement, and took it down to the part of the yard in which he was to work.

When any of these workmen fell down for three or four days in succession, tho old way would be to call him up and say, "Here, John, you are no good; get out of this; you are not doing a day's work. I don't have any man here who is not doing a day's work. Now get out of this." But that is not the way with Scientific Management. The moment the management sees that this man has fallen down, that it is something more than an accident, then a teacher—not a bulldozer, but a *teacher*—is sent out to him to find out what is the matter, and to study the man for the purpose of correcting his fault. In nine cases out of ten that teacher would perhaps find that the man had simply forgotten something about the art of shoveling. I suppose you are skeptical about this "art of shoveling," but let me tell you there is a great deal to it. We have found that the most efficient method of shoveling is to put your right arm down on your right hip, hold your shovel on your left leg, and when you shovel into the pile throw the weight of your body upon the shovel. It does not take any muscle to do that; the weight of your body throws it if you get your arm braced. But if you attempt to do as most shovelers do, take it with your arms and shove it into a stubborn pile, you are wasting a great deal of effort. Time and again we found that a man had forgotten his instructions and was throwing the weight of his arms instead of the weight of his body. The teacher would go to him and say, "You have forgotten what I told you about shoveling; I don't wonder you are not getting your premium; you ought to be getting 60 percent more money. You are falling out of the first class. Now I want to show you again. Just watch the way this thing is done." The teacher would stand by him *as a friend* and show him how to earn his premium. Or perhaps if he found that the man was really not suited to that work, for instance that he was too light for it, the man would then be transferred to a lighter kind of work for which he was suited. It is in that way, by kindly and intimate personal study of them, that we find to what workmen are adapted.

All of that takes money, and it is an important and very fair question whether it pays. Can you pay for all these time study men who are developing the art of shoveling? Can you pay for your shovel tool room, for the telephone system, and all the clerks and teachers? The only answer to that is these facts. At the end of about three years we had practically the whole of the yard labor of the Bethlehem Steel Works transferred from the old piecework and day work plan to the new scientific plan. Those workmen under the old plan had earned $1.15 a day. Under the new plan they earned $1.85 a day, an increase of more than 60 percent in wages. We had them studied and a report made. We found that they were practically all sober, that most of them were saving some little money, that they lived better than they ever had before, and that they were as contented a set of men as could be found together anywhere, a magnificent body of carefully selected men. That is what the men got out of it.

What did the company get out of it? The old cost for handling a ton of materials in the yard of the Bethlehem Steel Company was between 7 and 8 cents a ton. The new cost, after all the costs of the clerical work in the office and the tool room, of the teaching, the telephone system, the new implements, and the higher wages, were taken into consideration, was between 3 and 4 cents a ton. And the actual cash saving to the Bethlehem Steel Company during the last year was between $70,000 and $80,000. That is what the company got out of it, and therefore the system is justified from the points of view both the men and the management.

I am very sure that I could convince you that the ratio of gain of Scientific Management when applied to a trade that requires a high-class mechanic, is far greater than when applied to work like shoveling. The difficulty which I find is to convince men of the universality of these principles, that *they are applicable to all kinds of human effort.* I should like to convince you, I am sure that I could convince you, that with *any* of the more intricate kinds of work, the gain must be enormously greater than with the simple work; that no high-class mechanic can possibly do what he should for his own sake and for the employer's sake, without the friendly cooperation of a man on the management side. That is what I should like to prove to you, prove beyond the shadow of a doubt.

Take the case of a machinist who is doing work that is repeated, we will say, over and over again. He is not the highest class mechanic, but he is fairly well up. It may be questioned whether it is possible for any scientific knowledge to help an intelligent mechanic, a man, for instance, who has had a high school education and who has worked for his whole life as a machinist. I want to show you that that man needs the help of—not a higher order of man, nothing of that sort, but of a man with a different type of education from his own; that the skilled workman needs it far more even than the cheap laborer needs it in order to do his work right.

I take an actual case, that of a shop manufacturing small machines. This was a department of a large company which had been running under the old system many years. The article was a patented device that had been manufactured in this department about 12 years, perhaps more, by some 300 workmen. These articles varied somewhat in size but they were made by the thousands. The men would naturally become highly skilled. Each man had his own machine, ran it from year end to year end, made comparatively few parts, and therefore became skilled in his work.

Now the owner of this establishment was a very progressive man, and he came to the conclusion that he wanted to investigate Scientific Management. So he sent for my friend, Mr. Barth* to see what Mr. Barth could do for him. After they had had a little sparring on the subject, Mr. Barth rather mortified the owner by telling him that he could come pretty close to doubling the output of his shop. After they had sparred a little over that, Mr. Barth suggested that he make a test to show the men in the shop what he could do. So a typical machine was selected, a machine which they both agreed was fairly representative of the machines in the shop, and the work which was then being done noted; the kind of work, the character of it, and the time which

---

*Carl George Lange Barth, 1860–1939, mechanical engineer and instructor in manual work and mathematics. He introduced the Taylor System in machine shops.

it should take to do it was written down. Then Mr. Barth proceeded to study the machine, in just the way under Scientific Management and machines are analyzed in all shops that we go to. We do not go to some foreman or super-intendent, or to the maker of the machine, and ask, "How fast do you think we should run this machine?" Not at all. A careful, thorough analysis was made of the possibilities of that machine, and to do that Mr. Barth used four slide rules. One slide rule will solve any problem in gearing in almost no time. It is a gear slide rule. Another solves any problem about belts in a fraction of a minute. Another tells you how many pounds pressure a chip of any shape or kind will exert on the cutting tool, and therefore shows you how much resis-tance you have to overcome with your machine. The fourth slide rule tells you what cutting speed you can use with any kind of metal, with any depth of cut, with any feed, and with any shape tool.

Now with these four rules it is possible scientifically to analyze the machine, to know how it should be speeded for the particular kind of work that is in hand. And let me tell you—this may seem an extraordinary state-ment—let me tell you that there is not one machine in fifty in the average machine shop in this country that is speeded right. I say that with all confi-dence. I say it with perfect confidence, because last spring I was invited by the tool builders, the makers of these machines, to address them at their annual meeting, and I challenged them to contradict that fact. They were there, representatives of the tool builders of this country, and not one man took up my challenge. They knew, just as well as I know, that their speeds are nine-tenths guess and one-tenth knowledge, that they do not take into considera-tion the peculiarities of the shop their machines go into, in one case in fifty. They have no means of knowing the kind of material the machines are to cut, and the machines are speeded practically the same for every shop they go to, whereas each machine should be speeded to suit the average of the work that is to be done in a particular shop.

After Mr. Barth had inspected that machine by means of these slide rules, in two or three hours he was able to write the prescription for it, showing what should be done to have it right. And then, after he had given direc-tions to have the machine speeded right, he went home and made a slide-rule by means of which, when he returned to the shop, he was able to show the workmen, the foreman, and the owner of that shop just how the machine should be run in various cases. Pieces of metal were put into the machine, similar to those which were ordinarily run in it, and his smallest gain was two and a half times as much, and his largest gain nine times as much work as had been done before. That is typical of what can be done in the average machine shop in this country.

Why? Because the science of cutting metals is a true science, and because the machine shops of this country are run, we can almost say, without the slightest reference to that science. They are run by the old rule-of-thumb method just as they were fifty years ago. The science is almost neglected, and yet it is true science.

I want to show you in a general way what that science is, so that you will understand why it is that a man who had never seen that particular machine, who had never seen that work, was able to compete with the workman who had been working for ten or twelve years on the same machine, who had the help of the foreman and of his superintendent,—for it was a well-run establishment; how a man who had never seen that work, but who was equipped with a knowledge of the science, was able to make it do from two and a half to nine times as much work as had been done before. I want to show you what it is, because that is the essence of Scientific Management, the development of a science which is of real use when applied with the cooperation of the management to help the workmen.

I spoke at the beginning about an ordinary piecework fight which went on between a foreman who tried to do his duty and his men. At the end of that bitter fight of two or three years, I obtained permission from William Sellers, who was then the president of the Midvale Steel Works, to spend some money in educating the foreman of the Midvale Steel Works so that he should have at least a fraction of the knowledge of his men. And one of the subjects which we took up at that time, one in which the foreman needed most education, was the science of cutting metals, for metal cutting was the whole work of the shop. And I believed, just as Mr. Sellers believed, just as almost every mechanic at that time believed, that the science of cutting metals consisted mainly if not entirely in finding the proper cutting angles of the tool.

As you all know, each metal-cutting tool has, properly speaking, three cutting angles. It has the clearance angle, the side slope, and the hack slope. And it was my opinion, just as it was the opinion of almost every machinist that I knew, that if you could get the right combination of cutting angles you could cut steel and iron a great deal faster than we were then doing. So we started out to make a careful investigation as to what those cutting angles should be.

We were exceedingly fortunate in having what hardly any shop in the United States had at that time, a very large boring room. We were then making locomotive tires. That was a considerable part of the business of the Midvale Steel Works at that time. We had a very large boring mill available, sixty-six inches in diameter, and a very large uniform body of metal and tires weighing two thousand pounds to put on it. So we had an opportunity to do what very few people had the opportunity to do. A sixty-six-inch diameter mill was at that time an unusually large one, so we put our tire on that mill and, having enough metal in that one piece to run three or four months, we could eliminate possible errors resulting from variability of the metal. At the end of six months we found that these angles which we supposed were of the greatest consequence counted for but little in the art of cutting metals. The two things which every machinist must know every time he puts a piece of work into his lathe, if he wishes to do it right, are the speed he should run his machine and the feed he should use in order to do his fastest work. Those two things sound very simple indeed. But to know them is to know the science of cutting metals. At the end of six months we found that the thing we were hunting for, the question of angles, had very little bearing on the problem, but we had unearthed a gold mine of possible information. And when I was able to show Mr. Sellers the possibilities of knowledge ahead, he said at once, "Go right ahead, go on spending the money." And for practically twenty-six years, with here and there a year or two of intermission, went on that series of experiments to determine the laws of the science of cutting metals. It was found that there were twelve great variable elements which enter into metal-cutting operations. All that was done in twenty-six years was to investigate these twelve elements, to find out the facts connected with them, to record and tabulate these facts, to reduce them to mathematical formulae, and finally to make those mathematical formulae applicable in everyday work.

I know that it will seem almost inconceivable that such a time should be taken, and I want to show you how it is possible that it took that length of time. At various times in this investigation ten different machines were built and equipped and run for the purpose of determining the various elements of this science. While we were at the Midvale Steel Works we had no trouble at all because they knew the value of the elements which we were studying; they knew the commercial value of them; but after we left there our only means of continuing these experiments was to give the information which we had up to date in payment to anyone who would build us a machine and furnish the labor and materials to continue the investigation. So most of these ten different machines were built in that way by men who were willing and anxious to trade their money, in the shape of new equipment, new forgings, new castings, and new labor, for the knowledge that had been obtained from previous experiments.

Let me briefly call your attention to some of the variable elements. I will not bother you with all the twelve, but I want to let you see enough of them to appreciate what I mean by this science of cutting metals. Investigations similar to this are bound to be made in every industry in this country, scientific investigations of those elements which go to make up the science, whatever that science is; that is the reason why I am dwelling on it. It is not an isolated case. It is perhaps the longest drawn out investigation that has been made, but it is simply typical of what is bound to take place in every industry.

One of the first discoveries which we made—and it seems an exceedingly simple one—was that if you throw a stream of water on the chip and tool at the point at which the shaving of iron is being cut off from the forging, you can increase your cutting speed 40 percent. You have a 40 percent gain just by doing that little thing alone. That we found out within the first 6 months. Mr. Sellers had the courage of his convictions; he did not believe it at first, but when we proved to him that it was true, he tore down the old shop and replaced it with another so as to get that 40 percent increase in the cutting speed. He built a shop with water drains extending under the floor to carry off the water with which the tools were cooled to a central settling tank; from there it was pumped up again to a tank in the roof and carried from there through proper piping to every tool, so that the workman did not need to spend much time in adjusting a stream which would flow on to any tool in any position. He was a broad enough man to see that it paid him to build a new shop to get that 40 percent.

Now our competitors came right to the Midvale Steel Works without any hesitation. They were invited to come there, and in 20 years just one competitor used that knowledge and built a shop in which it was possible to throw a heavy stream of water on the tools, and that was a shop started by men who had left the Midvale Steel Works and who knew enough to do this. That shows the slowness of men, in that trade at least, to take advantage of a 40 percent gain in cutting.

That is one of the twelve elements, a very simple one, the simplest of all. Let me show you one or two more.

There is the old diamond-point tool, used when I was a boy in practically all shops throughout the country. One of the first suggestions that I had for an experiment was from Mr. John Bancroft,* now one of the ablest engineers in the country. He suggested that I try the effect of using a round-nose tool, with a round cutting edge. Hardly a single piece of original work was done by us in Scientific Management. Everything that we have has come from the suggestion of someone else. There is no originality about Scientific Management. And, gentlemen, I am proud of it; I am not ashamed of it, because the man who thinks he can place his originality against the world's evolution, against the combined knowledge of the world, is pretty poor stuff.

Now, that diamond-point tool was almost universally used at that time, and I do not believe there is one mechanic in fifty now who knows why it was used. It was used because in the primitive shops, such as the one in which I served my apprenticeship, we all had to make and dress our own tools. There was no tool dresser. We would heat the metal, lay it on the edge of the anvil one way and ask a friend to hit it a crack, and then turn it around and

---

*John Sellers Bancroft, 1843-1919, mechanical engineer and inventor. Member ASME.

repeat the process, and simply turning it and hitting it with the sledge would give it the diamond point. That is the only reason why a tool of that shape was in use. It was a tradition. It had no scientific basis.

After a sufficient number of experiments, we found that a roundnose tool was far superior to a diamond-point tool, but it took a long time after we made that discovery before we found what kind of a round-nose tool. It took years before we were through with the experiment to determine what curve was the best when all things were considered, because there are many considerations which come in. There is the speed, the convenience of handling, the kind of work to be done, and so on.

Having, then, decided that a round-nose tool was the best, we had to make another investigation. If you have a light cut taken on your tool in one case, a heavy cut in another, and a still heavier one in another, it is a matter of plain common sense that you could of course in one case run a very much higher cutting-speed than in another. How fast can you run? That is a question for accurate scientific investigation. The investigation, simply to determine that fact, took altogether, I think, as much as two years. And even after we had determined the facts, it was many years before we finally got the proper mathematical expression of those facts. That is a totally different matter. Before we had reduced our knowledge to a true mathematical formula which could be worked with, it was a question of years.

The next investigation, perhaps the most spectacular of all, was to answer the question, what is the effect of the chemical composition of the tool and its best treatment? The old-fashioned tools when I served my apprenticeship were all made of carbon steel. But it has been found that by putting tungsten in those tools one can make them withstand a higher amount of heat and still not lose their cutting edge. A part, then, of the study of the art or science of cutting metals was to make a thorough, scientific investigation of the possibilities of alloy steel, not only with the new metal tungsten, but with other alloys which presented possibilities; so we varied the quantities of tungsten, chromium, molybdenum and one or two other elements, until at the end of three years of continuous experimenting the modern high-speed steel was developed; that is, a certain kind of steel which when heated in a certain revolutionary way would enable you to run, to be accurate, just seven times as fast as with the carbon steel. The discovery of high-speed steel and its treatment was the result of investigations. Most people think it was a mere accident, that some fools were fooling around and by accident discovered this thing; but I assure you three or four years of hard study and investigation by chemists and metallurgists working according to the most scientific methods were required. In these various experiments $200,000 were spent and from 800,000 to 1,000,000 pounds of metal were cut up into chips.

Perhaps the most difficult phase of the experiments was getting steel of uniform hardness for experimental purposes. To carry on our elaborate experiments when high-speed steel came in, we had to have at least 20,000 pounds of metal to experiment on, and it is almost impossible to get 20,000 pounds which are uniform. We finally solved it and obtained metal which was sufficiently uniform by using exactly the same processes which are used in making the great high-power cannon for the army and navy. That is, we forged metal under a forging press, and then oil-tempered and annealed it until we got a uniform body of metal. The tempering and annealing resulted in making the steel finer and finer and making all the crystallized structure uniform.

I want to explain why twenty-six years were necessary to carry out these experiments. Time after time we would have to throw away six months' work because eleven of these elements had slipped up while we were experimenting with the twelfth. If hard spots appeared in the steel, a whole line of experiments was thrown out and we would have to get a new forging and start all over again. It was the difficulty of that sort of thing, holding eleven elements constant while we were getting the twelfth, which made that problem as difficult as it was. When those experiments had first been reduced to facts, and then the facts to diagrams, and then curves drawn through the diagrams and finally mathematical formulae made to fit those diagrams, then we were on the road toward the development of a science. We finally developed twelve formulae to represent the twelve variables, of which this is a specimen:

$$V = \frac{11.9}{F^{0.665} \left(\frac{48}{3} D \right)^{0.2373 + \frac{2.4}{18 + 48D}}}$$

When one has a lot of mathematical formulae of that sort, it seems at first the idea of a lunatic to imagine that anyone could get any use out of them. That is, all of our friends, when they found that our experiments were resulting in such formulae as these, said, "Why, you are nothing but rank crazy; you will never be able to use these things." And a great work, greater than the experiments which gave us these formulae, was the work of giving these formulae a form which would make them usable for the ordinary machinist. We kept mathematicians working on that problem for about eighteen years.

Now you must realize that a mathematical problem with twelve variables is a big thing. During that time we went to the great mathematicians in the country, the professors in our universities, and offered them any price to solve that problem for us. Not one of them would touch it; they all said, "You can solve a problem with four variables if you have your four equations, possibly; beyond that it is an indeterminate problem, and it is all nonsense thinking of getting a mathematical solution for it." I dare say you people think I am trying to prove that Mr. Barth and Mr. Gantt and these other gentlemen are very remarkable men. Nothing of the kind. This is the point I want to make: that it is a long, tedious operation to solve a problem of that sort, or to solve any of the intricate problems connected with the mechanic arts, or those that are going to arise in any art. It is a difficult thing to do. But very ordinary men with ordinary equipment can solve and make useful any problem, I do not care how difficult it is, if they will only give the time and the money and the patience; they will solve it.

At the end of 18 years these men had devised a little machine, a slide-rule, which solves the problem with 12 independent variables in about 20 seconds. That is put into the hands of an ordinary lathe man who knows nothing about mathematics, and by means of it that man determines under which one of 800 or 900 conditions pertaining to the particular job he will do his fastest work. It was for that reason that Mr. Barth, with his slide rule, was able to more than compete with the mechanic who had spent 12 years in the old-fashioned rule-of-thumb way of cutting a particular kind of metal on his particular kind of machine; just for that reason, because the amount of knowledge which that machinist needed to have in order to solve that problem was utterly impossible for any one to have.

What I am trying to show you is, that the more intelligent the high-class mechanic the more he needs the help of the man with the theoretical knowledge; he must have it even more than the ordinary laborer must have it. And that is why this cooperation, in which the management does one part of the work and the workman another, must accomplish overwhelmingly more work in all cases than the old method of leaving to the workman both the determining how and the performance.

There is just one thing more that I want to say; something that I am sure you are all thinking of. I find this question in the mind of every one who is considering Scientific Management. It may be that this combination of the science and the workman turns out more work than before, but doesn't it make a wooden man out of the workman? Doesn't it make him a machine? Doesn't it reduce him to the level of an implement?

I want to give one or two answers to that. The first is this: that under the new system every single working man is raised up, is developed, is taught, so that he can do a higher, a better, and a more interesting class of work than he could before. The ordinary laborer is taught to run the drill-press in the machine shop, the drill press hand becomes a lathe hand, the lathe hand becomes a toolmaker; the toolmaker—now I am speaking of types of men, you understand, not literally—the toolmaker becomes one of the teachers. He is the man in the planning room. He is the man who makes up this one out of three who is transferred to the management side, so that the best workmen, who before would have remained workmen, are on the management side and become teachers and helpers of the other workmen. I want to emphasize the brotherly feeling which exists under Scientific Management. It is no longer a case of master and men, as under the old system, but it is a case of one friend helping another and each fellow doing the kind of work that he is best fitted for. You boys have here in the college one pretty good piece of Scientific Management, and that is football—a good case of cooperation, training, and teaching and that is the fine feature about football, that it does enforce a fine method of friendly cooperation.

Does this make workmen into wooden men? Let us answer the second question. I have said, and I repeat, that no one claims any originality for Scientific Management; it was all done before. I do not know of a person who claims any originality for it whatever. It has simply taken what other people were doing before. Long before we had any development of Scientific Management, there was in existence a far finer case of Scientific Management than we have ever succeeded in developing. The finest mechanic in the world had developed Scientific Management long before we touched it or ever dreamed of it. You all know him, every one of you; he is the modern surgeon. In his operations five or six men cooperate, each one doing in turn just what he should do. How does that finest mechanic teach his apprentices? Do you suppose that when the young surgeons come to their teachers, the skilled surgeons, they are told first of all: "Now, boys, what we want first is your initiative; we want you to use your brains and originality to develop the best methods of doing surgical work. Of course you know we do have our own ways of performing these operations, but don't let that hamper you for one instant in your work. What we want is your originality and your initiative. Of course you know, for example, when we are amputating a leg and come to the bone, we take a saw and cut the bone off. Don't let that disturb you for a minute; if you like it better, take an axe, take a hatchet, anything you please; what we want is originality. What we want of all things is originality on your part."

Now that surgeon says to his apprentices just what we say to our apprentices under Scientific Management. He says: "Not or your life. We want your originality, but we want you to invent upward and not downward. We do not want any of your originality until you know the best method of doing work that we know, the best method that is now known to modern surgery. So you just get busy and learn the best method that is known to date under modern surgery; then, when you have got to the top by the present method, invent upward; then use your originality."

That is exactly what we say to our men. We say, "We do not know the best; we are sure that within two or three years a better method will be developed than we know of; but what we know is the result of a long series of experiments and careful study of every element connected with shop practice; these standards that lie before you are the results of these studies. We ask you to learn how to use these standards as they are, and after that, the moment any man sees an improved standard, a better way of doing anything than we are doing, come to us with it; your suggestion will not only be welcome but we will join you in making a carefully tried experiment, which will satisfy both you and us and any other man that your improvement is or is not better than anything before. If that experiment shows that your method is better than ours, your method will become our method and every one of us will adopt that method until somebody gets a better one."

In that way you are able to apply a true science to mechanical work, and only in that way. If you allow each man to do his own way, just exactly as he pleases, without any regard to science, science melts right away. You must have standards. We get some of our greatest improvements from the workmen in that way. The workmen, instead of holding back, are eager to make suggestions. When one is adopted it is named after the man who suggested it, and he is given a premium for having developed a new standard. So in that way we get the finest kind of teamwork, we have true cooperation, and our method, instead of inventing things that were out of date forty years ago, leads on always to something better than has been known before.

SCIENCE IN MANAGEMENT FOR THE ONE BEST WAY TO DO WORK

FRANK B. GILBRETH

FALLACY OF THE DRIFTING PROCESS TOWARD EFFICIENCY

In the past, progress in management has been made largely by the "drifting process." This drifting process is the slowest process. The drifting process has never once led to the One Best Way to do work—*never once*. Everybody knows this, yet only a small percentage of the world is applying science to methods of work and to management, as has been done to so many of her material things.

ACTUAL MEASUREMENT SHOULD BE THE BASIS FOR DECISIONS FOR OBTAINING EFFICIENCY

Times have changed, and are changing, and the engineer has now shown how greater changes for progress in methods of work and in management can be made in a year than have formerly been made in centuries. For greatest results, the best of present practice must be recorded, measured, judged, and conserved. In the past, there has been no nation which has attempted to standardize, as a result of measurement, the best that is known regarding methods of work and management.

Published by Società Umanitaria, Milan, 1923. Paper presented at Illème Conférence Internationale de Psychotechnique Appliqué à l'Orientation Professionelle, Milan, Italy, October 2–4, 1922. Original pamphlet made available through the courtesy of the Gilbreth Collection, Engineering Library, Purdue University, Lafayette, Indiana. Used by permission of Mrs. Lillian M. Gilbreth.

A NATION SHOULD MEASURE AND INVENTORY ITS EFFICIENCY

This is the age of measurement.

An epoch in the development of a nation is marked when it inventories its efficiency and gathers detailed records of successful methods and devices for doing work, in order that all may use the One Best Way available, or extant, wherever it be found, and improve constantly and cumulatively from the best that is known at any time; but unless measurement is applied, and the causes and reasons for success or efficiency are recorded sufficiently in detail for others than those who did the recording to understand, real, constant, cumulative, and lasting progress cannot result.

THOROUGHNESS IS NECESSARY

It is necessary not only to observe present conditions carefully but to *"think things through,"* to get back to fundamentals, and to ask not only *what* is efficient but *how* and *why* it is efficient, and what can be standardized that will automatically cause the conditions that will enable those efficient happenings to exist continuously, to be permanent and repetitive.

SCIENCE OF MANAGEMENT TELLS THE "WHAT," "HOW," AND "WHY"

It is for this reason that the science of management is an indispensable aid in understanding and using efficiency methods and devices, because it tells *what* is efficient, decides exactly *how* efficient it is, and explains the *why*.

The Science of Management consists of applying measurement to management and of abiding by results of measurement. National prosperity can be maintained only if it measures its development and plans its progress as a result of this measurement.

PURPOSE OF THIS PAPER

It is the purpose of this paper to show why the science of management forms an important part in attaining, and especially in maintaining, national prosperity.

HOW SCIENTIFIC MANAGEMENT GOT ITS NAME

"Scientific Management" is merely a name for an attempt to enlist science in the solving of the complicated problem of increasing the productivity of all for the greatest good of the greatest number and for justice, increased opportunity, comfort, and happiness for all. As it is known today, it dates in the minds of most people from the time when successful methods of work were investigated in America, and especially when the Interstate Commerce Commission and Congress were holding hearings on the claims, merits, and possibilities of the Taylor and other systems of management in relation to increases in efficiency, particularly of the railroads in opposition to proposed increases of railroad freight rates.

In planning the hearings before the Interstate Commerce Commission, it was found desirable to decide upon a short title, or name, by which the subject of "science applied to management" could be identified and discussed. At a small meeting of a few of the early advocates of the movement at which we were present, prior to the hearings, Mr. Louis Brandeis, now Justice Brandeis, who advocated better management instead of increasing freight rates, presented the need for such a name. The term "Scientific Management" was finally decided upon as being suitable, free from personal entanglements, and embodying the underlying ideas of this new "decision by measurement" type of management. As a consequence, the name "Scientific Management" was used and was flashed and mailed around the world by news and technical writers, although the name "measured functional management," suggested at the time, would perhaps have been better for the cause of science in management, as well as being more appropriate and more truly descriptive.

The "Science of Management" includes much more than what is included in the term "Scientific Management."

AGE AND ORIGIN OF EARLY ATTEMPTS AT DEFINITE AND SYSTEMATIC MANAGEMENT

The science of management far antedates Taylor and the other leaders of the movement of this generation. We find it well under way in the work of Babbage and of Adam Smith. In 1776 Adam Smith wrote "An Inquiry into the Nature and Cause of the Wealth of Nations," a masterpiece for its time and in many respects still a masterpiece not only of economics but of industrial efficiency. In 1832 Charles Babbage, in his "Economy of Machinery and Manufacture," gave not only a masterly description and discussion of conditions in industry at that time but a model method of studying such conditions. These clear thinkers and finished writers were able to put into words thoughts that intelligent men everywhere had been working toward and struggling to express and use for ages. Learned men were also giving this subject their attention in France and Italy, as is clearly seen in the works of Coulomb and in the handbook of Leonardo da Vinci.

Management has for centuries been a subject that held popular attention, the complicated managerial problems of pay systems and cooperation being clearly described in the Parable of the Vineyard. It is not surprising that management has always been an essential element of work and of production.

ANCIENT RECORDS OF METHODS OF MANAGEMENT

All existing records of methods in arts and trades show unmistakable signs of an advanced development in management and motion study, as may be seen even in the sculptured pictures of the Assyrian, Babylonian, and Egyptian monuments, executed in the dawn of written history, which show a certain type of efficiency and which may well have served not only as records but also as teaching devices. In these records there are numerous examples of recognition of the factor of rhythm as a variable of motions and of efficiency. In many instances these records show that the different kinds and classes of workers were distinguishable by their different kinds of dress. The records show, in part, the accepted and apparently highly standardized methods of enforcing order of those days, for the gang bosses are repeatedly shown as each possessing one large club and two long daggers. The large club is poised in the air in the right hand, and one long dagger in the left, and the second dagger is always so located and positioned that it can be grasped with the shortest and quickest motions, in case at any time it was desired in the hand more than was the club.

UNITS, METHODS, AND DEVICES FOR JUDGING MANAGEMENT

We cannot properly compare, or "rate," or judge management without *measurement*. For constant, cumulative improvement and progress, this measurement of efficiency and management must consider three factors: first, the units to measure, the numerical measures of which indicate the quality of management; second, the methods of measuring, the measures of which, in many different units, determine their value and desirability; third, the measuring devices, the measures of which determine their desirability as tools of measuring. The *unit* selected indicates the results desired to be achieved or eliminated. The *method* used shows the state of perfection of the theory. The *device* shows the existing state of the practice.

To be efficient, the units must be as elementary as possible and selected with special regard to their facilitating the holding of all units constant except the one which is being measured at that time. The units should foster accuracy and be readily transferable for the solving of other, similar problems. The *method* must insist on such a degree of accuracy as the results desired demand. Any error should be toward the practice of too great accuracy, because of the possibility of utilizing accurate records for many more problems than the original one for which they were specially intended. For the same reason, the devices must attain as great a degree of accuracy as is possible, but must be as cheap and available as is consistent with such accuracy. As far as possible, these devices must be free from human error.

EXAMPLE OF SELECTION OF WRONG UNIT OF MANAGEMENT

For a definite illustration of the importance of this, consider the original records of Assyrian and Egyptian management already referred to and still available to the world in the British Museum. These records show that the *unit* to be measured selected by these ancient managers was improperly and unwisely chosen. This unit considered, apparently, the amount of time worked and, secondarily, *the amount of output accomplished*, the emphasis being upon the amount of effort exerted, rather than upon the continuity of effort. The quality of output was judged from the standpoint of the finished work and not the method by which it was done. The human element was not only not considered, but the subject was apparently discarded as being entirely unworthy of attention. Apparently there was not the least consideration given to measuring any units that reduce fatigue or labor turnover, for the workers were drafted and impressed in accordance with royal edicts which were issued in some cases, after a careful census of the inhabitants had been taken.[1] Their "employment psychology" was apparently based upon no such scheme as dismissal for disobedience, insubordination, or lack of cooperation. Their plan was apparently to make a horrible example of each act that the ever present gang boss considered a breach of discipline. This practice can be paralleled in some organizations today, but public sentiment prevents going so near the limit as was apparently customary in ancient times.

Human life, in the earliest records of management, was the cheapest of commodities, and work was done either by slaves of foreign extraction, or by [native?] slaves, or the equivalent of slaves, or prisoners of war, who were undergoing punishment or who belonged to a class expected to live lives of drudgery.

ETHICS, NOT SCIENCE, FURNISH STANDARDS OF RIGHT AND WRONG

We note that while science is not called upon to furnish a standard of right and wrong, this being the task of ethics, science can be utilized for measuring the data submitted and comparing them to the established standard, and publishing the

---

[1] King, Williford, "The Elements of Statistical Method," page 2.

facts for all to see. Such a standard having been determined, it is thus possible to judge whether the units, methods, and devices selected are ethical or otherwise.

THE BEST UNIT FOR SCIENCE TO USE TO MEASURE ETHICAL STANDARDS IS A MINUTE OF HAPPINESS

In scientific management the most constructive, desirable, successful, and ethical unit of measurement is a "Minute of Happiness,"[2] here or hereafter. In many instances a reward hereafter has been found sufficient for obtaining the workers' best efforts, serving instead of the customary wage in money for that kind and quantity of output in the vicinity.

Obviously, other things being equal, that which affects favorably the largest number of people will cause the greatest quantity of happiness minutes. It must be remembered that to enlist the ability and zeal of those fitted to lead an aggregation or organization to greatest success, sufficient motivation must be offered; or the *one best leader,* as desired in each division of the organization, will devote his efforts and time to something which will bring him what he thinks will be greater returns.

This brings us to the great problem of "pay for results," the discussion of which is out of place in this paper. For further details of this, see Chapter entitled "Incentives in Psychology of Management."

A method in management is ethical when it gives those concerned a square deal. Even the *devices* can be judged as honest or dishonest, as well as accurate or inaccurate, and condemned as unethical, as the spying stopwatch book has been where it disregards or infringes human rights.

SCIENCE DETERMINES UNITS OF EFFICIENCY

While the science of management may not determine standards of right and wrong, it can, and actually does, determine standards of efficiency, such as the One Best Way to learn, do, or teach any kind of work. In its most approved and advanced forms, the science of management has been more just and ethical in defining the subject matter of implied, as well as actual, contracts between employer and employee based upon "pay for results" than has any other form of management.

To determine these standards of just and ethical procedure, management must, first, *conserve the best of the past;* second, *organize the present;* and, third, *forecast and plan for the future.*

---

[2]See "Fatigue Study," Routledge & Co., London; "Etude des mouvements appliqué," Dunod, Paris; "Ermüdungstudlen," Berlin.

It has often been thought that the science of management, like some unfortunate improperly prepared and planned attempts in "Scientific Management," is a destructive force—a critical force—that aims to do away with whatever exists, root and branch, and to start something entirely new on a new foundation. This is not the case at all when the management is installed by one who properly understands it. The aim of the science of management is to submit to measurement what already exists in the plant under examination, in order to discover and conserve those things which are worth keeping and perpetuating.

When this is not done, there is always an astounding unnecessary waste, because time and individual conditions and differences bring to pass many standards, customs, and methods of great value, which could be utilized with profit. It must not be forgotten that nothing is exempt from inspection and judgment by measurement because of its aim or its long use as a standard, and that sometimes things which are of less than no value have been allowed to go on continuously for years because no one has had the combination of the thought, the desire, and the proper authority to make a change. On the other hand, a method or a device that has worked satisfactorily for many years should be most carefully investigated, in order that the demands which it fulfills, as well as the manner in which it fulfills them, may be most carefully estimated. "Hold fast to that which is good" might well be a slogan of the science of management, though it is not generally understood to be one.

RECOGNITION OF SOME LAWS OF MOTION STUDY BY THE PEOPLE OF THE STONE AGE AS SHOWN BY THEIR IMPLEMENTS

Scores of definite instances illustrating the above can be cited from existing evidences of tool efficiency in the days of the stone age, due consideration being given to the handicap that stone instead of metal was the material of which these tools were made. The tools of the expert workmen of that age, found in the archaeological museums of the world, indicate certain features relating to motion study, fatigue study, and causes of skill—developed during the many thousands of years of the stone age—that have not been equalled or appreciated as yet, even by the designers, makers, and users of the later bronze tools or of the steel tools of today. The reason for this is that the tool designers of today have not actually had these tools in their hands and examined them from the standpoint of the laws of motion study, fatigue study, and standardization. Such definite instances should be recognized, measured, and recorded in the survey of all existing evidences of the One Best Way to do work.

TYPES OF SURVEYS FOR EFFICIENCY

Systematizing and organizing all existing desirable conditions calls for a careful survey which can also assist in conservation. A survey may be anything from a more or less unsystematic record or list of what occurs to what is known as a technical survey, made by experts who are experienced in finding, recording, and using data. Such surveys as those made by the Russell Sage Foundation, under the brilliant leadership of Dr. Leonard Ayers, furnish an excellent example of what a scientific survey is and can accomplish. The advantage of having a survey made by someone in the plant is that the making of the survey is of itself a highly educative process. The advantage of having the survey made by a survey expert is that he is already trained to note minute likenesses and differences. He is able not only to record what exists but also to deduce valuable recommendations for improvement from his experience in similar problems in other organizations, particularly regarding the adoption of fewer and better standards and methods for the same kind of work.

EVERYTHING SHOULD BE STANDARDIZED AND ALL STANDARDS NOTED IN THE SURVEY

This does not mean fewer standards for different kinds of work. On the contrary, the best results come only when everything is standardized down to the smallest and most insignificant details. This means that decisions on often repeated questions should be standardized wherever possible. For example: Before starting to work one's first minute on a typewriter, calculating, or accounting machine, the decisions as to which fingers shall strike each individual key should be standardized and settled, once and for all.

A SURVEY SHOULD RECORD "WHAT IS" SEPARATE FROM "WHAT SHOULD BE" OR "WILL BE"

It is almost impossible for the amateur survey maker to give an unprejudiced record of what occurs, not only because of his limited experiences, but also because he is constantly tempted to put down not that which he actually does but, rather, that which he obviously ought to do or would like to do, or what he thinks he does, or what he thinks will be the method in the near future—or something in some degree different from a survey of what actually is being done. The ideal conditions exist when as many members of the organization as possible make an amateur survey, each of his own work, as part of and in accordance with a complete outline in process chart form; and when, to supplement this, a survey expert makes a survey of the entire plant and organization in order to "check up" and supplement the individual surveys and individual process charts.

SURVEYING, CLASSIFYING, AND FILING INFORMATION

A most important part of the organization work of the science of management consists of planning, gathering, arranging, and systematizing all this and similar information and filing it under a complete interrelated mnemonic classification filing system. This is specially adapted for all existing and all future notes and information specifically related to any work in question and classified and subclassified by subject, so that all data differing by one variable only are as nearly contiguous as possible. In this way, related matter comes automatically to the attention of the searcher, even if he does not suspect the existence of such information, in accordance with the laws of modern filing of information.

It is possible that much of this organizing of information and of the methods and processes throughout the plant can be done without the aid of a professional expert in the science of management. By this we mean that all successful and progressive plants of today have undoubtedly systematized their procedure to some extent. However, the science of management is fortunate in being able to provide the complete skeleton and mechanism for handling all procedure, with units, methods, and devices already standardized for visualizing, filing, and using. This means that both materials and information can be stored or used with ease.

FILING, CONNECTING, AND VISUALIZING INTERRELATIONS OF SEPARATE PIECES OF INFORMATION

A cursory study of many types of management charts will illustrate this very clearly. For example, take the typical organization chart, showing methods of visualizing and grouping responsibilities and lines of authority and counsel. Take, for example, our functional organization chart, illustrating grouped interrelated subdivisions of the Taylor system, which recognizes the functional division of the planning from the performing and which shows plainly such divisions as the "what," "who," "where," "when," "how," "why," and "how much" of the problem. Take, again, our subfunctional chart, which shows the various types of work or subfunctions that are performed under each function. Take, for example, a typical chart of our three-position plan of promotion. See also the chapter on "Units, Methods and Devices," in "Applied Motion Study," which shows the financial and promotion relations of each type of work to every other type, and exactly along which regular and optional or exceptional-principle lines the employee must advance to reach any predetermined function. Take our master and individual process charts, which show the various stages in the manufacture of the product. These are but a few of many charts which show how information is recorded, grouped, visualized, and filed, and which indicate the degree to which it is available when needed.

A close study of these charts shows that in every case they depict logical and definite relationships; that is, they show the relation of cause to effect, and they give the valid cause for each desired effect. They conform not only to the laws of logic but to those of psychology, and of least waste in education, in that they afford the best method of imparting ideas and facts and of memorizing the information. Here, again, it is impossible for an organization to do much for itself in putting its information into a more orderly state. In fact, a series of more or less complete charts, showing, in comparable form, possible and planned changes, may be made a most valuable by-product of the survey.

Facts as Shown by the Surveys and Collected Information Must Be Faced

It requires something like courage for one to record and study the actual existing conditions in his own plant, whether in chart form or not, and to record the present and proposed future position of each and of every member of the organization engaged in management—his present and probable titles and functions; the work that he actually does now; the work that he could or should do; and the relation of his work to that of the other members of that branch of the organization. It takes courage to walk personally with open mind and eyes through one's plant and to cause to have made and to study the actual records and charts of the various processes. These should begin where the requisition for raw material originates and the material enters the plant, and end as the finished product leaves the plant for transportation elsewhere. In the case of a blank form, these start with the first filling in and state exactly, step by step, workplace by workplace, where it goes when it reposes in or travels through current or obsolete files; who or what transports it there; why it goes to each place; how long it remains there; what happens to it there; when, where, and with what it is inspected and overinspected for quantity or quality, or both, etc.

The Best Way Is Always the Simplest Way After It Is Learned

By studying these things one realizes, as never before, the ramifications of and the many complications that beset even the simplest problems in production, and how numerous the instances are which are handled in a complicated way simply because there is no definite system recorder in detail for maintaining the simplest way.

It must not be forgotten also that "putting things in order" implies two things; first, getting them *into* the place desired; second, getting them *out of* the place without delay when they are needed. In most cases, the important thing is to be able to get the thing out and ready for use in the shortest amount of time possible when it is needed. The test of the efficiency of "filing," for example, is not in how short a time any specific item can be put into a resting place, but rather in how short a time it can be found and taken from its resting, or storage, place to the place where it is to be used. As an example of this let us consider the repair and storage of tools.

A TOOL ROOM MUST BE COMPLETELY STANDARDIZED FOR BEST RESULTS

The advantage of a tool room, under the most scientifically planned practice, is that a tool can be taken to the workplace a short time before it is needed, in that predetermined standard condition described by the written and otherwise recorded standard as essential to doing the best work in the shortest amount of time possible. True, it takes time to have the tool carried to the tool room, to have it inspected to see if it complies in every respect with the requirements of the written standards and, if it does not, to have it put into the standardized condition, then re-inspected and put away.

With a few standardized exceptions, which are also thoroughly provided for, each tool should be stored in the tool room when not in use, and when stored should be so placed in the tool rack

1. that the part showing its working condition will be most easily seen during the regular inspection and over-inspection trips arranged on the exception principle for an executive;
2. that it can be taken out in the shortest amount of time possible; and
3. that it conforms. while in storage in the tool room, to the laws of least waste for the motion cycle elements, such as "search," "find," "select," "grasp,"[3] just as it does while being used.

If at any time it is not in the condition that has been standardized and specified in writing, it is not to be put into storage until so conditioned and again

---

[3] See the chapter on "Motion Study for Crippled Soldiers" in the book *Motion Study for the Handicapped,* Routledge, London.

inspected. When it conforms to the written standard made for that tool, it is to be put away in the standard position, which is the easiest way, after the tool bin has been constructed in accordance with the requirements of the standard.

The cost of the time of sharpening, conditioning, transporting, storing, and inspecting is as nothing compared with the benefits—direct and indirect—resulting from putting this standardized, properly sharpened and conditioned, automaticity-causing tool in the hand of the worker at the moment when he needs it; and the assurance that, as a result, he will be able to perform his part of the production schedule and program in the expected and allotted time.

THE ASTOUNDING LOSS TO THE WORLD BY REASON OF LACK OF APPRECIATION OF THE PART THAT PROPER TOOLS PLAY IN THE ONE BEST WAY TO DO WORK

The hindrance to the productivity of all nations due to those in responsible charge of workers neither understanding the needs for, nor the solutions of, the problem of maintaining the best tools constantly in the proper condition undoubtedly amounts in money to more than an average of twenty percent of the payroll of the world's workers. We have estimated this figure carefully, and we believe that 20 percent is much below the true amount. The resulting figures are astounding. Some people are so constituted that they cannot look wastes squarely in the face, simply because these wastes are astoundingly large. As an example of this, last year we stated that the loss in the United States due to unnecessary fatigue of all workers is a matter of hundreds of millions of pounds sterling per year. However, after due consideration one of the officers of the National Safety Council, a great organization for the prevention of accidents and unnecessary fatigue, in their official organ said our statement was reasonable and unanswerable.

These facts, when visualized in actual total money waste, are astounding, but we have seen many cases in motion study laboratory investigations of some of the best organizations where the loss has been more than fifty of the workers' payroll, and we know of organizations where it is probably more. The motion study variable of automaticity is so important that it is better to have all one kind of an inferior class of tools in perfect condition than to have some first and some second class tools in varying states of condition.

THE QUALITY OF TOOLS IS NOT CHANGED BY REASON OF THEIR HAVING ORIGINATED OUTSIDE OF ONE'S OWN COUNTRY

One thing that hinders efficiency and fosters the continuation of the deplorably inefficient system of *"drifting toward efficiency"* is that in practically all nations there is evidence of the belief that it is something resembling a lack of patriotism and loyalty to acknowledge that any other nations have better tools than has one's own nation. Nevertheless, the facts bear out the economic law that those nations as a whole, and those parts of nations in particular which have paid the highest wages continuously for long periods, have the best tools with which to work. If a worker is paid low enough wages, it matters comparatively little what kind of tools he has, from a cost standpoint, but if his wages are unusually high, his managers and foremen insist that he be provided with the most suitable tools obtainable.

MOTION STUDY LABORATORIES FOR RESEARCH IN THE WORLD'S TOOLS SHOULD BE AT THE DISPOSAL OF EVERY EARNEST WORKER

The difference in tools is everywhere so evident that it would pay any nation, any city, or even any Employers' Board of Trade or Workers' Association to be ever cognizant of the best tools and best methods of conditioning tools, regardless of whence the necessary information must come. Any organization is lucky that can obtain a man, at almost any price, who can analyze tools from the motion study, fatigue study, and skill study standpoint, instead of relying upon the prejudice and preference of workers, due to habit and dexterity in spite of their wrong and poor tools, which influence their attempts to be perfectly fair in their judgment.

TOOL STUDY APPLIES TO ALL DEPARTMENTS

At present, first cost is the test of tools. Even a broom is made to that width which will sell to best advantage, not sweep with fewest motions. Where is the broom maker who has had his broom's motion studied? The same general criticism applies to many other tools. The maker of tools is not the only one asleep. How many executives have provided sweepers with a properly selected assortment of different sized brooms to be used by the same sweeper in different parts of the sweeping? How many great organizations have furnished their purchasing departments with clearly circumscribed super standards for tools to be purchased? No large organization can avoid losing money that has not hundreds of such standards for its purchasing department. This does not mean merely for hatchets, saws, and wrenches. It means everything down to the smallest item used—that automaticity may be achieved for big outputs and least fatigue. Our clients have invariably been surprised when they have seen the simple money-saving standards that could be substituted for their unsystematized practices. The executive who does not also, personally, use a dictating machine instead of a stenographer exclusively, thus enabling his typist to earn higher wages because of his and her higher outputs, the man who still prefers the old-fashioned razor because he has neither personally acquired automaticity with the one best safety razor, nor counted the relative number of motions while shaving; the man who has not accustomed himself to walking on the one best kind of rubber heels and noted carefully the extra amount of work which he is capable of performing because he is less fatigued—these are examples of the types who cannot be expected to realize the amount of money that the world is losing by reason of its workers not being provided with the *best tools in proper condition.*

This is not a matter to be decided by a few minutes' consideration, for a short time review of this subject will give the same sort of decision as that of the American Indian who tried sleeping with one feather between his head and the rock that supported it. His conclusion was, you remember, that sleeping on a bed full of feathers would give him a similar disastrous result, proportionate to the relative number of feathers used. All mankind is prone to say, as did this Indian, "You can't change my mind. I've tried it." It must be remembered that a *trial is not a trial until the condition of automaticity has been achieved, and even then measurement must be used instead of judgment.* There are still many men who act as though it were as necessary to be present personally when their boots are cleaned as it is for them to be personally present when they are shaved.

THE SUBJECT OF TOOL STUDY IS TOO LARGE FOR THIS PAPER

This paper is not the place to describe in detail the differences in output of contented workers, both in the shops and in the offices when they are furnished with superstandardized tools, maintained in condition in the One Best Way, and in sufficient quantity and with proper routines that eliminate delays. Superstandardized tools permit learning their use in less time—a point of great importance to the learner and the nation. Superpractice with few tools makes greater skill in the same time. It also makes sooner the state of automaticity which is the greatest free asset of the worker. This gives more time for learning the use of more tools.

LETTER FILES ARE TOOLS OF THE MENTAL WORKER AND ARE SUBJECT TO ALL THE LAWS OF TOOL STUDY

The hindrance due to improperly standardized and operated tool systems is a no more flagrant example of causes of inefficiency than is the method of handling of letters for and by executives in the majority of organizations.

The value of the time taken to put a letter properly into the file is trifling compared with the value of the time required to find that letter and place it before the man at the moment he requires it if the letter is not filed in the One Best Way together with related information.

It is not expedient to write here the details of the necessity nor the process of having all letters in all departments put away properly into the files within one day from the day that they are received, regardless of the size of the organization, nor is it wise to start any argument about the possibility of this with those executives who have not seen it done in great organizations as well as in small ones.

It is not wise to dwell here upon the usual and customary arguments to the effect that a letter cannot be filed until after it has been answered, nor to discuss the admission that, in many files, filing means "probably lost" or "lost for a long time."

It is also not wise to dwell here upon the unnecessary delay and the cost of the ordinary routine in organizations where inefficient outing, filing systems, and handling of inward and outward correspondence testify to a general lack of appreciation of the fact that the usual practice to be found almost everywhere was not designed by the methods of motion study but, on the contrary, appears to be designed with the idea of *making* motions instead of *saving* them.

THE COST PER PIECE FOR HANDLING MAIL SHOULD BE WATCHED

It will pay any organization to have a careful record made of the cost of handling each piece of mail. The results of such a cost investigation have never, in our experience, failed to turn doubters of the value of the science of management into enthusiastic exponents, at least so far as process charts and a standardized standing order system are concerned.

PRESENT METHODS SHOULD BE VISUALIZED AND COMPARED WITH PLANNED METHODS

We note here only the importance of visualizing, measuring, and comparing the existing methods with a well-thought-out logical plan for all details of administration. We emphasize, as we must repeatedly, the benefits of specific standard mechanisms and installations, such as those referred to in the two examples just given, as a stimulus to thought and imitation. They are a starting point from which improvements are to be made and suggestions and inventions considered; and must be understood, installed, and working smoothly before real progress can be assured.

WATCHING FOR INDICATIONS OF THE PROBABLE TREND OF EVENTS

The third function of management, following conservation and organization, is the forecasting of and planning for the trend of future developments. The study of statistics in graphical form shows that a careful investigation and comparison of the past and the present permits the prediction of at least the *trend* of future developments. Elderton, King, Secrist, among the recent writers on statistics, make this extremely plain even to the lay mind. The admirable books and papers of such men as Brinton and the Graphical Standards Committee show exactly how to present statistics graphically and not only *what* can be done but *how* it can be done, in the simplest and most impressive fashion.

GRAPHS OF THE PAST AND PRESENT MEASUREMENTS INDICATE THE TRENDS OF SIMILAR EVENTS IN THE FUTURE

A careful study of the past history and the present practice in a plant will enable one, to some extent, to predict future development or at least show present trends. It will probably be said that much of this development depends on conditions peculiar to the individual plant, upon the prosperity of the country, upon the business and labor conditions, upon the demand for the product, and upon all sorts of outside factors. This is undoubtedly true, but two things should be said.

1. A man should be able to estimate what he will do if conditions remain the same as they are at present; and
2. He should be prepared to meet almost any emergency by some planned-for expedient in his program.

The science of management is fortunate in being able not only to forecast a trend for any individual enterprise more scientifically than can be done without scientific management, but also in being able to tell what the trend *ought to be,* as well as what it probably *will be.* Thus, it is possible to plan ahead for such action as may be desirable only when the quantity plotted falls outside the zone of exclusion on the graphical exception-principle charts,[4] and present the case for action to an executive on the exception principle, automatically notifying the executive whose rank is comparable with the quantity of deviation.

---

[4]See "Graphical Control on the Exception Principle for Executives," A. S. M. E.

PREPAREDNESS FOR MEETING EMERGENCIES AND OTHER EXCEPTIONS FROM CLASS

Scientific Management is also fortunate in having definite and proved methods with which to meet an emergency. Such terms as "automatic notification," "exception principle," "zones of exclusion," "elasticity station," "standard deviation," "Flying Squadron in Management," represent the standardized methods already provided for meeting and handling the unexpected. Perhaps it might better be said, "expecting the unexpected to happen" and getting ready to handle it when it does occur. After all, statistics seem to show that "chance" is really no longer "chance" but happens fairly closely in accordance with the laws of expected variation from the normal curve of the class.

PLANNING FOR PROBABLE DEVELOPMENT

Much can be said of the value of statistics in assisting in the making of correct decisions regarding lines of probable development and planning accordingly. Take, for an actual example of this, the future need for and the building of a great Western University. A loyal citizen, a regent of the University, instituted a competition, which was engaged in by architects from many countries, to plan for the development of the buildings and grounds of this University. Every department of the University outlined its present and future needs; everyone interested in the University contributed information as to its possible, probable, and desired development. All of these data were assembled and studied, and the resulting needs were met by the foremost leaders in their professions. The plans made were far ahead of the requirements at the time. Their effect, however, has been extremely successful. Not only has such development as has taken place in the twenty years since then followed the lines wisely laid down at that time, but undoubtedly much has found its way into the resources of the University, because those who had things to contribute knew that what they gave would be utilized in a directed, orderly fashion. As a result, these plans have served as a stimulus, as well as a conserving and guiding force, and have probably exceeded even the usefulness that their donor expected of them.

In the same way the science of management is already equipped to supply a plan for the development of an industry or an organization. It is able not only to meet the general demands but to consider the individual differences of the organization. The early recognition of the trend, the laying out of this plan, and the adaptation of the methods of the science to the individual needs is not work for an untrained, inexperienced executive, although such can be found in charge of this responsible work almost everywhere. The literature, of the subject of management contains the necessary information, but only the trained thinker and installer can use this information for the betterment of the plant. In some plants today management has developed to such a stage that experts are now at work making surveys, organizing, and forecasting the trend of future development. However, the majority of plants are as yet in an earlier stage, where the chief necessities are to arouse interest in progress in the plant towards better management; to make every member of the organization, in all fields of the work, *think* along the lines of measurement in management; and to stimulate the plant to take such preliminary steps as it can for itself.

PROCEDURE OF THE PRELIMINARY STAGE OF THE TRANSITORY PERIOD IN MANAGEMENT

We are informed on good authority that it is the belief of many of the leaders of thought in Europe that the majority of the plants abroad require most of all information as to the best procedure in this preliminary stage. We are, therefore, and by request, making this paper very definite and specific in its description of what can wisely be done in the first stages of thinking along the lines of the science of management and of preparing to make measurement and accept its results.

VISUALIZING THE PROBLEM

With this thought in mind, we shall review what we have already said on the subject, to emphasize the importance, in all three stages, of visualizing the problem. Charts, photographs, graphs, and other methods of recording have, as their prime object, presenting the existing state of things to the eye in the clearest possible way.

Those not intimately acquainted with present day investigations in education scarcely realize how many more people learn easier through their eyes than through their ears, or their muscles, or other sense avenues. Through our work with the crippled and blinded, especially the crippled and blinded soldier, we are now able to substitute the use of the other senses for the use of sight.[5] It still remains to be said, however, that the sighted in a large majority of cases learn things easiest through the eye. While we supplement eye teaching with teaching through the ear and teaching through the kinesthetic sensations—as in the use of motion models[6]—

---

[5]See "Motion Study for the Handicapped," 147.
[6]See "Applied M.S.," 91; Macmillan & Co., N.Y.; "Etudes des mouvements appliqué," Chap. VI, Dunod, Paris; "Angewandte Bewegungsstudien," Berlin.

we always stress the importance of visualization. Therefore, in the preliminary stage of introducing the science of management into a plant, we endeavor in every possible way to visualize the problems and to make the process of teaching visual.

So far we have outlined the relation of scientific management to the *past,* to the *present,* and to the *future* of the plant. It is now well to outline its relation to other existing activities. The science of management owes the chief part of its development to the work of the engineer. The leaders in the field have all been engineers—the leaders both in the theory and in the practice—and at the present time the installers are largely also recruited from the field of engineering. This is undoubtedly because the engineer has been accustomed, from his earliest instruction, to deal with measurement and to abide by the results of measurement. The engineer has, however, been ready and glad to acknowledge and is increasingly willing to acknowledge the value of cooperation in other fields.

COOPERATION STIMULATES PROGRESS

The science of management profits by using the results of other already existing activities. It must, of course, test these activities, not only for their validity, but for their usefulness in the field of management. It has, in this way, tested and cooperated with findings in the field of safety, of vocational guidance,[7] of betterment work, of teaching—both in full-time schools and colleges and in part-time and continuation schools—in the work of the industrial schools and institutes; in the work done by the public libraries; in fact, in all work done by teaching, betterment, philanthropic, and clinical activities in the community.

More than this, the engineer has welcomed investigators and thinkers in other lines into the field of management. The work of testing and investigating materials of all kinds is not new. The engineer has gladly cooperated with the chemist, the physicist, and with all other scientists whose work leads them into the field of materials. Increasingly, also, the engineer is cooperating with, and inviting into management, the educator, the physiologist, the psychologist,[8] the psychiatrist, and other scientists engaged in what are known as the human sciences—also, the economist and the statistician.

---

[7]See "Publications of National Safety Council," Chicago, Meyer Bloomfield.

[8]"Psychology of Management," Macmillan & Co., New York; German Edition, "Verwaltungspsychologie" by I. M. Witte, published by Verlag des Vereins Deutscher Ingenieure.

COOPERATION WITH PSYCHOLOGIST

The cooperation with the psychologist has been especially valuable, and it is a matter for congratulation that increasingly bodies of psychologists are devoting themselves to intensive study of the problems of industry. Courses in psychology are being introduced into the curriculum of the engineer. The fact that psychology is devoting itself to such a great extent to industrial problems insures teaching of young engineers that will be most profitable and allow them with the least expenditure of time to apply the results of the teaching to their individual problems.

It may be argued that scientific management as recorded in literature does not always show the influence of, or the results of, the cooperation that we advocate. To which the reply may be made that we are not here discussing so-called "Scientific Management," some instances of which are unquestionably in many respects faulty, but *the science of management.* The theory of management is evidently on the right trend if it is based upon science or upon accurate measurement.

The technique is often the honest though imperfect attempt to carry out that which is misunderstood to be the theory, and the practice does not always live up even to what is recognized and conceded to be best in the technique.

LACK OF COOPERATION CAUSES UNNECESSARY WASTES

But what we must emphasize here is not so much that cooperation does not exist as that an enormous waste occurs when it does not exist. The duplication and reduplication of effort is a pitiful waste of time and effort. Sometimes this is unavoidable, as it was in our own case, when after years of painstaking effort in devising many different methods for the photography of time and motion we discovered, too late to prove of use, though not too late to prove of interest and inspiration, the remarkable work of the French genius, Marey.[9] His work, unfortunately, had never been at our disposal until we had reinvented and abandoned many of its processes because they were unsuitable for our work. We finally invented and perfected our own units, methods, and devices for the solution of our problems and for their application to the needs in hand.

Management has many times experienced a similar waste of effort, as was the case in the early evolution of stopwatch time study without the proper

---

[9]The reference may possibly be to Jules Etienne Marey, 1830–1904, student of physiology, medicine, and photography.

knowledge of educational psychology and statistics.[10] Doubtless other fields have experienced a similar waste through failing to cooperate with management, but comments along these lines will come more appropriately from thinkers and investigators in these fields.

THE MANAGEMENT SHOULD COOPERATE WITH OUTSIDE EFFORTS TO INCREASE EFFICIENCY

As for the practical application, in making an investigation to any particular field we urge cooperation with all existing activities in the community, but it is not possible to list all of these. There are already functioning numerous philanthropic, social service, social, and other agencies engaged in betterment work who are glad to cooperate in many phases of the subject. For example: housing, feeding, lighting, heating, entertaining, insurance, service of doctor, dentist, and nurse, safety, social service, psychiatric clinic, the giving of psychological and fitness tests, together with all the educational forms of service. There are also the libraries—those housed in permanent habitations and the traveling libraries—the foreman's meeting held under such auspices as those of the Y.M.C.A. Again, there are the existing unions and other labor bodies, and all their many-sided activities.

It is a waste to install any new activity in a plant, or to assist in getting such activity going in the plant, if it can be handled better through cooperation with some already existing outside activity. Nothing but accurate measurement can determine whether the activity is better handled inside or outside the plant. The subject must come under serious consideration, and the waste of the duplication must be eliminated, for it is expensive not only in direct cost but in indirect cost, because it encourages a practice which is unprofitable, uncooperative, and unscientific.

It may be urged that such cooperation often does away with the "personal element," with the development of individuality, and with the "personal interest" in these activities. Very true. In such case, let the value of these mentioned traits be measured, and if their value proves to be greater than the value of other things gained through cooperation, by all means conserve the individuality, the personal element, but do not refuse to subject the problem under consideration to measurement.

Here again, we note the importance of units of measurement and their relation to the ethical side of the problem. We must be careful to make it plain that by cooperation we mean "working together" in the old-fashioned sense

---

[10]See "Time Study and Motion Study as Fundamental Factors in Planning and Control," Taylor Society, N. Y.

of the word, and that we do not attach any socialistic or other significance to the word. "Cooperation" is always used in the sense of "working together for the common good" in the literature, theory, and the practice of the science of management.

EFFICIENCY IS NOT LIMITED MERELY TO THE PRODUCTION OF GOODS

In order to set about this work of installing the science of management in the preliminary stage in a plant with the least handicap, it is necessary to be forearmed with information as to the field of such application. The science of management has, in the past, done its most important work in the field of production—and this for several reasons. The leaders in the movement were primarily interested in production. It was their life work; and it is still with difficulty that most engineers can be persuaded that production is not the great work of the world. At times, marketing, distribution, and other types of work may seem, for the moment, to hold the most important place; but, in the long run, *production is the universal need of all times.*

Because of the importance of production, and because the leaders were in the field of production, the vocabulary of the science of management is the vocabulary of production. More than this, because Dr. Taylor was an engineer engaged chiefly in machine shop work and preliminary interested in the machine shop, much of the terminology of management today appears to fit the needs of the machine shop rather than the needs for explaining the theory and the phenomena of management in general. For this reason, many have had the mistaken idea that the science of management applies only to production, and others have had the equally wrong notion that it applies only, or at least best, to work in the machine shop.

PRECISE MEASUREMENT FOR FINDING THE ONE BEST WAY IN THE WORK OF EXECUTIVES AND OFFICE WORK

This latter idea has not been common recently due to the growth of the literature of the movement, telling of micromotion studies of work of executives and managers themselves and of the standardization by photography and writing, and of the organization in the field, in the office, in accounting, in distribution, in sales, in advertising, in the hospitals and other institutions. This literature is becoming lengthy and important. As a matter of fact, since the early days management has been applied in all these fields and also in fields entirely outside the industries, as in the professions of surgery and nursing, and even in the sports.

OFFICE AND ALL OTHER KINDS OF MENTAL WORK CAN BE DONE MORE EFFICIENTLY, AND ARE SUBJECT TO THE SAME LAWS AS WORK IN THE SHOP

The office end is perhaps receiving special prominence, since the extensive micromotion and chronocyclegraph studies which we made in 1912 again proved, and beyond argument, that the underlying principles of obtaining and maintaining the One Best Way in office work are identical to those in any other work, so far as analysis, planning, routing, motion study, fatigue study, waste elimination, standardization, large outputs, management, and control are concerned. Further, the side of distribution is receiving great emphasis because of the need, nowadays, for consideration of this subject.

It is a sign of the times that the economist is arguing that the great waste of the war must ultimately be compensated for by extra production, at the same time that the manufacturers are unable to find a ready market for their wares, and while also there is much unemployment.

The Taylor Society, the Society of Industrial Engineers, and the Management Section of The American Society of Mechanical Engineers, all of them organizations in America for the study of problems of management, are now carefully collecting and exchanging data for the consideration of the special problems of distribution and salesmanship, and in the near future we may expect results which will be of international value.

THE SUPERSTANDARDIZATION OF EVERYTHING, EVERY TOOL, EVERY PRACTICE, EVERY PROCESS, DOWN TO THE MOST INSIGNIFICANT ITEM, IS NECESSARY FOR THE GREATEST EFFICIENCY

We have thus far pointed out the need for and the advisability of applying the science of management to all work. We have explained the advantages of the preliminary survey which presents a record of existing conditions and existing needs. What is the next step to be considered? Undoubtedly the selection of *units* to be measured and some knowledge of methods and of devices which make the measurements, so that the best practice may be known and the tools, machines, equipment, and surrounding conditions, down to the smallest item, may be superstandardized; that automaticity, the great variable of motion study, may be enlisted to increase skill and production and decrease fatigue.

MOTION STUDIES, FATIGUE STUDY, SKILL, AND TIME STUDY ARE INDISPENSABLE FOR DETERMINING THE ONE BEST WAY TO DO WORK

Motion study, fatigue study, skill study, and time study are methods of measurement under the science of management, and *without them it is absolutely impossible to find the One Best Way to do work,* or to make and enforce the superstandards and programs for the benefit of all. These have application in every field, are closely related, and must receive attention at the proper periods in the installation of scientific methods of management.

MOTION STUDY

Motion study is a method of increasing the efficiency of the worker. It is the science of determining and perpetuating the scheme of perfection; the performing of the One Best Way to do work.

FATIGUE STUDY

Fatigue study is a first step in motion study. It is the investigation of the causes and opportunities for the elimination of unnecessary fatigue, and the provision of rest from necessary fatigue. It is unreasonable to expect to obtain hearty cooperation in matters where the workers have not received proper consideration as to the elimination of their unnecessary fatigue.

SKILL STUDY

Skill study is an inquiry into the causes of, and the best way of acquiring and transferring, skill. It is a subject that affects everyone, whether he is apprentice, journeyman, laborer, manager, employer, or stockholder—and also the consumer. The accuracy of the *method of working* leads to the accuracy of the resulting workmanship. Too much emphasis during the learning period cannot be laid upon the importance of correcting the erroneous practice of saving material at the expense of later interference of habits of motions, and the postponement of the day of utilization of automaticity of decision as well as motions. In no other way can superstandardization of tools and working conditions be enforced so well as by putting the emphasis on the accuracy of methods to be used from the beginning. In no other way can such rapid fitness for promotion be achieved. In no other way can the best way known be improved by those who have the greatest craft skill and craft knowledge. We advocate the transference to other work of all trade teachers who do not appreciate this scientific fact as a prime requisite for fitness to teach the beginners in the arts, trades, and crafts. The practice of allowing the *average* method to be taught by the *average* teacher should be discouraged and abolished wherever possible, and the practice of having the One Best Way taught by the *best teacher available* should be encouraged by everyone. There have been no careful and systematized attempts by any nation to collect information about skill, similar to the attempt to find the best wheat, yet the field for synthesizing elements of skill offers opportunities of more importance to mankind than the cross fertilizations resulting in Marquis Wheat. There has been no nation or city that has had a definite system for conserving such information if it were offered to it. Rarely can a man be found who is able to distinguish skill of method from high speed of output in arts and crafts and trades. The workers of the world can now *make* anything. Let the emphasis *now*, during the learning process, be on the *method and not on the accuracy of the resulting product*. This is a problem in psychology, but apparently very few psychologists have more than a remote idea of what it is, yet it has been already proved by measurement, time and again, and solved to the point of standardization.

The best way to conserve the skill of the passing generations profitably is to establish a special department for encouraging the disclosure of unpatentable information, particularly regarding skill study; a department in the patent office should operate on the lines of a modern suggestion system in a motion study laboratory, with all the refinements of the present patent office, and subject to nearly all the same general principles and laws. This would furnish incentive, encouragement, and recognition, as well as a market for ideas pertaining to skill and to methods thought for the time being to represent the One Best Way to do work. Awards for disclosing full information regarding new and useful improvements in skill, which are not patentable, should be paid to the "Inventor" instead of requiring the "Inventor" to pay a fee, as is the custom in all patent offices, when he acquires exclusive rights to make and sell his invention for a term of years. Such a department could not be properly organized by anyone who does not know motion study and the methods of measuring its subdivisions and psychological variables. Neither could it be handled by anyone who does not know that *the One Best Way means the best way at present obtainable*. Nor could it be properly maintained by anyone who persists in believing that the individual differences in any one group of properly placed workers, due to heredity, are as great as their differences due to habit, education, wrong teaching, and automaticity.

It is to be expected that there will be a large number of people who will say that any such arrangement could not possibly work out in actual practice. Our answer is that it *is* already working in several very large organizations with such remarkable results that we venture to predict that a nation could afford to install it and could look for great benefits, even though it were muddled.

TIME STUDY

Time study is the art of determining "how long it takes to do work" or, stated in other words, "how much work can be done in a given time." Time is a variable of motion study, and correct time study is a subdivision and a by-product of micromotion study.[11] Time study should never be confused with motion study. They are quite distinct. Neither should *correct* time study, which is the byproduct of photographically recorded times, free from personal error, be confused with the inaccurate nonmethod recording stopwatch time study.

DEVELOPMENT OF MOTION STUDY AND TIME STUDY

The development of motion study and time study in their relation to each other, and to fatigue study, serves—as we have already shown—as an example not only of how much slower the methods and devices are developed than is the theory, but also of the ultimate development of methods and devices that fulfill the requirements and needs, once these are thoroughly understood. We find the practice of timing work early in the history of management. Dr. Taylor said he first received his idea of taking times from Mr. Wentworth, a teacher of his at Phillips Academy, Exeter, New Hampshire. Be this as it may, Dr. Taylor is undoubtedly, as he has been called, "The Father of Time Study." He was, undoubtedly, the first who had the idea of timing the work cycles and frequent rest periods separately, thus being able to predetermine with greater accuracy than it had hitherto been done how long it would take to do work. Time study should be used for making reasonable, achievable schedules and programs, according to which all can plan. In no other way can everyone assist in making the largest outputs. Time tables are necessary for railroads for greatest service to themselves and to the public, not for speeding up the trains to the point of destruction.

In spite of the fact that Taylor had no better device than the stopwatch, his idea marked a great step forward in management, the full possibilities of

---

[11]See *Engineering & Industrial Management,* "Time Study and Motion Study as Fundamental Factors in Planning and Control: An Indictment of Stopwatch Time Study." Also Bulletin of the Taylor Society.

which are little realized due to psychological defects of presentation and to objections which have nothing to do with the merit and value of the underlying principle involved. This great step of timing the work periods and the rest periods separately is *the* feature that distinguishes Taylor's plan of timing for prophesying how long it would take to do work from all the work of his predecessors. It is still so important that many great engineers continue to confuse time study with motion study, although the two are entirely different and even Dr. Taylor's theory must not be confused with his practice. The two must be analyzed and criticized separately.

SECRET TIME STUDY IS WORTHLESS AND SHOULD NEVER UNDER ANY CIRCUMSTANCES BE PRACTICED

Timing of work was done by Taylor, and by some of his immediate followers, by the use of a stopwatch. In the early days some secret timing of work was undoubtedly done, as the stopwatch book, described and repudiated in Taylor's "Shop Management" and in other works, shows.

It was sooner or later realized by most of its former advocators that secret time study is despised by the worker, that it never fosters hearty cooperation and therefore is valueless; and such time study was abandoned. There is, however, an additional reason for never making or using secret time study which, alone, should have been sufficient reason for dispensing with it from the very first. The times recorded are valueless, as they time a method and a rate of speed of motions at which the worker did not and could not cooperate, for the obvious reason that he had no knowledge that he was being timed.[12] There is no possibility of ever finding the One Best Way to do work by means of "secret" time study, neither is there any chance of determining causes of skill by its use. Any time records derived from "secret" time study are not worth the paper upon which they are written, to say nothing of the value of the time of the secret times observer.

MOTION STUDY ANTEDATES TIME STUDY

From our first interest in the subject of management, which began in 1885, we have specialized in motion study and the One Best Way to do the work; that is, in studying the motions made by the worker in doing his work and endeavoring to eliminate useless motions and to reduce the number of motions and the effort and resulting fatigue to the lowest amount possible.

---

[12]See Chapter on "Motion Study Instruments of Precision" in *Applied Motion Study,* Macmillan Co.

Since it so happened that heavy stone, concrete, brick, and steel construction, and more than a dozen other trades, formed an essential element of the specially provided practical part of the training of one of the writers in preparing to become a construction engineer, the early intensive applications of motion study were actually made under the most practical everyday conditions in those fields, under the constant training of the best mechanics obtainable, specially selected and assigned by the employer for the writer's intensive training for special progress.

TRANSFERENCE OF SKILL IS POSSIBLE

We have always believed that the writer's ability to earn more than the journeyman's pay in more than a dozen different trades was wholly due to the emphasis he placed upon transference of skill in the motions themselves, and that his progress in apprenticeship, his being made foreman before the expiration of the time of his apprenticeship, then superintendent at the expiration of his apprenticeship, and then highest of all the employees in the entire organization was due to his practice of submitting all of his working problems to the analytical method of motion study.

"HOW LONG IT TAKES TO DO WORK" IS NOT SO IMPORTANT AS "HOW TO DO IT IN THE ONE BEST WAY"

Through our acquaintance with Dr. Taylor, we first recognized the importance of prophesying the time it takes to do work in order to make schedules and programs. While we still recognize the importance of knowing the time it takes to do work, it should always be realized that the problem of prophesying the times of doing work will probably never have the importance of the problem of the One Best Way to do work.

We desire to emphasize again that the time required by any method is quite unimportant as compared with making the correct sequence of cycle subdivisions, the problem of least waste in energy involved, and the quality of the resulting product. However, we have always strenuously insisted that if times are recorded, they must be times of the smallest elements and they must be recorded with accuracy, if they are to be of permanent value. The micromotion process of motion study and its indirect by-product, photographically recorded time study, coupled with a search for greater information than merely what the eye can see and more permanent records regarding the actual behavior and the exact motions used, whether or not at the time the records are made there is knowledge enough to recognize and appreciate the information, is the outcome of this theory and practice.

At the present time, while we advocate the use of the stopwatch as a part of the preliminary education of the young engineer,[13] in order that he may appreciate the value and possibilities of the more accurate methods of micromotion study, in all our work we use micromotion method, as we find it is vastly superior to stopwatch time study no only from the standpoint of accuracy and permanent value but also from the standpoint of low cost, and especially from the standpoint of educational value, particularly the preservation of the best that has been done for future learners.

CHRONOCYCLEGRAPHS RECORD EFFECTS OF PSYCHOLOGICAL VARIABLES ON THE ELEMENTS OF BEHAVIOR AS SHOWN IN PATHS OF MOTION

Where it is desired to study the paths and the elements of the motion, and particularly the phenomena of skill, such as habit, conflict of habits, automaticity, distraction, and other psychological and motion study variables, we supplement micromotion study with the chronocyclegraph method of making records. Chronocyclegraphs were invented as a result of realizing the need for some form of recapitulation of the motions shown in the individual frames of the micromotion film. In no other way has the effect of one or more psychological variables been shown so plainly as by the cyclegraph method. In fact, the synthetic stereochronocyclegraph has already been used by us in research on the motion study variable of automaticity wherever data on the subject could be found, including studies of the motions of epileptics in seizures. The resulting analyses[14] have completely confirmed the opinions expressed in 1910 regarding our practice in teaching trades and have proved again, to our own satisfaction, that "the present apprenticeship system is pitiful and criminal from the apprentice's standpoint, ridiculous from a modern system standpoint, and there is no word that describes its wastefulness from an economic standpoint."[15]

CHRONOCYCLEGRAPHS CAN BE MADE AT THE SAME COST AS AMATEUR SNAPSHOTS

It has been said by some that the chronocyclegraph method is a scientific refinement of great accuracy which no manager should countenance in practice, because it deals with the minutiae of motions, but when it is realized that cyclegraphs can be made in a minute with even the cheapest of cameras, as a cost of a few cents, and that they furnish a permanent record

---

[13]See "Motion Study and Time Study," pp. 70 and 72 in this book.
[14]See Paper by Dr. Damon.
[15]See "Motion Study," p. 70 in this book.

that proves the fallacy of present methods, no further proof of their practicability is needed. These cyclegraph records assist in visualizing better methods. The actual results prove that there is no sound argument against them.[16]

INTERPRETATION OF CHRONOCYCLEGRAPHS REQUIRES KNOWLEDGE OF MOTION STUDY

They are, however, of little use in the hands of those who do not understand how to read and interpret them and compare the behavior of different demonstrators and workers under different conditions. Cyclegraphs are of greatest value only when they are made of the method of the most efficient worker demonstrating the One Best Way to do work. In no way, however, do they supplant or become a substitute for the usual procedure under the micromotion methods.

A FATIGUE SURVEY IS THE FIRST STEP IN FATIGUE STUDY

As an indispensable adjunct to all motion study and time study we have fatigue study, which, as we have already said, is really the first step in motion study. In the description of the making of a survey we spoke of the importance of a fatigue survey as a part of the general survey of the entire plant. We advise taking up this subject very early in the process of diagnosis and analysis, in order to enlist the self-interest and hearty cooperation of every member of the organization, as fatigue elimination is a subject upon which all can agree, for there are no interests against it. It is a very tangible, practical subject, easily visualized, and will pay big returns on the time and money invested.

In the making of the fatigue survey, we recommend recording everything that has ever been done to eliminate unnecessary fatigue and recording every idea for superstandardization of that which will cause less fatigue and greater comfort to the workers, for in no other way can the management start a new era of cooperation throughout the plant so successfully. There is no more practical way of actually fostering that first and greatest law for durable satisfactions of life and success in management, namely, "The Golden Rule." There is some misunderstanding as to the reduction of fatigue through

---

[16]Chronocyclegraph Motion Devices for Measuring Achievement, "Applied Motion Study," Chapter V, Macmillan Co., N. Y.; Etude des mouvements appliqué, Chap. V; Angewandte Bewegungsstudien, Berlin.

motion study. The prime aim of motion study is not to reduce the total amount of fatigue, although that of course is *very* desirable, but to eliminate that part of fatigue which is unnecessary, which does no one any good, and which reduces productivity and therefore earning power. Only by scientific investigation can it be determined how much fatigue any individual worker can endure day after day, without injury. If there is any question about the matter, our own recommended practice is to "provide facilities for rest, whether it is thought to be needed or not." The great thing in fatigue study, in which every one can participate, is to eliminate useless, unnecessary, unproductive fatigue, wherever possible, throughout the entire plant.

THERE IS TOO LITTLE ATTENTION GIVEN TO THE GREAT WASTE OF UNNECESSARY FATIGUE

It is surprising to read the interesting and valuable literature on the subject of fatigue, and the makings of investigations in fatigue, and to note how little thought has been directed toward the most important and most easily corrected waste, the *elimination of unnecessary fatigue*. Measurements of the periodicity and length of rest intervals and of the effects of overtime and night work—these are important and must be considered also; but emphasis on the old-fashioned method for cutting out or reducing unnecessary fatigue is essential, and this is absent, or practically absent, in the literature of fatigue, and absent also in a large percentage of all plants in all countries we have visited.

ENFORCING REPETITIVE UNPRODUCTIVE AND UNINTERESTING MOTIONS SPOILS MEN FOR REAL WORK LATER

It is interesting to note that the amount of unnecessary fatigue and indifference to the problem of fatigue existing is a good index of the civilization, education, general efficiency, and culture of a country, and of the intelligence and ethical standing of those in authority, whether in the factory, services, school, home, hospital, or other public institution. Such a deadening circle as selecting buttons to be polished, and polishing the buttons selected, should be eliminated everywhere or supplemented by work that stimulates the workers' brains and that fits them for promotion, or at least for transference to other more renumerative life works. Repetitive unnecessary motions that do not lead to valuable by-products, or to knowledge of the science of motion study, are deteriorating to the brain and insulting to the intelligence, and at best lead to habits of inefficient motions and inefficient processes of thought.

Never forget that fatigue study and the actual elimination of unnecessary fatigue *pays in actual money savings*. It pays in greater cooperation, which always means lower costs.

EMPLOYERS SHOULD BE MADE TO PROVIDE SEATS FOR ALL WORKERS SO THAT THEY MAY UTILIZE THEIR PERIODS OF UNAVOIDABLE DELAY FOR REST

Any country that seriously desires to help its working people to produce larger outputs with less fatigue and with more comfort and greater public health is recommended to tax the owner of each individual workplace that has not provided a suitable seat for occupancy during periods of "unavoidable delay." Each time that we have made this proposal we have had submitted to us a list of trades at which some one believes such practice not to be practical. We come to our recommendations after many years spent in the careful study of this subject, and we suggest that emphasis be put first on the places where it is easy to install chairs. The balance of cases will then be found to be suitable also for the same treatment. If a worker desires to loaf it is better that he should also at the same time rest instead of adopting a make believe work and a ca' canny policy. The general law of "making each industry pay the bill" has invariably caused invention to do away with the reason for the bill, although there may also be attempts temporarily to pass the tax on to the consumer by means of adding the amount to the price of the product. This, however, is always followed by an attempt to save the price of the tax.

A COMFORTABLE CHAIR WILL PERMIT LARGER OUTPUTS WITH LESS FATIGUE

It is invariably astonishing to see how many places can be supplied with special problem and special purpose chairs and stools, and how many kinds of work can be done alternately sitting and standing that have always been considered as standing jobs, when incentive to invention is brought to bear, and—most fortunately—*invariably with greater productivity as well as greater comfort to the worker.*

Only those who have studied the problems of the One Best Way to do work realize the increases in outputs, wages, and profits resulting from the elimination of unnecessary fatigue. We realize that this recommendation to tax each work place that is not provided with a proper seat specially designed for the kind of work done sounds radical. We have tried every other form of education, including maintaining a small museum for exhibits of devices for eliminating unnecessary fatigue, but the progress has been altogether too slow to satisfy us. The public must be made to think along the lines of eliminating unnecessary fatigue as a source of national health, as well as for their own health and comfort. We started the Fatigue Day Campaign in 1913. Professor Henry F. Spooner was the first to cooperate on a large scale in England, and each year he has addressed his students on the costs and discomforts of unnecessary fatigue. The Society of Industrial Engineers through its Fatigue Elimination Committee, of which Professor Spooner is a member and of which one of the authors is Chairman, is arousing public interest wherever possible on the subject of the Elimination of Unnecessary Fatigue. The Society, the Committee, and the Chairman will welcome cooperation on this subject. Membership in the Society is not a prerequisite for full opportunities for cooperation.

Professor George Blessing, head of the Mechanical Engineering Department at Swarthmore College and now with the Rockefeller interests, was the first to do noteworthy work in celebrating this "first Monday in December," or "Fatigue Elimination Day," in a college. He wrote a most interesting lecture to his students regarding the possibilities of eliminating unnecessary fatigue in his own and their daily lives, beginning with the automatic time clock and an electrical device that opens the furnace draft door before he and his family arise in the morning, and ending with the well-known advantages from an antifatigue standpoint of rubber heels on shoes for all members of the family, which every student of motion study and fatigue study knows to be an important factor in helping anyone to do more walking and standing with less fatigue.

RUBBER HEELS ELIMINATE UNNECESSARY FATIGUE

This factor of cushioning the feet of workers is so important that where rubber heels are too expensive for general use by them, similar but by no means such good results have in a measure been obtained by wearing, even in warm weather, extraheavy woollen socks and wooden-soled shoes.

Fatigue investigation cannot be too definite and concrete; no item is too small to consider; for the problem, to be successful, must be educational. It must be constantly emphasized that small individual outputs are often due largely to the discomfort and the fatigue of the worker. Fatigue investigations should consider also types of lighting and heating and its closely allied factor, accident prevention in the plant. Fear of accidents and constant watchfulness and unflagging attention to keep from being caught in an accident are very fatiguing, and it is now recognized that there is no sharp dividing line between accident prevention and fatigue prevention.

Description photographs and other records of chairs—particularly special-purpose chairs, such as three-way stools,[17] footrests, fatigue-eliminating work desks, individual tables, or work benches—are valuable; and these should include, wherever possible, some estimate of the fatigue prevented.

WORKERS HAVE NOT DONE THEIR BIT IN ELIMINATING THEIR OWN UNNECESSARY FATIGUE OR IN DISSEMINATING INFORMATION ABOUT IT

While the workers get immediate and ultimate comfort and satisfaction from the results of eliminating unnecessary fatigue, they have done less for themselves and for each other in this important subject than have the managers and the employers. There is an interesting reason for this, however. Workers have little time and opportunity for gaining scientific knowledge of the underlying causes of unnecessary fatigue, or of the best practice of fatigue elimination, or of the comparative fatigue-eliminating qualities of the various pieces of equipment or chairs which they use. This is proved without the question of a doubt through our own personal experience.

EXECUTIVES HAVE FAILED TO PROVIDE AND PRACTICE WHAT THEY PREACH

It is also remarkable to find that some of the executives, who have been most conscientious and insistent on providing the least fatiguing work places, so neglect their own work places that they become examples to be avoided.

LABOR WILL COOPERATE

If a square deal is assured, there is no doubt that labor will cooperate in every advance in the science of management affecting industry.

LABOR IS STUDYING THE SCIENCE OF ECONOMICS TODAY

Labor has representatives today who have enrolled as students in the science of economics. They have recently again had it proved conclusively to

---

[17]See "Transactions Society of Industrial Engineers," 1920.

them that neither strikes, lockouts, nor high pay and short hours furnish the permanent panacea for the working man's troubles. They have found that there is no permanent and cumulative improvement in the working man's conditions unless the higher pay and the shorter hours are accompanied with maximum production per man and the consequent low unit costs of manufacture, marketing, and distribution. This seeming paradox of high wages and low unit costs is not a contradiction at all. On the contrary, it is this combination that the science of management makes possible. A most valuable unit of measurement for comparing the quality of different managements is the amount that the wages are higher, and, at the same time, the costs are lower in one organization than in another, or under one regime than under another. When this is realized, hearty and strenuous cooperation between the management and the workers will be the rule and not the exception, and he who wastes either time, effort, or material will be treated as the enemy of all.

ECONOMISTS KNOW THAT ALL MUST SHARE IN PAYING FOR ANY AND ALL WASTES

Economists have known for a long time that the benefits from the elimination of every kind of individual and public waste of time, material, and human effort sooner or later are distributed to everyone, and the more savings of time and materials and the greater productivity the better the chance of having the benefits of the savings distributed sooner or later to everybody. All students of economics, in and out of the ranks of labor, realize that labor's prospects increase with the quality of the management, and it is for their interests especially to have all that science can offer applied to management.

It would seem reasonable to expect that all countries suffering from the wastes of war ought to realize this fact and begin by insisting upon the reorganization of their governmental departments and the rearrangement of interdepartmental relations in accordance with the best practices of scientific management to suit their present and future needs, instead of continuing the ill-fitting, outgrown, and unnecessarily wasteful traditional methods of organization and work handed down from times of different conditions.

Unfortunately, those on the outside, who nevertheless have to pay the bill, have insufficient power and realization of the facts, and those on the inside are also uninformed, although they are quite satisfied; yet the loss from waste of any kind is passed on to all, and the costs of the totals of inefficiency are well nigh unbearable in all countries at the present time.

The results of actual practice of motion study and science in management in large commercial and industrial organizations show beyond argument or doubt that the amount of money needed for taxes is actually small as compared with the amount of savings that can be made by motion study, scientific organization, and management.

SCIENCE IN MANAGEMENT IS A UNIFYING FORCE BECAUSE IT IS APPLICABLE TO ALL FIELDS OF ENDEAVOR

It perhaps never has been sufficiently emphasized that the science of management may serve as a great unifying force in industry. Because most students in management are specialists and are forced to be interested in any specialized field of their individual life work, if industry as a whole is to succeed, management has often been thought of largely in terms of application to specific fields. However, it must be recognized that when the producers of raw materials, the producers of machines and manufactured products, the users of the products, and ali the other producers in the country are thinking along lines of waste elimination and the science of management for obtaining the One Best Way and condition of doing work, a new type of cooperation will result, and an enormous amount of waste will be automatically, progressively, and constantly eliminated, if transferable information regarding the units of management is recorded. Take for the simplest sort of an illustration the question of *glare spots,* as induced for example by nickel parts of office devices and highly polished and varnished desks in highly lighted offices.

When the maker of equipment and also the public realize that glare spots and reflection prevent the user from achieving his full quota of possible production without unnecessary fatigue and perhaps also eye strain, when the user and the employer of the equipment know that the glare spots cut down production and cause unnecessary fatigue, these glare spots will be eliminated as being against good salesmanship and good practice. These highly polished surfaces are a matter of false ideas of what is demanded by the buyers of the product. They serve the short temporary demand of salesmanship, based on measuring the wrong units of what is desired in order to make sales, on wrong psychology, on selling something that is "bright and new and shiny," not something that is efficient—and they remain, to hinder the user, because of his mental inertia or ignorance of the conditions that hinder or permit the One Best Way to do work. The workers in most factories do not note the handicap of glare spots, because they have seen everywhere and have become accustomed to seeing workers at benches facing the bright sky through the window. The one who locates the benches against the windows instead of at or about right angles to windows probably does so because of his belief that the amount of floor space utilized is a more important unit to measure than visual acuity, fatigue, and quantity of resulting output.

When dark walls are painted white to enforce cleanliness, and to insure the proper amount and more even distribution of light for employees; when shiny metals, varnish, paint, and other glare spots are dulled so that the worker will not be handicapped by unnecessary eye strain; when scientifically designed chairs and seats are made to suit the needs of the individual user, with at least as much attention and regard as is given to fitting collars on horses, instead of the usual and customary practice of providing chairs for the indefinite, nonexisting "average man," then there will be a good beginning in creating standards that will be transferable to, and usable by, all organizations that desire to cooperate. Great progress has already been made in the design of some types of chairs by the American Posture League.

SUMMARY

We desire to emphasize the following:

First, the thought that the science of management is for everybody, everywhere, in every line of work, and that its underlying principles are those of education itself; that parts of it are teachable even in the lower grades of the schools; that the theory and practice of the One Best Way in sports is identical to that in the trades, industries, and in all kinds of work.

Second, the idea that while the application of the fine points of the science—the critical work—must be done by an expert, some of the preliminary steps can be taken by anyone, anywhere.

Third, that ultimately all successful establishments will be run along scientific lines, and that therefore everything done from this time onward should be in the line of adjusting the past and present along predetermined scientific plans, in order to determine the trend of, and plan for, the future. This is vitally important, for science is now applied to all work, and plants and organizations which have been and are run on rule-of-thumb, traditional, or "pure salesmanship" bases will have more difficulty in surviving in the future.

Greatest national prosperity depends upon greatest individual training in knowledge and in ability to contribute toward the public welfare. Such contributions may be, and often have been, more or less haphazard and still result in good. However, to be most profitable, activity must be planned and *directed,* must have ability, experience, and knowledge behind it. It must be based on measurement and willingness to abide by the result of measurement.

Nothing will stand for a long time and continue to exist and to give satisfaction unless there is a real reason for its so doing. It may stand for a long while because no one has changed it, but the day of comparison and struggle for survival will come, and unless it can show logical reason for its existence, it must go.

Therefore, development of national prosperity that is to have permanent stability, that is to be evolution and not revolution, that is to attain and perpetuate the all-essential element of maintenance, does depend upon science, upon measurement; and it is for this reason that the science of management is an essential factor in the development of national prosperity, of international prosperity and of the prosperity of the whole world.

The psychologist, who has done so much not only in his own field but in cooperating with others, can do much to further this development, and will doubtless prove not only an eloquent advocate but also an untiring participant in better management.

Manufacturing—Missing Link in Corporate Strategy

Wickham Skinner

A company's manufacturing function typically is either a competitive weapon or a corporate millstone. It is seldom neutral. The connection between manufacturing and corporate success is rarely seen as more than the achievement of high efficiency and low costs. In fact, the connection is much more critical and much more sensitive. Few top managers are aware that what appear to be routine manufacturing decisions frequently come to limit the corporation's strategic options, binding it with facilities, equipment, personnel, and basic controls and policies to a noncompetitive posture which may take years to turn around.

Research I have conducted during the past three years reveals that top management unknowingly delegates a surprisingly large portion of basic policy decisions to lower levels in the manufacturing area. Generally, this abdication of responsibility comes about more through lack of concern than by intention. And it is partly the reason that many manufacturing policies and procedures developed at lower levels reflect assumptions about corporate strategy which are incorrect or misconstrued.

Millstone Effect

When companies fail to recognize the relationship between manufacturing decisions corporate strategy, they may become saddled with seriously noncompetitive production systems which are expensive and time-consuming to change. Here are several examples:

- Company A entered the combination washer-dryer field after several competitors had failed to achieve successful entries into the field. Company A's executives believed their model would overcome the technical drawbacks

Reprinted by permission from *Harvard Business Review*, May–June 1969, 136–45.

which had hurt their competitors and held back the development of any substantial market. The manufacturing managers tooled the new unit on the usual conveyorized assembly line and giant stamping presses used for all company products.

When the washer-dryer failed in the market, the losses amounted to millions. The plant had been "efficient" in the sense that costs were low. But the tooling and production processes did not meet the demands of the marketplace.

- Company B produced five kinds of electronic gear for five different groups of customers; the gear ranged from satellite controls to industrial controls and electronic components. In each market a different task was required of the production function. For instance, in the first market, extremely high reliability was demanded; in the second market, rapid introduction of a stream of new products was demanded; in the third market, low costs were of critical importance for competitive survival.

  In spite of these highly diverse and contrasting tasks, production management elected to centralize manufacturing facilities in one plant in order to achieve "economies of scale." The result was a failure to achieve high reliability, economies of scale, or an ability to introduce new products quickly. What happened, in short, was that the demands placed on manufacturing by a competitive strategy were ignored by the production group in order to achieve economies of scale. This production group was obsessed with developing "a total system, fully computerized." The manufacturing program satisfied no single division, and the serious marketing problems which resulted choked company progress.

- Company C produced plastic molding resins. A new plant under construction was to come on-stream in eight months, doubling production. In the meantime, the company had a much bigger volume of orders than it could meet.

  In a strategic sense, manufacturing's task was to maximize output to satisfy large, key customers. Yet the plant's production control system was set up—as it had been for years—to minimize costs. As a result, long runs were emphasized. While costs were low, many customers had to wait, and many key buyers were lost. Consequently, when the new plant came on-stream, it was forced to operate at a low volume.

The mistake of considering low costs and high efficiencies as the key manufacturing objective in each of these examples is typical of the over-simplified concept of "a good manufacturing operation." Such criteria frequently get companies into trouble, or at least do not aid in the development of manufacturing into a competitive weapon. Manufacturing affects corporate strategy, and corporate strategy affects manufacturing. Even in an apparently routine operating area such as a production scheduling system, strategic considerations should outweigh technical and conventional industrial engineering factors invoked in the name of "productivity."

SHORTSIGHTED VIEWS

The fact is that manufacturing is seen by most top managers as requiring involved technical skills and a morass of petty daily decisions and details. It is seen by many young managers as the gateway to grubby routine, where days are filled with high pressure, packed with details, and limited to low-level decision making—all of which is out of the sight and minds of top-level executives. It is generally taught in graduate schools of business administration as a combination of industrial engineering (time study, plant layout, inventory theory, and so on) and quantitative analysis (linear programming, simulation, queuing theory, and the rest). In total, a manufacturing career is generally perceived as an all-consuming, technically oriented, hectic life that minimizes one's chances of ever reaching the top and maximizes the chances of being buried in minutiae.

In fact, these perceptions are not wholly inaccurate. It is the thesis of this article that the technically oriented concept of manufacturing is all too prevalent; and that it is largely responsible for the typically limited contribution manufacturing makes to a corporation's arsenal of competitive weapons, for manufacturing's failure to attract the top talent it needs and *should* have, and for its failure to attract more young managers with general management interests and broad abilities. In my opinion, manufacturing is generally perceived in the wrong way at the top, managed in the wrong way at the plant level, and taught in the wrong way in the business schools.

These are strong words, but change is needed, and I believe that only a more relevant concept of manufacturing can bring change. I see no sign whatsoever that we have found the means of solving the problems mentioned. The new, mathematically based "total systems" approaches to production management offer the promise of new and valuable concepts and techniques, but I doubt that these approaches will overcome the tendency of top management to remove itself from manufacturing. Ten years of development of quantitative techniques have left us each year with the promise of a "great new age" in production management that lies "just ahead." The promise never seems to be realized. Stories of computer and "total systems" fiascoes are available by the dozen; these failures are always expensive, and in almost every case management has delegated the work to experts.

I do not want to demean the promise—and, indeed, some present contributions—of the systems/computer approach. Two years ago I felt more sanguine about it. But, since then, close observation of the problems in U.S. industry has convinced me that the "answer" promised is inadequate. The approach cannot overcome the problems described until it does a far better job of linking manufacturing and corporate strategy. What is needed is some kind of integrative mechanism.

PATTERN OF FAILURE

An examination of top management perceptions of manufacturing has led me to some notions about basic causes of many production problems. In each of six industries I have studied, I have found top executives delegating excessive amounts of manufacturing policy to subordinates, avoiding involvement in most production matters, and failing to ask the right questions until their companies are in obvious trouble. This pattern seems to be due to a combination of two factors:

1. A sense of personal inadequacy, on the part of top executives, in managing production. (Often the feeling evolves from a tendency to regard the area as a technical or engineering specialty, or a mundane "nuts and bolts" segment of management.)
2. A lack of awareness among top executive that a production system inevitably involves trade-offs and compromises and so must be designed to perform a limited task well, with that task defined by corporate strategic objectives.

The first factor is, of course, dependent in part on the second, for the sense of inadequacy would not be felt if the strategic role of production were clearer. The second factor is the one we shall concentrate on in the remainder of this article.

Like a building, a vehicle, or a boat, a production system can be designed to do some things well, but always at the expense of other abilities. It appears to be the lack of recognition of these trade-offs and their effects on a corporation's ability to compete that leads top management to delegate often critical decisions to lower, technically oriented staff levels, and to allow policy to be made through apparently unimportant operating decisions.

In the balance of this article I would like to:

—sketch out the relationships between production operations and corporate strategy;

—call attention to the existence of specific trade-offs in production system design;

—comment on the inadequacy of computer specialists to deal with these trade-offs; and

—suggest a new way of looking at manufacturing which might enable the nontechnical manager to understand and manage the manufacturing area.

STRATEGIC IMPLICATIONS

Frequently the interrelationship between production operations and corporate strategy is not easily grasped. The notion is simple enough—namely, that a company's competitive strategy at a given time places particular demands on its manufacturing function, and, conversely, that the company's manufacturing posture and operations should be specifically designed to fulfill the task demanded by strategic plans. What is more elusive is the set of cause-and-effect factors which determine the linkage between strategy and production operations.

Strategy is a set of plans and policies by which a company aims to gain advantages over its competitors. Generally a strategy includes plans for products and the marketing of these products to a particular set of customers. The marketing plans usually include specific approaches and steps to be followed in identifying potential customers, determining why, where, and when they buy, and learning how they can best be reached and convinced to purchase. The company must have an advantage, a particular appeal, a special push or pull created by its products, channels of distribution, advertising, price, packaging, availability, warranties, or other factors.

CONTRASTING DEMANDS

What is not always realized is that different marketing strategies and approaches to gaining a competitive advantage place different demands on the manufacturing arm of the company. For example, a furniture manufacturer's strategy for broad distribution of a limited, low-price line with wide consumer advertising might generally require:

- Decentralized finished-goods storage
- Readily available merchandise
- Rock-bottom costs

The foregoing demands might in turn require:

- Relatively large lot sizes
- Specialized facilities for woodworking and finishing
- A large proportion of low- and medium-skilled workers in the work force
- Concentration of manufacturing in a limited number of large-scale plants

In contrast, a manufacturer of high-price, high-style furniture with more exclusive distribution would require an entirely different set of manufacturing policies. While higher prices and longer lead times would allow more leeway in the plant, this company would have to contend with the problems implicit in delivering high-quality furniture made of wood (which is a soft, dimensionally unstable material whose surface is expensive to finish and easy to damage), a high setup cost relative to running times in most wood-machining operations, and the need to make a large number of nonstandardized parts. While the first company must work with these problems too, they are more serious to the second company because its marketing strategy forces it to confront the problems head on. The latter's manufacturing policies will probably require:

- Many model and style changes
- Production to order
- Extremely reliable high quality

These demands may in turn require:

- An organization that can get new models into production quickly
- A production control group that can coordinate all activities so as to reduce lead times
- Technically trained supervisors and technicians

Consequently, the second company ought to have a strong manufacturing-methods engineering staff; simple, flexible tooling; and a well-trained, experienced work force.

In summary, the two manufacturers would need to develop very different policies, personnel, and operations if they were to be equally successful in carrying out their strategies.

IMPORTANT CHOICES

In the example described, there are marked contrasts in the two companies. Actually, even small and subtle differences in corporate strategies should be reflected in manufacturing policies. However, my research shows that few companies do in fact carefully and explicitly tailor their production systems to perform the tasks which are vital to corporate success.

Instead of focusing first on strategy, then moving to define the manufacturing task, and next turning to systems design in manufacturing policy, managements tend to employ a concept of production which is much less effective. Most top executives and production managers look at their production systems with the notion of "total productivity" or the equivalent, "efficiency." They seek a kind of blending of low costs, high quality, and acceptable customer service. The view prevails that a plant with reasonably modern equipment, up-to-date methods and procedures, a cooperative work force, a computerized information system, and an enlightened management will be a good plant and will perform efficiently.

But what is "a good plant"? What is "efficient performance"? And what should the computer be programmed to do? Should it minimize lead times or minimize inventories? A company cannot do both. Should the computer minimize direct labor or indirect labor? Again, the company cannot do both. Should investment in equipment be minimized—or should outside purchasing be held to a minimum? One could go on with such choices.

The reader may reply: "What management wants is a combination of both ingredients that results in the lowest *total* cost." But that answer, too, is insufficient. The "lowest total cost" answer leaves out the dimensions of time and customer satisfaction, which must usually be considered too. Because cost *and* time *and* customers are all involved, we have to conclude that what is a "good" plant for Company A may be a poor or mediocre plant for its competitor, Company B, which is in the same industry but pursues a different strategy.

The purpose of manufacturing is to serve the company—to meet its needs for survival, profit, and growth. Manufacturing is part of the strategic concept that relates a company's strengths and resources to opportunities in the market. Each strategy creates a unique manufacturing task. Manufacturing management's ability to meet that task is the key measure of its success.

TRADE-OFFS IN DESIGN

It is curious that most top managements and production people do not state their yardsticks of success more precisely, and instead fall back on such measures as "efficiency," "low cost," and "productivity." My studies suggest that a key reason for this phenomenon is that very few executives realize the existence of trade-offs in designing and operating a production system.

Yet most managers will readily admit that there are compromises or trade-offs to be made in designing an airplane or a truck. In the case of an airplane, trade-offs would involve such matters as cruising speed, takeoff and landing distances, initial cost, maintenance, fuel consumption, passenger comfort, and cargo or passenger capacity. A given stage of technology defines limits as to what can be accomplished in these respects. For instance, no one today can design a 500-passenger plane that can land on a carrier and also break the sonic barrier.

Much the same thing is true of manufacturing. The variables of cost, time, quality, technological constraints, and customer satisfaction place limits on what management can do, force compromises, and demand an explicit recognition of a multitude of trade-offs and choices. Yet everywhere I find plants which have inadvertently emphasized one yardstick at the expense of another, more important one. For example:

An electronics manufacturer with dissatisfied customers hired a computer expert and placed manufacturing under a successful engineering design chief to make it a "total system." A year later its computer was spewing out an inch-thick volume of daily information. "We know the location of every part in the plant on any given day," boasted the production manager and his computer systems chief.

Nevertheless, customers were more dissatisfied than ever. Product managers hotly complained that delivery promises were regularly missed—and in almost every case they first heard about failures from their customers. The problem centered on the fact that computer information runs were organized by part numbers and operations. They were designed to facilitate machine scheduling and to aid shop foremen; they were not organized around end products, which would have facilitated customer service.

How had this come about? Largely, it seemed clear, because the manufacturing managers had become absorbed in their own "systems approach"; the fascination of mechanized data handling had become an end in itself. As for top management, it had more or less abdicated responsibility. Because the company's growth and success had been based on engineering and because top management was R&D-oriented, policy-making executives saw production as a routine requiring a lower level of complexity and brainpower. Top management argued further that the company had production experts who were well paid and who should be able to do their jobs without bothering top-level people.

RECOGNIZING ALTERNATIVES

To develop the notion of important trade-off decisions in manufacturing, let us consider Exhibit 1, which shows some examples.

In each decision area—plant and equipment, production planning and control, and so forth—top management needs to recognize the alternatives and become involved in the design of the production system. It needs to become involved to the extent that the alternative selected is appropriate to the manufacturing task determined by the corporate strategy.

Making such choices is, of course, an on-going rather than a once-a-year or once-a-decade task; decisions have to be made constantly in these trade-off areas. Indeed, the real crux of the problem seems to be how to ensure that the continuing process of decision making is not isolated from competitive and strategic facts, when many of the trade-off decisions do not at first appear to bear on company strategy. As long as a technical point of view dominates manufacturing decisions, a degree of isolation from the realities of competition is inevitable. Unfortunately, as we shall see, the technical viewpoint is all too likely to prevail.

TECHNICAL DOMINANCE

The similarity between today's emphasis on the technical experts—the computer specialist and the engineering-oriented production technician—and yesterday's emphasis on the efficiency expert—time-study man and industrial engineer—is impossible to escape. For 50 years, U.S. management relied on efficiency experts trained in the techniques of Frederick W. Taylor. Industrial engineers were kings of the factory. Their early approaches and attitudes were often conducive to industrial warfare, strikes, sabotage, and militant unions, but that was not realized then. Also not realized was that their technical emphasis often produced an inward orientation toward cost that ignored the customer, and an engineering point of view that gloried in tools, equipment, and gadgets rather than in markets and service. Most important, the cult of industrial engineering tended to make top executives technically disqualified from involvement in manufacturing decisions.

Since the turn of the century, this efficiency-centered orientation has dogged U.S. manufacturing. It has created that image of "nuts and bolts," of greasy, dirty, detail jobs in manufacturing. It has dominated "production" courses in most graduate schools of business administration. It has alienated young men with broad management educations from manufacturing careers. It has "buffaloed" top managers.

Several months ago I was asked by a group of industrial engineers to offer an opinion as to why so few industrial engineers were moving up to the top of their companies. My answer was that perhaps a technical point of view cut them off from top management, just as the jargon and hocus-pocus of manufacturing often kept top management from understanding the factory. In

| EXHIBIT 1 | SOME IMPORTANT TRADE-OFF DECISIONS IN MANUFACTURING— OR "YOU CAN'T HAVE IT BOTH WAYS" |

DECISION AREA	DECISION	ALTERNATIVES
PLANT AND EQUIPMENT	Span of process	Make or buy
	Plant size	One big plant or several smaller ones
	Plant location	Locate near markets or locate near materials
	Investment decisions	Invest mainly in buildings or equipment or inventories or research
	Choice of equipment	General-purpose or special-purpose equipment
	Kind of tooling	Temporary, minimum tooling, or "production tooling"
PRODUCTION PLANNING AND CONTROL	Frequency of inventory taking	Few or many breaks in production for buffer stocks
	Inventory size	High inventory or a lower inventory
	Degree of inventory control	Control in great detail or in lesser detail
	What to control	Controls designed to minimize machine downtime or labor cost or time in process, or to maximize output of particular products or material usage
	Quality control	High reliability and quality or low costs
	Use of standards	Formal or informal or none at all
LABOR AND STAFFING	Job specialization	Highly specialized or not highly specialized
	Supervision	Technically trained first-line supervisors or nontechnically trained supervisors
	Wage system	Many job grades or few job grades; incentive wages or hourly wages
	Supervision	Close supervision or loose supervision
	Industrial engineers	Many or few such men
PRODUCT DESIGN/ ENGINEERING	Size of product line	Many customer specials or few specials or none at all

EXHIBIT 1	SOME IMPORTANT TRADE-OFF DECISIONS IN MANUFACTURING— OR "YOU CAN'T HAVE IT BOTH WAYS" (CONTINUED)	

DECISION AREA	DECISION	ALTERNATIVES
	Design stability	Frozen design or many engineering change orders
	Technological risk	Use of new processes unproved by competitors or follow-the-leader policy
	Engineering	Complete packaged design or design-as-you-go approach
	Use of manufacturing engineering	Few or many manufacturing engineers
ORGANIZATION AND MANAGEMENT	Kind of organization	Functional or product focus or geographical or other
	Executive use of time	High involvement in investment or production planning or cost control or quality control or other activities
	Degree of risk assumed	Decisions based on much or little information
	Use of staff	Large or small staff group
	Executive style	Much or little involvement in detail; authoritarian or nondirective style; much or little contact with organization

their isolation, they could gain only a severely limited sense of market needs and of corporate competitive strategy.

ENTER THE COMPUTER EXPERT

Today the industrial engineer is declining in importance in many companies. But a new technical expert, the computer specialist, is taking his place. I use the term "computer specialist" to refer to individuals who specialize in computer systems design and programming.

I do not deny, of course, that computer specialists have a very important job to do. I do object, however, to any notion that computer specialists have more of a top management view than was held by their predecessors, the industrial engineers. In my experience, the typical computer expert has been forced to master a complex and all-consuming technology, a fact which frequently makes him parochial rather than catholic in his views. Because he is so preoccupied with the detail of a total system, it is necessary for someone in top management to give him objectives and policy guidance. In his choice of trade-offs and compromises for his computer system, he needs to be instructed and not left to his own devices. Or, stated differently, he needs to see the entire corporation as a system, not just one corner of it—i.e., the manufacturing plant.

Too often this is not happening. The computer is a nightmare to many top managers because they have let it and its devotees get out of hand. They have let technical experts continue to dominate; the failure of top management truly to manage production goes on.

How *can* top management begin to manage manufacturing instead of turning it over to technicians who, through no fault of their own, are absorbed in their own arts and crafts? How can U.S. production management be helped to cope with the rising pressures of new markets, more rapid product changes, new technologies, larger and riskier equipment decisions, and the swarm of problems we face in industry today? Let us look at some answers.

BETTER DECISION MAKING

The answers I would like to suggest are not panaceas, nor are they intended to be comprehensive. Indeed, no one can answer all the questions and problems described with one nice formula or point of view. But surely we can improve on the notion that production systems need only be "productive and efficient." Top management can manage manufacturing if it will engage in the making of manufacturing policy, rather than considering it a kind of fifth, independent estate beyond the pale of control.

The place to start, I believe, is with the acceptance of a theory of manufacturing which begins with the concept that in any system design there are significant trade-offs (as shown in Exhibit 1), which must be explicitly decided on.

DETERMINING POLICY

Executives will also find it helpful to think of manufacturing policy determination as an orderly process or sequence of steps. Exhibit 2 is a schematic portrayal of such a process. It shows that manufacturing policy must stem from corporate strategy, and that the process of determining this policy is the means by which top management can actually manage production. Use of this process can end manufacturing isolation and tie top management and manufacturing together. The sequence is simple but vital:

EXHIBIT 2   THE PROCESS OF MANUFACTURING POLICY DETERMINATION

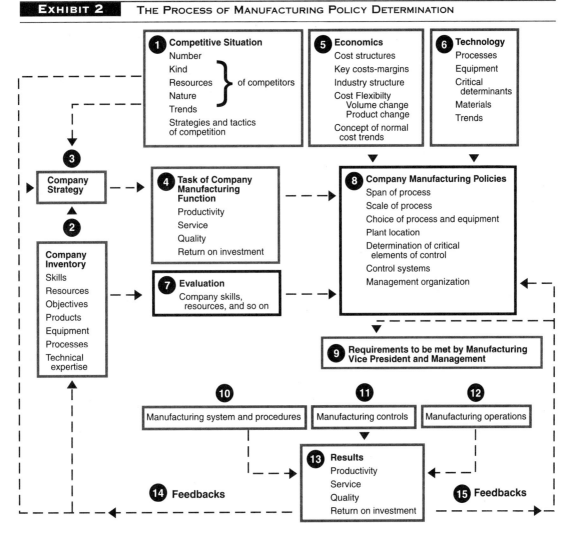

Key

1. What the others are doing
2. What have we got or can get to compete with
3. How can we compete
4. What we must accomplish in manufacturing in order to compete
5. Economic constraints and opportunities common to the industry
6. Constraints and opportunities common to the tecnnology
7. Our resources evaluated
8. How we should set ourselves up to match resources, economnics, and technology to meet the tasks required by our competitive strategy

9. The implementation requirements of our manufacturing policies
10. Basic systems in manufacturing (e.g., production planning, use of inventories, use of standards, and wage systems
11. Controls of cost, quality, flows inventory, and time
12. Selection of operations or ingredients critical to success (e.g., labor skills, equipment utilization, and yields)
13. How we are performing
14. Changes in what we have got, effects on competitive situation, and review of strategy
15. Analysis and review of manufacturing operations and policies

- It begins with an analysis of the competitive situation, of how rival companies are competing in terms of product, markets, policies, and channels of distribution. Management examines the number and kind of competitors and the opportunities open to its company.
- Next comes a critical appraisal of the company's skills and resources and of its present facilities and approaches.
- The third step is the formulation of company strategy: How is the company to compete successfully, combine its strengths with market opportunities, and define niches in the markets where it can gain advantages?
- The fourth step is the point where many top executives cut off their thinking. It is important for them to define the implications or "so-what" effects of company strategy in terms of specific manufacturing tasks. For example, they should ask: "If we are to compete with an X product of Y price for Z customers using certain distribution channels and forms of advertising, what will be demanded of manufacturing in terms of costs, deliveries, lead times, quality levels, and reliability?" These demands should be precisely defined.
- The fifth and sixth steps are to study the constraints or limitations imposed by the economics and the technology of the industry. These factors are generally common to all competitors. An explicit recognition of them is a prerequisite to a genuine understanding of the manufacturing problems and opportunities. These are facts that a nontechnical manager can develop, study, understand, and put to work. Exhibit 3 contains sample lists of topics for the manager to use in doing his homework.
- The seventh and eighth steps are the key ones for integrating and synthesizing all the prior ones into a broad manufacturing policy. The question for management is: "Given the facts of the economics and the technology of the industry, how do we set ourselves up to meet the specific manufacturing tasks posed by our particular competitive strategy?" Management must decide what it is going to make and what it will buy; how many plants to have, how big they should be, and where to place them; what processes and equipment to buy; what the key elements are which need to be controlled and how they can be controlled; and what kind of management organization would be most appropriate.
- Next come the steps of working out programs of implementation, controls, performance measures, and review procedures (see Steps 9-15 in Exhibit 2).

CONCLUSION

The process just described is, in my observation, quite different from the usual process of manufacturing management. Conventionally, manufacturing has

| EXHIBIT 3 | ILLUSTRATIVE CONSTRAINTS OR LIMITATIONS WHICH SHOULD BE STUDIED |

A. ECONOMICS OF THE INDUSTRY

Labor, burden, material, depreciation costs
Flexibility of production to meet changes in volume
Return on investment, prices, margins
Number and location of plants
Critical control variables
Critical functions (e.g., maintenance, production control, personnel)
Typical financial structures
Typical costs and cost relationship
Typical operating problems
Barriers to entry
Pricing practices
"Maturity" of industry products, markets, production practices, and so on
Importance of economies of scale
Importance of integrated capacities of corporations
Importance of having a certain balance of different types of equipment
Ideal balances of equipment capacities
Nature and type of production control
Government influences

B. TECHNOLOGY OF THE INDUSTRY

Rate of technological change
Scale of processes
Span of processes
Degree of mechanization
Technological sophistication
Time requirements for making changes

been managed from the bottom up. The classical process of the age of mass production is to select an operation, break it down into its elements, analyze and improve each element, and put it back together. This approach was contributed years ago by Frederick W. Taylor and other industrial engineers who followed in his footsteps.

What I am suggesting is an entirely different approach, one adapted far better to the current era of more products, shorter runs, vastly accelerated product changes, and increased marketing competition. I am suggesting a kind of "top-down" manufacturing. This approach starts with the company and its competitive strategy; its goal is to define manufacturing policy. Its presumption is that only when basic manufacturing policies are defined can the technical experts, industrial and manufacturing engineers, labor relations specialists, and computer experts have the necessary guidance to do their work.

With its focus on corporate strategy and the manufacturing task, the top-down approach can give top management both its entrée to manufacturing and the concepts it needs to take the initiative and truly manage this function. When this is done, executives previously unfamiliar with manufacturing are likely to find it an exciting activity. The company will have an important addition to its arsenal of competitive weapons.

THE FOCUSED FACTORY

WICKHAM SKINNER

The threat posed by foreign competition, the problem of industries suffering from "blue-collar blues," and the increasing complexity and frustration of life in the factory have forced public attention back to the industrial sector of the economy. Many years of taking our industrial health and leadership for granted abruptly ended in the 1970s when our declining position in world markets weakened the dollar and became a national issue.

In the popular press and at the policy level in government, the issue has been seen as a "productivity crisis." The National Commission on Productivity was established in 1971. The concern with productivity has appealed to many managers who have firsthand experience with our problems of high costs and low efficiency.

So pessimism now pervades the outlook of many managers and analysts of the U.S. manufacturing scene. The recurring theme of this gloomy view is that:

a. U.S. labor is the most expensive in the world,

b. its productivity has been growing at a slower rate than that of most of its competitors, and therefore

c. our industries sicken one by one as imports mushroom and unemployment becomes chronic in our industrial population centers.

In this article, I shall offer a more optimistic view of the productivity dilemma, suggesting that we need not feel powerless in competing against cheaper foreign labor. Rather, we have the opportunity to effect basic changes

Reprinted by permission from *Harvard Business Review*, May–June 1974, 113–121.

Author's note: This article is an analysis based on my cases written in the electronics, plastics, textile, steel, and industrial equipment industries, supplemented by recent project research in the furniture industry. Financial support for this was provided by the Harvard Business School Division of Research and course development funds is gratefully acknowledged.

in the management of manufacturing, which could shift the competitive balance in our favor in many industries. What are these basic changes? I can identify four:

1. Seeing the problem not as "How can we increase productivity?" but as "How can we compete?"
2. Seeing the problem as encompassing the efficiency of the *entire* manufacturing organization, not only the efficiency of the direct labor and the work force. (In most plants, direct labor and the work force represent only a small percentage of total costs.)
3. Learning to focus each plant on a limited, concise, manageable set of products, technologies, volumes, and markets.
4. Learning to structure basic manufacturing policies and supporting services so that they focus on one explicit manufacturing task instead of on many inconsistent, conflicting, implicit tasks.

A factory that focuses on a narrow product mix for a particular market niche will outperform the conventional plant, which attempts a broader mission. Because its equipment, supporting systems, and procedures can concentrate on a limited task for one set of customers, its costs and especially its overhead are likely to be lower than those of the conventional plant. But, more important, such a plant can become a competitive weapon because its entire apparatus is focused to accomplish the particular manufacturing task demanded by the company's overall strategy and marketing objective.

In spite of their advantages, my research indicates that focused manufacturing plants are surprisingly rare. Instead, the conventional factory produces many products for numerous customers in a variety of markets, thereby demanding the performance of a multiplicity of manufacturing tasks all at once from one set of assets and people. Its rationale is "economy of scale" and lower capital investment.

However, the result more often than not is a hodge-podge of compromises, a high overhead, and a manufacturing organization that is constantly in hot water with top management, marketing management, the controller, and customers.

A simple but telling example of a failure to focus is uncovered in this case study of a manufacturer, the American Printed Circuit Company (APC).

APC was a small company which had been growing rapidly and successfully. Its printed circuits were custom-built in lots of 1 to 100 for about 20 principal customers and were used for engineering tests and development work. APC's process consisted of about 15 operations using simple equipment, such as hand-dipping tanks, drill presses, and manual touch-ups. There was considerable variation in the sequence and processes for different products. Delivery was a major element for success, and price was not a key factor.

APC's president accepted an order from a large computer company to manufacture 20,000 printed circuit boards—a new product for the company—at a price equivalent to about one third of its average mix of products. APC made the decision to produce these circuit boards in order to build volume, broaden the company's range of markets, and diversify the line. The new product was produced in the existing plant.

The result was disastrous. The old products were no longer delivered on time. The costs of the new printed circuit boards were substantially in excess of the bid price. The quality on all items suffered as the organization frenetically attempted to meet deliveries. Old customers grew bitter over missed deliveries, and the new customer returned one third of the merchandise for below-spec quality. Such heavy losses ensued that the APC company had to recapitalize. Subsequently, the ownership of the company changed hands.

The purpose of this article is to set forth the advantages of focused manufacturing. I shall begin with the basic concepts of the focused factory, then follow with an analysis of the productivity phenomenon, which tends to prevent the adoption of the focused plant concept. Finally, I shall offer some specific steps for managing manufacturing to accomplish and take advantage of focus.

BASIC CONCEPTS

From my study of approximately fifty plants in six industries, I can pinpoint three basic concepts underlying focused manufacturing. Consider:

1. *There are many ways to compete besides by producing at low cost.* This statement may be self-evident to the reader (particularly, to one in an industry which has been badly hit by low-priced foreign imports and has been attempting to compete with better products, quality, or customer service and delivery). Nevertheless, it still needs saying for two reasons.

   One is simply the persistent attitude that ways of competing other than on the basis of price are second best. The other is that a company which starts out with higher manufacturing costs than its competitors is in trouble regardless of whatever else it does.

   While these assumptions may be true of industries with mature products and technologies, they are not at all true of products in earlier stages of their life cycles. In fact, in many U.S. industries, companies are being forced to shift to products in which technological innovation in the form of advanced features is a more critical element of competitive advantage than cost.

2. *A factory cannot perform well on every yardstick.* There are a number of common standards for measuring manufacturing performance. Among these are short delivery cycles, superior product quality and reliability, dependable delivery promises, ability to produce new products quickly, flexibility in adjusting to volume changes, low investment and hence higher return on investment, and low costs.

These measures of manufacturing performance necessitate trade-offs—certain tasks must be compromised to meet others. They cannot all be accomplished equally well because of the inevitable limitations of equipment and process technology. Such trade-offs as costs versus quality or short delivery cycles versus low inventory investment are fairly obvious. Other trade-offs, while less obvious, are equally real. They involve implicit choices in establishing manufacturing policies.

Within the factory, managers can make the manufacturing function a competitive weapon by outstanding accomplishment of one or more of the measures of manufacturing performance. But managers need to know: "What must we be especially good at? Cost, quality, lead times, reliability, changing schedules, new-product introduction, or low investment?"

Focused manufacturing must be derived from an explicitly defined corporate strategy which has its roots in a corporate marketing plan. Therefore, the choice of focus cannot be made independently by production people. Instead, it has to be a result of a comprehensive analysis of the company's resources, strengths and weaknesses, position in the industry, assessment of competitors' moves, and forecast of future customer motives and behavior.

Conversely, the choice of focus cannot be made without considering the existing factory, because a given set of facilities, systems, and people skills can do only certain things well within a given time period.

3. *Simplicity and repetition breed competence.* Focused manufacturing is based on the concept that simplicity, repetition, experience, and homogeneity of tasks breed competence. Furthermore, each key functional area in manufacturing must have the same objective, derived from corporate strategy. Such congruence of tasks can produce a manufacturing system that does limited things very well, thus creating a formidable competitive weapon.

MAJOR CHARACTERISTICS

Five key characteristics of the focused factory are:

1. *Process technologies:* Typically, unproven and uncertain technologies are limited to one per factory. Proven, mature technologies are limited

to what their managers can easily handle, typically two or three (e.g., a foundry, metal working, and metal finishing).

2. *Market demands:* These consist of a set of demands including quality, price, lead times, and reliability specifications. A given plant can usually only do a superb job on one or two demands at any given period of time.

3. *Product volumes:* Generally, these are of comparable levels, such that tooling, order quantities, materials handling techniques, and job contents can be approached with a consistent philosophy. But what about the inevitable short runs, customer specials, and one-of-a-kind orders that every factory must handle? The answer is usually to segregate them. This is discussed later.

4. *Quality levels:* These employ a common attitude and set of approaches so as to neither overspecify nor overcontrol quality and specifications. One frame of mind and set of mental assumptions suffice for equipment, tooling, inspection, training, supervision, job content, and materials handling.

5. *Manufacturing tools:* These are limited to only one (or two at the most) at any given time. The task at which the plant must excel in order to be competitive focuses on one set of internally consistent, doable, noncompromised criteria for success.

My research evidence makes it clear that the focused factory will outproduce, undersell, and quickly gain competitive advantage over the complex factory. The focused factory does a better job because repetition and concentration in one area allow its work force and managers to become effective and experienced in the task required for success. The focused factory is manageable and controllable. Its problems are demanding, but limited in scope.

PRODUCTIVITY PHENOMENON

The conventional wisdom of manufacturing management has been and continues to be that the measure of success is productivity. Now that U.S. companies in many industries are getting beaten hands down by overseas competitors with lower unit costs, we mistakenly cling to the old notion that "a good plant is a low-cost plant." This is simply not so. A low-cost plant may be a disaster if the company has sacrificed too much in the way of quality, delivery, flexibility, and so forth, in order to get its costs down.

Too many companies attempt to do too many things with one plant and one organization. In the name of low investment in facilities and spreading their overheads, they add products, markets, technologies, processes, quality levels, and supporting services which conflict and compete with each other and compound expense. They then hire more staff to regulate and control the unmanageable mixture of problems.

In desperation, many companies are now "banging away" at anything to reduce the resulting high costs. But we can only regain competitive strength by stopping this process of increasing complexity and overstaffing.

This behavior is so illogical that the phenomenon needs further explanation. Our plants are generally managed by extremely able people; yet the failure to focus manufacturing on a limited objective is a common managerial blind spot. What happens to produce this defect in competent managers? Engineers know what can and cannot be designed into planes, boats, and building structures. Engineers accept design objectives that will accomplish a specific set of tasks which are possible, although difficult.

In contrast, most of the manufacturing plants in my study attempted a complex, heterogeneous mixture of general and special-purpose equipment, long- and short-run operations, high and low tolerances, new and old products, off-the-shelf items and customer specials, stable and changing designs, markets with reliable forecasts and unpredictable ones, seasonal and nonseasonal sales, short and long lead times, and high and low skills.

LACK OF CONSISTENT POLICIES

It is not understood, I think, that each of the contrasting features just noted generate conflicting manufacturing tasks and hence different manufacturing policies. The particular mix of these features should determine the elements of manufacturing policy. Some of these elements are the following:

- Size of plant and its capacity
- Location of plant
- Choice of equipment
- Plant layout
- Selection of production process
- Production scheduling system
- Use of inventories
- Wage system
- Training and supervisory approaches
- Control systems
- Organizational structure

Instead of designing elements of manufacturing policy around one manufacturing task, what usually happens? Consider, for example, that the wage system may be set up to emphasize high productivity, production control to maximize short lead times, inventory to minimize stock levels, order quantities to minimize setup times, plant layout to minimize materials handling costs, and process design to maximize quality.

While each of these decisions probably looks sensible to the professional specialist in his field, the conventional factory consists of six or more inconsistent elements of manufacturing structure, each of which is designed to achieve a different implicit objective.

Such inconsistency usually results in high costs. One or another element may be excessively staffed or operated inefficiently because its task is being exaggerated or misdirected. Or several functions may require excess staff in order to control or manage a plant which is unduly complex.

But often the result is even more serious. My study shows that the chief negative effect is not on productivity but on ability to compete. The plant's manufacturing policies are not designed, tuned, and focused as a whole on that one key strategic manufacturing task essential to the company's success in its industry.

REASONS FOR INCONSISTENCY

Noncongruent manufacturing structures appear to be common in U.S. industry. In fact, my research revealed that a fully consistent set of manufacturing policies resulting in a congruent system is highly rare. Why does this situation occur so often? In the cases I studied, it seemed to come about essentially for one or more of these reasons:

- Professionals in each field attempted to achieve goals which, although valid and traditional in their fields, were not congruent with goals of other areas.
- The manufacturing task for the plant subtly changed while most operating and service departments kept on the same course as before.
- The manufacturing task was never made explicit.
- The inconsistencies were never recognized.
- More and more products were piled into existing plants, resulting in an often futile attempt to meet the manufacturing tasks of a variety of markets, technologies, and competitive strategies.

Let me elaborate on the first and last set of causes we have just noted.

'PROFESSIONALISM' IN THE PLANT

Production system elements are now set up or managed by professionals in their respective fields, such as quality control, personnel, labor relations, engineering, inventory management, materials handling, systems design, and so forth.

These professionals, quite naturally, seek to maximize their contributions and justify their positions. They have conventional views of success in each of their particular fields. Of course, these objectives are generally in conflict.

I say "of course" not to be cynical. These fields of specialty have come into existence for many different reasons—some to reduce costs, others to save time, others to minimize capital investments, still others to promote human cooperation and happiness, and so on. So it is perfectly normal for them to pull in different directions, which is exactly what happens in many plants.

This problem is not totally new. But it is changing because professionalism is increasing; we have more and more experts at work in different parts of the factory. So it is a growing problem.

PRODUCT PROLIFERATION

The combination of increasing foreign and domestic competition plus an accelerating rate of technological innovation has resulted in product proliferation in many factories. Shorter product life, more new products, shorter runs, lower unit volumes, and more customer specials are becoming increasingly common. The same factory which 5 years ago produced 25 products may today be producing 50 to 100.

The inconsistent production system grows up, not simply because there are more products to make—which is of course likely to increase direct and indirect costs and add complexity and confusion—but also because new products often call for different manufacturing tasks. To succeed in some tasks may require superb technological competence and focus; others may demand extremely short delivery; and still others, extremely low costs.

Yet, almost always, new products are added into the existing mix in the same plant, even though some new equipment may be necessary. The rationale for this decision is usually that the plant is operating at less than full capacity. Thus the logic is, "If we put the new products into the present plant, we can save capital investment and avoid duplicating overheads."

The result is complexity, confusion, and worst of all a production organization which, because it is spun out in all directions by a kind of centrifugal force, lacks focus and a doable manufacturing task. The factory is asked to perform a mission for Product A which conflicts with that of Product B. Thus the result is a hodgepodge of compromises.

When we may have, in fact, four tasks and four markets, we make the mistake of trying to force them into one plant, one set of equipment, one factory organization, one set of manufacturing policies, and so on. We try to cram into one operating system the ability to compete in an impossible mix of demands. Each element of the system attempts to adjust to these demands with variation, special sections, complex procedures, more people, and added paperwork.

In my opinion this syndrome, starting with added market demands and ending with incongruent internal structures, to a large extent accounts for the human frustrations, high costs, and low competitive abilities we see so much of in U.S. industry today.

Who gets the blame? The manufacturing executive, of course, gets it from corporate headquarters for high costs, poor productivity, low quality and reliability, and missed deliveries. In turn he tends to blame the situation on anything which makes sense, such as poor market forecasts, subpar labor, unconcern over quality, inept engineering designs, faulty equipment, and so forth.

Probably all such factors contribute and, undoubtedly, they all add to the pressure on production people. But what is not perceived is that a given production organization, as we noted earlier, can only do certain things well; trade-offs are inevitable.

Experience accomplishes wonders, but a diffused organization with conflicting structural elements and competing manufacturing tasks accumulates experience and specialized competence very slowly.

TOWARD MANUFACTURING FOCUS

A new management approach is needed in industries where diverse products and markets require companies to manufacture a broad mix of items, volumes, specifications, and customer demand patterns. Its emphasis must be on building competitive strength. One way to compete is to focus the entire manufacturing system on a limited task precisely defined by the company's competitive strategy and the realities of its technology and economics. A common objective produces synergistic effects rather than internal power struggles between professionalized departments. This approach can be assisted by these guiding rules:

- Centralize the factory's focus on relative competitive ability.
- Avoid the common tendency to add staff and overhead in order to save on direct labor and capital investment.
- Let each manufacturing unit work on a limited task instead of the usual complex mix of conflicting objectives, products, and technologies.

This management approach can be thought of as focused manufacturing, for it is the opposite of the under-one-roof diffusion process of the conventional factory. Instead of permitting the whirling diversity of tasks and ingredients, top management applies a centripetal force, which constantly pulls inward toward one central focus—the one key manufacturing task. The result is greater simplicity, lower costs, and a manufacturing and support organization that is directed toward successful competition.

ACHIEVING THE FOCUSED PLANT

In my experience, manufacturing managers are generally astounded at the internal inconsistencies and compromises they discover once they put the concept of focused manufacturing to work in analyzing their own plants.

Then, when they begin to discern what the company strategy and market situation are implicitly demanding and to compare these implicit demands with what they have been trying to achieve, many submerged conflicts surface.

Finally, when they ask themselves what a certain element of the structure or of the manufacturing policy was designed to maximize, the built-in cross-purposes become apparent.

At the risk of seeming to take a cookbook approach to an inevitably complex set of issues, let me offer a recipe for the focused factory based on an actual but disguised example of an industrial manufacturing company which attempted to adapt its operations to this concept.

Consider this four-step approach of, say, the WXY Company, a producer of mechanical equipment.

1. *Develop an explicit, brief statement of corporate objectives and strategy.* The statement should cover the next three to five years, and it should have the substantial involvement of top management, including marketing, finance, and control executives.

   In its statement, the top management of the WXY Company agreed to the following:

   "Our corporate objective is directed toward increasing market share during the next five years via a strategy of (1) tailoring our product to individual customer needs, (2) offering advanced and special product features at a modest price increment, and (3) gaining competitive advantage via rapid product development and service orientation to customers of all sizes."

2. *Translate the objectives-and-strategy statement into "what this means to manufacturing."* What must the factory do especially well in order to carry out and support this corporate strategy? What is going to be the most difficult task it will face? If the manufacturing function is not sharp and capable, where is the company most likely to fail? It may fail in any one of the elements of the production structure, but it will probably do so in a combination of some of them.

   To carry on with the WXY Company example, such a manufacturing task might be defined explicitly as follows:

   "Our manufacturing task for the next three years will be to introduce specialized, customer-tailored new products into production, with lead times which are substantially less than those of our competitors.

"Since the technology in our industry is changing rapidly, and since product reliability can be extremely serious for customers, our most difficult problems will be to control the new-product introduction process, so as to solve technical problems promptly and to maintain reliability amid rapid changes in the product itself."

3. *Make a careful examination of each element of the production system.* How is it now set up, organized, focused, and manned? What is it now especially good at? How must it be changed to implement the key manufacturing task?

4. *Reorganize the elements of structure to produce a congruent focus.* This reorganization focuses on the ability to do those limited things well which are of utmost importance to the accomplishment of the manufacturing task.

To complete the example of the WXY Company, Exhibit 1 lists each major element of the manufacturing system of the company, describes its present focus in terms of that task for which it was implicitly or inadvertently aimed, and lists a new approach designed to bring consistency, focus, and power to its manufacturing arm.

What stands out most in this exhibit is the number of substantial changes in manufacturing policies required to bring the production system into total consistency. The exhibit also features the implicit conflicts between many manufacturing tasks in the present approach, which are the result of the failure to define one task for the whole plant.

The reader may perceive a disturbing implication of the focused plant concept—namely, that it seems to call for major investments in new plants, new equipment, and new tooling, in order to break down the present complexity.

For example, if the company is currently involved in five different products, technologies, markets, or volumes, does it need five plants, five sets of equipment, five processes, five technologies, and five organizational structures? The answer is probably *yes*. But the practical solution need not involve selling the big multipurpose facility and decentralizing into five small facilities.

In fact, the few companies that have adopted the focused plant concept have approached the solution quite differently. There is no need to build five plants, which would involve unnecessary investment and overhead expenses.

The more practical approach is the "plant within a plant" (PWP) notion in which the existing facility is divided both organizationally and physically into, in this case, five PWPs. Each PWP has its own facilities in which it can concentrate on its particular manufacturing task, using its own workforce management approaches, production control, organization structure, and so forth. Quality and volume levels are not mixed; worker training

EXHIBIT 1			
CONFLICTING MANUFACTURING TASKS IMPLIED BY INCONGRUENT ELEMENTS OF THE PRESENT PRODUCTION SYSTEM			
PRODUCTION SYSTEM ELEMENTS	**PRESENT APPROACH (CONVENTIONAL FACTORY)**	**IMPLICIT MANUFACTURING TASKS OF PRESENT APPROACH**	**CHANGED APPROACH (FOCUSED FACTORY)**
Equipment and process policies	One large plant; special purpose equipment; high-volume tooling; balanced capacity with functional layout.	Low manufacturing costs on steady runs of a few large products with minimal investment.	Seperate old, standardized products and new customized products into two plants within a plant (PWP). For new PWP, provide general purpose equipment, temporary tooling, and modest excess capacity with product-oriented layout.
Work-force management policies	Specialized jobs with narrow job content; incentive wages; few supervisors; focus on volume of production per hour.	Low costs and efficiency.	Create fewer jobs with more versatility. Pay for breadth of skills and ability to perform a variety of jobs. Provide more foremen for solving technical problems at workplace.
Production scheduling and control	Detailed, frequent sales forecasts; produce for inventory economic lot sizes of finished goods; small, decentralized production scheduling group.	Short delivery lead times.	Produce to order special parts and stock of common parts based on semi-annual forecast. Staff production control to closely schedule and centralize parts movements.
Quality control	Control engineers and large inspection groups in each department.	Extremely reliable quality.	No change.
Organizational structure	Functional; production control under superintendents of each area; inspection reports to top.	Top performance of the objectives of each functional department, i.e., many tasks.	Organize each PWP by program and project in order to focus organizational effort on bringing new products into production smoothly and on time.

and incentives have a clear focus; and engineering of processes, equipment, and materials handling are specialized as needed.

Each PWP gains experience readily by focusing and concentrating every element of its work on those limited essential objectives which constitute its manufacturing task. Since a manufacturing task is an offspring of a corporate strategy and marketing program, it is susceptible to either gradual or sweeping change. The PWP approach makes it easier to perform realignment of essential operations and system elements over time as the task changes.

CONCLUSION

The prevalent use of "cost" and "efficiency" as the conventional yardsticks for planning, controlling, and evaluating U.S. plants played a large part in the increasing inability of many of the approximately 50 companies included in my research to compete successfully. However, such goals are no longer adequate because competition is getting rougher and, in particular, because a strictly low-cost, high-efficiency strategy is apparently becoming less viable in many industries.

While the economy has moved toward an era of more advanced technologies and shorter product lives, we have not readjusted our concepts of production to keep up with these changes. Instead, we have continued to use "productivity" and "economies of scale" as guiding objectives. Both feature only one element of competition (i.e., costs), and both are now obsolete as general, all-purpose guides in manufacturing management.

But I have concluded that the focused plant is a rarity. With the mistaken rationale that the keys to success are limited investment, economies of scale, and full utilization of existing plant resources to achieve low costs, we keep adding new products to plants which were once focused, manageable, and competitive.

Reversing the process, however, is not impossible. In most of the cases I have studied, capital investment in facilities is not difficult to justify when payoffs that will result from organizational simplicity are taken into account. Resources for simplifying the focus of a manufacturing complex are not hard to acquire when the expected payoff is the ability to compete successfully, using manufacturing as a competitive weapon.

Moreover, better customer service and competitive position typically support higher margins to cover capital investments. And when studied carefully, the economies of scale and the effects of less than full utilization of plant equipment are seldom found to be as critical to productivity and efficiency as classical economic approaches often predict.

The U.S. problem of "productivity" is real indeed. But seeing the problem as one of "how to compete" can broaden management's horizon. The focused factory approach offers the opportunity to stop compromising each element of the production system in the typical general-purpose, do-all plant which satisfies no strategy, no market, and no task.

Not only does focus provide punch and power, but it also provides clear goals which can be readily understood and assimilated by members of an organization. It provides, too, a mechanism for reappraising what is needed for success, and for readjusting and shaking up old, tired manufacturing organizations with welcome change and a clear sense of direction.

In many sectors of U.S. industry, such change and such a new sense of direction are needed to shift the competitive balance in our favor.

REFLECTING CORPORATE STRATEGY IN MANUFACTURING DECISIONS

STEVEN C. WHEELWRIGHT

In spite of the fact that manufacturing frequently accounts for the majority of a firm's human and financial assets, top management often overlooks the role that operations can play in accomplishing corporate objectives. The problem is not that top management ignores manufacturing, but rather that marketing and finance are expected to play a major role in formulating corporate plans, with manufacturing simply reacting to those plans as best it can. This failure to consider manufacturing to be a key resource in realizing corporate objectives seldom represents an explicit decision to restrict it to a reactive role. The reasons for such shortsightedness and its consequences have been described by Wickham Skinner:*

> Top management unknowingly delegates a surprisingly large portion of basic policy decisions to lower levels in the manufacturing area. Generally, this abdication of responsibility comes about more through a lack of concern than by intention. And it is partly the reason that many manufacturing policies and procedures developed at lower levels reflect assumptions about corporate strategy which are incorrect or misconstrued.
>
> The conventional factory produces many products for numerous customers in a variety of markets, thereby demanding the performance of a multiplicity of manufacturing tasks all at once from one set of assets and people. Its rationale is "economy of scale" and lower capital investment.

Reprinted by permission from *Business Horizons,* February 1978, 57–66.

---

*Wickham Skinner, "Manufacturing—Missing Link in Corporate Strategy," *Harvard Business Review* (May–June 1969) 136–45; and "The Focused Factory," *Harvard Business Review* (May–June 1974) 113–121.

Unfortunately, even a company that recognizes these problems and has first-rate managers to work on them faces a major challenge in establishing procedures to ensure that manufacturing decisions mesh with corporate plans and goals. While operating decisions may make sense individually, they may not work cumulatively to reinforce the corporate strategy. The basic problem is that most decisions, particularly those in manufacturing, require trade-offs among various criteria. All too often the trade-offs that are made in such decisions reflect priorities that are internally inconsistent or that run counter to corporate strategy. Management needs a procedure for developing and implementing plans that support and reinforce corporate strategy.

Research and experience suggest that it is not enough just to communicate strategy throughout the organization. Some intermediate mechanism is needed for translating strategy into a form directly applicable to manufacturing decisions. One approach that several firms have applied utilizes a set of criteria that are appropriate for evaluating operations decisions. When the company assigns weights to these criteria that reflect the priorities of corporate strategy, these priorities can be used to ensure that tradeoffs associated with operation decisions are consistent with strategy. This approach has been successfully used both by corporate manufacturing staff and by line management charged with making improvements in manufacturing decision making.

The remainder of this article describes and illustrates this approach. The major emphasis is on implementing proven concepts so that the problems cited earlier can be avoided and the full strategic potential of manufacturing can be realized. As a starting point, four typical production decisions are described, and for each one the course of action initially selected by manufacturing management is indicated. The modifications in those decisions that resulted when a broader corporate perspective was considered are then examined. Following these illustrations of what it means to have manufacturing decisions reinforce corporate strategy, a conceptual framework is described that assists managers to accomplish systematically that desired congruence. Finally, two alternative procedures are presented for implementing that framework. In the first, the corporate manufacturing staff takes the initiative; in the second, line management.

SOME IMPORTANT DECISIONS

In each of the following decision situations, manufacturing management had identified those actions they thought would be most appropriate. However, a subsequent review of each decision's compatibility with corporate goals and strategy indicated that a different course of action would be more appropriate. These four situations suggest the range of operating decisions which are typically made independently, but which have a major cumulative impact on the corporation's success in accomplishing its overall strategy.

SITUATION A: MAJOR EQUIPMENT PURCHASE

Production output was approaching the capacity of a major piece of equipment at a wholly owned subsidiary of a diversified company. This subsidiary sold 85 percent of its output to other divisions within the corporation. The other 15 percent, which represented outside sales, was an important source of profits for the subsidiary because of the transfer price arrangement established for corporate business and because the in-house business was at the low-priced end of the market. It was agreed that the division would soon need new equipment, and management was about to propose a multipurpose machine. This equipment offered more capacity per dollar invested than other alternatives and promised a chance to expand outside business and thereby increase return on investment. The only question appeared to be whether to buy the new machine at once or to delay the purchase for a year.

As a first step in taking a broader view of this decision, division management determined that the goal for the subsidiary was to be a low-cost source of supply to the corporation for that particular product. Other firms were potential suppliers, but top management had originally established this subsidiary to obtain low-cost materials for specialized, high-volume needs.

Review indicated that purchase of the proposed machine was not the best decision if the subsidiary was to work only for the parent company in the future. The subsidiary's outside customers put quality ahead of cost, but corporate customers emphasized cost. The proposed multipurpose machine would raise the cost on corporate business because of its cost structure. Also, because of the natural desire to utilize expensive equipment as fully as possible, it would probably lead to less emphasis on sales to corporate customers (and on costs) and more emphasis on outside sales (and quality) in order to utilize the equipment's full capability.

SITUATION B: QUALITY CONTROL BUDGET

This company had grown substantially over several years but had recently noted that indirect and overhead costs were growing more rapidly than sales. Management was concerned that these costs were getting out of line. As part of the annual budgeting procedure, manufacturing management proposed that the quality control area be rationalized and streamlined to bring its costs more in line with what they had been historically. The plan was to use more final product sampling (and less components testing) to cut quality control cost per unit.

A broader examination of this situation revealed that the company's products were selling at a premium price with an image of quality and high reliability. In fact, when the use of the product was examined for the major customer segment, it became apparent that the cost of a motor breakdown for even a single day was more than the price of a new motor. Manufacturing concluded that quality had to be maintained and given top priority. Component reliability was identified as an integral part of quality because of the modular product design and customer maintenance procedures. As a result of this review, management decided that more, not less, quality control per unit was appropriate, and that reductions in overhead and indirect costs would have to come from areas other than quality.

SITUATION C: LABOR NEGOTIATIONS

In six months, the major production facility of a manufacturer of a perishable consumer product (shelf life about three months) would face its first labor contract renewal. The corporate labor relations staff, whose policy had always been one of firmness, considered the existing contract most attractive and wanted to keep the new contract equally favorable to the company. Unfortunately, the union had recently been agitating among employees, emphasizing that the existing contract, unlike most other contracts in that region and industry, had no cost-of-living adjustment clause. A group of employees had become vocal in demands for a substantial "catch-up" adjustment in the new contract. It was assumed that when the contract expired in six months, the normal procedure of having the corporate labor relations staff handle negotiations would be followed. That staff had already recommended that as much extra inventory as possible should be built up in anticipation of a three-to-four-week strike. Given current capacity constraints and the perishable nature of the product, manufacturing had indicated that no more than three weeks of finished goods inventory could be accumulated by the time the current contract expired.

A more thorough examination of this situation indicated that the market was growing at about 60 percent annually and that there were two other major firms in the business. This company and its two competitors each had about the same market share and were seeking to build national distribution as quickly as possible. In addition, recent studies of similar products and their economies suggested that there might only be room for two major firms once the growth rate began to slow. Manufacturing concluded that to achieve reliable, uninterrupted supply was the key task of production if corporate goals were to be met. Consequently, manufacturing decided to take an active role in urging labor relations to open negotiations early and, if at all possible, to resolve the contract issues before a strike became inevitable.

SITUATION D: MAJOR CAPACITY EXPANSION

The established manufacturer of a branded household product suddenly found its market growing rapidly, severely taxing its outdated production process. An engineering firm had been hired to develop process equipment that would improve the consistency of the product and provide substantial productivity improvement. A new process design had been completed and, although the equipment was new to this application, it was based on known technologies from other fields. To meet the coming year's substantially increased capacity requirements, manufacturing management planned to replace the old production process with the new one. This promised twice the output per square foot of plant and per employee, with an investment per unit of capacity that was slightly lower than for the old equipment. The new process appeared to more than meet cost goals, and manufacturing management was planning to move ahead with it as quickly as possible.

In this situation, a broader look at the corporate strategy and the environment identified the critical role of additional capacity. There was no contingency plan in the event that the new production process met unexpected start-up problems, a fact that signaled danger. Further investigation indicated that the cost of excess capacity was minimal compared with the product's gross margin of almost 50 percent, and the maintenance of 30 percent excess capacity would add only 1 or 2 percent to product cost. Management concluded that if the firm was unable to meet all of the demand for its products, the penalty would not only be a loss in market share but a waste of advertising dollars equivalent to the capital investment required for 30 percent idle capacity. Manufacturing concluded that the new process might be appropriate in the longer term; initially, however, it should be added as excess capacity, not as a replacement for the existing process.

A CONCEPTUAL FRAMEWORK

The four decisions described above illustrate a range of situations where individual decisions must be reviewed in the context of corporate goals and strategy if those decisions are to have the desired reinforcing effect. In each instance, manufacturing management thought it had identified the appropriate action; yet a more comprehensive strategic review indicated that a major change in that action was needed. These situations suggest the need to develop a framework that triggers such a review, establishes company-specific criteria to be applied in that review, and provides a means of using those criteria effectively.

The ability of a company's manufacturing function to reinforce corporate strategy is determined by a number of decisions over an extended period of time. Understanding these decisions is the first step in using them to accomplish corporate goals. The following are among the most important factors in determining whether a firm's manufacturing actions will be truly supportive.

Facilities.   The rationalization and focus of individual plants and their sizes and locations are major manufacturing commitments. These decisions are often the most visible examples of manufacturing strategy selection, in that options are often first defined at this point.

Choice of Process.   A major set of manufacturing decisions concerns the matching of the company's choice of equipment and processes with its products' characteristics and competitive pressures. Choices must be made regarding the degree of automation, the level of product-line specificity, and the degree of interconnectedness among different stages in the process.

Aggregate Capacity.   Both type of capacity and the timing of capacity changes are important elements in this category. Should the production rate be level or should it chase demand? Should capacity lead or follow changes in demand? Should overtime, second shift, or subcontracting be used for peak capacity requirements?

Vertical Integration.   The number of production and distribution stages to be managed by a single firm, and the balance and relationships between vertically linked stages, are critical manufacturing decisions with an impact on corporate strategy.

Manufacturing Infrastructure.   Molding the bricks, mortar, equipment, and people into a coordinated whole requires that the firm specify policies for production planning and control, quality control, inventory and logistic systems, and work-force management. Labor policies and materials-management procedures are important related topics.

Interface with Other Functions.   Manufacturing must work closely with the other corporate functions. The operations manager and the manufacturing executive must facilitate these relations while balancing them against their own priorities.

These six choices determine corporate strategy in a company's manufacturing operations. They are the points at which key trade-offs are made. If they are to support corporate aims, they must consistently reinforce the desired competitive focus and goals—a simple achievement in firms in which the chief executive is involved in all decisions of significance. In larger firms with functional or divisionalized structures, a systematic effort is needed to insure this consistency. This effort is particularly critical as products and businesses grow, develop, or shrink, requiring change in the corporate strategy and in the manufacturing decisions to support that change.

Unfortunately, simply giving manufacturing management a statement of the corporate objectives and strategy is not particularly effective in achieving this desired consistency in decision making. The gap between operating decisions and their impact on corporate strategy is just too great. Some intermediate step is needed.

Manufacturing decisions reflect trade-offs among different performance criteria. Thus, identifying these criteria and prioritizing them has proven effective in bridging this gap. The most important performance criteria are the following:

> *Efficiency.* This criterion encompasses both cost efficiency and capital efficiency and can generally be measured by such factors as return on sales, inventory turnover, and return on assets.
> *Dependability.* The dependability of a company's products and its delivery and price promises is often extremely difficult to measure. Many companies measure it in terms of the "percent of on-time deliveries."
> *Quality.* Product quality and reliability, service quality, speed of delivery, and maintenance quality are important aspects of this criterion. For many firms this is easy to measure by internal standards, but as with the other criteria, the key is how the market evaluates quality.
> *Flexibility.* The two major aspects of flexibility changes are in the product and the volume. Special measures are required for this criterion, since it is not generally measured.

The four situations described earlier illustrate how an initially narrow view may lead to decisions that are not most appropriate for the corporation as a whole. As is frequently the case, in three of those four situations manufacturing management erred initially in assuming that the appropriate trade-offs were those that minimized the production cost per unit. A broader perspective for the last three situations indicated that the single criterion of lowest cost did not identify the best overall decision for those companies.

Every corporate situation is unique; no single procedure will guarantee that manufacturing decisions always reinforce corporate strategy. However, utilizing this framework that seeks to establish manufacturing priorities has been helpful in many situations. A first step in implementing the framework for an individual company is to answer two important questions: *Who* will apply the framework? *When and where* in existing planning and decision-making procedures will it be applied?

Among those who might take responsibility for applying the framework are the division general manager, the director of the corporate manufacturing staff, the division controller, and the division's director of manufacturing. These positions can be grouped into two main categories—line and staff. The division general manager and the director of manufacturing represent line management; the corporate manufacturing manager or a member of the controller's office represents staff. Who can best assume this responsibility depends on the organization of the company and its normal split of staff and line assignments. Even when a staff group facilitates and shepherds the application of this framework, it is always necessary to have the understanding and commitment of line management to make the framework useful.

When and where the implementation of this framework should be monitored depends largely on established management and decision-making procedures. For one company, the most logical time might be the annual budgeting or planning cycle. For another, it might best be incorporated in the periodic corporate review of divisional plans or in the division general manager's quarterly review of operations. How the framework can be used most effectively will depend both on the organization's motivation and management philosophy and on the manager (line or staff) most willing to take responsibility for seeing that significant progress is made.

APPLYING THE FRAMEWORK

Two separate applications of this conceptual framework will illustrate the range of approaches available for its implementation. The first was developed by a corporate manufacturing staff seeking to improve annual manufacturing plans. The second was designed and implemented by a vice president of manufacturing.

A STAFF APPROACH

The corporate manufacturing staff of a large diversified company with several autonomous divisions was concerned that manufacturing was not achieving its potential as a competitive weapon. Historically, the manufacturing staff had consisted of fewer than a dozen people whose major task was to make sure that requests for major capital appropriations were "complete." While the staff's charter continued to call for a limited staff, the vice president who had recently been put in charge of the group wanted to move quickly to help division manufacturing managers take a more active role in the accomplishment of corporate strategy.

As a first step in this direction, he decided that all the divisions had a similar problem: developing annual manufacturing plans consistent with marketing and product strategies. Subsequently, corporate manufacturing assumed responsibility for communicating the framework and concepts related to manufacturing performance priorities and for having each division's manufacturing manager make them operational.

Two major objectives motivated corporate manufacturing's pursuit of this framework in the company. First, the corporate staff wanted to provide the different manufacturing managers from each of the operating divisions with a common set of concepts and language. It was felt that the corporate manufacturing staff and top management, who are not familiar with the technical problems, pressures, and issues facing manufacturing management, would be better able to review and evaluate operations decisions if they mastered these concepts.

A second objective was to help operating managers recognize the specific competitive decisions faced by their division. This could then help such managers make manufacturing decisions and formulate action plans consistent with corporate and division strategies and objectives.

The staff's approach in accomplishing these goals consisted of two phases. The first phase was a two-day seminar for thirty-five key manufacturing and distribution managers selected from all of the company's divisions. The first step was to introduce the framework presented in Figure 1. Thereafter, through a variety of case studies, the manufacturing managers were able to see the concepts applied to different situations.

The second phase applied the framework to each of the individual operating units as a part of their annual five-year planning process. After the division's operating plan had been drafted, manufacturing management met for a day with the corporate manufacturing staff. Their purpose was to review the draft plan and to examine the interaction between anticipated operating decisions and the division's strategy. These follow-up sessions consisted of four steps, as illustrated in Figure 2.

Step 1 defined the basic business units of the division—those product-market groupings for which the division had a homogeneous strategy and for which a single set of priorities for the manufacturing performance criteria would be appropriate. Step 2 defined the four performance criteria for that division's manufacturing and marketing setting, determining what constituted quality, flexibility, cost, and dependability. Step 3 identified for each business unit the priorities customarily assigned to the four performance criteria. Identification was accomplished through a review of past manufacturing decisions and the relative emphasis those had given to each criterion. Future priorities for each business unit were also identified during this part of the session. Step 4 identified the key operating decisions to be made in the coming years and evaluated those using the performance priorities specified in Step 3.

FIGURE 1	MANUFACTURING STRATEGY AND OPERATING DECISIONS

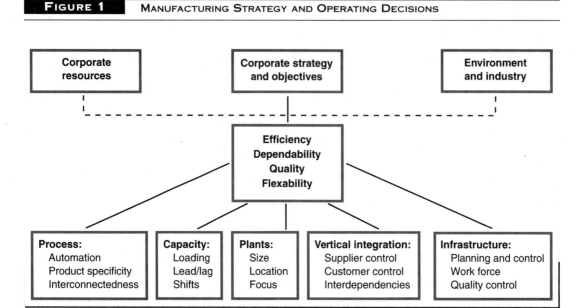

Manufacturing interface with other functions

In several instances, this process did no more than reinforce the actions tentatively planned by manufacturing management. In other instances, however, the priorities suggested that the proposed decisions should be altered so that actions would better reinforce the division's strategy and have the desired cumulative effect. Situations A, C, and D, described earlier, were among the proposed decisions that were reviewed and subsequently revised as a result of this exercise.

A LINE MANAGEMENT APPROACH

A second situation where the framework of Figure 1 proved effective did not involve any staff support. It was initiated and guided by the vice-president of manufacturing. The company, which manufactured four major industrial products and a line of spare parts, had found itself capacity-constrained for some time. Production bottlenecks were frequent, and manufacturing had been under substantial pressure to improve its performance and its support of the company's goals.

The motivation for this particular application came from the vice president of manufacturing, who had recently attended a two-week seminar on

FIGURE 2	APPLICATION OF MANUFACTURING CRITERIA BY CORPORATE MANUFACTURING STAFF

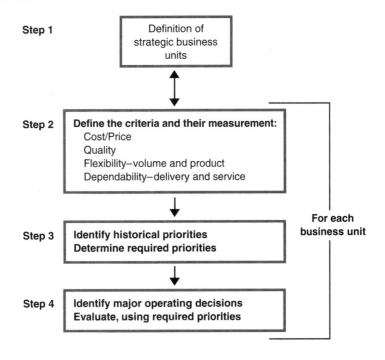

manufacturing in corporate strategy. Upon returning, he was asked, half jokingly, to tell some of the other members of top management what he had learned. He decided to respond by discussing the use of manufacturing priorities to support corporate strategy. He also wanted to determine the appropriate priorities for his own operations and to review major operating decisions.

The first step in his approach was to have company vice-presidents individually assess current manufacturing priorities. This was done by defining the four criteria described in the accompanying box and having them distribute points among these criteria. The assessment form identified the company's five separate business units and requested that 100 points be allocated for historical (as is) priorities and 100 points for required (should be) priorities for each. (The split into 5 product categories had been used frequently as part of the planning process.)

As might be expected, responses from the vice-presidents varied considerably. To reconcile the differences, discussion sessions were held among all of the members of top management. The result was a consensus

ELEMENTS OF MANUFACTURING STRATEGY AS DEFINED BY THE VICE-PRESIDENT OF MANUFACTURING

Cost. This criterion refers to low cost or even lowest possible cost, including cost of capital employed. This would imply minimum wages, particularly for hourly but also supervision. The amount of supervision would be determined by cost minimization rather than maintenance of quality or dependability levels. Capital equipment selections would be based on acquiring specialized machinery to produce at the lowest cost and would produce parts to the loosest possible acceptable tolerance levels. Equipment would be replaced only when completely worn out and would likely be overhauled once or twice prior to actual replacement. Inventories would be maintained at the minimum level needed to avoid idle shop time but would not necessarily be based upon needs for customer service levels. Emphasis of this criterion maximizes return and minimizes investment.

Quality. This criterion focuses on maintaining high levels of quality. High levels of quality can be defined as significantly higher than competitive products and sufficiently high to support sale of the product based upon its high quality, even if its price is unfavorable with respect to competition. Examples of primary emphasis on quality would be Mercedes automobiles and Hewlett-Packard calculators.

Dependability. This refers primarily to meeting all delivery commitments for new orders and parts. It includes not only the capability to stock products, but also the ability to manufacture replacement parts quickly.

Flexibility. Flexibility refers to the ability to make significant changes in manufacturing volumes and/or products. It entails high responsiveness to either increases or decreases in customer demand in the short term (substantially less than one year). It also may be related to flexibility to changes in product design such as the acquisition of new product lines and/or the significant modification of existing product lines.

as to past priorities and required priorities for each of the company's five business areas, as shown in the accompanying table. This step identified a number of areas in need of a change in emphasis so that manufacturing and its performance priorities would be most supportive of the corporate strategy.

Some of the actions that resulted from the identification of major differences in historical and required emphasis included the following:

Product 1 should have modest increases in quality and dependability at the expense of manufacturing cost efficiencies.

Products 2 and 3 should have no significant changes in manufacturing.

CURRENT AND REQUIRED PRIORITIES AS ASSESSED BY VICE PRESIDENTS
(VP)* AND MANUFACTURING MANAGERS (MM)*

	COST		QUALITY		DEPENDABILITY		FLEXIBILITY	
	VP	MM	VP	MM	VP	MM	VP	MM
PRODUCT 1								
As is	42	44	17	15	25	26	16	15
Should be	28	46	24	16	31	26	17	12
Needs more (less)	(14)	2	7	1	6	0	1	(3)
PRODUCT 2								
As is	26	20	37	43	24	22	13	15
Should be	26	30	36	38	26	20	12	12
Needs more (less)	0	10	(1)	(5)	2	(2)	(1)	(3)
PRODUCT 3								
As is	34	36	27	28	23	19	16	17
Should be	34	38	29	24	24	20	13	18
Needs more (less)	0	2	2	(4)	1	1	(3)	1
PRODUCT 4								
As is	24	34	30	22	19	17	27	27
Should be	39	44	20	25	23	15	18	16
Needs more (less)	15	10	(10)	3	4	(2)	(9)	(11)
PRODUCT 5 (Parts)								
As is	45	37	21	14	18	31	16	18
Should be	22	31	24	13	35	35	19	21
Needs more (less)	(23)	(6)	3	(1)	17	4	3	3

*Criteria totals for VP and MM for each priority = 100.

Product 4 should have a significant improvement in manufacturing cost efficiencies at the expense of quality and flexibility.

Product 5 (parts) should have a significant increase in dependability at the
expense of manufacturing cost efficiencies.

As a follow-up, the vice president of manufacturing used the same
approach with the manufacturing department heads who reporting to
him; the results are also shown in the table. This second application of the
framework convinced the vice president of manufacturing that his manufacturing managers were motivated primarily by the desire to achieve a
high degree of cost efficiency. Since manufacturing's action plan was
based on consensus reached by top management, the vice president of

manufacturing sought to convince his manufacturing subordinates that it was an appropriate plan of action since it was reached at the policy level in the company.

The vice president was very satisfied with the results he obtained from this process and concluded that his manufacturing people had gained a better understanding of the corporate strategy for each major product segment. He also felt that their ability to use the policies derived from this priority-setting procedure would continue to grow. Situation B, described earlier, is typical of the impact that this approach has had on his company.

In both of the companies described above, the managers involved found the establishment and application of priorities for manufacturing performance measures to be extremely valuable. This was particularly the case in the second example, where all of the vice-presidents had reached a consensus on the priorities for manufacturing. A significant reduction in the conflict resulted between manufacturing and marketing because both areas agreed on a common direction. The exercise also proved to have very useful organizational development benefits, many of which were greater than those obtained from programs designed only for organizational development purposes.

Upon reflection, the corporate manufacturing staff in the first situation felt its approach would have been strengthened had there been feedback to marketing for comment and appraisal. While they were uncertain how best to handle that, given their role as a staff group, they did agree that such marketing involvement should be obtained in future applications.

In both instances, there was some skepticism at the outset about the benefits obtainable from such an approach. In the first case, even the company's president had reservations in the beginning about the value of the exercise. After seeing its results, however, the president subsequently sought to make such an approach a more integral part of the company's annual planning and budgeting process. In the second case, the priorities are being used on an ongoing basis to help both staff and line management more adequately review division operating plans and ensure that major decisions submitted for corporate approval reflect appropriate priorities.

The four decision situations described initially illustrate how the establishment of manufacturing performance priorities allow such individual decisions to be made quickly and effectively in a manner that supports corporate strategy. Also, for those decisions already consistent with corporate strategy, the reinforcement gained through use of these priorities can often advertise their usefulness and appropriateness to other members of top management. By making these concepts an integral part of a company's planning and decision-making processes, manufacturing can realize its own strategic potential. Rather than simply being reactive to others' plans, manufacturing can itself be part of the plan.

MANAGING OUR WAY
TO ECONOMIC DECLINE

ROBERT H. HAYES AND WILLIAM J. ABERNATHY

During the past several years American business has experienced a marked deterioration of competitive vigor and a growing unease about its overall economic well-being. This decline in both health and confidence has been attributed by economists and business leaders to such factors as the rapacity of OPEC, deficiencies in government tax and monetary policies, and the proliferation of regulation. We find these explanations inadequate.

They do not explain, for example, why the rate of productivity growth in America has declined both absolutely and relative to that in Europe and Japan. Nor do they explain why in many high-technology as well as mature industries America has lost its leadership position. Although a host of readily named forces—government regulation, inflation, monetary policy, tax laws, labor costs and constraints, fear of a capital shortage, the price of imported oil—have taken their toll on American business, pressures of this sort affect the economic climate abroad just as they do here.

A German executive, for example, will not be convinced by these explanations. Germany imports 95 percent of its oil (we import 50 percent), its government's share of gross domestic product is about 37 percent (ours is about 30 percent), and workers must be consulted on most major decisions. Yet Germany's rate of productivity growth has actually increased since 1970 and recently rose to more than four times ours. In France the situation is similar, yet today that country's productivity growth in manufacturing (despite current crises in steel and textiles) more than triples ours. No modern industrial nation is immune to the problems and pressures besetting U.S. business. Why then do we find a disproportionate loss of competitive vigor by U.S. companies?

Our experience suggests that, to an unprecedented degree, success in most industries today requires an organizational commitment to compete in the marketplace on technological grounds—that is, to compete over the long run

---

Reprinted by permission from *Harvard Business Review*, July–August 1980, 67–77.

by offering superior products. Yet, guided by what they took to be the newest and best principles of management, American managers have increasingly directed their attention elsewhere. These new principles, despite their sophistication and widespread usefulness, encourage a preference for

1. analytic detachment rather than the insight that comes from "hands on" experience and
2. short-term cost reduction rather than long-term development of technological competitiveness. It is this new managerial gospel, we feel, that has played a major role in undermining the vigor of American industry.

American management, especially in the two decades after World War II, was universally admired for its strikingly effective performance. But times change. An approach shaped and refined during stable decades may be ill suited to a world characterized by rapid and unpredictable change, scarce energy, global competition for markets, and a constant need for innovation. This is the world of the 1980s and, probably, the rest of this century.

The time is long overdue for earnest, objective self-analysis. What exactly have American managers been doing wrong? What are the critical weaknesses in the ways that they have managed the technological performance of their companies? What is the matter with the long-unquestioned assumptions on which they have based their managerial policies and practices?

A FAILURE OF MANAGEMENT

In the past, American managers earned worldwide respect for their carefully planned yet highly aggressive action across three different time frames:

Short term—using existing assets as efficiently as possible.
Medium term—replacing labor and other scarce resources with capital equipment.
Long term—developing new products and processes that open new markets or restructure old ones.

The first of these time frames demanded toughness, determination, and close attention to detail; the second, capital and the willingness to take sizable financial risks; the third, imagination and a certain amount of technological daring.

Our managers still earn generally high marks for their skill in improving short-term efficiency, but their counterparts in Europe and Japan have started to question America's entrepreneurial imagination and willingness to make risky long-term competitive investments. As one such observer remarked to us: "The U.S. companies in my industry act like banks. All they are interested in is return on investment and getting their money back. Sometimes they act as though they are more interested in buying other companies than they are in selling products to customers."

In fact, this curt diagnosis represents a growing body of opinion that openly charges American managers with competitive myopia: "Somehow or other, American business is losing confidence in itself and especially confidence in its future. Instead of meeting the challenge of the changing world, American business today is making small, short-term adjustments by cutting costs and by turning to the government for temporary relief .... Success in trade is the result of patient and meticulous preparations, with a long period of market preparation before the rewards are available .... To undertake such commitments is hardly in the interest of a manager who is concerned with his or her next quarterly earnings reports."[1]

More troubling still, American managers themselves often admit the charge with, at most, a rhetorical shrug of their shoulders. In established businesses, notes one senior vice president of research: "We understand how to market, we know the technology, and production problems are not extreme. Why risk money on new businesses when good, profitable low-risk opportunities are on every side?" Says another: "It's much more difficult to come up with a synthetic meat product than a lemon-lime cake mix. But you work on the lemon-lime cake mix because you know exactly what that return is going to be. A synthetic steak is going to take a lot longer, require a much bigger investment, and the risk of failure will be greater."[2]

These managers are not alone; they speak for many. Why, they ask, should they invest dollars that are hard to earn back when it is so easy—and so much less risky—to make money in other ways? Why ignore a ready-made situation in cake mixes for the deferred and far less certain prospects in synthetic steaks? Why shoulder the competitive risks of making better, more innovative products?

In our judgment, the assumptions underlying these questions are prime evidence of a broad managerial failure—a failure of both vision and leadership—that over time has eroded both the inclination and the capacity of U.S. companies to innovate.

---

[1]Ryohei Suzuki, "Worldwide Expansion of U.S. Exports—A Japanese View," *Sloan Management Review*, Spring 1979, 1.
[2]*Business Week*, February 16, 1976, 57.

FAMILIAR EXCUSES

About the facts themselves there can be little dispute. Exhibits 1–5 document our sorry decline. But the explanations and excuses commonly offered invite a good deal of comment.

It is important to recognize, first of all, that the problem is not new. It has been going on for at least 15 years. The rate of productivity growth in the private sector peaked in the mid-1960s. Nor is the problem confined to a few sectors of our economy; with a few exceptions, it permeates our entire economy. Expenditures on R&D by both business and government, as measured in constant (noninflated) dollars, also peaked in the mid-1960s—both in absolute terms and as a percentage of GNP. During the same period the expenditures on R&D by West Germany and Japan have been rising. More important, American spending on R&D as a percentage of sales in such critical research-intensive industries as machinery, professional and scientific instruments, chemicals, and aircraft had dropped by the mid-1970s to about half its level in the early 1960s. These are the very industries on which we now depend for the bulk of our manufactured exports.

Investment in plant and equipment in the United States displays the same disturbing trends. As economist Burton G. Malkiel has pointed out: "From 1948 to 1973 the (net book value of capital equipment) per unit of labor

EXHIBIT 1	GROWTH IN LABOR PRODUCTIVITY SINCE 1960 (UNITED STATES AND ABROAD)

	AVERAGE ANNUAL PERCENT CHANGE	
	MANUFACTURING 1960–1978	**ALL INDUSTRIES 1960–1976**
United States	2.8%	1.7%
United Kingdom	2.9	2.2
Canada	4.0	2.1
Germany	5.4	4.2
France	5.5	4.3
Italy	5.9	4.9
Belgium	6.9(*)	—
Netherlands	6.9(*)	—
Sweden	5.2	—
Japan	8.2	7.5

(*)1960-1977.

Source: Council on Wage and Price Stability. *Report on Productivity* (Washington, D.C.: Executive Office of the President, July, 1979).

EXHIBIT 2	GROWTH OF LABOR PRODUCTIVITY BY SECTOR, 1948–1978		

| TIME SECTOR | GROWTH OF LABOR PRODUCTIVITY (ANNUAL AVERAGE PERCENT) | | |
	1948-65	1965-73	1973-78
Private business	3.2%	2.3%	1.1%
Agriculture, forestry, and fisheries	5.5	5.3	2.9
Mining	4.2	2.0	-4.0
Construction	2.9	-2.2	-1.8
Manufacturing	3.1	2.4	1.7
Durable goods	2.8	1.9	1.2
Nondurable goods	3.4	3.2	2.4
Transportation	3.3	2.9	0.9
Communication	5.5	4.8	7.1
Electric, gas, and sanitary services	6.2	4.0	0.1
Trade	2.7	3.0	0.4
Wholesale	3.1	3.9	0.2
Retail	2.4	2.3	0.8
Finance, insurance, and real estate	1.0	-0.3	1.4
Services	1.5	1.9	0.5
Government enterprises	-0.8	0.9	-0.7

Note: Productivity data for services, construction, finance, insurance, and real estate are unpublished.

Source: Bureau of Labor Statistics

grew at an annual rate of almost 3 percent. Since 1973, however, lower rates of private investment have led to a decline in that growth rate to 1.75 percent. Moreover, the recent composition of investment (in 1978) has been skewed toward equipment and relatively short-term projects and away from structures and relatively long-lived investments. Thus our industrial plant has tended to age .... "[3]

Other studies have shown that growth in the incremental capital equipment-to-labor ratio has fallen to about one-third of its value in the early 1960s. By contrast, between 1966 and 1976 capital investment as a percentage of GNP in France and West Germany was more than 20 percent greater than that in the United States; in Japan the percentage was almost double ours.

To attribute this relative loss of technological vigor to such things as a shortage of capital in the United States is not justified. As Malkiel and others have shown, the return on equity of American business (out of which comes the capital necessary for investment) is about the same today as 20

[3]Burton G. Malkiel, "Productivity—The Problem Behind the Headlines," *Harvard Business Review*, May-June 1979, 81.

| EXHIBIT 3 | NATIONAL EXPENDITURES FOR PERFORMANCE OF R&D AS A PERCENT OF GNP BY COUNTRY, 1961-1978* |

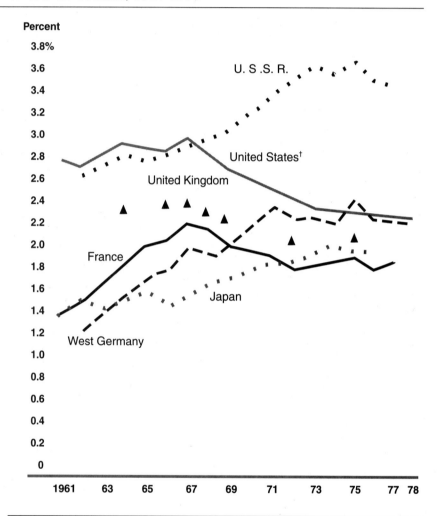

*Gross expenditures for performance of R&D including associated capital expenditures.

†Detailed information on capital expenditures for R&D is not available for the United States. Estimates for the period 1972–1977 show that their inclusion would have an impact of less than one-tenth of 1% for each year.

Source: *Science Indicators*—1978 (Washington, D.C.: National Science Foundation, 1979), p. 6.

Note: The latest data may be preliminary or estimates.

years ago, *even after adjusting for inflation*. However, investment in both new equipment and R&D, as a percentage of GNP, was significantly higher 20 years ago than today.

| **EXHIBIT 4** | INDUSTRIAL R&D EXPENDITURES FOR BASIC RESEARCH, APPLIED RESEARCH, AND DEVELOPMENT, 1960-1978 (IN $ MILLIONS) |

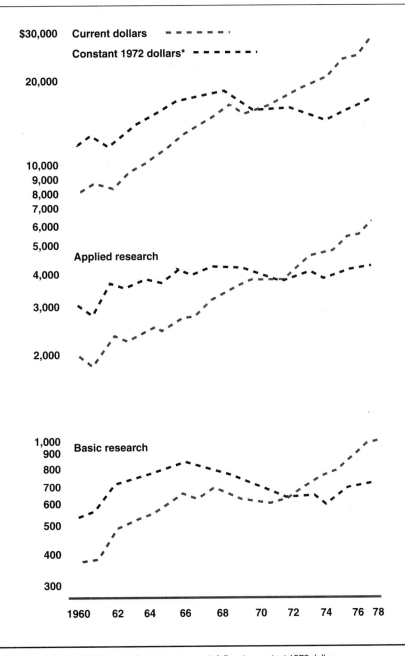

*GNP implicit price deflators used to convert current dollars to constant 1972 dollars.

Source: *Science Indicators*—1978, p. 87.

Note: Preliminary data are shown for 1977 and estimates for 1978.

The conclusion is painful but must be faced. Responsibility for this competitive listlessness belongs not just to a set of external conditions but also to the attitudes, preoccupations, and practices of American managers. By their preference for servicing existing markets rather than creating new ones and by their devotion to short-term returns and "management by the numbers," many of them have effectively forsworn long-term technological superiority as a competitive weapon. In consequence, they have abdicated their strategic responsibilities.

THE NEW MANAGEMENT ORTHODOXY

We refuse to believe that this managerial failure is the result of a sudden psychological shift among American managers toward a "super-safe, no risk" mind set. No profound sea change in the character of thousands of individuals could have occurred in so organized a fashion or have produced so consistent a pattern of behavior. Instead we believe that during the past two decades American managers have increasingly relied on principles which prize analytical detachment and methodological elegance over insight, based on experience, into the subtleties and complexities of strategic decisions. As a result, maximum short-term financial returns have become the overriding criteria for many companies.

For purposes of discussion, we may divide this new management orthodoxy into three general categories: financial control, corporate portfolio management, and market-driven behavior.

FINANCIAL CONTROL

As more companies decentralize their organizational structures, they tend to fix on profit centers as the primary unit of managerial responsibility. This development necessitates, in turn, greater dependence on short-term financial measurements like return on investment (ROI) for evaluating the performance of individual managers and management groups. Increasing the structural distance between those entrusted with exploiting actual competitive opportunities and those who must judge the quality of their work virtually guarantees reliance on objectively quantifiable short-term criteria.

Although innovation, the lifeblood of any vital enterprise, is best encouraged by an environment that does not unduly penalize failure, the predictable result of relying too heavily on short-term financial measures—a sort of managerial remote control—is an environment in which no one feels he or she can afford a failure or even a momentary dip in the bottom line.

CORPORATE PORTFOLIO MANAGEMENT

This preoccupation with control draws support from modern theories of financial portfolio management. Originally developed to help balance the overall risk and return of stock and bond portfolios, these principles have been applied increasingly to the creation and management of corporate portfolios—that is, a cluster of companies and product lines assembled through various modes of diversification under a single corporate umbrella. When applied by a remote group of dispassionate experts primarily concerned with finance and control and lacking hands-on experience, the analytic formulas of portfolio theory push managers even further toward an extreme of caution in allocating resources.

"Especially in large organizations," reports one manager, "we are observing an increase in management behavior which I would regard as excessively cautious, even passive; certainly overanalytical; and, in general, characterized by a studied unwillingness to assume responsibility and even reasonable risk."

MARKET-DRIVEN BEHAVIOR

In the past 20 years, American companies have perhaps learned too well a lesson they had long been inclined to ignore: businesses should be customer oriented rather than product oriented. Henry Ford's famous dictum that the public could have any color automobile it wished as long as the color was black has since given way to its philosophical opposite: "We have got to stop marketing makeable products and learn to make marketable products."

At last, however, the dangers of too much reliance on this philosophy are becoming apparent. As two Canadian researchers have put it: "Inventors, scientists, engineers, and academics, in the normal pursuit of scientific knowledge, gave the world in recent times the laser, xerography, instant photography, and the transistor. In contrast, worshippers of the marketing concept have bestowed upon mankind such products as new-fangled potato chips, feminine hygiene deodorant, and the pet rock ...."[4]

The argument that no new product ought to be introduced without managers undertaking a market analysis is common sense. But the argument that consumer analyses and formal market surveys should dominate other considerations when allocating resources to product development is untenable. It may be useful to remember that the initial market estimate for computers in 1945 projected total world-wide sales of only ten units.

---

[4]Roger Bennett and Robert Cooper, "Beyond the Marketing Concept," *Business Horizons*, June 1979, 76.

Similarly, even the most carefully researched analysis of consumer preferences for gas-guzzling cars in an era of gasoline abundance offers little useful guidance to today's automobile manufacturers in making wise product investment decisions. Customers may know what their needs are, but they often define those needs in terms of existing products, processes, markets, and prices.

Deferring to a market-driven strategy without paying attention to its limitations is, quite possibly, opting for customer satisfaction and lower risk in the short run at the expense of superior products in the future. Satisfied customers are critically important, of course, but not if the strategy for creating them is responsible as well for unnecessary product proliferation, inflated costs, unfocused diversification, and a lagging commitment to new technology and new capital equipment.

THREE MANAGERIAL DECISIONS

These are serious charges to make. But the unpleasant fact of the matter is that, however useful these new principles may have been initially, if carried too far they are bad for U.S. business. Consider, for example, their effect on three major kinds of choices regularly faced by corporate managers: the decision between imitative and innovative product design, the decision to integrate backward, and the decision to invest in process development.

IMITATIVE VS. INNOVATIVE PRODUCT DESIGN

A market-driven strategy requires new product ideas to flow from detailed market analysis or, at least, to be extensively tested for consumer reaction before actual introduction. It is no secret that these requirements add significant delays and costs to the introduction of new products. It is less well known that they also predispose managers toward developing products for existing markets and toward product designs of an imitative rather than an innovative nature. There is increasing evidence that market-driven strategies tend, over time, to dampen the general level of innovation in new product decisions.

Confronted with the choice between innovation and imitation, managers typically ask whether the marketplace shows any consistent preference for innovative products. If so, the additional funding they require may be economically justified; if not, those funds can more properly go to advertising, promoting, or reducing the prices of less-advanced products. Though the temptation to allocate resources so as to strengthen performance in existing products and markets is often irresistible, recent studies by J. Hugh Davidson and others confirm the strong market attractiveness of innovative products.[5]

Nonetheless, managers having to decide between innovative and imitative product design face a difficult series of marketing-related trade-offs. Exhibit 5 summarizes these trade-offs.

By its very nature, innovative design is, as Joseph Schumpeter observed a long time ago, initially destructive of capital-whether in the form of labor skills, management systems, technological processes, or capital equipment. It tends to make obsolete existing investments in both marketing and manufacturing organizations. For the managers concerned it represents the choice of uncertainty (about economic returns, timing, etc.) over relative predictability, exchanging the reasonable expectation of current income against the promise of high future value. It is the choice of the gambler, the person willing to risk much to gain even more.

Conditioned by a market-driven strategy and held closely to account by a "results now" ROI-oriented control system, American managers have increasingly refused to take the chance on innovative product/market development. As one of them confesses: "In the last year, on the basis of high capital risk, I turned down new products at a rate at least twice what I did a year ago. But in every case I tell my people to go back and bring me some new product ideas."[6] In truth, they have learned caution so well that many

EXHIBIT 5	TRADE-OFFS BETWEEN IMITATIVE AND INNOVATIVE DESIGN FOR AN ESTABLISHED PRODUCT LINE

IMITATIVE DESIGN	INNOVATIVE DESIGN
Market demand is relatively well and predictable.	Potentially large but unpredictable known demand; the risk of a flop is also large.
Market recognition and acceptance are rapid.	Market acceptance may be slow initially, but the imitative response of competitors may also be slowed.
Readily adaptable to existing market, sales, and distribution policies.	May require unique, tailored marketing, distribution and sales policies to educate customers or because of special repair and warranty problems.
Fits with existing market segmentation and product policies.	Demand may cut across traditional marketing segments, disrupting divisional responsibilities and cannibalizing other products.

[5]J. Hugh Davidson, "Why Most New Consumer Brands Fail," *Harvard Business Review*, March–April 1976, 117.
[6]*Business Week*, February 16, 1976, 57.

are in danger of forgetting that market-driven, follow-the-leader companies usually end up following the rest of the pack as well.

BACKWARD INTEGRATION

Sometimes the problem for managers is not their reluctance to take action and make investments but that, when they do so, their action has the unintended result of reinforcing the status quo. In deciding to integrate backward because of apparent short-term rewards, managers often restrict their ability to strike out in innovative directions in the future.

Consider, for example, the case of a manufacturer who purchases a major component from an outside company. Static analysis of production economies may very well show that backward integration offers rather substantial cost benefits. Eliminating certain purchasing and marketing functions, centralizing overhead, pooling R&D efforts and resources, coordinating design and production of both product and component, reducing uncertainty over design changes, allowing for the use of more specialized equipment and labor skills—in all these ways and more, backward integration holds out to management the promise of significant short-term increases in ROI.

These efficiencies may be achieved by companies with commodity-like products. In such industries as ferrous and nonferrous metals or petroleum, backward integration toward raw materials and supplies tends to have a strong, positive effect on profits. However, the situation is markedly different for companies in more technologically active industries. Where there is considerable exposure to rapid technological advances, the promised value of backward integration becomes problematic. It may provide a quick, short-term boost to ROI figures in the next annual report, but it may also paralyze the long-term ability of a company to keep on top of technological change.

The real competitive threats to technologically active companies arise less from changes in ultimate consumer preference than from abrupt shifts in component technologies, raw materials, or production processes. Hence those managers whose attention is too firmly directed toward the marketplace and near-term profits may suddenly discover that their decision to make rather than buy important parts has locked their companies into an outdated technology.

Further, as supply channels and manufacturing operations become more systematized, the benefits from attempts to "rationalize" production may well be accompanied by unanticipated side effects. For instance, a company may find itself shut off from the R&D efforts of various independent suppliers by becoming their competitor. Similarly, the commitment of time and resources needed to master technology back up the channel of supply may distract a company from doing its own job well. Such was the fate of Bowmar, the pocket calculator pioneer, whose attempt to integrate backward into semiconductor production so consumed management attention that final assembly of the calculators, its core business, did not get the required resources.

Long-term contracts and long-term relationships with suppliers can achieve many of the same cost benefits as backward integration without calling into question a company's ability to innovate or respond to innovation. European automobile manufacturers, for example, have typically chosen to rely on their suppliers in this way; American companies have followed the path of backward integration. The resulting trade-offs between production efficiencies and innovative flexibility should offer a stern warning to those American managers too easily beguiled by the lure of short-term ROI improvement. A case in point: the U.S. auto industry's huge investment in automating the manufacture of cast-iron brake drums probably delayed by more than five years its transition to disc brakes.

PROCESS DEVELOPMENT

In an era of management by the numbers, many American managers— especially in mature industries—are reluctant to invest heavily in the development of new manufacturing processes. When asked to explain their reluctance, they tend to respond in fairly predictable ways. "We can't afford to design new capital equipment for just our own manufacturing needs" is one frequent answer. So is: "The capital equipment producers do a much better job, and they can amortize their development costs over sales to many companies." Perhaps most common is: "Let the others experiment in manufacturing; we can learn from their mistakes and do it better."

Each of these comments rests on the assumption that essential advances in process technology can be appropriated more easily through equipment purchase than through in-house equipment design and development. Our extensive conversations with the managers of European (primarily German) technology-based companies have convinced us that this assumption is not as widely shared abroad as in the United States. Virtually across the board, the European managers impressed us with their strong commitment to increasing market share through internal development of advanced process technology—even when their suppliers were highly responsive to technological advances.

By contrast, American managers tend to restrict investments in process development to only those items likely to reduce costs in the short run. Not all are happy with this. As one disgruntled executive told us: "For too long

U.S. managers have been taught to set low priorities on mechanization projects, so that eventually divestment appears to be the best way out of manufacturing difficulties. Why?

"The drive for short-term success has prevented managers from looking thoroughly into the matter of special manufacturing equipment, which has to be invented, developed, tested, redesigned, reproduced, improved, and so on. That's a long process, which needs experienced, knowledgeable, and dedicated people who stick to their jobs over a considerable period of time. Merely buying new equipment (even if it is possible) does not often give the company any advantage over competitors."

We agree. Most American managers seem to forget that, even if they produce new products with their existing process technology (the same "cookie cutter" everyone else can buy), their competitors will face a relatively short lead time for introducing similar products. And as Eric von Hippel's studies of industrial innovation show, the innovations on which new industrial equipment is based usually originate with the user of the equipment and not with the equipment producer.[7] In other words, companies can make products more profitable by investing in the development of their own process technology. Proprietary processes are every bit as formidable competitive weapons as proprietary products.

THE AMERICAN MANAGERIAL IDEAL

Two very important questions remain to be asked:

1. Why should so many American managers have shifted so strongly to this new managerial orthodoxy? and
2. Why are they not more deeply bothered by the ill effects of those principles on the long-term technological competitiveness of their companies?

To answer the first question, we must take a look at the changing career patterns of American managers during the past quarter century; to answer the second, we must understand the way in which they have come to regard their professional roles and responsibilities as managers.

THE ROAD TO THE TOP

During the past 25 years the American manager's road to the top has changed significantly. No longer does the typical career, threading sinuously up and

---

[7]Eric von Hippel, "The Dominant Role of Users in the Scientific Instrument Innovation Process," MIT Sloan School of Management Working Paper 75-764, January 1975.

EXHIBIT 6	CHANGES IN THE PROFESSIONAL ORIGINS OF CORPORATE PRESIDENTS (PERCENT CHANGES FROM BASELINE YEARS [1948-1952] FOR 100 TOP U.S. COMPANIES.)

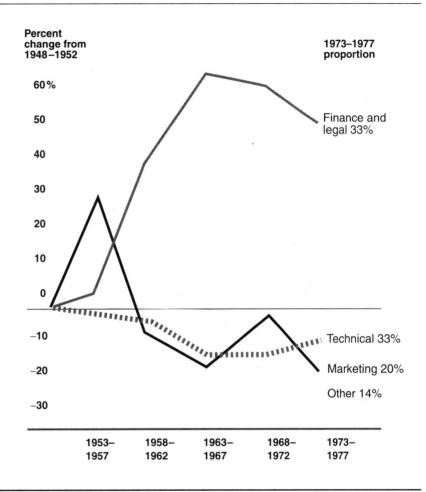

Source: Golightly & Co. International (1978).

through a corporation with stops in several functional areas, provide future top executives with intimate hands-on knowledge of the company's technologies, customers, and suppliers.

Exhibit 6 summarizes the currently available data on the shift in functional background of newly appointed presidents of the 100 largest U.S. corporations. The immediate significance of these figures is clear. Since the mid-1950s there has been a rather substantial increase in the percentage of new company presidents whose primary interests and expertise lie in the financial and legal areas and not in production. In the view of C. Jackson Grayson, president of the American Productivity Center, American management has for 20 years "coasted off the great R&D gains made during World War II, and constantly rewarded executives from the marketing, financial, and legal sides of the business while it ignored the production men. Today (in business schools) courses in the production area are almost nonexistent."[8]

In addition, companies are increasingly choosing to fill new top management posts from outside their own ranks. In the opinion of foreign observers, who are still accustomed to long-term careers in the same company or division, "High-level American executives... seem to come and go and switch around as if playing a game of musical chairs at an Alice in Wonderland tea party."

Far more important, however, than any absolute change in numbers is the shift in the general sense of what an aspiring manager has to be "smart about" to make it to the top. More important still is the broad change in attitude such trends both encourage and express. What has developed, in the business community as in academia, is a preoccupation with a false and shallow concept of the professional manager, a "pseudo-professional" really—an individual having no special expertise in any particular industry or technology who nevertheless can step into an unfamiliar company and run it successfully through strict application of financial controls, portfolio concepts, and a market-driven strategy.

THE GOSPEL OF PSEUDO-PROFESSIONALISM

In recent years, this idealization of pseudo-professionalism has taken on something of the quality of a corporate religion. Its first doctrine, appropriately enough, is that neither industry experience nor hands-on technological expertise counts for very much. At one level, of course, this doctrine helps to salve the conscience of those who lack them. At another, more disturbing level it encourages the faithful to make decisions about technological matters simply as if they were adjuncts to finance or marketing decisions. We do not believe that the technological issues facing managers today can be meaningfully addressed without taking into account marketing or financial considerations; on the other hand, neither can they be resolved with the same methodologies applied to these other fields.

Complex modern technology has its own inner logic and developmental imperatives. To treat it as if it were something else—no matter how comfortable

---

[8] *Dun's Review*, July 1978, 39.

one is with that other kind of data—is to base a competitive business on a two-legged stool, which must, no matter how excellent the balancing act, inevitably fall to the ground.

More disturbing still, true believers keep the faith on a day-to-day basis by insisting that as issues rise up the managerial hierarchy for decision they be progressively distilled into easily quantifiable terms. One European manager, in recounting to us his experiences in a joint venture with an American company, recalled with exasperation that "U.S. managers want everything to be simple. But sometimes business situations are not simple, and they cannot be divided up or looked at in such a way that they become simple. They are messy, and one must try to understand all the facets. This appears to be alien to the American mentality."

The purpose of good organizational design, of course, is to divide responsibilities in such a way that individuals have relatively easy tasks to perform. But then these differentiated responsibilities must be pulled together by sophisticated, broadly gauged integrators at the top of the managerial pyramid. If these individuals are interested in but one or two aspects of the total competitive picture, if their training includes a very narrow exposure to the range of functional specialties, if—worst of all—they are devoted simplifiers themselves, who will do the necessary integration? Who will attempt to resolve complicated issues rather than try to uncomplicate them artificially? At the strategic level there are no such things as pure production problems, pure financial problems, or pure marketing problems.

MERGER MANIA

When executive suites are dominated by people with financial and legal skills, it is not surprising that top management should increasingly allocate time and energy to such concerns as cash management and the whole process of corporate acquisitions and mergers. This is indeed what has happened. In 1978 alone there were some 80 mergers involving companies with assets in excess of $100 million each; in 1979 there were almost 100. This represents roughly $20 billion in transfers of large companies from one owner to another—two-thirds of the total amount spent on R&D by American industry.

In 1978 *Business Week* ran a cover story on cash management in which it stated that "the 400 largest U.S. companies together have more than $60 billion in cash—almost triple the amount they had at the beginning of the 1970s." The article also described the increasing attention devoted to—and the sophisticated and exotic techniques used for—managing this cash hoard.

There are perfectly good reasons for this flurry of activity. It is entirely natural for financially (or legally) trained managers to concentrate on essentially financial (or legal) activities. It is also natural for managers who subscribe to the portfolio "law of large numbers" to seek to reduce total corporate risk by parceling it out among a sufficiently large number of separate product lines, businesses, or technologies. Under certain conditions it may very well make good economic sense to buy rather than build new plants or modernize existing ones. Mergers are obviously an exciting game; they tend to produce fairly quick and decisive results, and they offer the kind of public recognition that helps careers along. Who can doubt the appeal of the titles awarded by the financial community; being called a "gunslinger," "white knight," or "raider" can quicken anyone's blood.

Unfortunately, the general American penchant for separating and simplifying has tended to encourage a diversification away from core technologies and markets to a much greater degree than is true in Europe or Japan. U.S. managers appear to have an inordinate faith in the portfolio law of large numbers—that is, by amassing enough product lines, technologies, and businesses, one will be cushioned against the random setbacks that occur in life. This might be true for portfolios of stocks and bonds, where there is considerable evidence that setbacks *are* random. Businesses, however, are subject not only to random setbacks such as strikes and shortages but also to carefully orchestrated attacks by competitors, who focus all their resources and energies on one set of activities.

Worse, the great bulk of this merger activity appears to have been absolutely wasted in terms of generating economic benefits for stockholders. Acquisition experts do not necessarily make good managers. Nor can they increase the value of their shares by merging two companies any better than their shareholders could do individually by buying shares of the acquired company on the open market (at a price usually below that required for a takeover attempt).

There appears to be a growing recognition of this fact. A number of U.S. companies are now divesting themselves of previously acquired companies; others (for example, W.R. Grace) are proposing to break themselves up into relatively independent entities. The establishment of a strong competitive position through in-house technological superiority is by nature a long, arduous, and often unglamorous task. But it is what keeps a business vigorous and competitive.

THE EUROPEAN EXAMPLE

Gaining competitive success through technological superiority is a skill much valued by the seasoned European (and Japanese) managers with whom we talked. Although we were able to locate few hard statistics on their actual practice, our extensive investigations of more than 20 companies convinced us that European managers do indeed tend to differ significantly from their American counterparts. In fact, we found that many of them were able to articulate these differences quite clearly.

In the first place, European managers think themselves more pointedly concerned with how to survive over the long run under intensely competitive conditions. Few markets, of course, generate price competition as fierce as in the United States, but European companies face the remorseless necessity of exporting to other national markets or perishing.

The figures here are startling: manufactured product exports represent more than 35 percent of total manufacturing sales in France and Germany and nearly 60 percent in the Benelux countries, as against not quite 10 percent in the United States. In these export markets moreover, European products must hold their own against "world class" competitors, lower-priced products from developing countries, and American products selling at attractive devalued dollar prices. To survive this competitive squeeze, European managers feel they must place central emphasis on producing technologically superior products.

Further, the kinds of pressures from European labor unions and national governments virtually force them to take a consistently long-term view in decision making. German managers, for example, must negotiate major decisions at the plant level with worker-dominated works councils; in turn, these decisions are subject to review by supervisory boards (roughly equivalent to American boards of directors), half of whose membership is worker elected. Together with strict national legislation, the pervasive influence of labor unions makes it extremely difficult to change employment levels or production locations. Not surprisingly, labor costs in Northern Europe have more than doubled in the past decade and are now the highest in the world.

To be successful in this environment of strictly constrained options, European managers feel they must employ a decision-making apparatus that grinds very fine—and very deliberately. They must simply outthink and outmanage their competitors. Now, American managers also have their strategic options hedged about by all kinds of restrictions. But those restrictions have not yet made them as conscious as their European counterparts of the long-term implications of their day-to-day decisions.

As a result, the Europeans see themselves as investing more heavily in cutting-edge technology than the Americans. More often than not, this investment is made to create new product opportunities in advance of consumer demand and not merely in response to market-driven strategy. In case after case, we found the Europeans striving to develop the products and process capabilities with which to lead markets and not simply responding to the current demands of the marketplace. Moreover, in doing this they seem less inclined to integrate backward and more likely to seek maximum leverage from stable, long-term relationships with suppliers.

Having never lost sight of the need to be technologically competitive over the long run, European and Japanese managers are extremely careful to make the necessary arrangements and investments today. And their daily concern with the rather basic issue of long-term survival adds perspective to such matters as short-term ROI or rate of growth. The time line by which they manage is long, and it has made them painstakingly attentive to the means for keeping their companies technologically competitive. Of course they pay attention to the numbers. Their profit margins are usually lower than ours, their debt ratios higher. Every tenth of a percent is critical to them. But they are also aware that tomorrow will be no better unless they constantly try to develop new processes, enter new markets, and offer superior—even unique—products. As one senior German executive phrased it recently, "We look at rates of return, too, but only after we ask 'Is it a good product?'"[9]

CREATING ECONOMIC VALUE

Americans traveling in Europe and Asia soon learn they must often deal with criticism of our country. Being forced to respond to such criticism can be healthy, for it requires rethinking some basic issues of principle and practice.

We have much to be proud about and little to be ashamed of relative to most other countries. But sometimes the criticism of others is uncomfortably close to the mark. The comments of our overseas competitors on American business practices contain enough truth to require our thoughtful consideration. What is behind the decline in competitiveness of U.S. business? Why do U.S. companies have such apparent difficulties competing with foreign producers of established products, many of which originated in the United States?

For example, Japanese televisions dominate some market segments, even though many U.S. producers now enjoy the same low labor cost advantages of offshore production. The German machine tool and automotive producers continue their inroads into U.S. domestic markets, even though their labor rates are now higher than those in the United States and the famed German worker in German factories is almost as likely to be Turkish or Italian as German.

The responsibility for these problems may rest in part on government policies that either overconstrain or undersupport U.S. producers. But if our

---

[9] *Business Week,* March 3, 1980, 76.

foreign critics are correct, the long-term solution to America's problems may not be correctable simply by changing our government's tax laws, monetary policies, and regulatory practices. It will also require some fundamental changes in management attitudes and practices.

It would be an oversimplification to assert that the only reason for the decline in competitiveness of U.S. companies is that our managers devote too much attention and energy to using existing resources more efficiently. It would also oversimplify the issue, although possibly to a lesser extent, to say that it is due purely and simply to their tendency to neglect technology as a competitive weapon.

Companies cannot become more innovative simply by increasing R&D investments or by conducting more basic research. Each of the decisions we have described directly affects several functional areas of management, and major conflicts can only be reconciled at senior executive levels. The benefits favoring the more innovative, aggressive option in each case depend more on intangible factors than do their efficiency-oriented alternatives.

Senior managers who are less informed about their industry and its confederation of parts suppliers, equipment suppliers, workers, and customers or who have less time to consider the long-term implications of their interactions are likely to exhibit a noninnovative bias in their choices. Tight financial controls with a short-term emphasis will also bias choices toward the less innovative, less technologically aggressive alternatives.

The key to long-term success—even survival—in business is what it has always been: to invest, to innovate, to lead, to create value where none existed before. Such determination, such striving to excel, requires leaders—not *just* controllers, market analysts, and portfolio managers. In our preoccupation with the braking systems and exterior trim, we may have neglected the drive trains of our corporations.

RESEARCH IN OPERATIONS MANAGEMENT

ELWOOD S. BUFFA

The launching of a new journal says something about the maturity of the operations management field. The journal will become the most visible expression of what the field is and where it is going. Therefore, we should attempt to chart a course rather than be defined merely by the drift of what people in the field happen to be doing. Where should the field go? What should we be doing? Which directions for research seem the most useful and productive at the present state of our development?

WHERE HAVE WE BEEN?

It would not be productive to recycle the past research directions, so I would like to spend some space in reviewing the past. In fact, production and operations management is one of the oldest disciplines in the general study of management. The earliest research in managerial systems deal with production and indeed the managerial system was though of as the production system by Adam Smith and Charles Babbage, and down through the decades to Taylor. In the modern era, it is no accident that "operations" research was so named, and defined and developed the methods of management science/operations research (MS/OR) initially on production systems.

Why then has there been such a rocky road for operations management in defining and establishing itself? I believe one of the reasons is in the original breadth of the field. Perhaps most of those currently in the field were never exposed to the descriptive phase of operations management that held

Reprinted by permission from *Journal of Operations Management,* vol. 1 (August 1980): 1–7.

Author's Note: I wish to thank colleagues who reviewed and reacted to earlier drafts: James S. Dyer, Jeffrey G. Miller, Rosser T. Nelson, and Rakesh Sarin.

sway until the middle 1950s. The definition of the field as expressed by the introductory textbooks was virtually the entire field of industrial management. A review of the tables of contents of those textbooks reveals the inclusion of important chapters on personnel management, finance, marketing, organization and general management. As curricula developed, it was not illogical that the descriptive course would be dismantled and differentiated into the several functional fields of management and the field of general management. The offspring turned on the parent and questioned its "raison d'etre." Being left with what we knew about production systems at that time was to be left with a nearly empty basket of techniques: time and motion study, plant layout, Gantt's production control boards, the simple EOQ model, and simplistic descriptions of how production systems worked. The main emphasis in what could pass for research dealt with methods or motion study, led by Ralph Barnes.

The savior that rescued the field from extinction was the development of MS/OR. Overlapping with the descriptive phase (the death of which I place in 1961), MS/OR provided the scientific methodology that allowed us to develop something akin to the "natural science" or physics of operating systems. MS/OR also opened the door to the study of service systems as a natural broadening of production management into the present scope of operations management. For at least 20 years we have enjoyed the pleasure of ample researchable topics with publishing outlets in the MS/OR journals. A scanning of the MS/OR literature of the past 30 years shows rather clearly the development of that field within the context of productive systems, both in terms of methodology and applications. Indeed, in *Management Science* the production field has dominated. In a recent survey of the first 25 years of that journal, Nelson states: "Production management problems have consistently been in a class by themselves as the most studied area (27 percent). Finance (8 percent) and marketing (6 percent) are the only other areas with consistent frequency."[1]

To be scientific was to be an academic success. For example, when *Management Science* diversified its journal into "Theory" and "Application," it was not uncommon for individuals to carefully note in their bibliographies that their papers appeared in the theory series.

During this phase of the development of OM there evolved a strong relationship and dependence on MS/OR, to the point where it was often difficult to tell if there was a difference between OM and MS/OR. Indeed, many people, including myself, taught OM in the context of quantitative methodology. But, MS/OR has also been a false prophet for operations management. Not

---

[1]Rosser T. Nelson, "Management Science Journal: The First Twenty Five Years," *Management Science*, 1980.

because the methodology is not applicable—extremely important contributions have been made—but because MS/OR methodology does not define the OM field nor point the way of the future. When curricula matured one more step and required courses in MS/OR became common, there was no longer a logic to teaching such methodology in OM since it was being presented in broader context in other courses. Again the nagging questions: What is left? What is OM? Future research and publication in our journals needs to reflect the latest evolution of the field.

WHERE WE ARE

The past 20 years has produced great progress in terms of an understanding of how productive systems work, and the development and improvement of many very useful techniques. Operations management has benefitted greatly from the impact of MS/OR. I believe, however, that we are emerging from the MS/OR phase into a clear recognition of OM as a functional field of management. True, it is a field where quantitative methodology is particularly useful, but the field is a managerial one and I feel that it is in the process of finding itself as such.

Looking at research in the field before and after the MS/OR revolution it appears we have become expert at defining a problem of relatively narrow scope, building a model to represent it, and evaluating the results by a single-valued criterion. The implied advice to managers is that if they will narrow their horizon they will see things our way, or if they do not agree with the narrow definition, they can engage in something we call tradeoff analysis to take account of factors or variables not in the model, but that problem seems to be theirs, not ours. The best of these kinds of analyses provide sensitivity analyses and the evaluation of alternatives through the change of parameters in the model to aid managers in the trade-off process.

Again, looking at research in the field before and after the MS/OR revolution, it appears that we have learned a great deal about inventories, scheduling, aggregate planning, quality control, capacity planning, and so on, in the sense of models of those isolated subsystems. We have not learned very much about the relationship between these subsystems; we view the field as a collection of seemingly unrelated subsystems rather than as whole systems (there are exceptions). In addition, we have seldom attempted to deal with interfunctional relationships, though I feel that we do this as well or better than our colleagues in other functional disciplines. Of course, it is understandable why we view the research problems in this disconnected way. It is much more difficult to define and implement more global projects that recognize the multiple criterion character of managerial problems, where values may be as important as "optimum" solutions. It is an anomaly that the teaching of OM is somewhat more effective in dealing with the broader managerial implications of decisions in productive systems than the leading edge research.

Finally, there have been some important developments of quite complex models that are usually extensions of the simpler ones. The more complex models we presume are more realistic, since they take into account more variables. But managerial acceptance of the more complex models has not been very good. Indeed, the acceptance of the simpler (presumably less effective) models has been greater. If there is greater realism in these more complex models, it seems as though managerial acceptance should be greater. The lack of acceptance is not surprising since the more complex model is not as easy to understand as the simple one. Good managers do not want simply to know "the answer," but wish to gain insight into why a solution is what it is.

WHERE SHOULD WE BE GOING?

The very essence of operations management is contained in its apt title. Management is its focus. But, we need to capitalize on our close relationship with MS/OR as we refocus on the *management* of operations. At the broadest level, I choose the word "implementation" to characterize the direction that productive research should take. If the results of research can be implemented, then it has obvious useful implications for management. This does not mean that we should strive to produce only applications research. It does suggest that we should take our objectives and criteria set from real systems. When we idealize situations in order to make them tractable, we should attempt to account for the effects of the resulting losses of reality. There will always be a need for new theory, but it should narrow the reality gap.

The kinds of research that are likely candidates for implementation will recognize the multiple criterion nature of the managerial world. The results will seldom use the word "optimum" nor will they purport to make managerial decisions; rather, I believe that they should provide managers with a process for making rational decisions by identifying the impact of environmental, intra- and inter-functional factors. Interactive computing systems provide one vehicle for the process I envision, where managers can interact with a model in such a way that alternatives other than those resulting from the single-valued criterion may be considered, valued, and traded-off. We have a magnificent base from which to launch these kinds of research studies, since most of our colleagues are at home with MS/OR methodology. Having been the beneficiaries of MS/OR, perhaps we can now repay the debt by showing how it should be used appropriately in the decision-making process in managing operations.

Many of the research projects that have the implementation characteristic will be complex by their nature, if they attempt to reflect intra- and interfunctional factors, and if they build on previous work. It would be most unfortunate if we failed to gain managerial acceptance of our work in our finest hour. One technique that has been used is for the researcher to build a parallel but simpler model that captures the essence of the problem being considered and provides insights to the managers in aggregate terms. Greater understanding may provide greater acceptance. This suggests that the current research on aggregation-disaggregation should be encouraged and expanded.

FINDING VIABLE RESEARCH PROJECTS

Where does one find the kinds of projects that are likely to have the implementation characteristics? Popeye's wisdom may be a guide—"I looks where it is and I finds it!" The best source of viable projects is where the problems are. If we look for research projects that arise from practice we will find ourselves constrained to deal with broader problem definitions and the criteria faced by practicing managers. The probability for implementation should improve. If we abstract situations that we find in practice, we should be in a better position to account for the differences between models developed and reality.

Additional insight comes from the reports of a panel discussion at the Northeast AIDS meeting in Boston dealing with research perspectives on MRP.[2] The managers of the panel "described their dominant problems in terms of long range capacity planning, centralized vs. decentralized control, organizational issues, workforce management, and vendor relationships. When the academics on the panel noted that much OM research is focused on lot-sizing rules, safety stock levels, and optimizing, one of the managers replied, 'Our issues are complex, your algorithms aren't.'" Managers want realities reflected in our research that are necessarily complex. Also, I believe that research is a highly personal thing, but can we continue to ignore the issues that managers say are uppermost in their needs?

SCANNING THE HORIZON

In the call for papers for the *Journal of Operations Management* announced in the initial issue of *The Operations Management Newsletter,* the area of OM was

---

[2]Linda Sprague, "Simple Algorithms, Compels Issues," *The Operations Management Newsletter,* 1 (1), May–June 1979, 13.

defined to include, but not necessarily be limited to the subject areas in Exhibit 1, for both *manufacturing* and *service* organizations.

Who could argue with this list? The introductory textbooks deal with this set of topics in one way or another. However, I see a danger in the list if we generate more papers that define a problem of relatively narrow scope, build a model to represent it, and evaluate the results by a single-valued criterion. In other words, I fear that we will recycle the kind of research that has typified the past 20 years, in a situation that I see as needing change.

The list of topics need not be viewed in a narrow way, however. I shall place myself in harms way by suggesting possible researchable topics from the list that are meant to be consistent with the proposed directions, for both manufacturing and service systems. Then, there is another way of looking at the list, or in a sense, not looking at it. The list is topical in the traditional sense. But, where are the issue-oriented topics? Can OM researchers contribute to the solution of societal problems? I shall also suggest issue-oriented topics as a third category.

MANUFACTURING SYSTEMS

STRATEGIC PLANNING DECISIONS

There has been relatively little attention given to strategic issues in operations management, yet these are the most important in terms of the long-term effects on organizations, their competitive strength, and the level of management personnel involved. Four general topic areas come to mind:

Manufacturing strategy and technological choice,
Job design,
Capacity planning,
Location choice.

They are not independent of each other. Indeed, that is the challenge, to design research projects that may have a focus but which recognize the inter- and intra-relationships. These four topics involve several of the items from the list in Exhibit 1. They all involve relationships with one or more other functional units such as marketing, finance, and personnel. They all involve a careful assessment of risk.

Manufacturing Strategy and Technological Choice.   Should a given manufacturer choose a production strategy that emphasizes flexibility, consumer choice, and quality or one that emphasizes cost and off-the-shelf availability? These are

EXHIBIT 1	SUBJECT AREAS IN OPERATIONS MANAGEMENT

1. Inventory Control
   a. order point systems
   b. material requirements planning systems
   c. multi-echelon inventory systems
   d. lot sizing
2. Aggregate Planning
   a. production planning
   b. staff sizing
3. Forecasting
4. Scheduling
   a. master production scheduling
   b. single machine, flow shop, and job shop scheduling
   c. large project scheduling
   d. shift scheduling
   e. priority planning
   f. shop floor control system
   g. scheduling services
5. Capacity Planning
   a. plant and equipment investment
   b. loading systems
   c. service systems
6. Purchasing
7. Facility Location
   a. manufacturing
   b. service
8. Facility Layout
   a. manufacturing
   b. service
9. Process Design
   a. line balancing
   b. process selection
   c. job design
   d. job enlargement
   e. labor/capital mix
   f. organizational structure
10. Maintenance and Reliability
11. Quality Control
12. Work Measurement

Source: *The Operations Management Newsletter,* 1 (1), May–June 1979, 14.

two points in a solution space that is defined by the nature of the market (custom versus highly standardized products as extreme points), and production technology (job shop versus highly automated systems as extreme points). There is a wide choice available in most situations, and the joint strategy has far-reaching significance. Yet the strategies that I have observed in organizations seemed to have "grown up" like Topsy rather than having been "decided" by managers. This important strategic decision interacts with the facility design and layout, job design, and capacity planning. It involves a careful assessment of markets, contingencies depending on future technological developments, and other possible events. While the decision is clearly in the production domain, it interacts and impacts the finance, marketing, and personnel functions. Can OM provide a rational theoretical structure for such decisions? A rational decision process for managers?

Job Design.   Of course, an integral part of the issue of technological choice and manufacturing strategy is in the human side of production. But in addition, job design is itself an important issue. It has societal and possible individual enterprise productivity implications, and impacts directly the facility design and layout. Like the more general strategy decision, there is a choice. But based on simple observation of what happens, it seems to me that managers are unaware of possible choices. More research is needed to indicate choices of technology and human factors that are acceptable. Can OM produce guidelines for choice? Can we continue to ignore the fact that people are an integral part of productive systems? Should we go to our colleagues in the behavioral sciences for collaboration, or should we wait for them to come to us?

Capacity Planning.   The previous question of strategy and technological choice cannot avoid the issue of capacity planning, and vice versa. Technological choice is a dynamic factor that must enter capacity planning together with other contingencies. Then there is the issue of location which should be an integral part of capacity planning. How should managers predict contingencies and take them into account in capacity planning. The capacity planning decision must involve the finance and marketing functions, and where labor supply is an issue, the personnel function. Of course, we (the OM community) know that the theoretical structure is not a secret, but have we shared it with practicing managers in a way that they can use it? Can we develop a generalized decision process, perhaps in interactive mode, that would help managers make these important decisions?

Locational Choice.   A great deal of theoretical research has been done on plant location, physical distribution systems, and warehouse location. Yet somehow, the benefits have been reaped by only a small minority of enterprises. As with capacity planning, perhaps translations of the present state of the art are needed in order to convert theory to practice. The conversion would be a worthy accomplishment in itself.

OPERATIONS PLANNING AND CONTROL

I have selected three topics that seem interesting to me in a managerial sense:

Aggregate planning,
Personnel and shift scheduling,
Dependent product structure systems.

Each of these topics is in Exhibit 1, and a great deal of work has already been done on each of them. While other functions such as marketing, finance, and personnel are involved in the first two, the last one is internal to the production function.

Aggregate Planning. One of the favorite topics of the last 20 years still needs work. Why? No one uses it in the form that we, in our infinite wisdom, constructed these models. The decision processes that we proposed simply do not meet the requirements of managers. It is not that good managers do not plan in aggregate terms, for there is ample evidence that they do, but they do not do it our way. Perhaps the first thing that we should do is to spend time with managers responsible for these important short-term capacity planning decisions. We know that they are sensitive to costs and want to minimize them in the general sense, but they must be including some costs that are not in our models. For example, are they sensitive to a labor force fluctuation cost over and above the hiring-layoff cost that we include? We expect them to engage in trade-off analysis on this issue, but instead they reject the entire system. What level of disaggregation is required by them? What other expectations do managers have in aggregate planning systems?

I suspect that managers would prefer an entirely different decision process than we have provided. Perhaps managers need a richer model that includes all of the other factors that they think are important, in combination with a computational algorithm that computes costs for alternatives that are acceptable to them. Such a model could also compute the minimum cost as a reference point, recognizing that this is an idealized cost that gives no weight to the other factors that managers wish to trade off. Such an interactive system would make the trade-off process a rational part of the planning decisions.

Personnel and Shift Scheduling. How would a modified work week affect productivity, flexibility of operations, manufacturing strategy, and so on? We know that our society may be in for a change. We may change the work week in order to save energy, spread the work, or enjoy more leisure time. The pressures come from organized labor, politicians and others who are not in a position to assess the impact of alternatives on important aspects of manufacturing management. We have already generated algorithms for personnel and shift scheduling. Perhaps they can be used in connection with the evaluation of alternate proposals.

Dependent Product Structure Systems. The development of MRP is a good example of something developed for managerial use. Unfortunately, academics had little or nothing to do with its development. Operating managers found our research on inventory models and scheduling to be of little value to them. We did not consult them to find out what their problems really were, nor even the nature of demand patterns in dependent systems. Managers rejected statistical inventory control in these situations and created their own systems.

But, we now have MRP concepts firmly established and a whole generation of research needs to be repeated in a sense, in the environment of dependent demand systems. The old job shop simulators are obsolete. The general simulation methodology is valid, but we need new simulators to test lot sizing alternatives, priority rules, shop floor procedures, labor assignment procedures, labor-machine ratios, the effects of lot splitting, and on and on. The traditional assumptions of Poisson arrivals and negative exponential service need to be reexamined. What happens when labor is not interchangeable? What are the effects of capacity changing actions such as the use of overtime, second shifts, hiring and firing, switching operators between job classifications, subcontracting, and whatever else managers really do?

SERVICE SYSTEMS

The prime research areas in service systems may be somewhat different than for manufacturing systems, both because very little has already been done, and because service systems have some special characteristics. The special characteristics that I refer to are the familiar ones: the output cannot be inventoried; extremely variable demand on a short-term basis; backlogging and/or smoothing of demand is often difficult or impossible; operations are usually labor intensive; and system location is dictated by the location of users, resulting in local, decentralized operations, and smaller units that have difficulty in taking advantage of economies of scale.

Perhaps the easy way out for me is to say that service systems are virgin territory and virtually everything needs to be done. We all engage service systems in our daily lives and observe an appalling lack of scheduling of personnel, simple recognition of good flow patterns, capacity planning on a short- or long-term basis, control of quality or even the recognition of what constitutes quality, location planning, availability of parking, capacity lane, and so on. Some of these lacks would be relatively easy to correct through better managerial training and practices and may not be good research projects. For example, decent layout and flow patterns can result with a little careful thought. "Ordinarily good" line balance can be achieved without sophisticated models in the usual simple situation. Student projects might improve service systems and university-community relations simultaneously.

But, there are many generic problems in service systems that justify research effort, and many more industry-oriented problems. I pick out three, but I am sure that there are many more:

Positioning strategy,
Capacity planning, and
Quality control.

These three topics involve one or more of the other functions of marketing, finance, and personnel. In some instances these functions are not highly developed or differentiated from the operating function, except in large organizations with centralized staffs that provide services to local operating units.

Positioning Strategy.   While service operations do not have the options of producing "to order" or "to stock," they do often have options in the way the service is packaged. It can be offered production line style with everything standardized at one extreme, or custom designed to the users needs at the other extreme. Also, the quality of the service can be high or low, and this dimension is not necessarily correlated with the degree of standardization of the service. The choices made have an important bearing on the marketing of the service, the design of the productive system, the capacity, the capital costs, and so on.

The positioning decision is crucial since the service and its productive systems are so completely bound together. Yet the more usual procedure is to design the nature of the service and then figure out how to produce it, which makes little more sense than designing the productive system and then figuring out what product it is producing. Since the nature of services is so diverse, perhaps the need is for a rational decision process that may be made specific to any situation by entering specific variables and data. Alternately, it may make more sense to develop such studies in specific industries, since services are so diverse in their nature. In any case, the contact with managers of service systems would be very important.

Capacity Planning. Currently, we discuss capacity for service systems largely in relation to waiting-line models. But, service system capacity must be growing at a phenomenal rate, based on the growth of services versus products in GNP. Therefore, managers of service systems need to plan for future capacity. What are the rational bases for such plans? What kinds of forecasts are needed? What are the planning contingencies? What are logical alternate sources of capacity near a capacity limit? What is the effect of adding larger versus smaller capacity increments? Will larger or smaller units give the best service? What capacity are customers and clients willing to pay for in relation to service time? Where should the new capacity be located? Can we develop a decision process that would help service system managers?

Quality Control. The entire field of quality control in service operations needs attention. The organizational function usually does not exist in any formal sense as it does in manufacturing. Standards of quality do not exist, perhaps because the dimensions of quality have not even been identified. The human element is very important and different than the human element in manufacturing quality control. The quality of services depends so much on the attitudes of personnel and the way service is given. This field seems to be wide open.

ISSUES FOR THE FUTURE

Many of the managerial problems in the future will be centered on the impact of factors that we have usually felt were outside our province, the exogenous factors that we take as given. Yet the operations manager may spend more time and effort in the future on the kinds of issues I will suggest than on the designing of the internal systems that have been our focus in the past.

Energy. We have traditionally focused attention on the inputs of labor, materials, and technology. Another input that is commonly included in general models of productive systems is energy, but we have seldom dealt with it. The efficient productive system of tomorrow may be one that is energy efficient. While we have concentrated on cost trade-offs in the past, we may design systems in the future where energy tradeoffs are the focus. Such systems might impact our traditional topical list by influencing location decisions, transportation and distribution systems, aggregate planning and schedules, and so on.

Productivity. The changing mix of manufacturing and services in GNP has diluted our national annual increase in productivity. Services seem less susceptible to productivity increase through mechanization and automation. At the same time there has been a tremendous impact on costs and productivity by federal and state regulatory bodies such as OSHA, EPA, CPSC, and others. There is a growing acceptance of job designs that may be satisfying, even at the expense of productivity. What is the role of OM research in this general field? Can we help evaluate the impact on productivity of the directions currently taken? Can we help guide the directions?

Inflation.   What are the strategic choices that operations managers should make in an inflationary economy? How does inflation affect capacity planning, investment in new production processes, and so on. Even shorter range plans might be impacted, such as inventory policy, hiring and layoff practices, and other short range capacity adjustment policies. We have usually repressed the inflation issue by an "other things being equal" assumption. But, in today's economy, the possible future effects of inflation need to be accounted for. What is the methodology? What are the effects?

Uncertain supply.   If *The Limits to Growth*[3] study is right, materials will become more and more scarce. Good operations management may be the result of managing with scarce or uncertain supply. Managers are used to interruptions of supply because of strikes or catastrophes, but these events occur only once in a while. If the environment were to change so that uncertainty of supply were a common factor, then the focus of operations management would also need to change.

CONCLUDING COMMENTS

The refocusing of OM as a functional field of management must have an impact on the nature of research in the field. There will always be an important place for theoretical research, but even theoretical research in OM needs a strong element of relationship to the practicing world. Research hypotheses need to be developed with the input of practicing managers, and an important general objective might be the packaging of decision processes for managerial use. We need to think about how research that results in complex models can be made more acceptable, and therefore useful. Issue-oriented research may well be some of the most useful to operations managers. Managers' input on which topics are likely to be more useful to them may have funding implications.

---

[3]D.L. Meadows, D.H. Meadows, J. Randers, and N.W. Behrens III, *The Limits to Growth,* Universe Books, New York, 1972.

GLOBAL PRODUCTION AND OPERATIONS STRATEGY

MARTIN K. STARR

New competitive pressures exist for normally nationally-constrained (domestic) enterprises to innovatively engage in global production operations. Why is this so? First, new technologies that lower operating costs require greater capital investment. To pay for the increased investments, greater sales volumes are essential. Since many countries have far smaller domestic consumer markets than the U.S., they must compete abroad to achieve sales that justify the large investments. This is particularly true when competition at home (say in Japan) is greater than in other countries, like the U.S. The global competing companies set standards that the domestic producers must match. As they raise their standards to compete at home, these domestic producers recognize the advantages of adopting global strategies. Second, various governments support their export industries with industrial policies that make them highly competitive so that their trade balances can be very profitable.

Third, the global setting has produced international suppliers with advantages over domestic vendors. Fourth, it has increased the volume of goods shipped, which has lowered the costs of distribution. This can provide marginal advantages to those engaged in high-volume, long-distance distribution which often circumvents union and governmental regulations. Fifth, global firms can enjoy the fluctuation of exchange rates, inflation rates and other volatile factors that provide advantages precisely because they do fluctuate, if they know how to benefit from the ups-and-downs. Volatility of fundamental economic factors challenges those who rely on stability and provides great opportunities for those who do not build strategies based on stability. For simplicity, we can assume that the production operations are associated with manufacturing. However, much of what we say in this article applies to services as well. For example, consider McDonald's which makes and sells

Reprinted by permission from *Columbia Journal of World Business* 19.4 (Winter 1984): 17–22.

hamburgers in many parts of the world. This product line and its packaging are about as different from computers and software as one can imagine. Nevertheless, comparisons can be drawn between the way McDonald's does its global thing, and say IBM. The IBM pattern of manufacture has high local content in a great variety of countries, but production of components is not constrained to be exclusive, and transfers occur between countries. The study of many companies reveals great strategic differences between them, in how they allocate the global resources, and for each company incessant, dynamic, evolutionary change, reflecting opportunities to innovate.

What Is Global Production?

The definition of global production is not cut and dried. Variability of product design to satisfy each country's UL (Underwriting Laboratory) requirements, different food and drug regulations, and even national taste anomalies, create complexities that lead to questions of how many factories make sense, and where they should be located. Decisions to license, export or produce within foreign country are clear choices of different global strategies. When mixed together, they comprise so great a potential number of combinations across many countries, that ordinary rationality is challenged and defeated.

Production management includes distribution, although in such applications it is often called operations management (OM). The OM designation is also used for process management in banking, transportation, and other services, as well as for managing services that support manufacturing operations. World-wide distribution systems provide an excellent example of global operations. Specialized carriers can significantly alter the direct costs of goods sold and delivered to customers. Toyota, for example, has shown that when export volume warrants the investment, ships specially designed to carry automobiles from plant to market can efficiently provide a strategic advantage that affects the decision of where to manufacture, *how much* to produce, and destined for *which* markets.

Also to be included in global production strategy is the issue of global sourcing. Who can be chosen to supply raw materials and components to a manufacturer is clearly a function of who that manufacturer considers to be part of the list of potential vendors. In the past, regional (and at most, national) familiarity led to "safe" decisions, meaning comfortable with the language and culture of the supplier. But now, options that are reasonable (and/or essential) to consider exist all over the world. Supplier selection must be dictated by analyses of comparative factor advantages of cost, quality, variety, service, delivery, warranties, realiabilities, and flexablities. Competitive advantages as they appear in the factor list are derived from superior technology, methodology, and management. More specifically, there are lots of factors that contribute to comparative advantage, for example, lower labor costs, higher worker skill, more favorable exchange rates, better lead times for delivery including carriers' reliability; and less danger of supply interruption through vendor or carrier strikes, etc. As risk exposure increases, multiple vendor selection becomes a necessity. Thus, with the vendor selection menu being global in scope, and growing, this aspect of the production problem allows unique opportunities for innovating to achieve competitive advantages.

GLOBAL LIFE CYCLE FACTORS

A manufacturer, with a strictly domestic market, deciding to order from a vendor located in another country—and this for the first time—may acquire information which then leads to the development of new markets abroad. Suppliers of manufactured goods can ship components or finished goods. The latter, as exporters, need no intermediate fabrication or assembly locations outside of their home base. Eventually, export strategies can change to plans to manufacture in that export country, with imports of at least some components from home base. Alternatively, by licensing the production process, fabrication and assembly can be conducted in the country which previously had been supplied by export. But licensing has a contractual end-date, at which time, the best decision may have changed to plant ownership abroad.

These are a few of the many dynamic systems that have to be reviewed continuously, with the distinct likelihood of major capital investment reconfiguration decisions. The reason is that country economics, industry concentrations, technological improvements, and consumer markets change with age and experience, in what are aptly called "life cycles". Such life cycles have always been around, but, for global systems, they are more volatile waves of greater volume that are speeded up by various new forces.

First, more countries, with their own governmental support, introduce new players in the competitive global game. On a broader canvas, national economies worldwide are experiencing faster and broader change than ever before.

Second, industry concentrations are significantly altered by global producers and marketers who cross national boundaries. Worldwide, a greater number of producers have assembled increasingly larger aggregate volumes as a result of their global activities. This translates into more competition between companies having better production processes, yielding higher quality and lower costs for consumers. These benefits start dissipating when governmental regulations are invoked to protect domestic producers. Protecting domestic producers increases concentrations and decreases competition and consumer benefits. However, increasingly, tariffs and quotas have shifted global marketing efforts into production investments inside the protected zone. The domestic proponents of protectionism find themselves (unexpectedly) involved in greater competition. They must invest in improvements of their production systems to match the competition.

Third, technological change, driven by semiconductor capacity and circuit design developments, decreasing computer costs and growing software intelligence, have no historical counterpart with respect to their impact and rate of change. Worldwide, individual governments are sponsoring research. Such R&D accomplishments cannot be overlooked, although their effects upon the global market are significantly less now than they will become in the future.

Fourth, with more options to choose from, especially as induced by global competition among technologically vaulting countries, consumers shorten product lives faster than ever.

There is a fifth point to be treated, as well. New technology alone is not responsible for the dynamics of life cycles. Global production systems have been unique in the extent to which they reflect changed process configurations and management principles. The Japanese model of management (job rotation, lifetime security, worker production-goal bonuses, consensus, etc.) has received major coverage by business publications.

Only slightly less journalistic attention has been paid to production techniques and procedures which include JIT (Just-in-Time), Kanban (cards) for production scheduling, and TQC (Total Quality Control) with workers organized in Quality Circles.

GLOBAL NETWORK MODELS

Ricardo (about 1800) formulated the notion of comparative advantage to explain international trading patterns. (An updated simplistic example: OPEC countries export oil and import autos from the countries that need oil to produce and export cars.) Nationally-owned physical resources dominate this early viewpoint, but tradeoffs with technological know-how do occur. Cost advantages are the primary focus, although some generalized quality standards and reliable delivery lead times must be assumed. Ricardo's insights still apply, but what constitutes comparative advantage for global firms engaged in international trade has taken on many new dimensions.

The point to be made is that sourcing, fabricating, assembling, and distributing decisions are becoming increasingly interdependent and critical in terms of the differences available between the best, the average, and the worst, with respect to: costs, quality, variety, service, deliveries, warranties, reliabilities, and flexibilities. The global environment contributes significantly to the dimensional enrichment of what constitutes comparative advantage. As some examples:

- increasing numbers of international suppliers appear with technological advantages in production processes, distribution (delivery) systems, and warehousing methods,
- new technology factories become feasible that (sometimes) can be installed abroad more easily than at home—this is because of many reasons, including union/management difficulties, national regulations, and lack of domestic competition that can match the global incursions,
- high-tech assembly systems can be installed in various parts of the world using computer software that can be created in one country and then shipped to the others; modifications can originate anywhere and go everywhere else; remote entry programming via satellite is not only economically feasible, it may be nearing optimality. Such computer control applies to new technology (fabrication) factories as well.

The model that allows total consideration of global sourcing, making, assembling, and marketing (including distribution) alternatives is that of a network, as shown in Chart 1.

The network is a rational expression of all possible combinations of the hierarchical chain of supply and demand which starts with raw materials and ends with markets. Not all possible connections (links) are drawn between the (nodes) suppliers, fabricators, assemblers, and marketers, but they all could be drawn and considered. The reason for considering less than all possible combinations is that constraints exist which may be real or imaginary. For example, it should be noted that a strictly domestic arrangement might look as shown in Chart 2. In any case, management seldom wishes to allow all possible options. Further, the list of existing suppliers, factories, and markets provides a foundation to which other nodes can be added. If you don't know about a potentially important new supplier in Korea, you can't add that node to the network; once known, you will add it.

The means of solving these complex network models exist, assuming that the costs and benefits can be determined. The costs, in most instances can be catalogued for various suppliers. However, global sourcing involves an exchange rate interface, which is difficult to predict because it is volatile and subject to many forces that transcend single company or even industry-wide knowledge.

Inflation rates differ by nations which can also affect purchasing as well as producing and marketing decisions. Sometimes good predictions of inflation

| **CHART 1** | CONSIDERS MOST POSSIBLE COMBINATIONS |

International   Domestic

Supplier

Fabricator

Assembler

Market

rates are easy to come by; namely, when the rates of change are fairly constant over time. When this is not the case, and with exchange rate volatility, many decisions are made irrationally. Yet, in every spin of the roulette wheel, some players win. And, for those who know more about such subjects, knowledge of the past plus sound intuition may provide substantial leverage.

The use of a global network model requires global market data which is needed to determine the marginal contribution of total revenues less total production costs. Such figures are somewhat less difficult to estimate on a global scale if there exist national markets for each production subsidiary. Problems of translating quality into costs and benefits, are another example of difficulties encountered in using models. However, there are tricks which take us a good distance of the way, and in this instance sensitivity analysis which tests performance for different levels of costs and benefits, provides insights concerning the effects of quality levels. So, in general, while we have emphasized measurement problems, we have also noted that they are not insuperable. By chance, there will be winners and losers. By skill, the probabilities of winning can be increased manyfold.

TRANSPORTATION AND TRANSSHIPMENT MODELS

The transportation model is a simple way of determining the optimal pattern of shipping from a set of origins to a set of destinations. This could be from a list of potential suppliers (global and domestic) to existing as well as potential production facilities (global and domestic) as represented by the top two levels of Chart 1. It could also be from fabricators (say domestic only) to assembly plants in strategic international locations. In many instances, the fabricators and assemblers would be located in the same plant. However, when the transportation costs of moving finished goods to the marketplace are high, (as in automobiles) it is not unusual to locate assembly plants near the market. This would alter Chart 1 as shown in Chart 3. In this case, the company's own production facilities become alternative (or constrained) suppliers to the assembly operations. The costs and benefits derived for the transportation model, where origins are assemblers and destinations are markets, clearly influences the

CHART 2   A STRICTLY DOMESTIC ENTERPRISE IS SHOWN BY SOLID FILLED-IN NODES

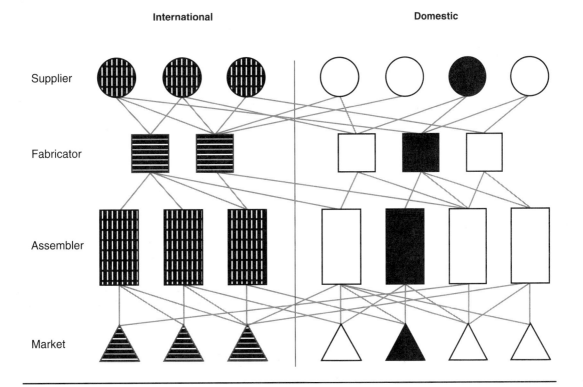

location decisions for suppliers, company fabrication plant (and even sub-assembly plants, say for auto engines, to provide a realistic example), assembly plants, and targeted markets.

To capture the entire four-tier hierarchy in the network requires a modification of the transportation model which is called a transshipment model.[1] It encompasses the total network, i.e., suppliers, to (fabrication and assembly) producers, to markets. A simple alteration of the well-known transportation model, takes care of the more complicated situation. We will not deal with the transshipment problem in this paper. Every major computer company has software that works for sizeable problems.

CHART 3	SUPPLIER CAN SHIP DIRECTLY TO ASSEMBLERS

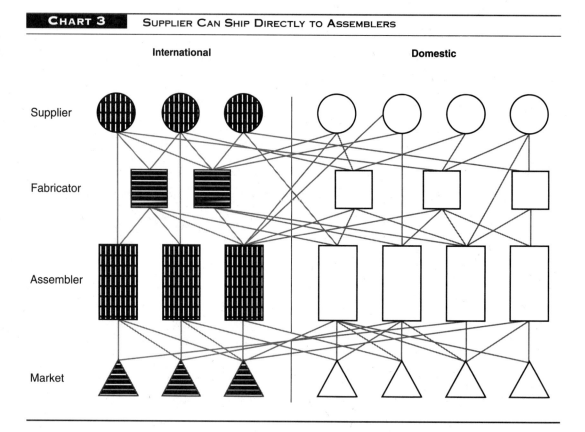

---

[1]Transshipment problem is a transportation problem that is modified to allow either supply or demand points to serve as transshipment points, receiving units that are to be eventually shipped elsewhere. From Dannenbring and Starr, *Management Science: An Introduction,* 1981, 347–49.

COMPETITIVE ADVANTAGE

Innovation does not have to originate in-company. Finding supplier innovations, anywhere in the world, is a new responsibility which many organizations cannot yet meet. In the past decade, competitive analysis has been adopted by many companies, and perfected by a few. The focus was on the market. Substitutability in the consumers' minds for "what they will buy" defined competition. As the global perspective emerged, it became clear that competitive advantage included more than marketing. Zenith Radio, in the 1960s, scrutinized RCA and GE. By the 1970s, RCA and Zenith were looking abroad, studying Sony's products, and Panasonic's, etc. Now, in the mid-1980s, these companies no longer look only at each other. They also look to alternative:

- raw material suppliers
- machine tool and other process technology suppliers
- component suppliers
- arrangements with co-producers
- R&D sources (see Chart 4)
- other opportunities for unique basic advantages (called UBA's)

THE EFFECTS OF NEW TECH, NEW PRODUCTION THEORY, AND NEW MANAGEMENT PRINCIPLES

Previously, companies located their production facilities in line with many established rational principles. One of the most significant forces for global production was to assemble sufficient marketing volume to permit a large production facility to be built which could reflect economies of scale that were inherent in the manufacturing process.

Now, in an increasing number of industries there exists profoundly new technology known as FMS (Flexible Manufacturing Systems). FMS has altered established production theory by using tools and transfer lines operated by computer software that can produce many different designs in low volumes (often 1 at a time) with exceptionally high quality. The investment is high, but it yields production configurations with the same economies of scale as formerly achieved by the large volume producers who could only produce a single output. Thus *economies of scope* can become more important in providing UBA's than economies of scale which no longer dominate all production investment decisions. The key to understanding these changes is the ability of new technology to achieve near-zero set-up times and cost.

CHART 4   GLOBAL VIEWS OF R&D CAN ORIGINATE FROM DOMESTIC AND/OR INTERNATIONAL SOURCES

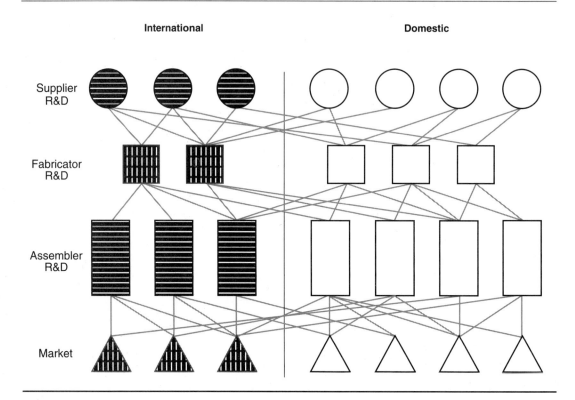

In the purest cases, many FMS factories can be built in different countries to comply with local content pressures—whether regulated or just bowing to social pressures. Assembly operations are moving in the same direction, and many industries are finding ways to shift their local content.

The key differences are based on ways to reduce waste. Work in process (WIP) must be brought to a minimum level. Defectives can be decreased by using the total quality control concept. Just in time deliveries by suppliers is an external criterion that requires special relations between vendors and users. Managers begin to work with employees to continually improve the production process. Especially, the effort is to drive set-up costs to near zero, while improving quality.

When all is in place, optimal producers emerge. They have the comparative advantage of achieving maximal margin contribution both short- and long-term. Opportunities for innovation at a strategic level have never been greater. The crucial variables belong to production and operations strategies.

In summary, if national companies want to survive and remain competitive they must look at global opportunities—because if they don't do this others are already getting ready to grab their markets with superior strategies that include lower costs, sharper market penetration in quality and design variability, and better distribution. Global networking is crucial for gaining the competitive edge.

REFERENCES

David G. Dannenbring and Martin K. Starr, *Management Science: An Introduction*, McGraw-Hill Book Company, NY, 1981.

Subhash C. Jain and Louis R. Tucker, Jr., *International Marketing: Managerial Perspectives*, CBI Publishing Co., Inc., Boston, MA.

John D. Daniels, et al., *International Business: Environments & Operations* (3rd ed.), Addison-Wesley Publishing Co., 1952.

Michael F. Porter, *Competitive Strategy*, Free Press, NY 1980.

THE VITAL ELEMENTS OF WORLD-CLASS MANUFACTURING

RICHARD J. SCHONBERGER

From the 1950s to the end of the 1970s, running manufacturing companies became gentlemen's work. Decisions and policies were made by people twice and thrice removed from the manufacturing arena. Authority was in the hands of staff people who sifted data from other staff people. Venturing out into the plant was, well, venturing. It was prudent to stick around offices and conference rooms and make sure your backside was covered. Excitement in industry was confined to high-tech R&D. Manufacturing was stagnant.

How quickly things change. While the changes have scarcely touched small companies, the well-known manufacturers are caught up in revival, renewal, recovery, and renaissance. A popular term among those caught up is *world-class manufacturing* (WCM) or a term like it. World-class manufacturing may sound like American hyperbole, but it is not.

The term nicely captures the breadth and the essence of fundamental changes taking place in large industrial enterprises. A full range of elements of production are affected: management of quality, job classifications, labor relations, training, staff support, sourcing, supplier and customer relations, product design, plant organization, scheduling, inventory management, transport, handling, equipment selection, equipment maintenance, the product line, the accounting system, the role of the computer, automation, and others.

I have conducted seminars and provided consultancy at manufacturing plants in a number of European and Pacific Basin (besides Japan) countries and have found WCM to be globe-spanning.

World-class manufacturing has an overriding goal and an underlying mind set for achieving it. The overriding goal may be summed up by a slogan suggested to me by a manager at the Steelcraft Division of American Standard, where I was recently presenting a seminar. During the afternoon break, the

---

Reprinted by permission from *International Management*, May 1986, 76–78.

fellow told me that he had digested all that had been said, and he concluded that the whole thing was like the motto of the Olympic Games: *citius, altius, fortius.* From the Latin the English translation is "faster, higher, stronger". The WCM equivalent is *continual and rapid improvement.*

A few years ago we didn't even know the factors of manufacturing that ought to improve. There was little agreement on what excellence in manufacturing is, because we thought in terms of trade-offs. Plant managers or their corporate overseers picked one set of high-priority targets one year (for example, defect rates and warranty costs) and another, seemingly conflicting, set to work on the next (perhaps overhead costs and customer service rates). The high priorities were where problems seemed most severe.

Today there is wide agreement among the WCM "revisionists" that continual improvement in quality, costs, lead time, and customer service is possible, realistic, and necessary. There is now good reason to believe that those goals may be pursued in concert, that they are not in opposition.

One more primary goal, improved flexibility, is also a part of the package. While some of our leading manufacturers have trouble avoiding pitfalls that lead to inflexibility (pitfalls that *are* avoidable), the goal itself is not an issue. With agreement on goals, the management challenge is reduced to speeding up the pace of improvement.

FOLLOWING A CLEAR PATH

The improvement journey follows a surprisingly well-defined path. The journey requires clearing away obstacles so that production can be simplified. A fast growing body of writings (including my own 1982 book, *Japanese Manufacturing Techniques: Nine Hidden Lessons in Simplicity*) offers lists of obstacles to remove and ways to simplify: fewer suppliers, reduced part counts, focused factories (focused on a narrow line of products or technologies), scheduling to a rate instead of scheduling by lots, fewer racks, more frequent deliveries, smaller plants, shorter distances, less reporting, fewer inspectors, less buffer stock, fewer job classifications.

There is reseeding going on, and there seems to be a single year that could be called the turning point: 1980. In that year, a few North American companies (and perhaps some in Europe) began overhauling their manufacturing apparatus. Those first WCM thrusts followed two parallel paths. One was the quality path, and the other was the just-in-time (JIT) production path.

One of the first to try just-in-time in North America was General Electric Co., which started up two JIT projects in 1980. Kawasaki Heavy Industries Ltd. in Nebraska and Toyota Motor Corp. in Long Beach, California, began shifting from standard to JIT production in the same year.

World-class manufacturing could not become the third major event if it were to peter out. The signs that it will not, that WCM is much more than a fad, are persuasive. The list of companies that have already made order-of-magnitude improvements in quality and manufacturing lead time is getting long. For example, I have compiled (and continue to update) a list of the "5-10-20s," which refers to companies, factories, or parts of factories where fivefold, tenfold, or twentyfold reductions in manufacturing lead time have been achieved.

With so short a history, WCM has not had a chance to mature in all of its natural habitats. What surprises many is the progressive unearthing of more and more natural habitats, different industries, and types of production. That is, what makes a world-class manufacturer in one industry also seems to work in other industries. That should not be surprising.

A machine shop, a sheet metal shop, a printed-circuit-board shop—any shop or factory that makes to order—is just the same. As long as the shop or factory is small, production is usually quite fast. But who wants to stay small? We have plants—for final goods and component parts alike—with thousands of employees and hundreds of thousands of square feet of space. Now the work goes through the plant at a snail's pace. Plant management has its hands full trying to prevent gridlock.

Growth is not the problem. The problem is the more-of-the-same approach to growth. A restaurant is a little *job shop*, to use the manufacturing term. It will not work if it becomes a big job shop—where a job (platter) has to traverse vast distances from one shop to another, waiting for one thing or another at most of the shops. Growth must be accompanied by a transformation to preserve speed, to avoid stop-and-go production.

CUSTOMERS ARE FICKLE

Over the years we came to believe that stop-and-go production was the fate of the job shop. We also believed that job shops were the fate of industry, because customers are fickle; they want the variety that job shops can provide. Job shop people looked enviously at the flow shops, where work just flows down a production line or through pipes continuously (as patrons flow down a cafeteria line).

That view is out of fashion because we have learned how to streamline our job shops, to make them behave more like flow shops. Some go so far as to simplify products and regularize schedules, and thereby transform themselves into flow shops. Many others—those that stick with customers who demand variety—will not become flow shops, but they can come close. The chameleon cannot ever be a leaf, but it can look like one. So it is in manufacturing.

WCMs Pattern of Improvement

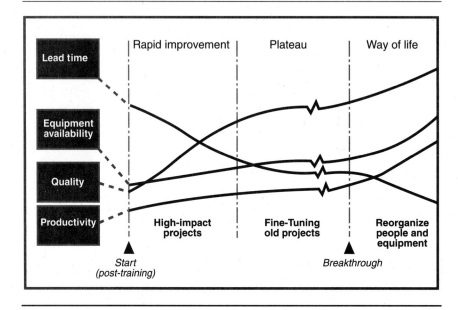

What tools and techniques make job shop transformations possible? At the top of the list are the set known as just-in-time production techniques. They were perfected by Toyota in Japan in the 1960s and 1970s. Toyota's techniques caused work to move through parts fabrication processes fast and get to final assembly just in time for use.

JIT was shaped in the flow shop mould. Continuous industries—the "pure" flow shops—have been around for a hundred or two hundred years. Examples are bottling, tableting, and canning; extruding and weaving; milling and refining. Some of the processes are tightly coupled. The work leaves one process and flows, perhaps through a pipe, to arrive just in time for the next. In that sense, JIT was around long before the people at Toyota thought of it.

In reality the flows are usually not all that continuous. The grain mills, the food processors, the medicine makers, the cloth producers, and the rest are stop-and-go producers, too. They go for a time on one size, style, model or chemical formulation, then shut down for a complete changeover in order to run another. Shutdowns for changeover are one concern. The massive quantities that build between changes—the raw and semiprocessed material, and especially the finished goods pushed out well in advance of customer needs—are a greater concern. All are forms of costly waste.

THE SMALLER, THE BETTER

There are dominant WCM precepts for treating the ailment. One is a JIT principle: the smaller the lot size, the better. World-class manufacturers of cars, tractors, and motorcycles have some lot sizes down to one unit by becoming adept at changeovers between models. This permits making some of every model everyday, almost like continuous-flow processing. With the capability, they outdo the flow processors they started out trying to copy.

A second precept is the total quality control (TQC) principle: do it right the first time. In the flow industries this means setting up for a new run so that the first yard of cloth, linear foot of sheet steel, length of hose, or can, bottle or tablet is good.

A third set of precepts is called "total" preventive maintenance (TMP). Maintain the equipment so often and so thoroughly that it hardly ever breaks down during a production run. There is nothing like an equipment failure to turn a continuous processor into its opposite number.

While the JIT *concept* (if not the application) is natural in the flow industries, it took Henry Ford and his lieutenants to get JIT worked out in discrete goods manufacturing. Ford has been called the father of mass production. His plants mass-produced the parts just in time for assembly, and his assembly lines pulled work forward to next assembly stations just in time, too.

By 1914 the Highland Park facility was unloading a hundred freight cars of materials each day, and the materials flowed through fabrication, subassembly and final assembly back on to freight cars. The product was the Model T, and the production cycle was 21 days. At River Rouge, about 1921, the cycle was only 4 days, and that included processing ore into steel in the steel mill that Ford built there.

That roughly equals the best Japanese JIT auto manufacturing plants today. But it was much easier for Henry Ford, because his plants followed his now famous dictum, "They can have it any color they want, so long as it's black."

The Model-T factories were what is known as *dedicated* plants and production lines. Where capacity is cheap (cheap equipment or labor) or volume is high, dedicated JIT lines make sense. Most producers of television sets, radios, videotape recorders, and personal computers today have enough volume to follow the easy dedicated-line path to JIT.

Whether making things that pour (the flow industries) or things that are counted in whole units (discrete goods), a WCM precept is to produce some of every type every day and in the quantities sold that day. Making more than can be sold is costly and wasteful, and the cost and waste are magnified manifold as the resulting lumpiness in the demand pattern ripples back through all prior stages of manufacture, including outside suppliers.

Makers of highly seasonal goods sometimes have sound reason for building at least some stock days or weeks before use or sale. Most of industry's chronic mismatches between demand rate and production rate are not caused by seasonality, however. Those mismatches are fixable. Companies in the flow industries need to figure out how to change overflow lines so fast that there is no reason for a long production run of one type. Since the flow industries have been investing for years in inflexible equipment that resists quick changeover, it is not an easy fix.

AN EASY FIX

In the assembly industries it tends to be an easy fix. Assembly—of personal computers, washing machines, boats, trucks, furniture, and hundreds of thousands of other products—is still largely manual. Humans are adaptable and can change from one model to another with ease—and efficiency, too. Assembly is efficient, however, only if the work place is orderly, with every part and tool exactly placed. If the assembler has to search, the efficiency is gone.

In *Japanese Manufacturing Techniques* I told of working for the fastest bricklayer in North Dakota and how he yelled at me if I didn't place bricks so that he could reach and find them without looking. The concept—exact placement of all the parts to eliminate search—has enabled the world's motorcycle manufacturers and some tractor producers to change models after each unit. That is called *mixed-model production*, and the lot size is one.

Ten years ago, all motorcycle and tractor manufacturers produced in large lots: maybe five hundred of model A; then shut down for a day or two to change over for a run of five hundred of model B; and so on.

Now, at Harley-Davidson, Honda, Kawasaki, Yamaha, John Deere tractor, and the others, some of every model is made every day. Marketing therefore has some to sell every day. If marketing comes to manufacturing and says, "Can you increase Model E by 10 percent and decrease A by 10 percent next week?" manufacturing says, "Yes, we can." The assemblers are quick-change artists. The makers of the components parts could still be obstacles, but they can learn quick-change artistry, too.

Some plants or parts of plants seem doomed to have long manufacturing lead times. Western manufacturers of machine tools and thousands of kinds of industrial components, from motors to pumps to hydraulics, take weeks, often months, to produce something. The problem is that those manufacturers are high-variety, low-volume job shops. Ten thousand different part numbers is normal, fifty thousand is not uncommon, and no one knows which ones are going to be needed in the next customer order. There may be four thousand work orders open in the plant at any given time, with a hundred completed and a hundred new ones added every day. How can such a production environment be anything but chaotic?

We know the answer. It is to divide the ten thousand part numbers into families—production families, not marketing families. A production family is a group of parts that follow about the same flow path. The result is a cell, a mini-production line, almost a pipeline that similar parts flow through.

Next, find another family and move the needed machines and work stations into cell 2. Then create cell 3, and so on. Engineers sometimes call this approach *group technology*, although many prefer to use the more descriptive *cellular manufacturing*.

The approach is much more than industrial engineering and plant layout, however. Cells create responsibility centers where none existed before. A single supervisor or cell leader is in charge of matters that used to be fragmented among several shop managers. The leader and the work group may be charged with making improvements in quality, cost, delays, flexibility, worker skills, lead time, inventory performance, scrap, equipment "up time," and a host of other factors that distinguish the world-class manufacturer.

Large numbers of Western manufacturers are following this path in their quest to become world-class. The machine-tool, aerospace, and shipbuilding industries are especially active in reorganizing their plants into cells. That is natural in view of the mind-boggling numbers of parts that go into large machines, ships, aircraft, and rockets.

'DO IT RIGHT THE FIRST TIME'

The metal-fabrication industries have no prior claim on cellular manufacturing. It is emerging as a prescription for much of the world of work, on a par with "Do it right the first time." Most of our plants' facilities and people are organized with giant barriers to problem-solving, and the same goes for most of our offices. No one is in charge. Distances between processes are too long for decent coordination. Flow times are too long for us to reconstruct chains of causes and effects when things go wrong—and they go wrong so often.

The task would be daunting if we were unsure of what paths to take. We *know* what paths to take, because there are many role models. Western manufacturers that have executed the WCM formula have been getting the same spectacular results that Japanese manufacturers did a bit earlier: product defects down from several percentage points to just a few per million pieces, and lead times cut by orders of magnitude. Knowing what it takes to get such results turns on the adrenalin pumps. The competitor whose pump does not get primed is the loser.

This reads, I suppose, like a pep talk, Olympic motto and all. If there were no substance to the message, it would fall on deaf ears, because we've all heard many pep talks—followed by business as usual. There *is* substance to the talk about world-class manufacturing. If a poll were taken to ask people to name the 20 best manufacturers (not marketers, not financial empires) in the world, how many would be American, Canadian, French, English, German, Italian, Swedish? Chances are good that many or most would be Japanese. There is substance to the Japanese formula for success in manufacturing.

It took Japanese industry three decades to make its remarkable climb. It used a collection of Western basics, plus common sense, high literacy, and lack of space and natural resources to spur them on. Now the rest of the world is stirred out of its complacency. In some cases manifold improvements have come after just a year or two of real effort.

WCM clearly is not reserved for the Japanese. In fact, I believe the Western temperament is better suited for rapid and continuous improvement than the Japanese temperament. We in the West have badly misused a chief asset, namely inquisitive minds and innovative spirits. Our greatest challenge is to undo the harm, to change a work culture, and unleash natural tendencies.

SELECTED READINGS

Adam, E., Jr. and Paul M. Swamidass, "Assessing Operations Management from a Strategic Perspective," *Journal of Management,* vol. 13, no. 2, (1989), 181–203.

Buffa, E., *Meeting the Competitive Challenge: Manufacturing Strategies for U.S. Companies.* Illinois: Richard D. Irwin, 1984.

Buffa, E., *Modern Production Management.* New York: John Wiley and Sons, 1961.

Chase, R. B. and J. J. Aquilano, *Production and Operations Management,* 6th Ed. Homewood, IL: Irwin, 1992.

Garvin, D., *Operations Strategy: Text and Cases.* New Jersey: Prentice-Hall, Inc. 1992.

Goldratt, E. M. and Jeff Cox., *The Goal.* Croton-on-Hudson, New York: North River Press, 1986.

Hayes, R. and Schmenner, R., "How Should You Organize Manufacturing?" *Harvard Business Review,* January–February 1978, 107–108.

Hayes, R. H. and S. C. Wheelwright, "Link Manufacturing Process and Product Life Cycles," *Harvard Business Review,* January–February 1979, 133–40.

Hayes R. and Wheelwright, S., *Restoring Our Competitive Edge.* New York: John Wiley & Sons, 1984.

Hayes R., Wheelwright, S. and Clark, K., *Dynamic Manufacturing: Creating the Learning Organization.* New York: The Free Press, 1988.

Hill, T., *Manufacturing Strategy.* Homewood, IL: Irwin, 1989.

Locke, E., "The Ideas of Frederick W. Taylor: An Evaluation," *Academy of Management Review,* vol. 7 (1982), 14.

Schonberger, R., *Japanese Manufacturing Systems.* New York: Free Press, 1982.

Schonberger, R., *World Class Manufacturing.* New York: Free Press, 1986.

Schonberger, R., *World Class Manufacturing: The Lessons of Simplicity Applied.* New York: Free Press, 1987.

Swamidass, P., "Manufacturing Strategy: Its Assessment and Practice," *Journal of Operations Management,* 1986, 471–84.

Taylor, F., *The Principles of Scientific Management.* New York: W.W. Norton & Company, 1947.

Wheelwright, S., "Manufacturing Strategy: Defining the Missing Link," *Strategic Management Journal,* vol. 5, 1984. 77–91.

Wheelwright, S. and Hayes, R., "Competing through Manufacturing," *Harvard Business Review,* January–February 1985, 99–109.

CHAPTER THREE

QUALITY

he explosion of research and publications on the subject of quality since about 1980 can lead students to believe that quality is a new revolution. Colleges and universities have only recently begun adding courses on quality to their business and engineering curricula. While some texts trace the quality field back to the building of the pyramids in Egypt, the subject of quality utilizing statistical techniques has only been in existence since the early 1920s.[1]

Two incidents appear to have significantly affected the attention paid to the subject of quality in the United States. The first of these was World War II. The need for highly reliable weapons systems with interchangeable parts provided high visibility for the kind of work conducted at Bell Laboratories by Walter Shewart and others. The armaments producers implemented these new ideas and techniques and proved their worth. However, after the war, the United States' dominant position in the world market for manufactured goods resulted in a retreat from these methods as U.S. industry found that it could sell virtually anything it produced regardless of the quality.

The second incident occurred with the revitalization of Japanese industry and the emergence in the world market of high quality products manufactured in Japan. This incident, which occurred during the late 1960s and early 1970s, raised competition to a new level. By the mid-to-late 1970s there was great concern among U.S. manufacturing companies about how to compete with the wave of low cost, high quality products flowing from Japanese factories. This wave resulted in the recognition of leaders in the quality field to whom U.S. industry was now prepared to listen.

This chapter uses the results of the surveys reported in Chapter One to identify the classic contributors to the quality field. Much has been written about these classic contributors in reporting and interpreting their messages. A greater understanding of the work of these contributors may be gained by reading a selection of the works themselves.

The second survey identified classic contributors to the quality portion of the field of production/operations management (POM). Based on this study, seven contributors, W. Edwards Deming, J.M. Juran, Walter A. Shewhart, Armand V. Feigenbaum, Shigeo Shingo, Phillip B. Crosby, and David A. Garvin, comprise the classic contributors to the quality portion of the field of POM.

Shewhart was one of the founders of the modern quality discipline. His work at Bell Laboratories, summarized in his book, *Economic Control of Manufactured Product,* is the seminal work underlying modern statistical quality control.

Deming was an early disciple of Shewhart, and in 1939 edited a book, *Statistical Method from the Viewpoint of Quality Control,* consisting of a series of four lectures delivered by Shewhart during the previous year at the Graduate School of the Department of Agriculture. Deming and Juran are credited with taking these

---

[1]Society of Automotive Engineers, *Quality Control in Manufacturing*, Warrendale, PA, 1981.

concepts to Japan and fueling Japanese industry's emergence as a powerful competitor in the global marketplace. The Deming Prize, awarded in Japan to individuals and companies for accomplishment in statistical theory and application, was instituted "in commemoration of [Deming's] contributions to Japanese industry," according to Kenichi Kayanagi. Deming went beyond Shewhart's statistical approach ["He that starts with statistical methods alone will not be here in three years [2]] to develop a comprehensive philosophy of management. This philosophy is embodied in his fourteen points and seven deadly diseases.

Juran gained widespread recognition somewhat earlier (early 1970s) than Deming (early 1980s) by modern quality practitioners in the United States who used his *Quality Control Handbook* and read his articles in the early volumes of *Quality Progress*. In his Juran [Quality] Trilogy® he adapted the processes used to manage for finance for use to manage for quality.

Feigenbaum is credited with developing the concept of total quality control (TQC). He began developing the TQC concept as "Modern Quality Control" in the 1951 book *Quality Control Principles, Practice, and Administration.* He expanded this early concept in the *Harvard Business Review* article, "Total Quality Control" and in his later book, *Total Quality Control: Engineering and Management.*

Shingo was first exposed to the concepts of statistical quality control in Japan in 1951. He later developed the single-minute exchange of die (SMED) and poka-yoke concepts at Toyota Motor Co. in Japan and contributed to the development of the concept of zero quality control. Shingo has been invited to the United States on a number of occasions to discuss his concepts and to "help [U.S. companies] search for ways to improve the efficiency of their production systems." The English translation of his book, *Zero Quality Control: Source Inspection and the Poka-yoke System*, is a detailed accounting of the development and use of his quality assurance concepts in Japan.

Crosby, while at Martin Marietta Corporation's Martin Company, participated in the development of the Zero Defects Program which he later popularized in his book, *Quality is Free*. Zero defects is a cornerstone of Crosby's fourteen step quality program. Garvin contributed to the new definition of product quality as a multidimensional concept in his articles, "What Does Product Quality Really Mean?" and "Competing on the Eight Dimensions of Quality."

Genichi Taguchi developed a new approach to design of experiments (DOE) for robust product/process design as well as developing the concept of the Loss Function. Although Taguchi's name is notably absent from the list of classic contributors determined by the survey, several of Taguchi's works are included in the bibliography.

An analysis of the survey data for these seven classic contributors in the quality field indicates that the POM professionals who participated in the survey that

---

[2]M. Walton. *The Deming Management Method* (New York: Perigee Books, 1986), 33.

identified them as classic contributors feel that there are degrees of "classicness." Analysis of the mean scores in Table 3–1 indicate three levels which we shall refer to as Type I, Type II, and Type III.

While there is overlap among these levels, as illustrated in Figure 3–1, there is justification for assigning each of the seven classic contributors to a specific level.

TABLE 3–1   SURVEY SCORES FOR CLASSIC CONTRIBUTORS

The survey score denotes the degree of agreement with the following statement: This person is a classic contributor to the field of POM. A score of 3 indicated No Opinion; a score of 4 indicated Agree Somewhat; a score of 5 indicated Agree.

CONTRIBUTOR	MEAN SCORE	STANDARD DEVIATION
Deming	4.50	1.01
Juran	4.15	1.14
Shewhart	3.87	1.21
Feigenbaum	3.67	1.18
Shingo	3.67	1.20
Crosby	3.38	1.09
Garvin	3.26	0.09

FIGURE 3–1   CURRENT CLASSIFICATIONS OF CLASSIC CONTRIBUTORS—QUALITY

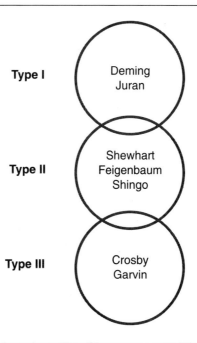

Assignment to a specific level does not represent a hierarchy of relative merit of the contributions made by the individual, rather it represents the current classification of that individual's contribution relative to other classic contributors in the minds of today's POM professionals.

The work of two classic contributors, Crosby and Shingo, is not included in this chapter because their work is primarily published in book form rather than in article form. Books by these classic contributors are included in the bibliography at the end of the chapter.

EXCERPTS FROM *ECONOMIC CONTROL OF QUALITY OF MANUFACTURED PRODUCT*

WALTER A. SHEWHART

PREFACE

Broadly speaking, the object of industry is to set up economic ways and means of satisfying human wants and in so doing to reduce everything possible to routines requiring a minimum amount of human effort. Through the use of the scientific method, extended to take account of modern statistical concepts, it has been found possible to set up limits within which the results of routine efforts must lie if they are to be economical. Deviations in the results of a routine process outside such limits indicate that the routine has broken down and will no longer be economical until the cause of trouble is removed.

This book is the natural outgrowth of an investigation started some six years ago to develop a scientific basis for attaining economic control of quality of manufactured product through the establishment of control limits to indicate at every stage in the production process from raw materials to finished product when the quality of product is varying more than is economically desirable. As such, this book constitutes a record of progress and an indication of the direction in which future developments may be expected to take place.

CHARACTERISTICS OF A CONTROLLED QUALITY

1. WHAT IS THE PROBLEM OF CONTROL?

What is the problem of control of quality of manufactured product? To answer this question, let us put ourselves in the position of a manufacturer

Excerpt from *Economic Control of Manufactured Product* (New York: D. Van Nostrand Co., Inc., 1931).

turning out millions of the same kind of thing every year. Whether it be lead pencils, chewing gum, bars of soap, telephones, or automobiles, the problem is much the same. He sets up a standard for the quality of a given kind of product. He then tries to make all pieces of product conform with this standard. Here his troubles begin. For him standard quality is a bull's-eye, but like a marksman shooting at a bull's-eye, he often misses. As is the case in everything we do, unknown or chance causes exert their influence. The problem then is: how much may the quality of a product vary and yet be controlled? In other words, how much variation should we leave to chance?

To make a thing the way we want to make it is one popular conception of control. We have been trying to do this for a good many years and we see the fruition of this effort in the marvelous industrial development around us. We are sold on the idea of applying scientific principles. However, a change is coming about in the principles themselves and this change gives us a new concept of control.

A few years ago we were inclined to look forward to the time when a manufacturer would be able to do just what he wanted to do. We shared the enthusiasm of Pope when he said "All chance is but direction thou canst not see," and we looked forward to the time when we would see that direction. In other words, emphasis was laid on the *exactness* of physical laws. Today, however, the emphasis is placed elsewhere as is indicated by the following quotation from a recent issue, July, 1927, of the journal *Engineering*:

> Today the mathematical physicist seems more and more inclined to the opinion that each of the so-called laws of nature is essentially statistical, and that all our equations and theories can do, is to provide us with a series of orbits of varying probabilities.

The breakdown of the orthodox scientific theory which formed the basis of applied science in the past necessitates the introduction of certain new concepts into industrial development. Along with this change must come a revision in our ideas of such things as a controlled product, an economic standard of quality, and the method of detecting lack of control or those variations which should not be left to chance.

Realizing, then, the statistical nature of modern science, it is but logical for the manufacturer to turn his attention to the consideration of available ways and means of handling statistical problems. The necessity for doing this is pointed out in the recent book[1] on the application of statistics in mass production, by Becker, Plaut, and Runge. They say:

---

[1]Julius Springer, *Anwendungen der Mathematischen Statistik auf Probleme der Massenfabrikation* (Berlin, 1927).

It is therefore important to every technician who is dealing with problems of manufacturing control to know the laws of statistics and to be able to apply them correctly to his problems.

Another German writer, K. H. Daeves, in writing on somewhat the same subject says:

> Statistical research is a logical method for the control of operations, for the research engineer, the plant superintendent, and the production executive. [2]

The problem of control viewed from this angle is a comparatively new one. In fact, very little has been written on the subject. Progress in modifying our concept of control has been and will be comparatively slow. In the first place, it requires the application of certain modern physical concepts; and in the second place, it requires the application of statistical methods which up to the present time have been for the most part left undisturbed in the journals in which they appeared. This situation is admirably summed up in the January, 1926 issue of *Nature* as follows:

> A large amount of work has been done in developing statistical methods on the scientific side, and it is natural for anyone interested in science to hope that all this work may be utilized in commerce and industry. There are signs that such a movement has started, and it would be unfortunate indeed if those responsible in practical affairs fail to take advantage of the improved statistical machinery now available.

2. NATURE OF CONTROL

Let us consider a very simple example of our inability to do exactly what we want to do and thereby illustrate two characteristics of a controlled product.

Write the letter *a* on a piece of paper. Now make another *a* just like the first one; then another and another until you have a series of *a*'s, *a, a, a, a,*... You try to make all the *a*'s alike but you don't; you can't. You are willing to accept this as an empirically established fact. But what of it? Let us see just what this means in respect to control. Why can we not do a simple thing like making all the *a*'s just alike? Your answer leads to a generalization which all of us are perhaps willing to accept. It is that there are many causes of variability among the *a*'s: the paper was not smooth, the lead in the pencil was not uniform, and the unavoidable variability in your

---

[2] "The Utilization of Statistics," *Testing*, March, 1924.

external surroundings reacted upon you to introduce variations in the a's. But are these the only causes of variability in the a's? Probably not.

We accept our human limitations and say that likely there are many other factors. If we could but name all the reasons why we cannot make the a's alike, we would most assuredly have a better understanding of a certain part of nature than we now have. Of course, this conception of what it means to be able to do what we want to do is not new; it does not belong exclusively to any one field of human thought; it is commonly accepted.

The point to be made in this simple illustration is that we are limited in doing what we want to do; that to do what we set out to do, even in so simple a thing as making a's that are alike, requires almost infinite knowledge compared with that which we now possess. It follows, therefore, since we are thus willing to accept as axiomatic that we cannot do what we want to do and cannot hope to understand why we cannot, that we must also accept as axiomatic that a controlled quality will not be a constant quality. Instead, a controlled quality must be a *variable* quality. This is the first characteristic.

But let us go back to the results of the experiment on the a's and we shall find out something more about control. Your a's are different from my a's; there is something about your a's that makes them yours and something about my a's that makes them mine. True, not all of your a's are alike. Neither are all of my a's alike. Each group of a's varies within a certain range and yet each group is distinguishable from the others. This distinguishable and, as it were, constant variability *within limits* is the second characteristic of control.

3. Definition of Control

For our present purpose *a phenomenon will be said to be controlled when, through the use of past experience, we can predict at least within limits, how the phenomenon may be expected to vary in the future. Here it is understood that prediction within limits means that we can state, at least approximately, the probability that the observed phenomenon will fall within the given limits.*

In this sense the time of the eclipse of the sun is a predictable phenomenon. So also is the distance covered in successive intervals of time by a freely falling body. In fact, the prediction in such cases is extremely precise. It is an entirely different matter, however, to predict the expected length of life of an individual at a given age; the velocity of a molecule at a given instant of time; the breaking strength of a steel wire of known cross section; or numerous other phenomena of like character. In fact, a prediction of the type illustrated by forecasting the time of an eclipse of the sun is almost the exception rather than the rule in scientific and industrial work.

In all forms of prediction an element of chance enters. The specific problem which concerns us at the present moment is the formulation of a scientific basis for prediction, taking into account the element of chance, where, for the purpose of our discussion, *any unknown cause of a phenomenon will be termed a cause.*

SCIENTIFIC BASIS FOR CONTROL

1. THREE IMPORTANT POSTULATES

What can we say about the future behavior of a phenomenon acting under the influence of unknown or chance causes? I doubt that, in general, we can say anything. For example, let me ask: "What will be the price of your favorite stock thirty years from today?" Are you willing to gamble much on your powers of prediction in such a case? Probably not. However, if I ask: "Suppose you were to toss a penny one hundred times, thirty years from today, what proportion of heads would you expect to find?", your willingness to gamble on your powers of prediction would be of an entirely different order than in the previous case.

The recognized difference between these two situations leads us to make the following simple postulate:

Postulate 1—All chance systems of causes are not alike in the sense that they enable us to predict the future in terms of the past.

Hence, if we are to be able to predict the quality of product even within limits, we must find some criterion to apply to observed variability in quality to determine whether or not the cause system producing it is such as to make future predictions possible.

Postulate 2—Constant systems of chance causes do exist in nature.

To say that such systems of causes exist in nature, however, is one thing; to say that such systems of causes exist in a production process is quite another thing. Today we have abundant evidence of the existence of such systems of causes in the production of telephone equipment. The practical situation, however, is that in the majority of cases there are unknown causes of variability in the quality of a product which do not belong to a constant system. This fact was discovered very early in the development of control methods, and these causes were called *assignable*. The question naturally arose as to whether it was possible, in general, to find and eliminate such causes. Less than ten years ago it seemed reasonable to assume that this could be done. Today we have abundant evidence to justify this assumption. We shall, therefore, adopt as our third postulate:

Postulate 3—Assignable causes of variation may be found and eliminated.

Hence, to secure control, the manufacturer must seek to find and eliminate assignable causes. In practice, however, he has the difficulty of judging from an observed set of data whether or not assignable causes are present. A simple illustration will make this point clear.

2. WHEN DO FLUCTUATIONS INDICATE TROUBLE?

In many instances the quality of the product is measured by the fraction nonconforming to engineering specifications or, as we say, the fraction defective.

What we need is some yardstick to detect in such variations any evidence of the presence of assignable causes. Can we find such a yardstick? Experience of the kind soon to be considered indicates that we can. It leads us to conclude that it is feasible to establish criteria useful in detecting the presence of assignable causes of variation or, in other words, criteria which when applied to a set of observed values will indicate whether or not it is reasonable to believe that the causes of variability should be left to chance. Such criteria are basic to any method of securing control within limits. Let us, therefore, consider them critically. It is too much to expect that the criteria will be infallible. We are amply rewarded if they appear to work in the majority of cases.

Generally speaking, the criteria are of the nature of limits derived from past experience showing within what range the fluctuations in quality should remain, if they are to be left to chance. For example, when such limits are placed on the fluctuations in the qualities shown in Figure 3,* we find, as shown in Figure 4, that in one case two points fall outside the limits and in the other case no point falls outside the limits.

Upon the basis of the use of such limits, we look for trouble in the form of assignable causes in one case but not in the other.

However, the question remains: Should we expect to be able to find and eliminate causes of variability only when deviations fall outside the limits? First, let us see what statistical theory has to say in answer to this question.

Upon the basis of Postulate 3, it follows that we can find and remove causes of variability until the remaining system of causes is constant or until we reach that state where the probability that the deviations in quality remain

---

*Figures in this article do not appear in a sequential numerical order as this article is not printed in its entirety—EDITOR.

| **FIGURE 4** | **SHOULD THESE VARIATIONS BE LEFT TO CHANCE?** |

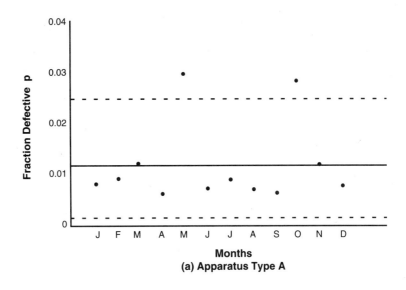

(a) Apparatus Type A

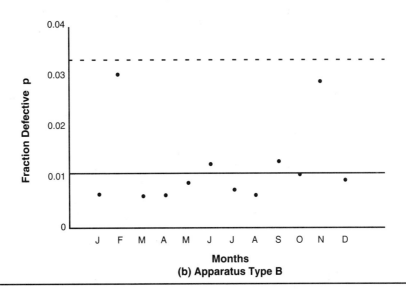

(b) Apparatus Type B

within any two fixed limits (Fig. 5) is constant. However, this assumption alone does not tell us that there are certain limits within which all observed values of quality should remain provided the causes cannot be found and eliminated. In fact, as long as the limits are set so that the probability of falling

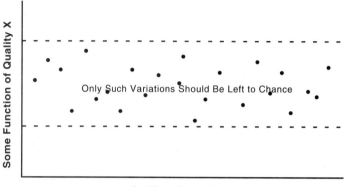

within the limits is less than unity, we may always expect a certain percentage of observations to fall outside the limits even though the system of causes be constant. In other words, the acceptance of this assumption gives us a right to believe that there is an objective state of control within limits but in itself it does not furnish a practical criterion for determining when variations in quality, such as those indicated in Figure 3, should be left to chance.

Furthermore, we may say that mathematical statistics as such does not give us the desired criterion. What does this situation mean in plain everyday engineering English? Simply this: such criteria, it they exist, cannot be shown to exist by any theorizing alone, no matter how well equipped the theorist is in respect to probability or statistical theory. We see in this situation the long recognized dividing line between theory and practice. The available statistical machinery referred to by the magazine *Nature* is as we might expect, not an end in itself but merely a means to an end. In other words, the fact that the criterion which we happen to use has a fine ancestry of highbrow statistical theorems does not justify its use. Such justification must come from empirical evidence that it works. As the practical engineer might say, the proof of the pudding is in the eating. Let us therefore look for the proof.

3. EVIDENCE THAT CRITERIA EXIST FOR DETECTING ASSIGNABLE CAUSES

A. Figure 6 shows the results of one of the first large scale experiments to determine whether or not indications given by such a criterion applied to

| **FIGURE 6** | EVIDENCE OF IMPROVEMENT IN QUALITY WITH APPROACH TO CONTROL |

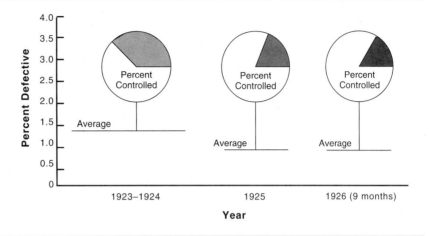

quality measured in terms of fraction defective were justified by experience. About thirty typical items used in the telephone plant and produced in lots running into the millions per year were made the basis for this study. As shown in this figure, during 1923–24 these items showed 68 percent control about a relatively low average of 1.4 percent defective.[3] However, as the assignable causes, indicated by deviations in the observed monthly fraction defective falling outside of control limits, were found and eliminated, the quality of product approached the state of control as indicated by an increase of from 68 percent to 84 percent control by the latter part of 1926. At the same time the quality improved; in 1923–24 the average percent defective was 1.4 percent, whereas by 1926 this had been reduced to 0.8 percent. Here we get some typical evidence that, in general, as the assignable causes are removed, the variations tend to fall more nearly within the limits as indicated by an increase from 68 percent to 84 percent. Such evidence is, of course, one sided. It shows that when points fall outside the limits, experience indicates that we can find assignable causes, but it does not indicate that when points fall within such limits, we cannot find causes of variability. However, this kind of evidence is provided by the following two typical illustrations.

B. In the production of a certain kind of equipment, considerable cost was involved in securing the necessary electrical insulation by means of materials previously used for that purpose. A research program was started to secure a cheaper material. After a long series of preliminary experiments, a

---

[3]R. L. Jones, "Quality of Telephone Materials," *Bell Telephone Quarterly,* June 1927.

TABLE 2			ELECTRICAL RESISTANCE OF INSULATION IN MEGOHMS—SHOULD SUCH VARIATIONS BE LEFT TO CHANCE?								
5,045	4,635	4,700	4,650	4,640	3,940	4,570	4,560	4,450	4,500	5,075	4,500
4,350	5,100	4,600	4,170	4,335	3,700	4,570	3,075	4,450	4,770	4,925	4,850
4,350	5,450	4,110	4,255	5,000	3,650	4,855	2,965	4,850	5,150	5,075	4,930
3,975	4,635	4,410	4,170	4,615	4,445	4,160	4,080	4,450	4,850	4,925	4,700
4,290	4,720	4,180	4,375	4,215	4,000	4,325	4,080	3,635	4,700	5,250	4,890
4,430	4,810	4,790	4,175	4,275	4,845	4,125	4,425	3,635	5,000	4,915	4,625
4,485	4,565	4,790	4,550	4,275	5,000	4,100	4,300	3,635	5,000	5,600	4,425
4,285	4,410	4,340	4,450	5,000	4,560	4,340	4,430	3,900	5,000	5,075	4,135
3,980	4,065	4,895	2,855	4,615	4,700	4,575	4,840	4,340	4,700	4,450	4,190
3,925	4,565	5,750	2,920	4,735	4,310	3,875	4,840	4,340	4,500	4,215	4,080
3,645	5,190	4,740	4,375	4,215	4,310	4,050	4,310	3,665	4,840	4,325	3,690
3,760	4,725	5,000	4,375	4,700	5,000	4,050	4,185	3,775	5,075	4,665	5,050
3,300	4,640	4,895	4,355	4,700	4,575	4,685	4,570	5,000	5,000	4,615	4,625
3,685	4,640	4,255	4,090	4,700	4,700	4,685	4,700	4,850	4,770	4,615	5,150
3,463	4,895	4,170	5,000	4,700	4,430	4,430	4,440	4,775	4,570	4,500	5,250
5,200	4,790	3,850	4,335	4,095	4,850	4,300	4,850	4,500	4,925	4,765	5,000
5,100	4,845	4,445	5,000	4,095	4,850	4,690	4,125	4,770	4,775	4,500	5,000

tentative substitute was chosen and an extensive series of tests of insulation resistance were made on this material, care being taken to eliminate all known causes of variability. Table 2 gives the results of 204 observations of resistance in megohms taken on as many samples of the proposed substitute material. Reading from top to bottom beginning at the left column and continuing throughout the table gives the order in which the observations were made. The question is: "Should such variations be left to chance?"

No *a priori* reason existed for believing that the measurements forming one portion of this series should be different from those in any other portion. In other words, there was no rational basis for dividing the total set of data into groups of a given number of observations except that it was reasonable to believe that the system of causes might have changed from day to day as a result of changes in such things as atmospheric conditions, observers, and materials. In general, if such changes are to take place, we may readily detect their effect if we divide the total number of observations into comparatively small subgroups. In this particular instance, the size of the subgroup was taken as four and the black dots in Figure 7-a show the successive averages of four observations in the order in which they were taken. The dotted lines are the limits within which experience has shown that these observations should fall, taking into account the size of the sample, provided the variability should be left to chance. Several of the observed values lie outside these limits. This was taken as an indication of the existence of causes of variability which could be found and eliminated.

| FIGURE 7 | SHOULD THESE VARIATIONS BE LEFT TO CHANCE? |

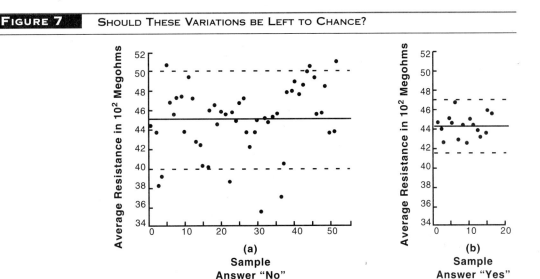

(a)
Sample
Answer "No"

(b)
Sample
Answer "Yes"

Further research was instituted at this point to find these causes of variability. Several were found, and after these had been eliminated another series of observed values gave the results indicated in Figure 7-b. Here we see that all of the points lie within the limits. We assumed, therefore, upon the basis of this test, that it was not feasible for research to go much further in eliminating causes of variability. Because of the importance of this particular experiment, however, considerably more work was done, but it failed to reveal causes of variability. Here then is a typical case where the criterion indicates when variability should be left to chance.

C. Suppose now that we take another illustration where it is reasonable to believe that almost everything humanly possible has been done to remove the assignable causes of variation in a set of data. Perhaps the outstanding series of observations of this type is that given by Millikan in his famous measurement of the charge on an electron. Treating his data in a manner similar to that indicated above, we get the results shown in Figure 8. All of the points are within the dotted limits. Hence the indication of the test is consistent with the accepted conclusion that those factors which need not be left to chance had been eliminated before this particular set of data were taken.

4. ROLE PLAYED BY STATISTICAL THEORY

It may appear thus far that mathematical statistics plays a relatively minor role in laying a basis for economic control of quality. Such, however, is not the case. In fact, a central concept in engineering work today is that almost every

---

FIGURE 8 VARIATIONS THAT SHOULD BE LEFT TO CHANCE—DOES THE CRITERION WORK? "YES."

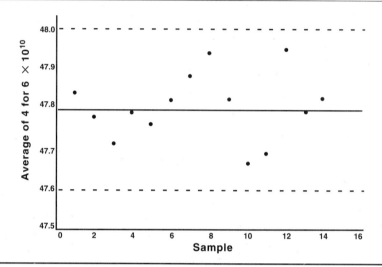

physical property is a *statistical distribution*. In other words, an observed set of data constitutes a sample of the effects of unknown chance causes. It is at once apparent, therefore, that sampling theory should prove a valuable tool in testing engineering hypotheses. Here it is that much of the most recent mathematical theory becomes of value, particularly in analysis involving the use of comparatively small numbers of observations.

5. CONCLUSION

Based upon evidence such as already presented, it appears feasible to set up criteria by which to determine when assignable causes of variation in quality have been eliminated so that the product may then be considered to be controlled within limits. This state of control appears to be, in general, a kind of limit to which we may expect to go economically in finding and removing causes of variability without changing a major portion of the manufacturing process as, for example, would be involved in the substitution of new materials or designs.

ADVANTAGES SECURED THROUGH CONTROL

I. REDUCTION IN THE COST OF INSPECTION

If we can be assured that something we use is produced under controlled conditions, we do not feel the need for inspecting it as much as we would if we did not have this assurance.

In the early stages of production there are usually causes of variability which must be weeded out through the process of inspection. As we proceed to eliminate assignable causes, the quality of product usually approaches a state of stable equilibrium somewhat after the manner of the two specific illustrations presented in Figure 11. In both instances, the record goes back for more than two years and the process of elimination in each case covers a period of more than a year.

It is evident that as the quality approaches what appears to be a comparatively stable state, the need for inspection is reduced.

2. Reduction in the Cost of Rejections

It may be shown theoretically that, by eliminating assignable causes of variability, we arrive at a limit to which it is feasible to go in reducing the fraction defective. It must suffice here to call attention to the kind of evidence indicating that this limiting situation is actually approached in practice as we remove the assignable causes of variability.

Let us refer again to Figure 6 which is particularly significant because it represents the results of a large scale experiment carried on under commercial conditions. As the black sectors in the pie charts decrease in size, indicating progress in the removal of assignable causes, we find simultaneously a decrease in the average percent defective from 1.4 to 0.8. Here we see how control works to reduce the amount of defective material.

3. Attainment of Maximum Benefits from Quantity Production

The quality of the finished product depends upon the qualities of raw materials, piece-parts, and the assembling process. It follows from theory that so long as such quality characteristics are controlled, the quality of the finished unit will be controlled, and will therefore exhibit minimum variability. Other advantages also result. For example, by gaining control, it is possible, as we have already seen, to establish standard statistical distributions for the many quality characteristics involved in design.

Suppose we consider a simple problem in which we assume that the quality characteristic Y in the finished product is a function f of m different quality characteristics, $X_1, X_2, \ldots, X_m$, representable symbolically by

$$Y = f(X_1, X_2, \ldots, X_m).$$

If, for example, it is desirable to minimize the variability in the resultant quality Y by proper choice of materials, and if standard distribution functions for the given quality characteristics are available for each of several

---

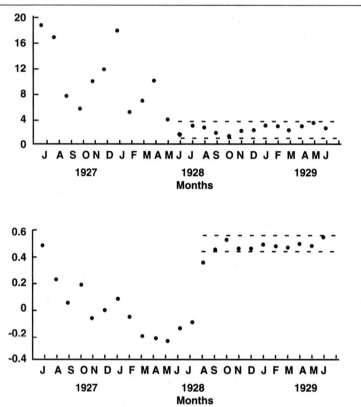

materials, it is possible to choose that particular material which will minimize the variability of the resultant quality at a minimum of cost.

4. ATTAINMENT OF UNIFORM QUALITY EVEN THOUGH INSPECTION TEST IS DESTRUCTIVE

So often the quality of a material of the greatest importance to the individual is one which cannot be measured directly without destroying the material itself. How are we to know that a product which cannot be tested in respect to a given quality is satisfactory in respect to this same quality? How are we to know that the fuse will not blow at a given current; that the steering rod of your car will not break under maximum load placed upon it? To answer such questions, we must rely upon previous experience. In such a case, causes of variation in quality are unknown and yet we are concerned in assuring ourselves that the quality is satisfactory.

Enough has been said to show that here is one of the very important applications of the theory of control. By weeding out assignable causes of variability, the manufacturer goes to the feasible limit in assuring uniform quality.

5. REDUCTION IN TOLERANCE LIMITS

By securing control and by making use of modern statistical tools, the manufacturer not only is able to assure quality even though it cannot be measured directly, but is also often able to reduce the tolerance limits in that quality as one very simple illustration will serve to indicate.

6. CONCLUSION

It seems reasonable to believe that there is an *objective state of control,* making possible the prediction of quality within limits even though the causes of variability are unknown. Evidence has been given to indicate that through the use of statistical machinery in the hands of an engineer artful in making the right kind of hypotheses, it appears possible to establish criteria which indicate when the state of control has been reached. It has been pointed out that by securing control, we can secure the following advantages:

1. Reduction in the cost of inspection.
2. Reduction in the cost of rejection.
3. Attainment of maximum benefits from quantity production.
4. Attainment of uniform quality even though the inspection test is destructive.
5. Reduction in tolerance limits where quality measurement is indirect.

DEFINITION OF QUALITY

I. INTRODUCTORY NOTE

When we analyze our conception of quality, we find that the term is used in several different ways. Hence, it is essential that we decide, first of all, whether the discussion is to be limited to a particular concept of quality, or to be so framed as to include the essential element in each of the numerous conceptions. One purpose in considering the various definitions of quality is merely to show that in any case the measure of quality is a quantity which may take on different numerical values. In other words, the measure of quality, no matter what the definition of quality may be, is a variable.

2. HOW SHALL QUALITY BE DEFINED?

If we are to talk intelligently about the quality of a thing or the quality of a product, we must have in mind a clear picture of what we mean by quality. Enough has been said to indicate that there are two common aspects of quality. One of these has to do with the consideration of the quality of a thing as an *objective* reality independent of the existence of man. The other has to do with what we think, feel, or sense as a result of the objective reality. In other words, there is a *subjective* side of quality. For example, we are dealing with the subjective concept of quality when we attempt to measure the goodness of a thing, for it is impossible to think of a thing as having goodness independent of some human want. In fact, this subjective concept of quality is closely tied up with the utility or value of the objective physical properties of the thing itself.

For the most part we may think of the objective quality characteristics of a thing as being constant and measurable in the sense that physical laws are quantitatively expressible and independent of time. When we consider a quality from the subjective viewpoint, comparatively serious difficulties arise. To begin with, there are various aspects of the concept of value. We may differentiate between the following four [4] kinds of value:

1. Use
2. Cost
3. Esteem
4. Exchange

For example, although the air we breathe is useful, it does not have cost or exchange value, and until we are deprived of it we do not esteem it highly.

Although the use value remains comparatively fixed, we find that the significance of cost, esteem, and exchange values are relative and subject to wide variation. Furthermore, we do not have any universally accepted measures of such values. Our division of several different things of a given kind into two classes, good and bad, necessitates a quantitative, *fixed* measure which we do not have in the case of subjective value.

From the viewpoint of control of quality in manufacture, it is necessary to establish standards of quality in a quantitative manner. For this reason we

---

[4]For a thorough discussion of this division of economic value see C. M. Walsh, *The Four Kinds of Economic Value* (Cambridge: Harvard University Press, 1926).

are forced at the present time to express such standards, insofar as possible, in terms of quantitatively measurable physical properties. This does not mean, however, that the subjective measure of quality is not of interest. On the contrary, it is the subjective measure that is of commercial interest. It is this subjective side that we have in mind when we say that the standards of living have changed.

Looked at broadly, there are at a given time certain human wants to be fulfilled through the fabrication of raw materials into finished products of different kinds. These wants are statistical in nature in that the quality of a finished product in terms of the physical characteristics wanted by one individual is not the same for all individuals. The first step of the engineer in trying to satisfy these wants is, therefore, that of translating as nearly as possible these wants into the physical characteristics of the thing manufactured to satisfy these wants. In taking this step intuition and judgment play an important role as well as the broad knowledge of the human element involved in the wants of individuals. The second step of the engineer is to set up ways and means of obtaining a product which will differ from the arbitrarily set standards for these quality characteristics by no more than may be left to chance.

The discussion of the economic control of quality of manufactured product in this book is limited to this second step. The broader concept of economic control naturally includes the problem of continually shifting the standards expressed in terms of measurable physical properties to meet best the shifting economic value of these particular physical characteristics depending upon shifting human wants.

It seems reasonable to draw the following conclusions:

A. It is not feasible to make pieces of product identical one with another. Hence a controlled product must be one of variable quality.

B. To be able to say that a product is controlled, we must be able to predict, at least within limits, the future variations in the quality.

C. To be able to make such predictions, it is necessary that we know certain laws.

D. These laws may be exact, empirical, or statistical. Exact laws are generally stated in terms of the differential equations of physics and chemistry. Statistical laws are the frequency distributions arising from the very general law of large numbers. All other laws are empirical. The technique of finding and using exact and statistical laws is better established than that of finding and using what we term empirical laws.

STATISTICAL CONTROL

I. CONDITIONS FOR CONTROL

If there is a causal orderliness in events and phenomena as we postulate, then it follows that, to one with perfect knowledge, everything is predictable and therefore controlled. However, for practical purposes the quality of product is controlled only to the extent that we know the laws that make prediction possible. For one to be able to say that a phenomenon is controlled, it is necessary and sufficient that he know the laws which make prediction possible.

In practice, however, we must start with an observed set of data representing the fluctuations in some phenomenon and try to determine from these whether or not the product is controlled. Such a procedure involves, as do all scientific attempts to discover natural laws, logical induction in that we must employ some such argument as this: Since the observed fluctuations are such as might have occurred provided the phenomenon obeyed such and such laws, then it follows that these laws do control this phenomenon; whereas all that we are rigorously justified in saying is that these laws *may* control this phenomenon. For this reason we perhaps never can say that the behavior of a phenomenon in the past is sufficient to prove that the phenomenon is controlled by a given set of known laws. All that we can ever say is that experience has shown that such behavior appears to be sufficient.

Furthermore it is a significant fact, as we have seen in the previous chapter, that empirical laws do not make possible the prediction of erratic fluctuations upon the basis of probability theory. If product is controlled only in this empirical sense, it follows that we cannot obtain the economic advantages discussed in Part I. For this reason it is desirable to attain the state of statistical control in which the natural law of large numbers makes prediction possible.

2. NECESSARY AND SUFFICIENT CONDITIONS FOR STATISTICAL CONTROL

We shall assume that the necessary and sufficient condition for statistical control is that the causes of an event satisfy the law of large numbers as do those of a constant system of chance causes. If a cause system is not constant, we shall say that an *assignable cause of Type I* is present. Assignable causes of this type in an economic series are such things as trends, cycles, and seasonals; and in a production process, they are such things as differences in machines and in sources of raw material.

Stated in terms of effects of a cause system, it is necessary that differences in the qualities of a number of pieces of a product *appear* to be consistent with the assumption that they arose from a constant system of chance causes.

We say appear because, as is always the case in trying to find a law controlling a phenomenon, we can never be sure that we have discovered the law. Obviously such appearance is not sufficient in the logical sense although it must be in the practical sense.

3. Necessary and Sufficient Conditions— Continued

Let us see how the law of large numbers gives a basis for determining from the observed fluctuations in a phenomenon whether or not it is statistically controlled. For this purpose let us consider the practical problem presented in Part I, Chapter II, Paragraph 2.

If this product is statistically controlled, there is an objective probability **p** that a piece of this product will be defective. It follows, as we have seen in our previous discussion of experimental evidence for the existence of the law of large numbers, that the observed fractions defective in successive samples of size n should be clustered or distributed about the value $p = \mathbf{p}$ in accord with the terms of the point binomial $(q+p)^n$.

Graphically this means that, if we take the observed values of the fraction defective p as ordinances and a series of numbers corresponding to a sequence of samples of size n as abscissae, the observed fractions should be distributed about the ordinate **p** after the manner indicated schematically in Figure 51.

The frequency distribution of values of p observed in an infinite sequence of samples of size n should be some curve such as that indicated at the right of the figure. This is the picture of what happens in this very simple case deduced from the postulated law of large numbers.

The practical problem involves induction instead of deduction. We start with a sequence of observed values of the fraction defective, and from this we try to determine whether or not the quality as measured by fraction defective is statistically controlled. As indicated in part I, the method of attack is to establish limits of variability of p represented by the dotted lines parallel to the line $p = \mathbf{p}$ in Figure 51, such that, when a fraction defective is found outside these limits, looking for an assignable cause is worthwhile.

How to establish these limits is the question of utmost importance, because it must be satisfactorily answered if statistical control of a production process is to be a practical objective. Experience like that presented in Part I leads us to believe that it is feasible to establish workable rules for setting these limits. These rules will be presented in Part VI. For the present we shall confine our attention to a consideration of some of the fundamental problems which must be considered in the establishment of a scientific basis for setting such limits.

A. Obviously, it is not possible to observe an infinite sequence in order to discover the objective probability **p** even though it exists and is discoverable in this way. In practice, therefore, we must substitute some experimentally determined value for the objective value **p**.

B. Assuming for the sake of argument that in some manner we have found the true objective value **p**, it follows from what has previously been said that, no matter how we set the limits about the line $p = \mathbf{p}$ (so long as they are not outside the limits of the frequency distribution at the right of Fig. 51), some of the observed fractions will fall outside these limits. Therefore, if we look for trouble in the form of assignable causes of Type I every time an observed fraction falls outside these limits, we shall look a certain number of times even though none exists. Hence we must use limits such that through their use we will not waste too much time looking unnecessarily for trouble.

C. The fact that an observed set of values of fraction defective indicates the product to have been controlled up to the present does not prove that we can predict the future course of this phenomenon. We always have to say that this can be done provided the same essential conditions are maintained, and, of course, we never know whether or not they are maintained unless we continue to experiment. If experience were not available to show that a state of statistical equilibrium once reached is usually maintained, we could not attain most of the economic advantages of Part I. Evidence of the type given in Figures 6 and 11 seems to justify our belief in the constancy of the condition of statistical equilibrium when it is once attained, subject to the limitation that there is no *a priori* reason for believing that an assignable cause has entered the production process.

FIGURE 51	SCHEMATIC OF OBJECTIVE CONDITION

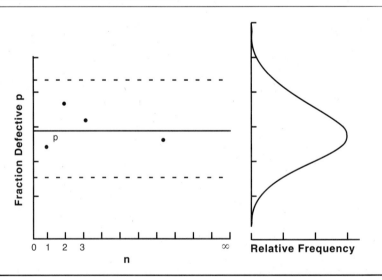

DETECTION OF LACK OF CONTROL IN RESPECT TO STANDARD QUALITY

I. THE PROBLEM

In Part V we saw that standard quality is characterized by the equation of control

$$dy = f(X, \lambda_1, \lambda_2, \ldots, \lambda i \ldots, \lambda_{m'}) dX. \quad (58)$$

In particular, we saw that it is desirable to maintain constancy of this distribution at least in respect to the average $\overline{X}$ and standard deviation σ. Of course the qualities of samples of n pieces of product of standard quality may be expected to show sampling fluctuations.

The problem to be considered in this chapter is that of establishing an efficient method for detecting the presence of a cause of variability other than one of the chance causes belonging to the group which gives the accepted standard distribution (58), or of determining when an observed sample is such that it is unlikely that it came from a constant cause system characterized by this distribution.

5. ADDITIONAL REASON FOR CHOOSING THE AVERAGE $\overline{X}$ AND STANDARD DEVIATION σ

We are now in a place to consider an additional and very important reason for choosing the average $\overline{X}$ of a sample to detect a change $\Delta\overline{X}$ and the standard deviation σ to detect a change $\Delta\sigma$. The previous discussion has been limited to the assumption that the universe or distribution (58) of standard quality is normal.

In Part IV, however, we saw that, no matter what the nature of the distribution function (58) of the quality is, the distribution function of the arithmetic mean approaches normality rapidly with increase in n, and in all cases the expected value of means of samples of n is the same as the expected value $\overline{X}$ of the universe. Hence the arithmetic mean is usable for detecting a change $\Delta\overline{X}$ almost equally well for any universe of effects which we are likely to meet in practice. It appears that the same cannot be said of any other known statistic.

We also saw in Part IV that, although the distribution function $f_\sigma(\sigma, n)$ of the standard deviation σ of samples of n is not known for other than the normal universe, nevertheless the moments of the distribution of variance σ^2 are known in terms of the moments of the universe. Hence we can always establish limits

$$\sigma^2 \pm \iota \sigma_{\sigma^2}$$

within which the observed variance in samples of size n should fall more than

$$100\left(1 - \tfrac{I}{t^2}\right)$$

percent of the total number of times a sample of n is chosen, so long as the quality of product is controlled in accord with the accepted standard.

This generality of usefulness is not shared by any other known estimate of σ or, more specifically, of σ^2.

THE CONTROL PROGRAM

1. RÉSUMÉ

Five important economic reasons for controlling the quality of manufactured product were considered in Part 1. In Chapter XXI of Part VI, we saw that, from the viewpoint of consumer protection, it is also advantageous to have attained the state of control. If only to assure the satisfactory nature of quality of product which cannot be given 100 percent inspection, the need for control would doubtless be admitted.

In a very general sense, we have seen that the scientific interpretation and use of data depend to a large extent upon whether or not the data satisfy the condition of control (58). The statistical nature of things and of relationships or natural laws puts in the foreground this concept of distribution of effects of a constant system of chance causes. For this reason, it is important to divide all data into rational subgroups in the sense that the data belonging to a group are supposed to have come from a constant system of chance causes.

We have considered briefly the application of five important criteria to check our judgment in such cases. We have seen, however, that such tests do not take the place of, but rather supplement, the inherent ability of the individual engineer to divide the data into rational subgroups. Thus we see clearly how statistical theory serves the engineer as a tool.

2. CONTROL IN RESEARCH

Since observed physical quantities are, in the last analysis, statistical in nature, it is desirable that the results of research be presented in a form easily interpreted in terms of frequency distributions. As a specific instance, the design engineer must depend upon the results of research to give him a basis for establishing the requisite standard of quality characterized, as we have seen in Part V, by the arithmetic mean $\overline{X}$ and the standard deviation σ of a controlled quality X.

Naturally the research engineer is always interested in detecting and eliminating causes of variability which need not be left to chance. Hence the criteria previously discussed often become of great assistance as is shown in Part VI. The data of research are good or bad, depending upon whether or not assignable causes of variability have been eliminated. In most instances the data which have been divided into rational subgroups can best be summarized by recording the average, standard deviation, and sample size for each subgroup.

3. Control in Design

Our discussion of this phase of the subject in Part V indicated the advantages to be derived through specification of the condition of control in terms of the arithmetic mean $\overline{X}$ and standard deviation σ of any prescribed quality characteristic X.

4. Control in Development

From the results of measurements of quality on tool-made samples supposedly produced under essentially the same conditions, we may attain tentative standards of quality expressible in terms of averages and standard deviations. These tentative standards may then be used as a basis for the construction of control charts in accord with Criterion I for the purpose of detecting and eliminating assignable differences of quality between tool-made samples and those produced under shop conditions.

5. Control in Commercial Production

It is obviously desirable that a method of detecting lack of control be such that it indicates the presence of assignable causes of variability before these causes have had time to affect a large percent of the product. For this reason, the method to be used on the job should involve a minimum number of computations. Here again Criterion I usually proves satisfactory.

6. Control in the Purchase of Raw Material

As is to be expected, a prevalent source of lack of control is selection of raw material. It not necessary that the different sources of material come from what could be considered to be the same constant cause system, but it is desirable that each source of a given material be controlled within itself. As an example, a physical property such as the tensile strength of a given species of timber may be assignably different for different sections of the country although within one section this variability may be such as to be attributable to a constant system of causes. In the same way, we may have sources of supply of piece-parts produced by different units of an organization or different manufacturers wherein there are assignable differences between the product coming from different sources even though each source represents a controlled product in itself. Such a condition can easily be taken care of in the use of the material, since the object of securing control from a design viewpoint is, as we have seen, the prediction of variability in the finished product.

7. QUALITY CONTROL REPORT

The quality report should, in general, do two things:

a. Indicate the presence of assignable causes of variation in each of the quality characteristics,
b. Indicate the seriousness of the trouble and the steps that have been taken to eliminate it.

EXCERPTS FROM
STATISTICAL METHOD
FROM THE VIEWPOINT
OF QUALITY CONTROL

WALTER A. SHEWHART
with the editorial assistance
of W. Edwards Deming

FOREWARD FROM THE EDITOR

In March of 1938 Dr. Shewhart, through the courtesy of the Bell Telephone Laboratories, delivered a series of four lectures under the title of this book at the Graduate School of the Department of Agriculture. Of late years there has been a tremendous interest among agricultural research workers in distribution theory and in statistical testing of hypotheses, as a consequence of which there has grown up a corresponding thirst for knowledge and new methods in inference. The Graduate School has persistently endeavored to supply the requisite academic courses, and to supplement them wherever possible by lecturers from other fields and other lands. Such is a brief description of the circumstances under which Dr. Shewhart came to Washington.

We found that though his experience had been in manufacturing, we in agriculture are faced with the same problems, but not with the same penalties for misuses and abuses of the theories that we apply. When machines are turning out piece parts by the thousands or even millions monthly, the industrial statistician does not have to wait long to see his predictions tested out. In agriculture, years are often required—a crop must be sowed and harvested again and again until the evidence is definitely for or against the prediction that one treatment is actually better than another, and by the time the question is settled, not only the statistician who made the prediction, but the prediction itself may be forgotten. With time in our favor it is easy to become careless about fundamentals.

Excerpt from *Statistical Method from the Viewpoint of Quality Control* (Washington: The Graduate School, The Department of Agriculture, 1939).

The page references throughout this article reflect those found in the original article.

An inference, if it is to have scientific value, must constitute a prediction concerning future data. If the inference is to be made purely with the help of the distribution theories of statistics, the experiments that constitute the evidence for the inference must arise from a state of statistical control; until that state is reached there is no universe, normal or otherwise, and the statistician's calculations by themselves are an illusion if not a delusion. The fact is that when distribution theory is not applicable for lack of control, any inference, statistical or otherwise, is little better than conjecture. The state of statistical control is therefore the goal of all experimentation.

Dr. Shewhart is in a position to speak with authority on some aspects of these questions. In his experience he has found that it is exceedingly more difficult that is commonly suppose to weed out the causes of large variation, but that it can usually be done through careful attention to the control chart and to the physical mechanism of the experiment or production process. Unfortunately not one but many experiments seem to be required.

The scientific view point is that every statement must be capable of being tested. If a statement cannot be put to a test, it has no value in practice. Dr. Shewhart kept this viewpoint throughout his lectures. Here for the first time we see operationally verifiable meanings for well-known statistical terms such as random variable, accuracy, precision, true value, probability, degree of rational belief, and the like, all of which are necessary if statistics is to take its rightful place as a tool of science. Here also we see a criterion of meaning that has been found useful in guiding the application of statistical technique in industry.

Most of us have thought of the statistician's work as that of measuring and predicting and planning, but few of us have thought it the statistician's duty to try to bring about changes in the things that he measures. It is evident, however, from the first chapter that this viewpoint is absolutely essential if the statistician and the manufacturer or research worker are to make the most of each other's accomplishments. What they are capable of turning out jointly is the sum of their independent efforts augmented by a strong positive interaction term. Likewise the value of a book is not just the sum of the values of the chapters separately; each chapter, even each paragraph, has a meaning that is conditioned by all the others. The subject of quality control is not fully expressed by any single idea, and the first chapter must be interpreted in the light of the last.

It has been the duty of the editor to promote clarity by altering the manuscript where it has seemed desirable to do so in order that the ideas expressed in the book will be understood, operationally, in the sense in which Dr. Shewhart understands them himself. Most of the cross-referencing, and many of the footnotes, signed and unsigned, are from the editor. It has been of particular satisfaction to work so closely with Dr. Shewhart on the production of this book, because it was he who introduced me to some of the modern statistical literature back in 1928.

In conclusion, it is fitting that attention should be drawn to the fact that this book is one more contribution to science from the staff of the Bell Telephone Laboratories. If the world were deprived of the contributions to science that have originated from the great organization, it would be a different one indeed.

W.E.D.

Washington
February 1939

STATISTICAL CONTROL

Introduction. Three steps in quality control. Three senses of statistical control.
Broadly speaking, there are three steps in a quality control process: the *specification* of what is wanted, the *production* of things to satisfy the specification, and the *inspection* of the things produced to see if they satisfy the specification. Corresponding to these three steps there are three senses in which statistical control may play an important part in attaining uniformity in the quality of a manufactured product:

a. as a concept of a statistical state constituting a limit to which one may hope to go in improving the uniformity of quality;
b. as an operation or technique of attaining uniformity; and
c. as a judgment.

Here we shall be concerned with an exposition of the meaning of statistical control in these three senses and of the role that each sense plays in the theory and technique of economic control.

Why, you may ask, do we find, some one hundred and fifty years after the start of mass production, this sudden quickening of interest in the application of statistical methods in this field? There are at least two important reasons. First, there was the rapid growth in standardization. The fundamental job of these standardizing organizations is to turn out specifications of the aimed-at quality characteristics. But when one comes to write such a specification, he runs into two kinds of problems:

1. *minimizing the number of rejections,* and
2. *minimizing the cost of inspection required to give adequate assurance of quality*

Hence the growth in standardization spread the realization of the importance of such problems in industry.

Second, there was a more or less radical change in ideology about 1900. We passed from the concept of the exactness of science in 1787, when interchangeability was introduced, to probability and statistical concepts which came into their own in almost every field of science after 1900. Whereas the concept of mass production of 1787 was born of an exact science, the concept underlying the quality control chart technique of 1924 was born of a probable science.

We may for simplicity think of the manufacturer trying to produce a piece of product with a quality characteristic falling within a given tolerance range as being analogous to shooting at a mark. If one of us were shooting at a mark and failed to hit the bull's-eye, and someone asked us why, we should likely give as our excuse, CHANCE. Had someone asked the same questions of one of our earliest know ancestors, he might have attributed his lack of success to the dictates of fate or to the will of the gods. I am inclined to think that in many ways one of these excuses is just about as good as another. perhaps we are not much wiser in blaming our failures on change than our ancestors were in blaming theirs on fate or the gods. But since 1900, the engineer has proved his unwillingness to attribute all such failures to chance. This represents a remarkable change in the ideology that characterizes the developments in the application of statistics in the control of quality.

Developments since 1870.   With the introduction of the go, no-go tolerance limits of 1870, it became the more or less generally accepted practice to specify that each important quality characteristic X of a given piece of product should lie within stated limits L_1 and L_2 represented schematically in Figure 4. Such a specification is of the nature of an end requirement on the specified quality characteristic X of a finished piece of product. It provides a basis on which the quality of a given product may be gauged to determine whether or not it meets the specification. From this viewpoint, the process

---

FIGURE 4

Quality X L_1 L_2

of specification is very simple indeed. Knowing the limits L_1 and L_2 within which it is desirable that a given quality characteristic X should lie, all we need to do is to put these limits in writing as a requirement on the quality of a finished product. With such a specification at hand, the next stop is to make the measurements necessary to classify a piece of product as conforming or nonconforming to specification.

At this point, however, two problems arise. Suppose that the quality under consideration, the blowing time of a fuse for example, is one that can be determined only by destructive tests. How can one give assurance that the quality of a fuse will meet its specifications without destroying the fuse in the process? Or again, even where the quality characteristic can be measured without destruction, there is always a certain fraction p falling outside the tolerance limits. How can we reduce this nonconforming fraction to an economic minimum? A little reflection shows that the simple specification of the go, no-go tolerance limits (p. 3) is not sufficient in such instances from the viewpoint of economy and assurance of quality.

As was mentioned at the beginning of this chapter, we shall consider control from the viewpoints of specification, production, and inspection of quality, as is necessary if we are to understand clearly the role played by statistical theory in the economic control of the quality of a manufactured product. To illustrate, suppose we fix our attention on some kind of material, piecepart, or physical object that we wish to produce in large quantities, and let us symbolize the pieces of this product by the letters

$$O_1, O_2, \ldots, Oi, \ldots, On, On{+}_1, \ldots, On{+}j, \ldots \, (1)$$

presuming that a given process of production may be employed to turn out an indefinitely large number of pieces. We shall soon see that corresponding to the three steps in control there are at lease three senses in which the phrase "statistical control" may be used in respect to such an infinite sequence of product.

In the first place, prior to the production of any of the O's, the engineer may propose to attain a sequence of O's that have the property of having been produced under a state of statistical control. In the second place, the engineer, before he starts the production of any specific sequence of objects, is pretty sure to focus his attention on the acts or operations that he wishes to be carried out in the production of the pieces of product. Often, when the aim is to produce a sequence of objects having a specified quality characteristic within some specified limits, the engineer will refer to the process of production as an *operation of control*. The available scientific and engineering literature, for example, contains many articles discussing "the control of quality" by means of gauges, measuring instruments, and different forms of mechanical technique: much of this literature makes no reference to the use of statistics, though in recent years the actual operations of control have often involved the use of statistical techniques such as, for example, the control chart. In order to distinguish the operation of control in the more general sense from that in which statistical techniques are used for the purpose of attaining a state of statistical control, it is customary to think of the latter as an *operation of statistical control.* That which transforms an operation of control into an operation of statistical control is not simply the use of statistical techniques, but the use of statistical techniques that constitute a *means* of attaining the end characterized here as a state of statistical control. It should be noted that the end desired may be conceived of prior to the production of any sequence of objects symbolized in (1) that have the desired characteristics, and independently of whether any such sequence can be produced. For example, we may conceive of a state of statistical control although we know of no way of attaining such a state in practice. In contrast, before we can describe an operation of statistical control, except to say that it is a means to an end, *we must find by experiment such an operation.*

A requirement regarding control.   Let us consider the following specified end *requirement:*

   A. The quality of the *O*'s shall be statistically controlled in respect to the quality characteristic *X.*

As an example, the product might be condensers and the quality characteristic *X* the capacity; the product might be pieces of steel and *X* the carbon content; or the product might be any other kind of object with an associated quality characteristic. The natural thing to do is to think of this requirement (A) as expressing a condition that the qualities of a sequence of pieces of product represented by the *O*'s in (1) shall be found to have *when made.* For example, we might, as we shall soon see, interpret this requirement as meaning that the sequence of values of the quality characteristic *X* belonging to the sequence of objects of (1) shall be random. On the other hand, we might interpret the requirement (A) as implying that the cause system underlying the operation of producing the objects satisfies certain physical requirements. In any case, the requirement itself may be, and usually is, stated prior to the production of any of the *O*'s in (1).

A probable inference regarding control.   Now let us contrast the requirement (A) with the following *statement* regarding control:

   B. The quality of the *O*'s is statistically controlled in respect to the quality characteristic *X.*

This is a *judgment* or *probable inference* that the quality of the product actually meets the requirement expressed by (A). Since we are here assuming that the process of manufacture is capable of turning out an indefinitely large number of pieces of product, it follows in practice that the statement (B) implies a prediction about *O*'s not yet made: as a probable inference *it is based on past evidence obtained in the process of making some pieces of product and in testing them*. In other words, it is an inference carried *from the product already made* to that which is to be made in the future. The full meaning of statement (B), as we shall see later, must depend upon a consideration not only of the sense of control implied as a requirement but also as an inference *based upon specific evidence* that this requirement has been met.

It is therefore essential that we examine carefully the three senses of statistical control: *first*, as a characterization of the state of control; *second*, as an operation; *third*, as a judgment. This is necessary if we are to see how the attainment of the economic control of the quality of a manufactured product involves the coordination of effort in the three steps: *specification*, *production*, and *inspection*.

THE STATE OF STATISTICAL CONTROL

The idea of control involves *action for the purpose of achieving a desired end*. Control in this sense involves both action and a specified end. For example, in the quotation at the head of this chapter we have an expression of the need for controlling the quality of steel to attain the end of greater *uniformity*. The man who is to do the controlling is likely to focus his attention on what he is supposed to do or on what action he is supposed to take in the process of making the steel, whereas the man who uses the steel may be primarily interested in the end result as determined by the quantitative measurements of the quality of the finished product. Hence there are two ways of viewing control in general and statistical control in particular; namely, from the viewpoint of the physical act of production, and from that of the end results as manifested in the uniformity of quality. Correspondingly, there are two ways of conceiving of the state of statistical control; namely, as a physical state describable in physical terms, and as a mathematical state characterized by the quantitative aspects of the end results and describable in mathematical terms and an operation of drawing at random.

Some may prefer to say that there is no mathematical state of control, but instead that there is simply a mathematical *description* of a physical state. This is perfectly satisfactory so far as I see *if* we think of the mathematical description as including an explanation of what the mathematical statistician means by the *operation* of drawing a sample at random and not simply the description of the results that he obtains mathematically. However, in much the same sense, there is no *observable* physical state of control except in descriptive terms characterizing some operation such as drawing a sample with replacement from a bowl, repeating an observation under the same essential conditions, or going as far as one can go in the process of controlling quality by finding and removing causes of variability. To be more exact, therefore, we should perhaps speak of the physical and mathematical *descriptions* of the state of control, but it will simplify matters to speak only of the "physical and mathematical states" in our attempt to relate the physical and mathematical operations.

As a background for our consideration of the two states of statistical control, we shall start with the aim of the engineer to manufacture a product of uniform quality. We shall take this to imply that the quality should be *reproducible within limits,*[1] or that the engineer should be able to predict with minimum error the percentage of the future product that will be turned out by a given process with a quality within specified limits. The engineer desires to reduce the variability in quality to an economic minimum. In other words, he wants

a. a rational method of prediction that is subject to minimum error, and
b. a means of minimizing the variability in the quality of a given product at a given cost of production.

Is it possible to control the production process so that these two wants may be satisfied? If so, how shall the engineer know when the production process is in such a state of control? How can this state be characterized? Shall it be by describing the physical operations that the engineer goes through in producing the product; shall it be in terms of quantitative data obtainable from the product in such a state of control; or shall it be by means of a combination of the two? As a basis for answering such questions, we must consider on the one hand the *physical aspects* of the state of control, and on the other hand the *mathematical aspects* of the quantitative data obtainable under a given state of control.

STATISTICAL CONTROL AS AN OPERATION[2]

Let us first see what the operation of control is designed to do. The statistician looking at the function or purpose of the operation of control will likely

---

[1]Sometimes the term homogeneous is used instead of the more descriptive phrase "reproducible within limits."

[2]This subject is discussed at length in my book, *Economic Control of Quality of Manufactured Product* (New York: Van Nostrand Co., Inc., 1931). It is also discussed in a most helpful way in *The Application of Statistical Methods to Industrial Standardization and Quality Control* by E. S. Pearson (London: British Standards Institution, 1935) and in the *Manual on Presentation of Data* (Philadelphia: American Society for Testing Materials, 260 S. Broad St., 1933).

see it as a procedure for attaining a state of statistical control of some variable whereas the engineer will see it as a means of effecting certain economies and attaining the highest degree of quality assurance at a given cost. Presumably both the statistician and the engineer are interested in understanding the operation of control as a scientific procedure. In what follows, an attempt is made to present the important characteristics of the operation from each of these viewpoints.

In the beginning of this chapter we noted the steps that had been taken in going from the concept of an exact fit of interchangeable parts based upon the concept of an exact science, to the concept of tolerances, Figure 4, p. 6. Statistical theory then stepped in (1924) with the concept of two action or control limits A and B that lie, in general, within L_1 and L_2, as shown in Figure 6 (next page). These limits are to be set so that when the observed quality of a piece of product falls outside of them, even though the observation be still within the limits L_1 and L_2, *it is desirable to look at the manufacturing process in order to discover and remove, if possible, one or more causes of variation that need not be left to chance.* In other words, whereas the limits L_1 and L_2 provide a means of gauging the product *already made,* the action limits A and B provide a *means of directing action toward the process* with a view to the elimination of assignable causes of variation so that the quality of the product *not yet made* may be less variable on the average.

Furthermore, the statistical theory of quality control introduces the concept of the expected value C lying somewhere between the action limits A and B. This point C serves in a certain sense as an aimed-at value of quality in an economically controlled state. We might pause a moment to note the importance of the point C from the viewpoint of design or the use of material that has already been made. Let us take, for example, a very simple problem of setting overall tolerance limits. Suppose that we start with the concept of the go, no-go tolerances of 1870 (Figure 4, p. 6) and that we wish to fix the overall tolerance limits for n pieceparts assembled in such a way that the resultant quality of the n parts is the arithmetic sum of the qualities of the component parts. An extremely simple example would be the establishment of tolerance limits on the thickness of a pile of n washers or, in general, any n laminated pieceparts in terms of the tolerance limits on one. The older method of fixing such limits was to take the sum of the tolerance limits on the individual pieceparts, but the tolerance range resulting from such practice is usually many times larger than it needs to be. The economical way of setting such tolerance limits for a product in a state of statistical control is in terms of the concept of the expected value C of the quality, and the expected standard deviation about this value. The concept of the expected value is of fundamental importance in all design work in which an attempt is made to fix overall tolerances in terms of those of pieceparts.

Thus we see that for reasons of economy and quality assurance it is necessary to go beyond the simple concept of the go, no-go tolerance limits of the customary specification and to include two action limits A and B and an expected value C, as shown schematically in Figure 6. Statistical theory alone is responsible for the introduction of the concept of the action limits A and B and the expected value C.

It should be noted that if there were no reason connected with economy or quality assurance for going beyond the concept of the go, no-go tolerance limits, statistical theory would have nothing to add. Likewise, it should be noted that, although the action limits A and B may lie within the tolerance limits L_1 and L_2, the product already produced and found by inspection to be within the limits L_1 and L_2 is still considered to conform, even if outside A and B. In other words, the action limits A and B do not apply as a gauge for product already made: their function is to call attention to evidence for believing that the manufacturing process includes assignable causes of variation in the quality that may give trouble in the future if they are not found and removed.

The operation of statistical control.   The use of statistical techniques in the way just described introduces a modification in the customary operation of control and in this sense constitutes an "operation of statistical control" directed toward the attainment of a state of statistical control.

The specification of an operation of statistical control consists of the following steps:

1. Specify in a general way how an observed sequence of n data is to be examined for clues as to the existence of assignable causes of variability.
2. Specify how the original data are to be taken and how they are to be broken up into subsamples upon the basis of human judgments about whether the conditions under which the data were taken were essentially the same or not.

FIGURE 6

3. Specify the criterion of control that is to be used, indicating what statistics are to be computed for each subsample and how these are to be used in computing action or control limits for each statistic for which the control criterion is to be constructed.
4. Specify the action that is to be taken when an observed statistic falls outside its control limits.
5. Specify the quantity of data that must be available and found to satisfy the criterion of control before the engineer is to act as though he had attained a state of statistical control.

In the next few paragraphs I shall consider briefly each of these steps and indicate the nature of the available evidence to show that the operation as a whole successfully accomplishes its objective in practice.

Let us think of a particular manufacturing process as an operation of making a given kind of object, and let us assume as above that this operation can be repeated again and again at will. Let us assume that we want to attain a state of statistical control of some quality characteristic X; that n pieces of the product have been made; and that the qualities of these n pieces in respect to the characteristic X are available in order that the pieces were produced. These n values of X may be thought of as constituting the first n terms of an infinite sequence (3) corresponding to what we should get under similar conditions by repeating again and again the operation of production.

It is essential for an understanding of the operation of control that we distinguish three kinds of acts that are involved. These are

a. mental operations or judgments typical of which is the judgment that two or more observations are made under the same or different conditions,
b. mathematical operations such as are involved in constructing a criterion of control, and
c. physical operations such as looking for an assignable cause when an observed point fails to satisfy a criterion of control.

THE RESULTS OF MEASUREMENT PRESENTED AS KNOWLEDGE—CUSTOMARY CONDITIONS

Complications in real measurements not in a state of statistical control. The problem of presenting the results of measurement of a physical quality characteristic or constant is much more complicated than that considered in the previous section dealing with samples from a bowl universe. This complication arises from the fact that measurements do not in general behave as though they arose under a state of statistical control. In fact, not only do repetitive measurements made by any one method of measuring usually show lack of control, but also measurements of the same quality characteristic or physical constant made by different methods usually indicate the existence of assignable causes of difference. For example, on page 89 we called attention to the fact that for any physical measurement X, there are three associated elements from the viewpoint of operational meaning, namely the condition C, under which the observation was taken, the human element H, introduced by the observer, and the order. Now to assume that an observation such as a drawing from a bowl arises from a state of statistical control implies operationally the assumption that for such an observation we may neglect the factors C, and H, as not contributing to knowledge. We shall soon see, however, that these factors play an important role in the problem of presenting the results of physical measurement. How to present C, and H, is a difficult problem. It goes without saying, however, that without knowing anything about C, and H, there is little ground for believing in any prediction that may be made upon the basis of a series of n repetitive measurements $X_1, X_2, \ldots, X_i, \ldots, X_n$. Here we shall confine our attention to certain aspects of the problem that are significant from the viewpoint of determining the usefulness of statistical theory as a guide in the presentation of the results of measurement.

In the first place, it should be noted in the light of the results presented in chapter II that if the formal rules for making predictions of the three types P_1, P_2, and P_3 are applied to an actual set of physical data, the expectancy of the percentage of valid predictions would be very low compared with the percentage attainable for drawings from a bowl. From the viewpoint of setting the most efficient tolerances, more knowledge is required than is contained in any tolerance set by such a rule, unless we have evidence to indicate that such observations are statistically controlled about a statistical limit which appears to be the same for all of the known methods of measuring. hence we shall here consider some of the ways statistical theory may be applied to advantage in the process of approaching the idealized condition of statistical control—that is, applied to advantage in the knowing process.

Although there are three component factors of knowledge as here considered, namely *evidence, prediction,* and *degree of belief* p_b, it is noteworthy that we have no quantitative way of measuring p_b. Let us consider the investigations in any new field of measurement. Many, many observations of an exploratory character are often taken before a scientist will even take time to record them. It is almost always a long experimental road between such initial efforts and the announcement of the final results as, for example, in the measurement of the velocity of light by Michelson. For our present purpose, perhaps the most important characteristic of such an approach to scientific knowledge is the fact that *the method of increasing knowledge does not consist in taking more and more repetitive measurements under presumably the same conditions as it does when one is making drawings from a bowl.* In fact, a scientist seldom bothers to take more than five or ten observations under what he considers to be the same essential conditions (drawings from a bowl), although often he experiments with what he thinks may be slightly different conditions. An illustration is provided by Heyl's measurements of G shown in Table 5 (p. 69) wherein the results are given for three different experimental arrangements which we might call conditions C_1, C_2, and C_3, provided it is permissible to conclude that the conditions remain the same for the measurements in each one of the three columns.

Consistency between different methods more important than consistency in repetition.   The degree of belief that a scientist holds in a prediction made upon the basis of measurements of some physical constant or property depends a lot more on the consistency between the results obtained under slightly different conditions and by different methods of measurement than it depends upon the number of repetitions made under what he considers to be the same essential conditions. In all such work it has long been recognized that the statistician may contribute to the efforts of the scientist in discovering assignable differences between two or more sets of observations. For example, in Table 5 the statistician might apply tests for determining whether the data obtained under the three possibly different conditions could reasonably have occurred as a result of sampling fluctuations; all he needs for this purpose are the average, standard deviation, and sample size for each of the three sets of measurements.

A word on the detection of constant errors by "tests of significance."   It is very difficult, however, to weigh the importance of this contribution of the statistician and to determine how much the results of his efforts contribute to a rational belief in the conclusion derived from the analysis of data. From the viewpoint of scientific inquiry, the validity attainable in predictions depends so much upon the skill of the experimentalist in selecting appropriate sense data on the one side and connecting principles or conceptual theories on the other, that unless this process is carried out successfully, almost nothing that the statistician contributes is significant. One must not place too much reliance upon the existence or nonexistence of so-called significant differences reached in any statistical test. However, if the scientist is successful in his choice of data and interpretative principles, the results of the application of statistical tests have the value customarily attributed to them and are successful to this extent. Hence in tabulating data from the viewpoint of providing knowledge, it is often desirable that summaries be made in terms of the average, standard deviation, and the sample size for each group of data taken under conditions assumed to be the same by the scientist, instead of summarizing all the data as though it constituted a single sample from a statistically controlled condition.

Need for the attainment of statistical control.   What seems to me a very important contribution of statistical theory to scientific methodology comes about when one tries to go further than the scientist customarily goes in looking to see whether repetitive observations made under presumably the same essential conditions satisfy the criteria of control referred to in chapter I. If one is to attain the kind of knowledge that is requisite for establishing the *most efficient* tolerances—the kind that could be established for drawings from a bowl—it is obvious that one must attain a close approximation to a state of statistical control. Furthermore, as I have said before, it is necessary to have a comparatively large sample, usually more than a thousand, as a basis for establishing the tolerance range if one is to keep within practical limits the error in setting such ranges. What I have termed in chapter I the "operation of control" constitutes an operational procedure for attaining this control and the knowledge requisite for establishing such tolerances. This application of statistics is inherently different from that of making the three kinds of prediction P_1, P_2, and P_3 from a single sample, referred to above. In fact, it is the function of the operation of statistical control to help attain with a minimum amount of human effort a state of control wherein we may with reasonable assurance of attaining valid results make these three kinds of prediction as if they were applied to drawings from an experimental bowl.

An interesting characteristic of this operation of attaining knowledge is that to begin with we cannot tell how many observations will be required. So long as we find any evidence of lack of control, we cannot estimate the degree of belief that we should hold in any prediction made upon the basis of accumulating data. However, this operational procedure of detecting and eliminating assignable causes provides a method of approaching a state of statistical control of a given repetitive operation in a more or less regular manner. So far as the claims for this operational technique are justified, it follows that the *available data should be so tabulated that criteria of control may be applied,* even when the scientist assumes that his data have been taken under the same essential conditions. An illustration of such a presentation if provided in Table 7 (p. 90), which gives the 204 observations of insulation resistance in the order in which the pieces were made. For investigating their state of control, the averages and standard deviations of the successive samples of four would have been a satisfactory summary of the original data.

It will be noted that in the previous section dealing with ideal conditions (pp. 101–110), the recommendation there given was to present the observed results in an ungrouped frequency distribution *f0,* but that no such recommendation is made in the present section; here we are not assuming that control exists, but rather we are attempting to attain it or prove it. The reason is obvious; the use of the observed frequency distribution *f0* is to give evidence concerning the nature of the distribution function is the experimental bowl, whereas in the initial stages of investigation, the condition of control has not yet been attained and *there is no universe (bowl) to be discovered.*

As we saw earlier, a prediction devoid of supporting evidence conveys no knowledge. And so it is that in order to convey to another person the knowledge that one obtains from a study of his own experimental work, *it is necessary to present the evidence as well as the prediction.* Since it is customary in experimental work to find that the state of statistical control can be approached only as a limit by discovering and weeding out assignable causes, the presentation of evidence that the assignable causes have been found and removed necessarily adds to one's rational belief that the end results represent a state of statistical control.

IMPROVEMENT OF QUALITY AND PRODUCTIVITY THROUGH ACTION BY MANAGEMENT

W. EDWARDS DEMING

WHY PRODUCTIVITY INCREASES WITH IMPROVEMENT OF QUALITY

Some simple examples will show how productivity increases with improvement of quality. Other benefits are lower costs, better competitive position, and happier people on the job. It is important to note that a gain in productivity is also a gain in capacity of a production line.

BEST EFFORTS ARE NOT SUFFICIENT

"By everyone doing his best."

This is the answer that someone in a meeting volunteered in response to my question, "And how do you go about it to improve quality and productivity?"

It is interesting to note that this answer was wrong—wrong in the sense that best efforts are not sufficient. Best efforts are essential, but unfortunately, best efforts alone will not accomplish the purpose. Everyone is already doing his best. Efforts, to be effective, must move in the right direction. Without guidance, best efforts result in a random walk.

Some folklore.   Folklore has it in America that quality and production are incompatible: that you cannot have both. It is either or. Insist on quality, and you will fall behind in production. Push production and you will find that your quality has suffered.

Reprinted with permission from W. Edwards Deming and *National Productivity Review* 1:1 (Winter 1981–1982): 12–22. Copyright 1982 by Executive Enterprises, Inc., 22 West 21st Street, New York, NY 10010-6990. 212-645-7880. All rights reserved.

The fact is that quality is achieved by improvement of the process. Improvement of the process increases uniformity of output of product, reduces mistakes, and reduces waste of manpower, machine-time, and materials.

Reduction of waste transfers man-hours and machine-hours from the manufacture of defectives into the manufacture of additional good product. In effect, the capacity of a production line is increased. The benefits of better quality through improvement of the process are thus not just better quality, and the long-range improvement of market-position that goes along with it, but greater productivity and much better profit as well. Improved morale of this work force is another gain: they now see that the management is making some effort themselves, and not blaming all faults on the production-workers.

A clear statement of the relationship between quality and productivity comes from my friend Dr. Yoshikasu Tsuda of Rikkyo University in Tokyo, who wrote to me as follows, dated 23 March 1980.

> I have just spent a year in the northern hemisphere, in twenty-three countries, in which I visited many industrial plants, and talked with many industrialists.
>
> In Europe and in America, people are now more interested in cost of quality and in systems of quality-audit. But in Japan, we are keeping very strong interest to improve quality by using statistical methods which you started in your very first visit to Japan.... When we improve quality we also improve productivity, just as you told us in 1950 would happen.

A simple example.   Some simple figures taken from recent experience will illustrate what happens [See Table 1]. Defective output of a certain production-line was running along at 11 percent (news to the management). A run-chart of proportion defective day by day over the previous six weeks showed good statistical control of the line as a whole. The main cause of the problem could accordingly only be ascribed to the system. This was also news to the management. The statisticians made the suggestion that possibly the people on the job, and inspectors also, did not understand well enough what kind of work is acceptable and what is not. The manager of the production-line and two supervisors went to work on the matter, and with trial and error came up in seven weeks with better definitions, with examples posted for everyone to see. A new set of data showed the proportion defective to be 5 percent. Cost, zero. Results:

Quality up
Productivity up 6 percent
Costs down
Profit greatly improved
Capacity of the production line increased 6 percent
(List continues)

TABLE 1	ILLUSTRATING GAIN IN PRODUCTIVITY WITH IMPROVED QUALITY	
ITEM	BEFORE IMPROVEMENT 11 PERCENT DEFECTIVE	AFTER IMPROVEMENT 5 PERCENT DEFECTIVE
Total cost	100	100
Spent to make good units	89	95
Spent to make defective units	11	5
Average number of good units per unit cost	.89	.95
Proportion of total cost spent to make defectives	.11	.05

Customer happier
Everybody happier

This gain was immediate (seven weeks); cost, zero: same work force, same burden, no investment in new machinery.

This is an example of gain in productivity accomplished by a change in the system, effected by the management helping people to work smarter, not harder.

REDUCTION IN COST

Taken from a speech delivered in Rio de Janeiro, March 1981, by William E. Conway, president of the Nashua Corporation.

At Nashua, the first big success took place in March 1980: improvement of quality and reduction of cost in the manufacture of carbonless paper.

Water-based coating that contains various chemicals is applied to a moving web of paper. If the amount of coating is right, the customer will be pleased with a good consistent mark when he uses the paper some months later. The coating-head applied approximately 3 pounds of dry coating to 3000 square feet of paper at a speed of approximately 1400 linear feet/minute on a web 6-8 feet wide. Technicians took samples of paper and made tests to determine the intensity of the mark. These tests were made on the sample both as it came off the coater and after it was aged in an oven to simulate use by the customer. When tests showed the intensity of the mark to be too low or too high, the operator made adjustments that would increase or decrease the amount of coating material. Frequent stops for new settings were a way of life. These stops were costly.

The engineers knew that the average weight of the coating material was too high, but did not know how to lower it without risk of putting on insufficient coating. A new coating-head, to cost $700,000, was under consideration.

There would be, besides the cost of $700,000, time lost for installation, and the risk that the new head might not achieve uniformity of coating much better than the equipment in use.

In August 1979, the plant manager decided to utilize the statistical control of quality to study the operation. It was thereby found that the coating-head, if left untouched, was actually in pretty good statistical control at the desired level of 3.0 dry pounds of coating on the paper, plus or minus .4.

Elimination of various special causes, highlighted by points of control, reduced the amount of coating and still maintained good consistent quality.

The coater had by April 1980 settled down to an average of 2.8 pounds per 3000 square feet, varying from 2.4 to 3.2, thereby saving 0.2 pounds per 3000 square feet, or $800,000 per year at present volume and cost levels.

What the operator of the coating-head had been doing, before statistical control was introduced and achieved, was to over-adjust his machine, to put on more coating, or less, reacting to tests of the paper. In doing his best, in accordance with the training and instructions given to him, he was actually doubling the variance of the coating. The control-charts, once in operation, helped him to do a much better job, with less effort. He is happy. His job is easier and more important.

All this was accomplished without making the proposed capital investment of $700,000, which might or might not have improved the process and the quality of the coated paper.

Engineering innovation.   Statistical control opened the way to engineering innovation. Without statistical control, the process was in unstable chaos, the noise of which would mask the effect of any attempt to bring improvement. Step by step they achieved:

- Improvement of the chemical content of the material used for coating, to use less and less coating.
- Improvement of the coating-head (without purchase of a new one) to achieve greater and greater uniformity of coating.

Today, only 1.0 pounds of improved coating is used per 3000 square feet of paper. This level is safe, as the variation lies only between .9 and 1.1. Reduction of a tenth of a pound means an annual reduction of $400,000 in the cost of coating.

The reader can do his own arithmetic to compute the annual reduction in cost from the starting point, namely, 3.0 pounds.

Before statistical control was achieved, the engineers had not entertained thought of improvement of coating-head. Once statistical control was achieved, it was easy to measure the effect of small changes in the chemistry of the coating and in the coating-head. The next step then became obvious—try to improve the coating and the coating-head, to use less coating with greater and greater uniformity.

LOW QUALITY MEANS HIGH COST

A plant was plagued with a huge amount of defective product. "How many people have you on this line for rework of defects made in previous operations?" I asked the manager. He went to the blackboard and put down 3 people here, 4 there, etc.—in total, 21 percent of the work force on that line.

Defects are not free. Somebody makes them, and gets paid for making them. On the supposition that it costs as much to correct a defect as to make it in the first place, then 21 percent of his payroll and burden was being spent on rework. In practice, it usually costs more to correct a defect than to make it, so the figure 21 percent is a minimum.

Once the manager saw the magnitude of the problem, and came to the realization that he was paying out good money to make defects as well as to correct them, he found ways to help the people on the line to understand better how to do the job. The cost of rework went down from 21 percent to 9 percent in a space of 2 months.

Next step: reduce the proportion defective from 9 percent to 0.

From 15 percent to 40 percent of the manufacturer's costs of almost any American product that you buy today is for waste embedded in it—waste of human effort, waste of machine-time, loss of accompanying burden. No wonder that many American products are hard to sell at home or abroad.

American industry (including service-organizations) can no longer tolerate mistakes and defective material at the start nor anywhere along the line, nor equipment out of order.

NEW MACHINERY IS NOT THE ANSWER

Lag in American productivity had been attributed in editorials and in letters in the newspapers to failure to install new machinery and the latest types of automation. Such suggestions make interesting reading and still more interesting writing for people that do not understand problems of production. There is a quicker and surer way, namely, better administration of man and whatever machinery is in use today. Then, after the present problems are conquered, talk about new machinery.

The following paragraph received from a friend in a large manufacturing company will serve as illustration.

This whole program (design and installation of new machines) has led to some unhappy experiences. All these wonderful machines performed their intended functions, on test, but when they were put into operation, they were out of business so much of the time for this and that kind of failure that our overall costs, instead of going down, went up. No one had evaluated the overall probable failure-rates and maintenance. As a result, we were continually caught with stoppages and with not enough spare parts, or with none at all; and no provision for alternate production-lines.

Comparison between American and Japanese production should take account of some important differences. Japanese manufacturers are already using their machinery to full advantage, not wasting materials, human effort, or machine-time. They have no unemployed people to draw upon for expansion. There are no unemployment agencies in Japan. The Monthly Report on the Labor Force for the United States, in contrast, shows at this writing 7 million unemployed. American industry can expand by drawing upon a supply of labor, a large part of it skilled, experienced, able, and willing to work. The Japanese manufacturer, on the other hand, can expand his production only by use of better machinery or improvement in design. He cannot hire more people: there are not any. The fact is that there is only a small amount of automation in Japan. They have been sensible about it.

If I were a banker, I would not lend money for new equipment unless the company that asked for the loan could demonstrate by statistical evidence that they are using their present equipment to full realizable capacity.

QUALITY CONTROL IN SERVICE INDUSTRIES

Eventually, quality control will assist not only the production of goods and food (the birthplace of modern statistical theory was agriculture) but the service industries as well—hospitals, hotels, transportation, wholesale and retail establishments, perhaps even the U.S. mail. Statistical quality technology has for many years contributed to telecommunications, both in the manufacture of equipment and in service. Statistical quality technology is improving service and lowering costs in the banking business. In fact, one of the most successful applications of statistical methods on a huge scale, including sample design and operations, is in the U.S. Census, not only in the decennial Census but in the regular monthly and quarterly surveys of people and of business, an example being the Monthly Report on the Labor Force.

It is interesting to note that some service industries in Japan have been active in statistical methods from the start, e.g., the Japanese National Railways, Nippon Telegraph and Telephone Corporation, the Tobacco Monopoly of Japan, the Post Office. Department stores have taken up statistical quality control. Takenaka Komuten (architecture and construction) won recognition in 1979 for thoroughgoing improvement of buildings of all types, and for decrease in cost, by studying the needs of the users (in offices, hospitals, factories, hotels) and by reducing the costs of rework in drawings and in the actual construction.

WHAT TOP MANAGEMENT MUST DO

The purpose here is to explain to top management what their job is. No one in management need ask again, "What must we do?" This section serves two purposes:

1. It provides an outline of the obligations of top management.
2. It provides a yardstick by which anyone in the company may measure the performance of the management.

Paper profits, the yardstick by which stockholders and Boards of Directors often measure performance of the president, make no contribution to material living for people anywhere, not do they improve the competitive position of a company or of American industry. Paper profits do not make bread: improvement of quality and productivity do. They make a contribution to better material living for all people, here and everywhere.

Short-term profits are not indication of good management. Anybody can pay dividends by deferring maintenance, cutting out research, or acquiring another company.

Ways of doing business with vendors and with customers that were good enough in the past must now be revised to meet new requirements of quality and productivity. Drastic revision is required.

What must top management do? As I noted at the beginning of this article, it is not enough for everyone to do his best. Everyone is already doing his best. Efforts, to be effective, must move in the right direction.

It is not enough that top management commit themselves by affirmation for life to quality and productivity. They must know what it is that they are committed to—i.e., what they must do. These obligations cannot be delegated. Mere approval is not enough, nor New Year's resolutions. Failure of top management to act on any one of the fourteen points listed ahead will impair efforts on the other thirteen. Quality is everybody's job, but no one else in the company can work effectively on quality and productivity unless it is obvious that the top people are working on their obligations.

"Let me emphasize that where top management does not understand and does not get personally involved, nothing will happen." *(From a speech made by William E. Conway, president of the Nashua Corporation.)*

THE 14 POINTS FOR TOP MANAGEMENT

Here are the obligations of top management. These obligations continue forever: none of them is ever completely fulfilled.

1. *Create constancy of purpose in the company.* The next quarterly dividend is not as important as existence of the company ten, twenty, or thirty years from now.
   a. *Innovate.* Allocate resources for long-term planning. Plans for the future call for consideration of:

   - Possible new materials, new service, adaptability, probable cost.
   - Method of production; possible changes in equipment.
   - New skills required, and in what number.
   - Training and retraining of personnel.
   - Training of supervisors.
   - Cost of production.
   - Performance in the hands of the user.
   - Satisfaction of the user.

   One requirement for innovation is faith that there will be a future. Innovation, the foundation of the future, cannot thrive unless the top management has declared unshakable policy of quality and productivity. Until this policy can be enthroned as an institution, middle management and everyone in the company will be skeptical about the effectiveness of their best efforts.

   The consumer is the most important part of the production-line. Japanese management took on a new turn in 1950 by putting the consumer first.

   b. Put resources into

   - research
   - education

   c. Put resources into maintenance of equipment, furniture, and fixtures, new aids to production in the office and in the plant.

   It is a mistake to suppose that statistical quality technology applied to products and services offered at present can with certainty keep an organization solvent and ahead of competition. It is possible and in fact fairly easy for an organization to go broke making the wrong product or offering the wrong type of service, even though everyone in the organization performs with devotion, employing statistical methods and every other aid that can boost efficiency.

Innovation generates new and improved services. An example is new and different kinds of plans for savings in banks, financial service offered by credit agencies, Meals on Wheels, day care in out-patient clinics. Leasing of automobiles is an example of service that did not exist years ago. Express Mail is a new service of the U.S. Post Office (equivalent to what a postage stamp would accomplish in Japan or in Europe). Mailgram by Western Union is another. Intercity and intracity messenger service is a growth industry, thriving on the delinquency of the U.S. Post Office. Services can and do have problems of mistakes, costly correction of mistakes, and consequent impairment of productivity associated with mistakes.

2. Learn the new philosophy.   We are in a new economic age. We can no longer live with commonly accepted levels of mistakes, defects, material not suited to the job, people on the job that do not know what the job is and are afraid to ask; handling damage; failure of management to understand the problems of the product in use; antiquated methods of training on the job; inadequate and ineffective supervision.

Acceptance of defective materials and poor workmanship as a way of life is one of the most effective roadblocks to better quality and productivity. The Japanese faced it in 1950. Unreliable and nonuniform were kind words for the usual quality of incoming materials. Japanese management took aim at the problem and in time reduced it to a level never before achieved. American industry today faces the same problem. The road that Japanese manufacturers paved would be a good one for American management to copy.

3. Require statistical evidence of process control along with incoming critical parts.   There is no other way for your supplier nor for you to know the quality that he is delivering, and no other way to achieve best economy and productivity. Purchasing managers must learn the statistical control of quality. They must proceed under the new philosophy: the right quality characteristics must be built in, without dependence on inspection. Statistical control of the process provides the only way for the supplier to build quality in, and the only way to provide to the purchaser evidence of uniform repeatable quality and of cost of production. There is no other way for your supplier to predict his costs.

Most purchasing managers do not know at present which of their suppliers are qualified. One of the first steps for purchasing managers to take is to learn enough about the statistical control of quality to be able to assess the qualifications of a supplier, to talk to him in statistical language. Don't expect him to carry on the conversation in French if you don't know French.

Some suppliers are already qualified and are conforming to this recommendation. Some follow their product through the purchaser's production-lines to learn what problems turn up, and to take action, so far as possible, to avoid problems in the future.

One company may have influence over hundreds of suppliers and over many other purchasers.

Vendors sometimes furnish reams of figures, such as records of adjustment, input of materials (2 kg. chromium added at 1000 h). Figures like these are as worthless to the buyer as they are to the vendor.

The manager of an important plant, which belongs to one of America's largest corporations lamented to me that he spends most of his time defending good vendors. A typical problem runs like this. A vendor has not for years sent to him a defective item, and his price is right. Some other manufacturer underbids this vendor by a few cents and captures the business. The corporate purchasing department awards the business to him because of price. The plant manager cannot take a chance, and must spend many hours and days arguing for the vendor that knows his business.

4. *The requirement of statistical evidence of process control in the purchase of critical parts will mean in most companies drastic reduction in the number of vendors that they deal with.*   Companies will have to consider the cost of having two or more vendors for the same item. A company will be lucky to find one vendor that can supply statistical evidence of quality. A second vendor, if he cannot furnish statistical evidence of his quality, will have higher costs than the one that can furnish the evidence, or he will have to chisel on his quality, or go out of business. A man that does not know his costs nor whether he can repeat tomorrow today's distribution of quality is not a good business partner.

We can no longer leave quality and price to the forces of competition—not in today's requirements for uniformity and reliability. Price has no meaning without a measure of the quality being purchased. Without adequate measures of quality, business drifts to the lowest bidder, low quality and high cost being the inevitable result. American industry and the U.S. government are being rooked by rules that award business to the lowest bidder.

The purchasing managers of a company are not at fault for giving business to the lowest bidder, nor for seeking more bids in the hope of getting a still better price. This is their mandate. Only the top management can change their direction.

Purchasing managers have a new job. It will take five years for them to learn it.

Made by Company A	Made by Company B
1000 pieces all meet specifications	1000 pieces all meet specifications

Example. An American manufacturer of automobiles may today have 2500 vendors. A Japanese automobile company may have 380. Rapid and determined reduction of the number of vendors in American manufacturing is already under way.

Problem 1. You wish to purchase 1000 pieces of xbae. You make calls to companies A and B that offer the product, and you explain the specifications. Each company submits 1000 pieces of xbae—all good, so the companies claim. You satisfy yourself, by your own inspection, that indeed all 2000 pieces meet your specifications. Which lot would you buy? Toss a coin?

Before you make a snap judgment, it might be wise to consider the fact that your specifications may not tell the whole story. There may be characteristics that are important to have in the pieces that you will buy, but not covered in your specifications. There may be other characteristics that you would wish to avoid, and your specifications may not protect you. Company A has been in the business and provides continuing evidence of process control. There may be persuasive arguments in favor of Company A. One must remember that the distribution of the important quality-characteristics of the 1000 parts made by Company A will be more uniform than the distribution of those made by Company B. Uniformity is nearly always important. If the price offered by Company B is the lower of the two, it would be wise to inquire how this could be, as Company A's costs will be lower. Perhaps Company B can offer a bargain. He may have had a cancellation from another customer, and has the material on hand.

Problem 2. Now, we come to a totally different problem. You plan to purchase 1000 pieces of xbae every week. Your requirements in this problem point definitely to selection of Company A. The distribution of the important quality-characteristic of the xbae is predictable. It will be steady week after week. If the distribution falls within your specifications, you can eliminate

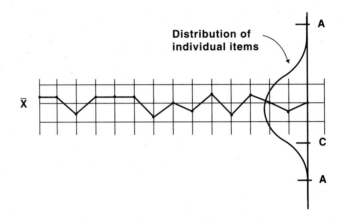

x̄-chart for a criitical quality-characteristic. If the specifications are at A, A, the output of Company A requires no inspection. Problems will arise (see text) if a specification were at C.

inspection of incoming parts except for routine observations and comparisons for identification. You will know from the control charts that came along with the product, far better than any amount of inspection can tell you, what the distribution of quality is and what it will be.

If a tail of the distribution falls beyond your specifications, you will require 100 percent inspection.

Company B? About Company B we know nothing.

Another advantage of statistical control is a better price and better quality than Company B can give. If Company B offers you a better price, it is because he knows not what his costs are. He may chisel you on quality, or he may go out of business trying to meet the price that he quoted, and leave you stranded.

You may decide, for protection, to give some of the business to Company B, just to have a second vendor to fall back on in case Company A suffers some hard luck. This is your privilege. You will have to pay the extra cost that Company B must charge you if he stays in business and delivers the quantity that you require, and you will have to inspect the material that comes from him. Whether it is wise to do business with Company B could be questioned, but you now have a rational basis for your decision.

In free enterprise you have a right to make a wrong decision, and to get beat up for it.

A request for bids usually contains a clause to say that quality may be considered along with price. That is, the award will not necessarily be given to the lowest bidder. Such a clause is meaningless without a yardstick by which to measure quality. The buyer and his purchasing manager usually lack such a yardstick. They are candidates for plunder by the lowest bidder.

A flagrant example is a request for professional help, to be awarded to the lowest bidder. Example (actual, from a government agency):

> For delivery and evaluation of a course on management for quality control for supervisors...
> An order will be issued on the basis of price.

5. Use statistical methods to find out, in any trouble spot, what are the sources of trouble.   Which are local faults? Which faults belong to the system? Put responsibility where it belongs. Do not rely on judgment. Judgment always gives the wrong answer on the question of where the fault lies. Statistical methods make use of knowledge of the subject matter where it can be effective, but supplant it where it is a hazard.

Constantly improve the system. This obligation never ceases. Most people in management do not understand that the system (their responsibility) is everything not under the governance of a local group.

6. Institute modern aids to training on the job.   Training must be totally reconstructed. Statistical methods must be used to learn when training is finished, and when further training would be beneficial. A man once hired and trained, and in statistical control of his own work, whether it be satisfactory or not, can do no better. Further training cannot help him. If his work is not satisfactory, move him to another job, and provide better training there.

7. Improve supervision.   Supervision belongs to the system, and is the responsibility of management.

- Foremen must have more time to help people on the job.
- Statistical methods are vital as aid to the foreman and to the production manager to indicate where fault lies: is it local, or is it in the system?
- The usual procedure by which the foreman calls the worker's attention to every defect, or to half of them, may be wrong—is certainly wrong in most organizations—and defeats the purpose of supervision.
- Supervision in large segments of American industry is deplorable. For example, a common practice is to look at the production records of people on the job, supervisors, managers, and to deliberately take aim at the lowest 5 percent or the lowest 10 percent. Claims of results from this procedure are nothing but reinvention of the Hawthorne effect. The ultimate result is frustration and demoralization of the organization.

8. *Drive out fear.*   Most people on a job, and even people in management positions, do not understand what the job is, nor what is right or wrong. Moreover, it is not clear to them how to find out. Many of them are afraid to ask questions or to report trouble. The economic loss from fear is appalling. It is necessary, for better quality and productivity, that people feel secure. *Se* comes from Latin, meaning without, *cure* means fear or care. Secure means without fear, not afraid to express ideas, not afraid to ask questions, not afraid to ask for further instructions, not afraid to report equipment out of order, nor material that is unsuited to the purpose, poor light, or other working conditions that impair quality and production.

Another related aspect of fear is inability to serve the best interests of the company through necessity to satisfy specified rules, or to satisfy a production quota, or to cut costs by some specified amount.

One common result of fear is seen in inspection. An inspector records incorrectly the result of an inspection for fear of overdrawing the quota of allowable defectives of the work force.

9. *Break down barriers between departments.*   People in research, design, purchase of materials, sales, receipt of incoming materials, must learn about the problems encountered with various materials and specifications in production and assembly. Otherwise, there will be losses in production from necessity for rework and from attempts to use materials unsuited to the purpose. Why not spend time in the factory, see the problems, and hear about them?

I only recently saw a losing game, 40 percent defective output, the basic cause of which was that the sales department and the design department had put their heads together and come through with a style whose tolerances were beyond the economic capability of the process. This lack of coordination helps a plant to become a nonprofit organization.

In another instance, the man in charge of procurement of materials, in attendance at the seminars, declared that he has no problems with procurement, as he accepts only perfect materials. (Chuckled I to myself, "That's the way to do it.") Next day, in one of his plants, a superintendent showed to me two pieces of an item from two different suppliers, same item number, both beautifully made, both met the specifications, yet they were sufficiently different for one to be usable, the other usable only with costly rework, a heavy loss to the plant. The superintendent was charged with 20,000 of each one.

Both pieces satisfied the specifications. Both suppliers had fulfilled their contracts. The explanation lay in specifications that were incomplete and unsuited to the requirements of manufacture, approved by the man that had no problems. There was no provision for a report on material used in desperation. It seems that difficulties like this bring forth solace in such remarks as:

This is the kind of problem that
we see any day in this business.

or

Our competitors are having the same kind
of problem.

What would some people do without their competitors? Surely one responsibility of management in production is to provide help in such difficulties, and not leave a plant manager in a state of such utter hopelessness.

Purchasing managers must learn that specifications of incoming materials do not tell the whole story. What problems does the material encounter in production? It is necessary to follow a sample of materials through the whole production process to learn about the problems encountered, and onward to the consumer's problems.

10. Eliminate numerical goals, slogans, pictures, posters, urging people to increase productivity, sign their work as an autograph, etc., so often plastered everywhere in the plant. ZERO DEFECTS is an example. Posters and slogans like these never helped anyone to do a better job. Numerical goals even have a negative effect through frustration. These devices are management's lazy way out. They indicate desperation and incompetence of management. There is a better way.

11. Look carefully at work standards. Do they take account of quality, or only numbers? Do they help anyone to do a better job? Work standards are costing the country as much loss as poor materials and mistakes.

Any day in hundreds of factories, men stand around the last hour or two of the day, waiting for the whistle to blow. They have completed their quotas for the day; they may do no more work, and they cannot go home. Is this good for the competitive position of American industry? Ask these men. They are unhappy doing nothing. They would rather work.

12. Institute a massive training program for employees in simple but powerful statistical methods. Thousands of people must learn rudimentary statistical methods. One in 500 must spend the necessary 10 years to become a statistician. This training will be a costly affair.

13. Institute a vigorous program for retraining people in new skills. The program should keep up with changes in model, style, materials, methods, and, if advantageous, new machinery.

14. Create a structure in top management that will push every day on the above thirteen points. Make maximum use of statistical knowledge and talent in your company. Top management will require guidance from an experienced consultant, but the consultant cannot take on obligations that only the management can carry out.

ACTION REQUIRED

The first step is for management to understand what their job is—the fourteen points. The next step is to get into motion on them. Quality and productivity are everybody's job, but top management must lead. Until and unless top management establish constancy of purpose and make it possible for everyone in the company to work without fear for the company and not just to please someone, efforts of other people in the company, however brilliant be the fires that they start, can only be transitory.

How soon? When?   A long thorny road lies ahead in American industry—ten to thirty years—to settle down to an accepted competitive position. This position may be second place, maybe fourth. Small gains will be visible within a few weeks after a company mobilizes for quality, but sweeping improvement over the whole company will take a long time, and will continue forever. Unmistakable advances will be obvious within five years, more in ten. Management must learn the new economics: likewise government regulatory agencies, and they may require thirty years. Meanwhile, American industry will continue to suffer under the supposition that competition is the secret to better quality and service, and to lower costs.

Products that have been the backbone of American industry may in time decline to secondary importance. New products and new technology may ascend to top place. Agriculture may move up further in foreign trade.

Tangible results from each of the fourteen points will not all be visible at the same time. Perhaps the best candidate for quickest results is to supplant work standards (No. 11) with statistical aids to the worker and to supervision. No one knows what productivity can be achieved with statistical methods that help people to accomplish more by working smarter, not harder.

A close second for quick results would be to start to drive out fear (No. 8), to help people to feel secure to find out about the job and about the product, and unafraid to report trouble with equipment and with incoming materials. Once top management takes hold in earnest, this goal might be achieved with 50 percent success, and with powerful economic results, within two or three years. Continuation of effort will bring further success.

A close third, and a winner, would be to break down barriers between departments (No. 9).

Survival of the fittest.   Companies that adopt constancy of purpose for quality and productivity, and go about it with intelligence, have a chance to survive. Others have not. Charles Darwin's law of survival of the fittest, and that the unfit do not survive, holds in free enterprise as well as in nature's selections.

CONSUMERISM AND PRODUCT QUALITY

JOSEPH M. JURAN

A huge storm is brewing, and the downpour has already begun. For some decades now, the accumulating grievances of consumers (i.e., "small" users of goods and services) have been gathering and shaping themselves into a striking force—a movement for which we have coined the name "consumerism." The movement has become sizeable enough to attract a wide assortment of new, bold consumer advocates who are emerging as leaders of the consumerism movement.

Let me at this point coin a new word, "consumerist," as a label for this new species of consumer advocates. These consumerists have successfully seized the initiative and have opened an attack on the established institutions which supply our goods and services, so that we are now in the early stages of what looks like a massive revolution in commercial and industrial practices.

In nearly half a century of close association with problems of product quality, I have never seen anything which towers as high as does this consumerism movement. The closest analogy is the wave of collective bargaining which struck industrial companies in the mid-1930's. Prior to the 1930's the accumulated grievances of industrial employes had been boiling and building up pressures. The shock of the Great Depression brought the explosion. Before it all settled down industrial companies discovered that a bargaining agent now stood between them and their employees.

The biggest fact about the consumerism movement is that before it all settles down the industrial companies may discover that a bargaining agent stands between them and their customers.

THE INDICTMENTS

The consumer has a wide list of grievances. Those which relate to quality can be grouped as follows:

> *Misrepresentation.* The advertising, package, sales pitch, and promotion are intended to confuse and deceive the consumer into buying something which will not live up to the representations.
> *Failures.* The products fail on receipt or in service.
> *No satisfaction.* When products do fail, the consumer cannot get satisfaction because of confused responsibility, incompetence, delay, and dishonesty.

(There are other grievances as well: deceptive pricing, financing, and quantities, etc., along with related matters, e.g., environmental pollution. These will not be considered in this article, which is restricted to product quality. "Product" is used here in the sense of both products and services.)

Evidence to support these indictments consists of legions of individual grievances but no summarized scoreboard. Emotion and bias can thrive in such an atmosphere, but not detached reflection and judgment. This state of affairs has predictably led us to some serious consequences:

1. Consumerists have been having a field day generalizing from selected grievances, publishing plausible but biased conclusions, thereby seizing the initiative.
2. Industrial managers, previously lulled into a false sense of security due to the lack of a scoreboard, have been unable to refute these charges due to this same lack of a scoreboard.
3. Consequently, while we have some very real consumer quality problems which require remedy, we are in grave danger of putting our efforts into channels which will serve to aggrandize the consumerists without helping the consumer.

It is my belief that this danger has already materialized in the case of automotive safety. New legislation requiring added equipment and controls is costing automobile purchasers more than a billion dollars per annum (a tax without a tax bill, actually). Yet there is no scoreboard. We literally do not know how much safety, if any, this has bought us.

With this introduction, let us now turn to: an examination of the validity of the indictments, a consideration of the causes of consumers' real quality problems, and an analysis of the means for providing remedies for these causes.

MISREPRESENTATION OF QUALITY

Let us start with the flat statement that advertising and promotion does in fact contain a great deal of exaggeration and confusion, along with some deceit. Why do we tolerate this? Why don't companies tell the truth about their products?

The main reason is that they are perpetuating a practice which, though once tolerable, is now largely obsolete. For centuries, sellers have exaggerated or "puffed" the merits of their products, and courts did little to stop them. The reason was that the ordinary user could do quite a bit to guard himself against deception. In those years the subjects of trade were mainly familiar materials and goods—natural foods, textiles, and the like. Users had been exposed to these products from childhood and could see, smell, and taste them in the village marketplace.

The rule of *caveat emptor* (let the buyer beware) was a sensible rule for such products. It forced the user to grow up and thereby kept the courts out of myriad small day-to-day transactions. (The rule is still sensible wherever buyer and seller meet in the village marketplace to haggle over beans, fish, or mules, as in villages in India, Greece, and Spain.) Not only was there a near equality of product knowledge between buyer and seller, they lived in the same village. The resulting clear identity of parties, in an atmosphere of village discipline, helped keep them both honest.

Our industrial civilization meanwhile has destroyed the premises justifying the rule of *caveat emptor,* i.e., near-equality of product knowledge, clear personal responsibility, and the pressures of village discipline. The small user is hopelessly ignorant of what the manufacturer did when he built the TV set, the tire, the automobile. In addition, the small user is caught in the confused interrelations of manufacturer, merchant, and service shops, without the benefit of village discipline to keep order. The exaggerations which once were tolerable are now misrepresentations which are no longer tolerable.

Some companies are unaware that for their present products the rule of *caveat emptor* has become obsolete and they should therefore quit the habit of centuries and start making their advertising "tell it like it is." Other companies know very well that they shouldn't exaggerate and would prefer to tell it straight. What stops them (so they say) is that the other fellow uses misleading advertising and is taking away customers. Seemingly, industry associations are unable to deal with the workings of this Gresham's law of ethics, since bitter competitors have great difficulty agreeing on rules of ethics and even more difficulty in carrying out the agreements.

Yet this helplessness is by no means universal. Some of our large merchant companies do tell it like it is, and they flourish mightily. Their practices suggest that reliability is marketable, whether in product or in advertising.

The analogy is striking. In the case of our products, we set up an independent inspection and test department to examine the product and determine its fitness for use. We are proud enough of this arrangement that we publicize it. The annual reports and institutional advertising of our companies often depict the test laboratories, torture tests and the stern "they shall not pass" inspectors, as evidence of the discipline which prevails with respect to product integrity.

In contrast, how often have we seen a picture of some stern advertising inspector as evidence of the discipline which prevails with respect to advertising integrity? I believe we have reached the stage where we now need a similar independent review of our advertising before we publish it. I doubt that this review needs to be imposed on those qualities which can be sensed by the user himself—size, shape, smell, taste, etc. As to such qualities the rule of *caveat emptor* is still a sensible rule in marketplace purchases. However, for the growing number of qualities which the user cannot sense, the rule of *caveat emptor* is obsolete, and so is the practice of puffing. It is to these qualities which the new discipline should be addressed.

If industries do not themselves see to the objectivity of their representations, they are creating the evidence needed by consumerists to make a case for regulation from the outside. Introducing an advertising inspector will likely have the same impact on marketing people as product inspection had on the production department or the design review concept had on the design department. These invasions of former monopolies were bitterly contested. In addition, it was necessary to develop the techniques of inspection—what to look for, what standards to apply, etc. We now face these same problems in reviewing advertising.

My conclusion on misrepresentation is that there is much merit to the charges, and a clear response is needed. The required response is not a change in technology but rather a change in business practice, consisting of application of strict objectivity to advertising and promotion. If enough companies go down this road, there may be no need for legislation. If a substantial minority of companies continue their present practices, then assuredly we will have legislation as a remedy.

PRODUCT FAILURES

A second major target of consumerism is product failures. ("It just stopped working.") These failures have given rise to a great deal of biting comment and a longing for the good old days of craftsmanship and the nostalgic rest. It is useful here to raise some pointed questions to which I will try to give objective answers.

1. Is product quality better or worse than it was years ago?   It is better. For any product line, today's quality usually is far better than it was years ago. Our lamps give better light, radio sets give greater fidelity, cameras give better pictures, appliances offer greater convenience than their predecessors.

Not only usage features, but product life also is better. Today's tires, lamps, TV sets, etc., all run longer before failure than their predecessor models. In technical jargon, the "failure rate" is going down. Failure rate is to products what mortality rate is to human beings.

2. If the failure rate really is going down, why do we seem to have more failures?   We seem to have more failures because we do have more failures. However, this is the result of the products population explosion.

In human mortality, despite the growing life span, the number of deaths rises annually because the growth in population more than offsets the decline in mortality rate. Similarly, in product mortality, the number of product failures rises because the growth in product population more than offsets the declining failure rate. The population explosion in products has been far more violent than the population explosion in people.

We see a quantified example of this in Chauncey Starr's[1] chart on the fatality rate of that much maligned device, the motor vehicle. Figure I shows that fatality rate per person-hour of exposure has been cut by several orders of magnitude since 1900. However, the number of people using motor vehicles has gone up even more orders of magnitude, and this has been multiplied further by growing vehicle usage in hours per year.

3. If failure rates are in fact going down, why aren't we better off than we used to be?   We *are* better off while products are working. However, we are worse off, much worse off, when products fail, because of some enormous, subtle changes:

   a. We have redesigned our patterns of life on the assumption that products and services will not fail. Like the Dutch, we now live behind numerous protective dikes, the dikes of quality control.[2]
   b. Our business policies and practices are largely designed to meet the needs of short-life not long-life products.
   c. We have not yet created service organizations adequate to give the small user prompt redress when things do fail.

---

[1]Chauncey Starr (Dean, School of Engineering and Applied Science, UCLA), "Social Benefit versus Technological Risk," *Science* 165 (Sept. 19, 1969): 1232–1238.
[2]Juran, J. M. "Mobilizing for the 1970s." *Quality Progress,* Aug. 1969.

FIGURE 1	**MOTOR VEHICLES**

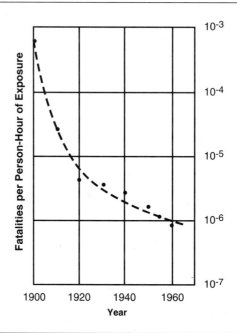

For these reasons (and others) the failures, though declining in rate, have grown in number and in impact on the consumers' well-being. It will help to reduce the failure rate still further, but the more immediate need is to improve machinery for dealing with service failures.

4. Are manufacturers knowingly putting out products which will give short life? Yes they are, for a variety of reasons, mostly "good":

a. They don't know how to increase the life, e.g., automotive spark plugs.
b. They know how, but to do so would deteriorate something else, e.g., a harsher ride from tires and shock absorbers.
c. They know how but it would clearly be a waste for the user, e.g., women's dress shoes, where style changes rather than technology decide the useful life.
d. They know how, and the result would be a long range cost reduction for the user. However, the tradition of emphasizing original price stands in the way, or so marketing managers say. (The early trade-in practice in some products greatly complicates this problem.)

This last approach requires some elaboration, since it contains the opportunity for failure reduction through a break with tradition. Emphasis on original price obviously is sound as applied to short-lived products for which follow-on costs are small. It is not "obvious" as applied to long-lived products. On the contrary, our sophisticated large users are abandoning the emphasis on original product price in favor of a new emphasis on *cost of service* over total useful life.

As matters stand, we have some high reliability designs which are not being marketed solely because of the tradition of emphasis on original price. We should become very suspicious about this tradition. Not only is it largely out of date; it also opens industry to charges of "planned obsolescence," i.e., that new models are created and through the hypnotism of advertising, consumers are forced to buy new models despite the adequacy of old models which they already own.

Let us note here that the term "planned obsolescence" is largely a piece of quackery used to sell the books of consumerists. (When it comes to marketing their wares, consumerists are at least as deceitful as those whom they accuse of being deceitful.) The crux of the matter is in the answer to "Who makes the decision to discard the old product?"

In the case of a new model car, refrigerator, etc., the manufacturer offers alternatives and tries to persuade the consumer to buy, but *the consumer makes the decision,* no matter what the consumerists say. However, in the case of short-life components which will not last the expected service life of the total apparatus, *the manufacturer makes the decision.*

This truly is a form of planned obsolescence, and there are plenty of evils lurking within this practice. One of them, the "profitable spare parts business," I described in some detail in another paper. The opportunity is present to give manufacturers a vested interest in product failures, and altogether too many instances of short-lived products are rooted in this vested interest, though defended on the grounds of avoiding increases in original costs.

Summarizing on product failures, I believe the industry record has been mostly good—a long, continuing record of lower failure rates through constant product improvement. However, there is a serious weakness inherent in the policy of designing and selling to emphasize original price. This policy is increasingly obsolete as applied to long-life products. There is a real marketing opportunity here for those manufacturers who are first to break with outmoded tradition.

Technological tools for reducing failure rates are well known and I believe we have done a good job in using them to date. We can go further in use of technology by improving maintainability, either by systems redesign (e.g., self-lubricating bearings) or by modular designs which simplify user self-maintenance. However, the main opportunity for improvement seems to be through abandoning the obsolescent policy of designing and marketing with emphasis solely on original selling price.

No Satisfaction

My conviction, which I am not able to prove by data, is that the consumer is tolerant on the matter of product failures. He doesn't like them, but he is aware that we have not yet learned how to make millions of units of product without some degree of product failure. However, as to providing satisfaction for the failures which do occur, I believe we are heading into a no tolerance era and it is high time.

Given a commitment to live behind the dikes of quality control, we simply must restructure our affairs to see that the consumer can get service restored promptly. I don't see how we can compromise with this. In my judgment, it is this lack of satisfaction, rather than the existence of failures, which has brought the consumerism movement to its present size and force.

The consumers' problems in getting service restored exist both during and beyond the guarantee period. During the guarantee period this problem is mainly bureaucratic in origin—how to locate the right man. To the consumer, the workings of a big company are just as mysterious as the workings of a television set. The need is to give the consumer a single address, a single phone number to contact. Some of our companies have set it up that way and it works. Failing this, the consumer can get lost in the labyrinth, whereupon he writes to his congressman or to some handy consumerist.

Outside of the guarantee period the problem is different and at its worst. Here the consumer is on his own and must discover a service shop that is competent, prompt and honest. It is a challenging assignment, to say the least.

Here again we soon see that the problems of restoring service are traceable mainly to outmoded policies and business practices. To understand this it is useful to look back at how the problems of restoring service were handled in centuries past, when mankind lived mainly in small villages.

In the village economy, the local craftsman performed completely the functions of product design, manufacture, sale, and service. The consumer had one man to deal with, so responsibility was undivided and clear. In turn, the undivided responsibility drove the village craftsman to do his job in a way which responded to the users' needs over the total product life, not just the infant mortality period.[3] Finally, the village discipline favored an honest response to this responsibility.

It is these same features of village life that we must now reinstate if we are to provide the consumer with satisfaction in case of failure: clear, one-man responsibility; responsibility for the useful life of the product, not just the infant mortality period; a discipline which favors meeting these responsibilities.

Two main obstacles stand between us and reinstating these conditions:

1. Present limited guarantees which cover only 10 percent or so of the useful life, requiring some different arrangement over the bulk of service life. The model for solving this already is in existence, i.e., an original limited guarantee as part of the purchase price, plus a term service contract thereafter. This model could take care of us if we had good service shops, which brings us to the second obstacle.

2. Our present service shops are seriously inadequate for the job and the situation may be getting worse, not better. This requires some elaboration.

While many of our manufacturers and merchants have created a service shop capacity adequate to handle in-guarantee failures, they have not expanded this capacity to out-of-guarantee failures. To fill this huge gap numerous independent repair shops have been created.

Many studies have been conducted to test the competence and integrity of these shops and the results are shocking. To illustrate—a simple malfunction was deliberately created in an automobile and the vehicle was then taken to 19 different New York City garages. Eleven of the 19 turned in false diagnoses at unconscionable prices. (One mechanic diagnosed the trouble immediately and corrected it at once—without charge.) This shocking variability in competence and integrity is probably aggravated by the operation of a Gresham's law of service—the dishonest shops drive out the honest, certainly in large cities.

There have been some attempts to deal with this problem through legislation. A few states now license their TV and appliance repairmen. The 1969 New York City Consumer Protection Act empowers the commissioner to sue on behalf of the user, and these suits can be applied to service repair shops. However, I am unimpressed by attempts to solve these matters by legislation since problems of independent service shops lie in inadequate management

---

[3]For a model of guarantee for service life, as well as of clarity, we might look at the guarantee of three jewelers in the Middle East: "As concerns the gold ring set with an emerald, we guarantee that for 20 years the emerald will not fall out of the gold ring. If the emerald should fall out of the gold ring before the end of 20 years we shall pay unto Bel-nadin-shumu an indemnity or 10 mana of silver." The date is 429 BC!

and technology. To be effective they need good diagnostic equipment, some of which has as yet not even been developed. They need specially designed tools. They desperately need technicians well trained in using this gear to diagnose and repair failures. Above all, they need good management.

On the record, small independents cannot solve such problems. Instead, they become extinct due to competition from other, more competent organization forms. In my lifetime I have seen entire species of small businesses become extinct: the corner grocer, the neighborhood butcher, and so on and on. The reasons for this were the superior efficiency of the central manufacturer, central merchant, or chain stores when compared to the small businesses as a class. Some small proprietors were superb and many were good. But most were not good and some were dreadful. The growth of the independent service shop as a species almost certainly will give us a re-run of this same scenario.

The challenge to independents will come from at least three other species:

1. *Manufacturers' service departments.* I believe we are seeing a trend for manufacturers to set up their own service shops to clarify responsibility, improve service, get better consumer feedback, and, significantly, improve product marketing.
2. *Merchants' service shops.* These likewise seem to be on the increase and for the same reasons as growth of manufacturers' service shops.
3. *Chain of service shops.* This would be a new application of the principle under which other services are now provided, e.g., restaurants, motels, laundries. To date this form has not made much headway, but I regard it as a neglected business opportunity.

Right now we cannot be sure which of these forms will succeed in dominating the service industry. However, we can confidently conclude that the dominant form will be characterized by:

Numerous shops geographically dispersed to provide locally convenient service,

Central staff specialists to plan the business and management structure and systems of the shops,

Central technology specialists to develop efficient machines, tools, and instruments for diagnosis and repair,

Central quality control specialists to establish quality plans (specifications, standards, procedures, etc.) and to audit performance of shops against these plans.

On the record, such organizations greatly outperform the small independents. Backed up by central technology and staff management assistance, their shops are able to secure better diagnostic instruments, better tools, better management systems. By offering a career they are able to recruit better candidates. They accept the need for training as a prerequisite to doing a job well. Not least, they adhere to a level of ethics that is well ahead of the independents as a species.

The foregoing may not be valid applied to small towns where something akin to village discipline favors competent honesty over incompetence and deceit. Neither is it valid as to repair services on products with which the consumer is familiar, e.g., shoes, clothing. Even in our giant cities we can get good repair service on such products.

ALTERNATIVE ROADS

Up to this point I have discussed consumer quality problems mainly from the standpoint of solutions to be provided by industry. However, the willingness and especially the ability of industry to solve these problems is open to serious question. In addition, the opportunities inherent in leadership of the consumerism movement have stirred the imagination of government departments, standards organizations, independent laboratories, consumer publications, etc. Extensive competition is in progress, the stakes being leadership of the consumerism movement and the post of bargaining agent between manufacturers and their customers. Since these stakes have enormous implications of economic power, we can be sure competition will be intense.

Now let's examine the potentialities of solution as offered by the principal contenders in this competition, including industry itself.

SOLUTION BY INDUSTRY

It would be a great simplification if industry itself could take the leadership of the consumerism movement. This would avoid creation of new regulatory devices, new advocates, and other intermediate agents, all of which add complication to something already complicated enough.

First let us clear ground by disposing of some industry actions that are assuredly *not* the solution.

1. Deny existence of the problem.   Consumerists have already outflanked this defense. Until a credible scoreboard can be developed, legislators will not accept the denials of industrialists.

2. Contend that government regulation is an evil.   This ideological defense is an exercise in futility; no one is listening except the cronies. During legislative hearings this contention, along with a wooden insistence that the situation is well in hand, leads legislators to conclude, quite properly, that they are dealing with men who are shockproof to the needs or are just stubbornly stupid about them. The legislators then proceed on the basis, "you are of no help, so we'll do the best we can without you."

3. Motivate workers.   Many managers cling tenaciously to a belief that product failures are the result of worker carelessness, blunder, indifference, and even sabotage. Under this belief the solution is to motivate the workers. Such was the thrust of zero defects programs of the 1960s. However, the facts are that the great majority of product failures are "management-controllable," e.g., poor design, inadequate processes, sale for the wrong application.

Turning away from these non-solutions, there are some constructive actions which companies can take.

1. Conduct the objective study.   There is a desperate need for industry to quantify the reasons for consumer agitation and unrest. I believe the main obstacle here has been the managers' belief that complaints, returns, and other such warning signals constituted adequate data sources. The rush of recent legislation should cause all managers to question these axiomatic beliefs—beliefs that are constantly reinforced by talking with other managers who share them.

The way out of this self-sealing thought system is through a fresh study insured for objectivity by participation of independent outsiders. Only such an objective study can reliably affirm the absence or presence of a real problem. It also can point to the vital few specifics which demand the bulk of the action.

The objective study may be sponsored by an industry group or even by a leading company that has decided to go it alone. Either way represents a vital first step without which the risk of false security or false solutions is high.

Lacking such an objective review, industry always faces the threat that some consumerist will make the study for them. These consumerist "studies" are commonly biased in the other direction; some of them are contemptibly biased. But strong bias tends to become well-publicized and, once publicized, attracts followers, including legislators.

2. Establish a scoreboard.   Just as desperately do we need a scoreboard on the extent of various consumer problems and on the various factors that influence these problems. At present we have good information only for what happens during the guarantee period, and even this is limited to whatever affects manufacturers' costs. This should be opened up to include the entire situation as seen by the user.

Such a new approach would require that we collect information over the entire useful life of the product, not just the guarantee period. We need information on users' costs no less than on manufacturers' costs. We also need to secure information on problems of restoring service—how easy it is to locate a service man, how prompt is his response, how competent is his repair, how honest is his invoice.

These scoreboards are needed not merely for defenses against the excesses of consumerists; they also are needed because a scoreboard is a tool basic to good management.

3. Establish new policies and standards. Objective studies and scoreboards will point to the need for new service policies and standards. Naturally, these will differ from industry to industry. However, we can safely suggest some likely universals:

  a. A policy of copy review for advertising and promotion. We need a formal review of copy for integrity just as we have for centuries formally inspected products before shipment and, more recently, have introduced formal design reviews.
  b. A policy of unified responsibility for service over the entire useful life of the product. At present the consumer deals with two sets of people— one group during the guarantee period and a second after the guarantee period. I doubt that this split can survive. To unify this responsibility may require that we "unbundle" the present guarantee from the original contract price. Alternatively, it may be done by providing a long range renewable guarantee as part of the original sales contract. Some experimentation is needed to test these and other alternatives.
  c. A policy of giving the consumer one sure number to call. This is the simple principle of eliminating any run-around for the consumer. Anything short of this seems to me to be an outrage.
  d. Standards for service performance: training and qualification of service men; time to respond to consumer calls; competence of repair; pricing, etc.
  e. A policy of audit of service shop performance and evaluation against standards.

Of course there will be some needs for improved technology. There is a widespread belief by companies that the service shop is unprofitable. Many do not set it up as a profit center, regarding it rather as an adjunct to product marketing. Yet when one visits various service shops, it soon becomes evident that we have not devoted the engineering effort needed to give them the diagnostic, repair, and paperwork tools and other essentials for efficient operation comparable to those of the factories. So we do need better technology.

However, the foregoing policies and standards are mainly concerned with business and management matters rather than with technology.

4. Set up executive seminars to help companies mobilize to solve these problems. Managers can learn much from each other during such seminars, but we also must guard against the self-sealing thought system.

Preparation for such seminars should include good staff work and, especially, objective studies of what bothers consumers. A helpful addendum is the study of what is done in other countries, notably Japan, western Europe, and the Soviet Union. The great variation in approach found in these diverse cultures is of great help in opening up rigid thought patterns.

I might add that, to my knowledge, there is no restraint of trade or anti-trust connotation in such industry seminars or even in a scheme of self-regulation by industry. What is decisive is the subject matter of the seminar or self-regulation. Obviously, the industry cannot establish standards for prices, share of market, or other matters of a commercial nature. However, quality controls and technology, per se, are not within these prohibitions.

5. Create the machinery for industry self-regulation. Here we get into controversial matters since there is a good deal of doubt that industries can become self-regulating. However, I will put down some ideas for exploration:

The clearinghouse to identify the bad guys. There is a widespread belief among managers that when it comes to dishonesty and incompetence, the Pareto principle holds, i.e., a small percent of the manufacturers, merchants, and service shops account for the bulk of the consumers' problems. I share this belief, but with caution, since we lack the data to be conclusive. However, if valid, the concept is of the greatest importance, since reforming or eliminating a few companies would greatly improve things for the consumer.

To this end I would like to see creation of an authoritative data bank or clearing house to receive information on company performance much as is now done by Dun & Bradstreet with credit ratings. The Better Business Bureaus now do some of this as applied to business practices, though their resources are as yet too limited to support a field force comparable to that of Dun & Bradstreet.

The use of these data would have to be a matter of evolution. However, precedents already set by Dun & Bradstreet and the Better Business Bureaus are suggestive of the path evolution will take. Provision would be made for consumers to draw information from the bank and to use this information as a guide in deciding with whom to do business.

As I will discuss later, I believe the separation of good guys from bad guys must be adopted not only by industry but by the regulators as well.

The ombudsman. This is the Swedish name for a man to call when all else fails. He is a sure friend. He is consumer-oriented. He knows how to find the right man in the labyrinth. And he has muscle through his access to top managers, government officials, and the press.

Some of our newspapers perform this function now, either by publishing letters to the editor or by providing an actual ombudsman for their readers. We should test this device on a much larger scale.

The dominant companies as leaders. In those industries where a few companies dominate the entire industry, the way is open for one or several companies to take the leadership for solving these problems through a bold (and risky) break with the past.

This is, of course, the very thing companies do in launching new products or new business practices. Their product or business leadership is based on exactly such breakthroughs. The challenge is presented for using this tried technique for securing leadership of the consumerism movement.

Some of these innovations are already in effect. The leading chemical fiber companies impose quality standards on converters as a condition of end-use licensing. In addition, the consumer is given the option of making his complaint direct to the nationally known chemical company rather than to the intermediate converters or merchants. One of the appliance manufacturers has similarly set up a direct communication link from user to manufacturer, bypassing the dealers in the process.

The industry association as leader. As we will see in the discussion of the standardization mark there is precedent for using the industry association to establish industry standards for matters affecting the consumer and to secure compliance. Because compliance is voluntary, the record in establishing standards has been much more distinguished than that in securing compliance. However, in deploring the latter, let us not overlook the former.

If we separate the setting of standards from the job of enforcement, we can make use of industry association machinery to help solve part of the problem. Certainly we need new standards for services to be rendered to the consumer. If companies can use association machinery to create such standards, that is already a progressive step forward. Once standards are available, there are alternatives for enforcement, as I will examine shortly.

We see from the foregoing that there are plenty of opportunities for constructive action by industry. The more that industry can take this action, the less is the need for bargaining agents and the more persuasive become industry defenses to regulation. However, it is unlikely that industry will do all that needs to be done. Hence let me turn to other forces contesting for leadership of the consumerism movement.

INDEPENDENT LABORATORY MARK

One candidate for providing added assurance to consumers is the independent test laboratory. The theory is that an unbiased laboratory can examine products, determine their fitness for use, and put its mark of approval on those fit for use. This mark, derived from such an unbiased source, offers users added assurance beyond that available from biased manufacturers.

Let me first distinguish between the mandatory and voluntary test laboratory. The former is backed by legislation or powerful economic forces to the extent that a manufacturer cannot market his products without laboratory approval. In contrast, the voluntary test laboratory offers its facilities and its mark of approval on the open market; manufacturers and consumers can take it or leave it, as they please.

Voluntary test laboratories have been around for a long time. They vary considerably in competence and especially in ethics. Collectively their impact on the economy has to date been quite limited. Now, under the agitation of the consumerism movement, independent laboratories are bustling with new energy, for they sense a big, rare opportunity to move in. An example of this new energy is seen in steps being taken by the American National Standards Institute (formerly the United States of America Standards Institute) to enter the certification arena.

To examine the potentialities of the independent laboratory mark we should look separately at the elements of fitness for use, since certification problems differ remarkably for each of these elements.

Quality of design. A good case in point is the mark of Underwriters Laboratories (UL) which is really a mandatory type of laboratory and is highly respected in the fields of fire hazards and other perils.

Along with analysis of designs, UL conducts qualification tests of samples by subjecting them to various environments and stresses dictated by codes and engineering judgment. Their mark is decisive in the ability to secure insurance at standard premiums.

However we must face squarely the fact that the test for quality of design is a one-shot test. It requires a laboratory equipped with the proper test gear and manned by professionals who know what to test for. It does not require continuing sampling of the product thereafter. It is a comparatively inexpensive form of assurance and can be of positive aid to the consumer.

Quality of conformance. Now we are in something radically different. What is required here is a continuing review of the product as distinguished from a one-shot study. The two main approaches for making this review are seen in the contrasting schemes for vendor relations:

a. A continuing independent inspection (detail or sampling) of the product plus acceptance based on the results of that inspection, or

b. The surveillance concept in which the independent laboratory (1) reviews and approves the manufacturer's control plan and (2) thereafter reviews data and decisions of the manufacturer, making (or observing) only such inspections as are needed to conduct an audit of decisions.

The inspection is a costly form of providing this assurance, and to date only regulatory agencies seem able to finance it. The surveillance concept is comparatively economical and we have much experience in its use due to its wide adoption by the military. I might note that use of the surveillance concept requires that the independent laboratory adopt the principle of treating good guys differently from bad guys.

The "abilities." In the case of long-life products, we still are in the early stages of setting standards for reliability, maintainability, and the rest. Until these standards have taken form, the conventional basis for awarding a mark is hardly complete. I suppose we might depart from convention and let laboratories award the mark on their best judgment. I cannot imagine our industrial companies accepting such a situation in the absence of legislation, and I can't imagine legislation on this topic in the absence of a provision for setting standards.

I doubt it has been thought through (including by myself) but it seems to me that in our present state of development independent laboratories are in no position to award the mark for the "abilities" aspect of fitness for use.

Customer service. In the case of customer service, the situation is at its worst. Here the laboratory with all of its test gear is academic to the issues. What is in question is the competence, promptness, and integrity of the service organizations. I cannot see the independent laboratory as being of any assistance here. We have to invent totally new forms of independent assurance.

The foregoing asserts that in our present state of development, the mark of the independent laboratory: can be effective as to quality of design, can be effective as to quality of conformance provided the surveillance principle is adopted, cannot be effective as to the "abilities" or as to customer service.

Even in the area of quality of design and quality of conformance, there are plenty of unsolved problems in applying the concept of the unbiased mark. Awarding the mark puts the laboratory in a position of legal risk. It intends the mark to be acted on by the consumer and, when there are failures, the consumer can and does make the laboratory a defendant. The problems of insuring the laboratory, of posting bonds to protect the laboratory, etc., are formidable and certainly not yet laid to rest.

In the capitalistic economies, independent laboratories are faced with getting their income from one of two basic sources—the consumers or the companies (really the manufacturers). Laboratories who derive their income from consumers have found that they must add the concept of value to their findings on quality. Their appeal to consumers is on the basis that the price of their publications is modest in relation to the benefit he gets through wiser purchases—a return on investment. Of course these publications must compete with the advertising and promotion of the companies.

The laboratories who wish to "sell" the mark to companies also face a return on investment criterion. Companies who buy the mark do so on the basis that they can recover costs through greater ease in marketing. In talking with some of our American companies (as well as companies in other capitalistic countries) I find that the powerful companies tend to scoff at the mark. They assert that their own name is better known and has better market appeal than does the mark of the independent laboratory; that this mark is useful only to shore up the weaknesses of other companies; that the strong actually demean their product by buying the mark.

Moreover, selling the mark to companies jeopardizes the laboratory's independence because of the conflict of interest, i.e., the laboratory cannot get full income unless the manufacturers' product gets good marks. Where the laboratory gets its income by selling advertising to the manufacturer the conflict is even worse and I, for one, have absolutely no confidence in the mark of such laboratories.

As matters stand, I see little likelihood that the voluntary independent laboratory can play a major role in solving the consumer's quality problems. They are at their best in evaluating short-life products for which laboratory testing is a reasonable simulation of use. For long-life, complex products, the problems of "abilities" and especially of securing satisfaction following failure are beyond the capacity of the laboratories until adequate data banks and scoreboards have been created.

Mandatory laboratories are another matter.

The Mandatory Mark

This form of solution is through a combination of national standardization plus a mandatory mark based on legislation. To understand this we must first part the dense foliage which surrounds the wide variety of activities vaguely labeled "standardization." These activities, along with who conducts them, are summarized in Table 1.

To date we in the United States have accepted the first three levels in the table with little resistance. We agree on the importance of a common reference base for the length of the meter if we are to avoid technological chaos. We agree that we must standardize voltages if we are to avoid economic

TABLE 1	STANDARDIZATION AND ENFORCEMENT		
PURPOSE OF STANDARDIZATION	**STANDARDS COMMONLY SET BY**	**ENFORCEMENT COMMONLY BY**	
1. Uniformity in metrology	National Bureau of Standards	National legislation	
2. National and local interchangeability e.g., household voltages	Various standardization committees	National and local legislation	
3. Technological definition, e.g., materials, testing	Broad based standardization committees	Voluntary compliance	
4. Minimal standards for safety, health	Government regulatory agencies	National and local legislation	
5. Minimal standards of fitness for use (not involving health or safety)	Broad based standards committees, or by competition in the marketplace	Voluntary compliance	

chaos. We agree we must have standard definitions for widely used materials and tests, again to avoid chaos.

The fourth level has been more troublesome and has met with grudging acceptance. The reason is not that our companies like their customers or employees to be maimed or diseased. Rather the resistance stems from two other reasons: a belief that enforcement of the standards will lead to economic suicide, and the past record of the regulators which so often has been to degenerate into trivial pursuits not related to human safety or health. However, these reasons have not turned out to be 100 percent valid, so the credibility of objectors has become suspect. Consequently, the list of standards for health and safety has kept growing.

We now are poised at the fifth level. At this level the purpose of minimum standards is to protect the citizen's purse. In the United States we have left it to the marketplace to carry out this function. The great quality debate of the 1970s will be on the question: *Are standards for fitness for use to be established by legislation or by the marketplace?* Both approaches are already in use and apply to domestic goods as well as to exports.

In the case of exports, many countries, both capitalistic and socialistic, have enacted legislation requiring that certain categories of products may not be exported unless they conform to minimal standards. Such export controls have for centuries been used to protect the purse of the national economy.

In the case of domestic products there has been a sharp cleavage in national practice. The capitalistic, market based economies have mainly left it to the marketplace to establish and enforce quality standards. In contrast, the socialistic, planned economies have left it to national standardization bodies to establish and enforce quality standards.

The most extensive form of this standardization activity I have witnessed has been in the Soviet Union. Here the committee for standards, measures, and measuring instruments has already established thousands of domestic quality standards and this goes on year after year. These standards have the force of law—compliance is mandatory, not merely voluntary. Moreover, the committee has the added responsibility of enforcing the standards. To this end it commands a network of hundreds of laboratories which are widely dispersed geographically and conduct product inspections, surveillance of factories, etc., to insure compliance.

In my travels I have seen no place on earth where mandatory regulation of fitness for use is as complete as in the Eastern European countries, particularly in the Soviet Union. Yet their visible products—furnishings in their hotels, goods in their domestic shops, building materials, packaging materials—exhibit shockingly low quality, the worst I have seen among industrialized countries.

This performance certainly is not due to the caliber of their people. The managers and engineers I have met are a competent, dynamic lot. They have worked out systems and technology that are a logical response to the limitations imposed by their planned society. In addition, they are actively searching for new ways of dealing with known problems. Let no one underestimate the competence and resourcefulness of these men!

They do face the problem of discovering a substitute for the advantages of the free market (as we do for its disadvantages). Their use of the mandatory mark has given us a living laboratory to study. It is my belief that their experience to date has disclosed weaknesses inherent in any system of a mandatory mark for consumer products.

1. *Companies tend to regard their mission as one of meeting specifications (as interpreted by the enforcement agency) rather than one of meeting the marketplace needs of fitness for use.* This tendency is the direct result of giving the agency the power to grant or withhold the mark.

2. *The pace of setting and maintaining standards does not conform to modern needs.* A basic principle of good standardization is the participation and practical unanimity of all interested parties. To carry out this wise provision has required that evolution of standards proceed at a glacial pace. Once issued, standards have tended to remain static since the revision of old standards commonly has a lower priority than the creation of new standards.

Such slow paced evolution was not too important in centuries past, when societies were mainly static anyhow. Neither is it too important today in those matters that are in the top three levels of our reference table, since they change slowly. However, product development has now reached a pace at which the rate of obsolescence is perilously close to the rate of standardization. For some products, the second and third generations are upon us before we have standardized the first, i.e., the standard is obsolete on the day it is issued.

No one knows better than the standardization bodies how long it takes to set a standard. Yet they can offer no easy way to make a drastic reduction. Instead, some of them hope that creation of standards for *multiple grades* will solve the problem, i.e., as affluence grows, users will promote themselves from one static grade to the next higher static grade. However, our technology and ingenuity do not pursue such convenient paths. A study of our consumption habits soon makes clear that an astonishing proportion of our products and grades of today did not even exist a decade ago.

To date I have seen no way around the need for drastically shortening the time interval for creating and revising standards. Unless this need can be met, it seems to me that the timetable alone remains as a fatal obstacle to using "standards plus enforcement" as a solution to the consumers' product quality problems.

3. *The consumers' main quality problems are traceable to slow restoration of service, incompetent repair, unconscionable pricing, etc.* In contrast, the historical emphasis and professional skills of the standards organizations have been concerned with technology: materials, products, metrology, testing. If the standards organizations are to contribute to solution of these main problems, it will not be through still more technology standards, but through a considerable change in emphasis.

Within our own market based economy, many industries have prepared standards of a technological nature, usually through the agency of broad based industry standardization committees. Compliance is voluntary, but natural economic forces have done a good deal toward achieving compliance.

Some industries have gone further and created a voluntary mark for those who choose to submit their products for test. American Gas Association and National Electrical Manufacturers Association are cases in point. Here again, natural economic forces have done much toward achieving compliance.

These voluntary schemes contain some defects—the very defects which have helped create the consumerism movement. But the voluntary structure also contains the genes for useful mutations. The real competition is not in conformance to specification but in superior fitness for use. The specification quickly becomes the minimum; the competition is to see who can exceed the minimum the most. In contrast, under mandatory conformance to standardization emphasis is on stability and the status quo rather than on dynamism and breakthrough. Meeting the unchanging standard and meeting the changing needs of the marketplace are two very different things.

From observations to date, it is my conclusion that the mandatory mark for consumer products is a detriment to the achievement of fitness for use in the free marketplace and that we should all resist its adoption. I can understand the need for this device in the planned societies to help insure that quality does not suffer in the urge to meet the production norms of national planning. In addition, I feel we should keep in close contact with their progress and the new tools they create.

I might add that to date there has been altogether too little contact between quality control and standardization specialists. Each has much to learn from the other and it is high time for the respective professional societies, conference managers, journal editors, etc., to throw some bridges across this gap.

GOVERNMENT REGULATION AND QUALITY

Government regulation of quality is as old as recorded history. Traditionally this regulation has been concerned with matters affecting the stability and purse of the government.

The consumerism movement is now thrusting government regulators into new areas—health, safety and, especially, the purse of the consumer. We can expect, and should tolerate, some awkwardness during their learning period. The agencies are faced with developing their policies and procedures, with recruiting and training their staffs, and with learning how to grapple with problems that are certainly new to them and for which precedents set by other regulatory agencies may not be fully applicable. Accordingly, while I will now propose some universals that seem pertinent to these new regulations, I do so with an awareness that they may turn out to be less than universal.

1. Regulate fitness for use, not conformance to specification.   To my knowledge, no consumer complains about conformance to specification—he complains because things don't work, because service is interrupted, because he is overcharged, etc. The entire purpose of enacting new legislation and of creating new regulatory bodies has been that they shall correct those ills that the unregulated industries have failed to correct. Such is the universally stated aim of the statutes, the speeches at ceremonial signings, the announcements of new administrators. These ills are not remedied by preoccupation with something other than fitness for use.

A clear departure from this principle is seen in the recent action to remove from the market cyclamates as an artificial sweetener. That action had nothing to do with fitness for use; there was literally no evidence that in years of usage by myriad people, any human being had been damaged by cyclamates. The real controversy was an economic contest between the sugar and the cyclamate interests. However, the surface action taken was a wooden conformance to standard—to a law that has no scientific relation to fitness for use.

In contrast, there is a great deal of evidence that cigarette smoking shortens human life, which is very much a matter of fitness for use, but no action has been taken by regulators to remove these from the market. Seemingly all we have proved is that the sugar lobby is stronger than the cyclamate lobby, and that the tobacco lobby is stronger than both. Of all the regulatory principles, we might list that of fitness for use as the most important. Regulatory agencies should never lose sight of it and we should bring them up short if they do.

2. Concentrate on the vital few qualities. A basic principle in control of anything is that a few really vital qualities are more important than the numerous trivialities. (I once misnamed this the Pareto Principle.) Our military quality regulators have greatly improved their effectiveness through use of this principle.

In contrast, I have recently seen reports of regulatory agencies which consist of nothing but the trivial many. In one series of surveillances the regulators observed, and the company verified, nearly 200 departures from standard practice: inadvertent errors, shortcuts, and the like. Not a single one of these instances affected fitness for use because the company in question made extensive use of redundancy and factor of safety in its control procedures. The main report to the company should have been, "fitness for use is well protected; keep up the good work, but continue also to keep after the kinds of errors that are set out in the appendix." Instead, the approach was to make a "federal case" out of each instance urging still more procedure and more redundancy. If the company gives in, the consumer will assuredly derive no benefit thereby. This maddening waste of energy has properly earned the contempt of the company's managers and professionals.

3. Set up to identify the bad guys. The great majority of people are law abiding, truthful, and sober. Only a relative few are criminals, liars, and sots. (The Pareto Principle again.) We make wide use of this fact. We believe the good guys; we extend credit to them; we accept their results with minimal review. We treat the bad guys differently. So useful is this principle that we go to pains to set up the scoreboards which will help us discover who are the good guys and who the bad guys. Often we go further—we make a presumption of innocence and assume someone is good until the evidence shows otherwise.

Many of our regulatory agencies make good use of this principle. Vendors are classified based on their past record and control practices are adjusted to this record. However, for reasons which are a mystery to me, some agencies reject this principle. Their explanation is that "we treat everyone alike."

We have a right and duty to insist that regulators concentrate their attention on the bad guys. At the outset they may need time to collect enough information to identify who these gentry are. However, once this time has gone by, we should demand that everybody *not* be treated alike, and we should publicly challenge the good faith of those regulators who persist in treating everyone, the reputable as well as the disreputable, as though they were permanent suspects.

4. Use surveillance, not retest.   Here again, military regulators have pioneered in evolving some valuable concepts. From control based almost exclusively on re-testing of the product, they have advanced to a surveillance concept in which the manufacturer has the dual responsibility of making the product fit for use and producing the proof that he did so. This same concept is available to new regulators and they would do well to study it carefully.

5. Develop the scoreboards.   We must have the means of knowing whether anything useful is happening to the consumer, since that is the purpose of it all. Lacking a scoreboard, the stage is set for all kinds of aimless action having no relation to fitness for use—the very thing that has likely happened with respect to automotive safety. The need for an adequate scoreboard is so fundamental that we should give regulators and companies no peace until they deliver.

6. No shift of responsibility.   Responsibility for achieving fitness for use should remain with industry and should not be taken over by the regulators. The more the regulators take on the job of detailed quality planning and detailed product testing, the more industrial companies are driven to shift their aim from achieving fitness for use to conformance to regulations.

In offering these principles for government regulation of quality, let me add that our regulatory agencies face severe pressures and criticisms from numerous insistent sources: consumerists, journalists, legislators, special pleaders of all sorts. Some of these critics are powerfully lodged and use their power recklessly to make cowardly, unwarranted attacks on regulatory agencies. All of us have a stern duty to respect the exposed position of public servants and to keep our comments on a factual, constructive level. This has been the intention in the foregoing comments.

A discussion of "Consumerism and Product Quality" would hardly be complete without some reference to the consumerists. They are very much in the scene, though their role is not understood by most and is certainly not welcomed by some.

A consumerist comes into being like any other advocate. He sees human beings who are troubled. They have needs which they cannot meet. They have problems which they cannot solve. They face threats for which they have no defense. If there are enough such human beings facing common problems, a power vacuum exists and some advocate will inevitably be drawn into this vacuum.

These advocates arise from a variety of sources, e.g., a reformer attracted by a potential cause, a journalist looking for a story, a legislator who sees a way to help his constituency, an industrialist who senses a business opportunity. One of those troubled human beings is so fed up he decides to go on the warpath.

The role of this advocate now becomes one of providing some essential services for these troubled human beings. These services include: a sympathetic understanding, diagnosis of the cause of the troubles, publicity, dramatization of the need for action, leadership.

For consumers who have been frustrated for years this collection of services must look worthwhile indeed. It should come as no surprise that they lend support to anyone who is able to provide such services. It is this collective support which has built the numerous frustrations of consumers into a "movement." In addition, the numbers of consumers (and hence voters) involved has stirred the interest of legislators who are understandably responsive to what appears to be a useful set of services for the public.

Those who deplore the emerging power of consumerists would do well to look back to the underlying forces as they existed (and still exist to a large degree). That background consisted of a widespread state of frustration due to unsolved consumer quality problems. There was a mystery about the extent of it, the cause, the remedy. No one in power even seemed to be concerned about it. The situation was made to order for any skilled consumerist who could offer the advocate's standard services. The situation created the consumerist, not the other way around.

Where the consumerist acts out his role in an objective way he deserves the support of all of us. However, there are some powerful forces tugging at the consumerist which urge him to be less than objective: his personal aspirations; the competition for leadership when the stakes are so high; the heady effect of sudden prominence and power, etc. If he yields to such forces he can do a great deal of damage to consumers, like any leader who marches his followers to an illusory goal derived from biased analysis.

I believe this is precisely what has happened with respect to automotive safety. In that area a skilled consumerist wrote a book purporting to show that the problems of automotive safety were the result of inadequate vehicle design and manufacture, that these inadequacies were the result of defective policies of the manufacturers, and that all this took place in an atmosphere of manufacturers' dominance over the forces which should have acted to restrain them. The book had a substantial sale and projected the author into national prominence. Without a doubt, the author and his book were highly influential in bringing about the recent legislation on automotive safety.

As I have noted earlier, this new legislation has been the equivalent of a tax of about a billion dollars per annum imposed on the buyers of motor vehicles. Right now no one can produce data to tell us how much safety this tax has brought us or can bring us. The data simply don't exist. They didn't exist when the legislation was enacted and they don't exist right now. Some studies are under way and they may shed light on this strange episode.

Here I venture to predict that we will discover we have been taken down a dead end, since the book in question was shockingly biased. What is significant here is not that this advocate came up with a biased book. Most of them do. What is significant is the fact that legislators were willing to act on this bias before taking steps to discover the facts, i.e.,

1. what were the relative contributions of the vehicle, motorist, road, etc., to the accident rate;
2. within these subcategories, what were the vital few causes that contributed most of the accidents; and
3. what would be the likely improvements from remedial legislation.

The action of legislators can be better understood if we look sideways at another situation in which the facts are not available. Some important discussions are held and vital decisions reached behind the closed doors of boards of directors, legislative committees, governmental offices. Many people are hungry for information on what goes on behind those closed doors. However, the official information released is incomplete, censored, and even distorted. The need for this missing information creates a vacuum filled by syndicated columnists, television commentators, and other merchants offering to provide the missing information.

Some of the information they provide is genuine, being derived from the official sources. Some is bootlegged, with all the risks inherent in unofficial sources. And some is pure fantasy, created by the merchant to enlarge his income, his ego, or his power. Merchants who are sufficiently cunning and ruthless can attract a wide audience, develop an extensive following, become widely influential, and thereby wield powers which cannot be ignored.

The lesson is that in any market where there is a shortage of an essential commodity, the human being will, in desperation, take what he can get rather than endure the shortage. When there are not enough quality goods to go around he accepts shoddy goods. Where there is a shortage of good food, he is driven to eat unspeakable things. When there is a shortage of good information, he is driven to accept rumors, fantasies, or biased books.

The remedy for all this lies not in deploring the biases of the merchant of information, the advocate, or the consumerist. The remedy lies in eliminating the conditions that create these men, i.e., the gaps between human needs and fulfillment. Of these gaps, very likely the most critical is the gap in information. Lacking information on what is the present status and what is the trend, the human being becomes fed up with his frustrations and commences to build up the pressures which will fuel the consumerist's power.

All industries, those that have already lost their leadership, and those whose turn may come next, should take seriously the need for an objective analysis and scoreboard on what is the status and trend of the consumers' problems. We need these data to squelch those consumerists who are misusing their newfound powers. We need these same data to head off the rise of new consumerists. Most of all, we need these data because we cannot be good managers when we are in a state of ignorance.

THE QUALITY TRILOGY

JOSEPH M. JURAN

Several premises have led me to conclude that our companies need to chart a new direction in managing for quality. These premises are as follows.

1. There is a crisis in quality. The most obvious outward evidence is the loss of sales to foreign competition in quality and the huge costs of poor quality.
2. The crisis will not go away in the foreseeable future. Competition in quality will go on and on. So will the impact of poor quality on society. In the industrialized countries, society lives behind protective quality dikes.
3. Our traditional ways are not adequate to deal with the quality crisis. In a sense, our adherence to those traditional ways has helped to create the crisis.
4. To deal with the crisis requires some major breaks with tradition. A new course must be charted.
5. Charting a new course requires that we create a universal way of thinking about quality—a way applicable to all functions and to all levels in the hierarchy from the chief executive officer to the worker in the office or the factory.
6. Charting a new course also requires extensive personal leadership and participation by upper managers.
7. An obstacle to participation by upper managers is their limited experience and training in managing for quality. They have extensive experience in management of business and finance but not in managing for quality.
8. An essential element in meeting the quality crisis is to arm upper managers with experience and training in how to manage for quality, and to do so on a time scale compatible with the prevailing sense of urgency.

"The Quality Trilogy," *Quality Progress* 9:8 (1986): 19–24. Reproduced with permission from the copyright holder, Juran Institute, Inc.

9. Charting a new course also requires that we design a basis for management of quality that can readily be implanted into the company's strategic business planning and that has minimal risk of rejection by the company's immune system.

A company that wants to chart a new course in managing for quality obviously should create an all-pervasive unity so that everyone will know which is the new direction, and will be stimulated to go there. Creating such unity requires dealing with some powerful forces which resist a unified approach. These forces are for the most part due to certain non-uniformities inherent in any company. These non-uniformities include:

- The multiple functions in the company: product development, manufacture, office operations, etc. Each regards its function as something unique and special.
- The multiple levels in the company hierarchy from the chief executive officer to the nonsupervisory worker. These levels differ with respect to responsibility, prerequisite experience, and training, etc.
- The multiple product lines: large and complex systems, mass production, regulated products, etc. These product lines differ in their markets, technology, restraints, etc.

Such inherent non-uniformities and the associated beliefs in uniqueness are a reality in any company, and they constitute a serious obstacle to unity or direction. Such an obstacle can be overcome if we are able to find a universal thought process—a universal way of thinking about quality—which fits all functions, all levels, all product lines. That brings me to the concept of the "quality trilogy."

(Let me add parenthetically that my colleagues in Juran Institute have urged me to let them call it the "Juran Trilogy." Their reasons are purely mercenary. I have yielded to their wishes. In Juran Institute we also need unity.)

The underlying concept of the quality trilogy is that managing for quality consists of three basic quality-oriented processes.

- Quality planning.
- Quality control.
- Quality improvement.

Each of these processes is universal: it is carried out by an unvarying sequence of activities. (A brief description of each of these sequences appears in the box on p. 281.) Furthermore, these universal processes are interrelated in ways we can depict on a simple diagram. (See Figure 1).

The starting point is quality planning—creating a process that will be able to meet established goals and do so under operating conditions. The subject matter of the planning can be anything: an office process for producing documents; an engineering process for designing products; a factory process for producing goods; a service process for responding to customers requests.

Following the planning, the process is turned over to the operating forces. Their responsibility is to run the process at optimal effectiveness. Due to deficiencies in the original planning, the process runs at a high level of chronic waste. That waste has been planned into the process, in the sense that the planning process failed to plan it out. Because the waste is inherent in the process, the operating forces are unable to get rid of the chronic waste. What they do instead is to carry out "quality control"—keep the waste from getting worse. If it does get worse (sporadic spike), a fire fighting team is brought in to determine the cause or causes of this abnormal variation. Once the cause(s)

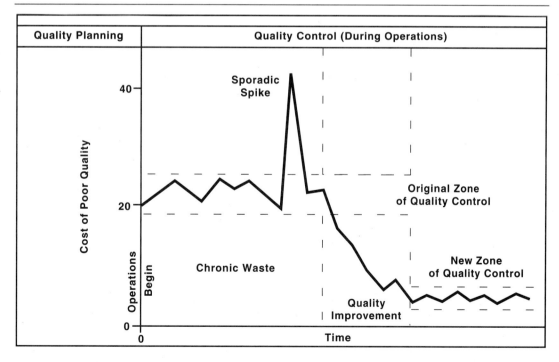

FIGURE 1   THE QUALITY TRILOGY

has been determined and corrective action is taken, the process again falls into the zone defined by the "quality control" limits.

Figure 1 also shows that in due course the chronic waste falls to a much lower level. Such a reduction does not happen of its own accord. It results from purposeful action taken by upper management to introduce a new managerial process into the system of managers' responsibilities—the quality improvement process. This quality improvement process is superimposed on the quality control process—a process implemented in addition to quality control, not instead of it.

We can now elaborate the trilogy descriptions somewhat as follows.

Process: Quality planning—the process for preparing to meet quality goals.

End result: A process capable of meeting quality goals under operating conditions.

Process: Quality control—the process for meeting quality goals during operations.

End result: Conduct of operations in accordance with the quality plan.

Process: Quality improvement—the process for breaking through to unprecedented levels of performance.

End result: Conduct of operations at levels of quality distinctly superior to planned performance.

The trilogy is not entirely "new." If we look sideways at how we manage finance, we notice some interesting parallels, as shown in Figure 2. (I have often used the financial parallels to help explain the trilogy to upper managers. It does help.)

In recent seminars, I have been collecting upper managers' conclusions on their companies' performance relative to the basic processes of the trilogy. The results are quite similar from one seminar to another, and they can be summarized as shown in Figure 3.

FIGURE 2   QUALITY AND FINANCE: PARALLELS

Trilogy processes
Quality planning
Quality control
Quality improvement
Financial processes
Budgeting
Cost control; expense control
Cost reduction; profit improvement

BASIC QUALITY PROCESSES

Quality Planning:

Identify the customers, both external and internal.

Determine customer needs.

Develop product features that respond to customer needs. (Products include both goods and services.)

Establish quality goals that meet the needs of customers and suppliers alike, and do so at a minimum combined cost.

Develop a process that can produce the needed product features.

Prove process capability—prove that the process can meet the quality goals under operating conditions.

Control:

Choose control subjects—what to control.

Choose units of measurement.

Establish measurement.

Establish standards of performance.

Measure actual performance.

Interpret the difference (actual versus standard).

Take action on the difference.

Improvement:

Prove the need for improvement.

Identify specific projects for improvement.

Organize to guide the projects.

Organize for diagnosis—for discovery of causes.

Diagnose to find the causes.

Provide remedies.

Prove that the remedies are effective under operating conditions.

Provide for control to hold the gains.

FIGURE 3 QUALITY PROCESS PERFORMANCE
(UPPER MANAGERS' RATINGS OF THEIR COMPANIES' PERFORMANCE)

TRILOGY PROCESSES	GOOD	PASSING	NOT PASSING
Quality planning	13%	40%	47%
Quality control	44	36	20
Quality improvement	6	39	55

These summarized data point to several conclusions.

1. The managers are not happy with their performance relative to quality planning.

2. The managers rate their companies well with respect to quality control, i.e., meeting the established goals. Note that since these goals have

traditionally been based mainly on past performance, the effect is
mainly to perpetuate past performance—the very performance which is
at the root of the quality crisis.

3. The managers are decidedly unhappy with their performance relative to
   quality improvement.

My own observations of company performance (during consultations)
strongly confirm the above self-assessment by company managers. During my
visits to companies I have found a recurring pattern of priorities and assets
devoted to the processes within the trilogy. This pattern is shown in Figure 4.

As Figure 4 shows, the prevailing priorities are not consistent with the
managers' self-assessment of their own effectiveness. That assessment would
suggest that they should put the control process on hold while increasing
the emphasis on quality planning and especially on quality improvement.

To elaborate on the need for raising the priority on quality improvement,
let me present several baffling case examples.

1. Several years ago the executive vice-president of a large multinational
   rubber company made a round-the-world-trip with his chairman. They
   made the trip in order to visit their major subsidiaries with a view to
   securing inputs for strategic business planning. They found much similarity with respect to productivity, quality, etc. except for Japan. The
   Japanese company was outperforming all others, and by a wide margin.
   Yet the Americans were completely mystified as to why. The Americans had toured the Japanese plant, and to the Americans' eyes the
   Japanese were using the same materials, equipment, processes, etc., as
   everyone else. After much discussion the reason emerged: the Japanese
   had been carrying out many, many quality improvement projects year
   after year. Through the resulting improvements they made *more and
   better products from the same facilities*. They key point relative to "ignorance" is that the Americans did not know what to look for.
2. A foundry that made aluminum castings had an identical experience.
   The foundry was losing share of market to a Japanese competitor,

FIGURE 4	**PRIORITIES FOR QUALITY PROCESSES**	
TRILOGY PROCESSES	**SELF-ASSESSMENT BY UPPER MANAGERS**	**PREVAILING PRIORITIES**
Quality planning	Weak	Limited priority
Quality control	Very strong	Top priority, by a wide margin
Quality improvement	Very weak	Very low priority

mainly for quality reasons. Arrangements were made for a delegation of Americans to visit the Japanese factory. The delegation came away completely mystified. The Japanese were using the same types of equipment and processes as were used by the Americans. Yet the Japanese results in quality and productivity were clearly superior. To this day the Americans don't know why.

3. A few years ago I conducted research into the yields of the process that make large scale integrated circuits. To assure comparability, I concentrated on a single product type—the 16K random access memory (16K RAM). I found that Japanese yields were two to three times the Western yields despite similarity in the basic processes. It came as no surprise to me that the Japanese have since become dominant in the market for 64K RAMs and up.

4. My final example relates to the steel industry. The managers of American steel companies report that their cost of poor quality (just for factory processes) runs at about 10–15 percent of sales. Some of these steel companies have business connections with Japanese steel companies, and the respective managers exchange visits. During these visits the Americans learn that in Japanese steel mills, which use comparable equipment and processes, the cost of poor quality runs at about 1–2 percent of sales. Again the American managers don't know why. Some of them don't even believe the Japanese figures.

My own explanation is that the Japanese, since the early 1950s, have undertaken to improve quality at a pace far greater than that of the West. The slopes of those two lines (Fig. 5) are an index of the rate of improvement. That rate is in turn dependent on the number of quality improvement projects completed. (A project is a problem scheduled for solution.) My estimate is that in terms of numbers of improvement projects completed, the Japanese pace has been exceeding that of the West by an order of magnitude, year after year.

It seems clear that we must change our priorities with regard to the three quality processes. This change in priorities represents a new course. Underlying this new course is the quality trilogy. As a universal way of thinking about quality, the trilogy offers a unified approach for multiple purposes. Let us look at two of these purposes: training in managing for quality, and strategic quality planning.

With respect to training, many of our companies have decided to break with tradition. In the past, their training in managing for quality has been limited to managers and engineers in the quality department. The break with tradition is to extend such training to all functions. Since this is a sizeable undertaking, the companies have set up corporate task forces to plan the approach.

| **FIGURE 5** | WORLD COMPETITION IN QUALITY |

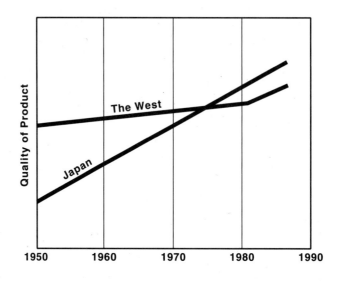

These task forces have run into serious obstacles due to those same systems of variables mentioned earlier. It is hopeless to establish numerous training courses in managing for quality, each specially designed to fit specific functions, specific levels in the hierarchy, specific product lines, etc. Instead, the need is for a universal training course that will apply to all audiences, but with provision for plugging in special case examples as warranted. The trilogy concept meets that need.

The training courses then consist of fleshing out the three sequences of steps described in the box on p. 281. Those sequences have been field tested and proven to be applicable to all functions, levels, and product lines.

We have already seen that the trilogy parallels our approach to strategic business planning. Our companies are experienced in business planning: they are familiar and comfortable with the concepts of financial budgets, cost control, and cost reduction. We can take advantage of all that experience by grafting the quality trilogy onto the existing business planning structure. Such a graft reduces the risk that the implant will be rejected by the company's immune system.

The usual starting point is to set up a quality planning council to formulate and coordinate the activity companywide. The council membership consists of high ranking managers—corporate officers. The chairman is usually the chief executive officer or an executive vice-president. The functions of this council parallel closely the functions of the company's finance committee, but apply to quality instead of finance.

The council prepares a written list of its responsibilities. These typically involve the following:

- Establish corporate quality policies.
- Establish corporate quality goals; review quality goals of divisions and major functions.
- Establish corporate quality plans; review divisional and functional plans.
- Provide the infrastructure and resources needed to carry out the plans.
- Review quality performance against plans and goals.
- Revise the managerial merit rating system to reflect performance against quality goals.

It is all quite logical, and some companies are already securing gratifying benefits from going into strategic quality planning. However, other companies are failing to get results, and the main reasons for these failures are becoming evident. They relate to some areas which I will now discuss: goal setting; providing the infrastructure; providing resources; upper management leadership.

Setting goals.   Goal setting has traditionally been heavily based on past performance. This practice has tended to perpetuate the sins of the past. Failure-prone designs were carried over into new models. Wasteful processes were not challenged if managers had met the budgets—budgets which had in turn assumed that the wastes were a fate to be endured.

All this must change. Goals for parameters that affect external customers must be based on meeting competition in the marketplace. Goals for parameters that affect internal customers must be based on getting rid of the traditional wastes.

Infrastructure.   Strategic quality planning requires an infrastructure to be set up. The nature of this is evident when we look sideways at the infrastructure needed for strategic business planning: a budgetary process; an accounting system to evaluate performance; associated procedures; audits, etc.

Much of this structure has long been in place to serve various local needs: divisions, functions, factories, etc. This structure must now be supplemented to enable it to meet strategic quality needs as well. This is especially the case in large corporations which traditionally have delegated matters of quality to the autonomous divisions. The quality crisis has caused some large corporations to revise this delegation. They now require corporate review of divisional quality goals, plans, and reports of performance. The new approach has required revision of the intrastructure.

Resources. It takes resources to carry out plans and meet goals. To date, companies have exhibited a selective response to this need. Let us look at several areas that require such resources.

- Training. Here the response of companies has generally been positive. Companies have invested heavily in training programs for special areas such as quality awareness, statistical process control, and QC circles. To get into strategic quality planning will require extensive training in the trilogy—how to think about quality. One can hope the response will continue to be positive.
- Measurement of quality. The quality crisis has required a major change in the basis for goal setting—the new basis requires measurement of market quality on an unprecedented scale. For example, some companies now have a policy that new products may not go on the market unless their reliability is at least equal to that of leading competitive products. Such a policy cannot be made effective unless resources are provided to evaluate the reliability of competing products.

Beyond the need to expand quality-oriented marketing research, there are other aspects of measurement which require resources: establishing the scorekeeping associated with strategic quality planning (the quality equivalent of the financial profit statements, balance sheets, etc.); extending measures of quality to the nonmanufacturing processes; and establishing means for evaluating the quality performance of managers, and fitting these evaluations into the merit rating system.

- Quality improvement. Here we have some puzzling contradictions. An emerging database tells us that quality improvement projects provide a higher return on investment than virtually any other investment activity. Yet many companies have not provided the needed resources.

    To be specific, that database comes mainly from the companies that have presented papers at the annual IMPRO conferences—conferences on quality improvement. Those published papers and related unpublished information indicate that in large organizations—sales of $1 billion or more—the average quality improvement project yields about $100,000 of cost reductions.[1]

    The same database indicates that to complete a project requires from $5,000 to $20,000 in resources. These resources are needed to diag-

---

[1]Eighteen case examples are cited in "Charting the Course." *The Juran Report* Number 4 (Winter 1985).

nose the cause of the problem and to provide the remedy. The return on investment is obviously attractive. Nevertheless, many companies—too many—have failed to provide the resources and hence have failed to get the results.

To go into strategic quality planning will require companies to create, for the quality function, a new role—a role similar to that of the financial controller. In all likelihood this new role will be assigned to the quality managers.

In part this new role will involve assisting the company managers to prepare the strategic quality goals—the quality equivalent of the financial budget. In addition the new role will involve establishing the continuing means of reporting performance against quality goals. This role parallels the financial reporting role of the financial controller.

Collateral with those two new responsibilities will be others, also of a broad business nature.

- Evaluation of competitive quality and of trends in the marketplace.
- Design and introduction of needed revisions in the trilogy of processes: quality planning, quality control, and quality improvement.
- Conduct of training to assist company personnel in carrying out the necessary changes.

For many quality managers such a new role will involve a considerable shift in emphasis: from technology to business management, from quality control and assurance to strategic quality planning. But such is the wave of the future. Those quality managers who choose to accept that responsibility, if and when it comes, can look forward to the experience of a lifetime. They will be participating fully in what will become the most important quality development of the century.

EXCERPTS FROM QUALITY CONTROL— PRINCIPLES, PRACTICE, AND ADMINISTRATION

ARMAND V. FEIGENBAUM

THE PRINCIPLES OF QUALITY CONTROL

A series of "principles" has begun to simmer out of industry's experience with Modern Quality Control.

An interpretation of these principles is presented below. It is offered as a summary of the administrative point of view toward quality control. It may also be used as a list of operating rules for organizing quality-control programs.

1. Quality control may be defined as

An effective system for coordinating the quality maintenance and quality improvement efforts of the various groups in an organization so as to enable production at the most economical levels which allow for full customer satisfaction.

2. In the phrase "quality control" the word *quality* does not have the popular meaning of "best" in any absolute sense. It means "best for certain customer conditions." These conditions are (a) the actual use and (b) the selling price of the product. Product quality cannot be thought of apart from product costs.

3. In the phrase, "quality control" the word *control* represents a management tool with four steps:

a. Setting quality standards.
b. Appraising conformance to these standards.
c. Acting when the standards are exceeded.
d. Planning for improvements in the standards.

Excerpt from *Quality Control—Principles, Practice, and Administration* (New York: McGraw-Hill, 1951).

4. Several of the quality-control methods have been carried on in industry for many years. What are new in the modern approach to quality control are integration of these often uncoordinated activities into an overall administrative program for a factory and the addition to the time-tested methods used of a few new techniques which have been found useful in dealing with and thinking about the increased emphasis upon precision in manufactured parts.

5. Modern Quality Control is an aid to, not a substitute for, the good engineering designs, good manufacturing methods, and conscientious inspection activity that have always been required for the production of high-quality articles.

6. The fundamentals of quality control are basic to any manufacturing process, and the tools have been and can be used in industries ranging from radios, electric motors, and turbines to bakery, drug, and brewery products. Although the approach is somewhat different if the production is job shop rather than large quantity, or small components rather than large apparatus, the same fundamentals still obtain. This difference in approach can be readily summarized: In mass-production manufacturing, quality-control activities center on the *product*, while in job-lot manufacturing, they are a matter of controlling the *process*.

7. The details for each quality-control program must be tailored to fit the needs of individual plants.

8. The core of the quality-control approach is control of product quality during the process of design and manufacture so as to *prevent* poor quality rather than to correct poor quality after an article has been produced.

9. Benefits often resulting from Modern Quality Control programs are improvements in product quality and design, reductions in operating costs and losses, improvement in employee morale, and reduction of production-line bottlenecks. By-product benefits are improved inspection methods, sounder setting of time standards for labor, definite schedules for preventive maintenance, the availability of powerful data for use in company advertising, and the furnishing of a factual basis for cost-accounting standards for scrap, rework, and inspection.

10. Cost reductions are possible results of quality control for two reasons.

a. Many of the "costs of quality" result from expenditures to correct mistakes or to police them.

b. Industry has often lacked quality standards. It has therefore unrealistically tilted the scales in the balance between the cost of quality in a product and the service that the product is to render.

11. Present-day factors affecting industrial product quality have developed around two major trends:

a. Toward customer demands for greater precision in the articles they purchase—a technological matter.

b. Toward the wide distribution of responsibility for product quality among a number of line, staff, and functional groups in contrast to the previous era, when this responsibility was largely in the hands of the factory foreman; and toward the substitution of green operators in once-stable work groups—a matter of human relations.

12. These two trends (see paragraph 11) can be handled by Modern Quality Control so that

a. Greater precision, involving more frequent and more accurate quality measurements, may be treated by practical common sense use of the "science of measurements"—statistics.

b. Greater distributions of responsibility for quality may be treated by new methods of organizing for quality control.

13. The factors affecting product quality may be divided into two major groupings:

a. the technological, that is, machines, materials, and processes;

b. the human, that is, operators, foremen, and other factory personnel.

Of these two factors, the human is of the greater importance by far. Quality control is primarily, therefore, a matter of human relations.

14. Quality control enters into all phases of the industrial production process, starting with the customer's specification and the sale to him on through design engineering and assembly and ending with the shipment of the product to a customer who is satisfied with it.

15. Effective control over the factors affecting product quality demands controls at all important stages of the production process. These controls may be termed the *jobs of quality control*, and they fall into four natural classifications:

a. New-design control.

b. Incoming-material control.

c. Product control.

d. Special process studies.

16. New-design control involves the establishment and specification of the desirable cost-quality and performance-quality standards for the product, including the elimination or location of possible sources of manufacturing troubles before the start of formal production.

17. Incoming-material control involves the receiving and stocking, at the most economical levels of quality, of only those parts the quality of which conforms to the specification requirements.

18. Product control involves the control of products at the source of productions, so that departures from the quality specification can be corrected before defective products are manufactured.

19. Special process studies involve investigations and tests to locate the causes of defective products and to determine the possibility of improving quality characteristics.

20. Statistics are used in an over-all quality-control program whenever and wherever they may be useful, but statistics are only one part of the over-all administrative quality-control pattern, they are not the pattern itself. The four statistical tools that have come to be used in quality-control activities are

  a. Frequency distributions,
  b. Control charts,
  c. Sampling tables,
  d. Special methods.

The point of view represented by these statistical methods has, however, had a profound effect upon the entire area of Modern Quality Control.

21. The statistical point of view in Modern Quality Control resolves essentially into this. Variation in product quality must be constantly studied—within batches of product, on processing equipments, between different lots of the same article, on critical quality characteristics and standards. This variation may best be studied by the analysis of samples selected from the lots of product or from units produced by the processing equipments.

22. An important feature of Modern Quality Control is its positive effect in stimulating and in building up operator responsibility for and interest in product quality.

23. Necessary to the success of quality control in a plant is the very intangible but extremely important spirit of "quality-mindedness," extending from top management right to the men and women at the bench.

24. Whatever may be new about the Modern Quality Control program for a plant must be sold to the entire plant organization so as to obtain its willing acceptance and cooperation. Participation by many members of the factory organization in developing details of the quality-control program is very desirable.

25. A plant quality-control program must have the complete support of top management. With lukewarm management support, no amount of selling to the rest of the organization can be genuinely effective.

26. Management must recognize at the outset of its Modern Quality Control program that the tool is not a temporary cost-reduction project.

Only when the inefficiencies represented by the cost reductions are out of the way can the quality-control program take over its long-range role of the management *control* over quality.

27. Organization-wise, quality control is management's tool for delegating authority and responsibility for product quality, thus relieving itself of unnecessary detail, yet retaining for itself the means of assuring that quality results will be satisfactory. The type of organization required to implement this program is a staff group reporting directly to top management.

28. From the human relations point of view, the quality-control organization is both

   a. A "channel of communication" for product-quality information among all concerned employees and groups.
   b. A "means of participation" in the over-all plant quality-control program by these employees and groups.

The quality-control organization is a means of breaking down the attitude sometimes held by factory operators and functional specialists that "our quality responsibility is so small a part of the whole that we're really not a part of the plant quality-control program or important to it."

29. The duty of the quality-control staff is that of acting in an advisory and a control capacity. It usually does not have any responsibility for the actual quality-control activities, which are carried on by groups such as Engineering and Manufacturing.

30. Modern Quality Control programs should be allowed to develop gradually within a given plant. It is often found wise to select one or two troublesome quality problems, to achieve successful results in attacking them, and to allow the quality-control program to grow step by step in this fashion.

SUMMARY OF MODERN QUALITY CONTROL

Management's product-quality goal can be simply stated. It is to manufacture a product into which quality is built and maintained at the most economical costs which yield full customer satisfaction.[1]

Such a goal is not a new one. Industrial history records a wide variety of plans developed by management to meet its product-quality problems. Operator education, foreman training, inspection in the sense of sorting the "bad"

---

[1]This chapter is expanded from a speech by the author before the American Institute of Electrical Engineers, which was later published as an article in *Electrical Engineering* for December, 1949.

pieces from the "good," preventive maintenance are a few of the more recent instances of such programs. While the term quality control was not usually applied to these plans, the control of quality was their major objective.

The one certainty about quality problems is that their content will change with the times. Results from these earlier versions of quality control are, in many plants, no longer adequate to meet management's quality objective.

The quality of products placed in the hands of customers has generally been relatively good. The price that manufacturers have paid to support this grade of quality has, however, been excessive.

Frictions arising out of quality squabbles have sometimes developed between Factory Supervision and Production Control and between Design Engineering and Manufacturing. Serious morale and personnel problems have been a result of such situations.

Internal factory costs for building and maintaining quality have far outstripped previous norms. The percentage of rejects occurring during factory operations has been on a steady increase. Many shops now take as a matter of course substantial losses due to material that must be scrapped and parts that must be reworked.

Neither this quality nor this cost picture is satisfactory. The present era of increasingly aggressive competition will not permit a plant to have a quality record that is only "relatively" good. Its record must be *very* good. With cost reduction a primary aim of management, this quality improvement cannot be accomplished simply by means of expenditures that will boost the already high quality costs. The job must be done in many instances at *less,* not more, cost.

The quality-control task which faces management today requires, therefore, a double-barreled solution:

1. A considerable improvement must be effected in quality of those products which require such improvement.
2. A substantial reduction must, at the same time, be made in the costs for supporting and improving the quality of these products.

THE ORIGINS OF PRESENT-DAY INTEREST IN MODERN QUALITY CONTROL

Why have these quality problems become so serious today? What are the industrial changes that have caused them to arise?

Two developments of the past several decades have impelled management to search for improvements in its older quality-control approaches.

The first development is a technical one. Customers' quality requirements have become far more precise than ever before. The relay that was acceptable in 1939 must perform with much greater accuracy today if it is to serve certain portions of the modern market. The machined part that could once be checked with a pocket scale must now be carefully measured with a pair of micrometers or even an air gage.

Material specifications have become more rigid. Tooling has become a more critical factor. "Intangibles" like dust in the air and humidity have now become both extremely tangible quality problems and the objective of elaborate safeguards. Many prewar methods for producing and measuring quality no longer meet present standards.

The second development is a matter of human relations. Plant expansion and war turnover wrought many changes in once-stable work groups. Green operators are still the rule of the day in many shops. The road back to the pride of workmanship, which is the core of any successful quality-control program, is one that is neither found automatically nor traveled over night.

Most product-quality responsibilities were once the exclusive province of the foreman. Some of these responsibilities are now widely scattered among many factory specialists. Poor quality of a part may be due to unsatisfactory specifications written by the design engineer, to faulty procurement by the purchasing agent, to inadequate testing by the laboratory technicians, to unsuitable processing equipment installed by Methods Engineering. With modern organizational practice, quality control can no longer be exclusively pinned down to the team of factory foreman and the old 100 percent "sort the bad from the good" inspection department.

Management's objective of better quality at lower cost is therefore complicated by the double-barreled problem of demand for greater product precision on the one hand and by the issues rising from more involved human relations on the other hand. Is management's quality objective attainable under present industrial conditions?

Practical experience has shown several instances where just such an objective has been obtained by management with a practical, common-sense program of Modern Quality Control. To summarize such a program with the principles, practice, and administration that have been discussed in the first 13 chapters of this book, the experience of the *X* company will be cited. *X* Company is taken to be representative of a typical present-day industrial concern, and its experience with quality control will be brought out by the discussion of several quotations.

QUESTION 1: WHAT IS THE DEFINITION OF QUALITY CONTROL?

Suppose that the management of the *X* Company decides to establish a quality-control program. It will want first to outline the scope and responsibilities of the new activity. How is quality control to be defined?

Management may immediately encounter a difficult problem. During the past several years, the term *quality control* has been applied to most of the proposals that have been advanced for improving product quality and for reducing the cost of its maintenance. The activity has come to have almost as many definitions as there have been systems proposed for its use.

Is quality control to refer to a series of sampling inspection methods? Is it to designate the trouble shooting of factory reject problems? Is the activity to be made synonymous with industrial statistics?

These definitions refer to individual methods for controlling quality. *X* Company management rejects them as being too restrictive.

It conceives of quality control as the over-all, factory-wide program for attaining management's quality goal. Such a broad program includes many of these individual methods.

Presence or absence of a method like acceptance sampling tables may be important to quality-control effectiveness. But it is not considered an indication of the presence or absence of a quality-control program.

X Company, therefore, visualizes quality control as an administrative device. The character of a management tool like production control is felt to be roughly analogous.

The technique of quality control is seen as a composite of sound human relations and effective technology.

Human relations activities include, among others, organizational planning and good administrative practice. These activities must invoke cooperative, coordinated activity among the individuals and groups engaged in the production process.

The technical activities must be directed toward preventing defective product quality. They must curb the practice of spending all effort on correcting troubles after they have occurred.

It may be noted that the "quality" which is being controlled does not have for management its popular meaning of "best there is." It means "best for some particular purpose."

Both end use by the customer and selling price are important among these purposes which establish industrial quality standards. Product quality cannot be thought of apart from product cost.

Scrap metal may, for example, be the "quality" raw material for a dimestore washer. An extremely expensive steel may be the "quality" raw material for a precision instrument washer.

X Company management wants its definition for quality control to mirror this administrative point of view. It accepts one such as the following:

Quality control is the X Company system for coordinating the quality-maintenance and quality-improvement efforts of the various groups in the organization so as to enable production at the most economical levels which yield full customer satisfaction.

Maintenance of tools so that they will produce satisfactory parts is felt by *X* Company to be a quality-control activity. So is the periodic check of thread gages, the analysis by draftsmen of tolerance build-ups, the use of machine floor inspectors, the determination of the accuracy of machine tools, the use of sampling inspection plans.

A more popular, sloganlike version of the *X* Company definition might be used. It states that "Quality control means coordinating the job of making the product right the first time at the best cost, which enables full customer satisfaction."

QUESTION 2: WHAT IS NEW ABOUT QUALITY CONTROL?

Is there anything genuinely new about Modern Quality Control as conceived by the *X* Company? Does it merely represent a new label applied to the reshuffling of well-known techniques?

Modern Quality Control differs from earlier versions of the activity in two important respects.

Modern Quality Control integrates the usually uncoordinated approaches to control of quality into an overall program for a factory. Quality-control activities have, like Topsy, "just growed" during the past decades. The value of an overall, coordinated plan in place of sprawling, disjointed activities is well known in factory administration.

This organization of effort is extremely important if not a single new quality-control method is added to the program of the factory. It is even more important if new techniques like the control chart are employed.

The second respect in which Modern Quality Control is different is just this: It may use in its programs a number of new techniques for dealing with, measuring, and thinking about the increased emphasis upon precision. Statistics is one of the most useful of these methods. Modern gaging practice is another.

QUESTION 3: WHAT IS A QUALITY-CONTROL PROGRAM?

Now that the hypothetical *X* Company has agreed upon its philosophy of quality control, its next step is the development of actual quality-control activities.

"Our long-range objective is a complete quality-control program for our shops," states *X* Company management. "Let's start by developing such a program for one of our products—an electric snapper."

What is this complete quality-control program? What methods are used in the program? Are its activities confined to inspection work? Are the production and engineering groups involved?

Answers here depend upon the determination of still more basic questions: What affects the quality of the electric snapper? Where is it affected? During design? During machining? In final assembly? How is the quality affected? Who affects it?

Those factors which may have important effects on snapper quality must be controlled if management is to attain its quality goal for the product. It is the consolidation into an overall program of various techniques for this control which constitutes a complete quality-control program.

The *X* Company electric snapper passes through many hands and processes before it is finally received by the customer. It is merchandised by a marketing group, which broadly establishes the product specifications. It is designed by an engineering group, which turns these requirements into actual factory standards.

Its materials are procured by a purchasing group, which has an important effect in determining the quality of these materials. The jigs, tools, and fixtures for its production may be developed by a methods group. Parts are manufactured and assembled by a production group.

Materials and life-test performance may be approved by a laboratory group. Conformance to standards is checked by mechanical inspection and electrical test groups. The container in which the snapper will be transported may be developed by a packaging group. The product is placed in its container by a shipping group.

Quality of the electric snapper may be affected at several of these stages in the production process. It may be affected by human beings—operator carelessness, inadequate supervision, poor design, unsound specifications by the sales manager. It may be affected by mechanical factors—inaccurate machine tools, decrepit jigs, and fixtures. It may be affected by natural causes—dust in the air which coats over the snapper contacts, excessive humidity which causes chemical action on the parts.

So a complete quality-control program starts with the design of the electric snapper and does not end until the snapper is placed in the hands of a customer who is satisfied with it. The activities to support this program fall into four natural classifications termed quality-control jobs. These jobs are listed below, with their definitions.

1. *New-design control* involves the establishment and specification of the desirable cost-quality and performance-quality standards for the product, including the elimination or location of possible sources of manufacturing troubles before the start of formal production.

2. *Incoming-material control* involves the receiving and stocking, at the most economical levels of quality, of only those parts whose quality conforms to the specification requirements.

3. *Product control* involves the control of processed parts and assemblies at the source of production so that departure from the quality specification can be corrected before defective products are produced.

4. *Special process studies* involve conducting investigations and tests to locate the causes of defective products and to determine the possibility of improving product-quality characteristics.

These four quality-control activities gear directly into the four major stages of producing the electric snapper.

Job 1—control of new designs and products—involves the quality-control work carried on while the snapper is being developed and designed. Tolerance analysis, pilot runs, the setting up and analysis of specifications and standards are a few of the methods that may be used here.

Job 2 concerns the quality-control work carried on while parts and materials for the product are being contracted for and received from outside vendors. Procedures for the procurement and use of the necessary measuring gages and standards, sampling inspection tables, vendor control and records are a few of the methods that can be used in this activity.

Job 3 is largely conducted in the shop while the snapper parts are being produced and assembled. Control-chart technique, process-operation-accuracy studies, and tool, jig, and fixture control are a few of the methods that can be used.

Job 4 is involved when trouble shooting is necessary on the quality problems which may occur at any stage in the production process. Methods used here include special studies of factory processes, the analysis of field reports and complaints, and also the use of certain statistical methods.

Each of these jobs is supported by a definite routine. These routines are approved by *X* Company management in accordance with a definite plan. They are part of factory practice just as are production-control or cost-control routines. The existence of these routines and their integration into an overall system are the very heart of electric-snapper quality control.

There is a definite approach at the core of these quality-control routines. It is that of preventing poor quality rather than correcting poor quality after an article has been manufactured.

A major feature of the quality-control jobs is their positive effect in building up operator responsibility for and interest in product quality. In the final analysis, it is a pair of human hands which performs the important operations affecting product quality. It is of paramount importance to successful quality control that those hands be guided in a skilled, conscientious, and quality-minded fashion.

QUESTION 4: IS QUALITY CONTROL GOOD ONLY FOR MASS PRODUCTION?

Suppose that the *X* Company decides to establish quality-control programs for products other than the electric snapper. Will this same framework of activities be applicable to these products? It is useful for large apparatus as well as small devices, for items built in mass quantities as well as those produced in job lots?

In the company which carries on both design and manufacture, roughly similar steps must be followed for all products. The articles must be designed, materials must be purchased, parts must be produced, these parts must be assembled together. A generally similar quality problem exists at each of these production stages, no matter what the nature of the product or the quantities in which it is to be built.

In mass-production operations, product quality can be effectively controlled by types of parts, since all parts will be the same. However, in job-lot manufacture, the parts differ from job to job and only the process by which they are produced is common to all types of products.

Therefore, in mass-production manufacturing, quality-control activities center on the *product*, while in job-lot manufacturing, it is a matter of controlling the *process*.

So the philosophy and framework and routines may remain comparable for all products. Individual quality-control methods used will, however, vary from product to product.

QUESTION 5: HOW DOES STATISTICS RELATE TO MODERN QUALITY CONTROL?

A wide variety of technical methods is available to the *X* Company for use in its quality-control program.

Industrial statistics is currently the most widely heralded of these methods. The statistical approach can be simply summarized: Variation in quality characteristics (inner diameter of bushings, hardness of studs, viscosity of varnish) must be expected among all processed parts, assemblies, and batches. This variation can best be studied by the selection and analysis of small samples of these parts and assemblies.

These sample studies may determine, for a given part or material, the amount of variation that is economically acceptable. They may aid in holding the actual variations occurring during product manufacture to these economic limits.

Four statistical techniques may be useful to *X* Company in this work.

The Frequency Distribution.   This is a tally of the number of times a given quality characteristic occurs within a sample of product. As a picture of the quality represented by the sample, it may be used to show at a glance

1. The average quality.
2. The spread of the quality.
3. The comparison of the quality with specification requirements.

The frequency distribution can be used in such instances as the study of the amount of deviation among batches of foundry sand and the analysis of the variability in the performance of relays at preshipment electrical test.

The Control Chart.   This is an hour-by-hour or day-by-day graphical comparison of actual product-quality characteristics with limits reflecting the ability to produce as shown by past experience on the characteristics. When the curve of the graph approaches or exceeds the limits, some process change is indicated which may require investigation.

The control chart is useful in such applications as the maintenance of a continuing check on the quality of articles produced by machine tools and painting equipments.

The chart may also furnish a valuable record of tool wear or other forms of process shifts.

The Sampling Tables.   These are a series of schedules for representing the probable quality relationships (usually expressed in percentage terms) of the entire lot to the samples properly selected from that lot.

Sampling tables have been useful in some of the more highly publicized quality-control projects. They are of value in replacing expensive 100 percent sorting and in the establishment for new products of inspection procedures which strike a balance between quality protection and inspection economy.

The Special Methods.   These comprise such techniques as correlation, significance tests, and analysis of variance. These methods have been hewn, for industrial quality-control use, out of the general body of statistics.

Special Methods are useful in many analyses of engineering designs and process troubles. Will experimental grid A have a better effect on electronic tube performance than will experimental grid B? Is hardness of the metal the cause of the breakage of screws being assembled to silicon-steel covers? Is furnace temperature a critical factor in causing variations in casting quality, while metal and furnace atmosphere are relatively unimportant?

Several applications of these statistical techniques have developed into full-fledged technical methods. *Process operational accuracy studies* are basically a special adaptation of the *frequency distribution.*

One object of process operational accuracy studies is to determine the amount of variation that must be normally expected from a machine-tool operation under a given set of circumstances. With these machine conditions—tooling, materials, coolant—held constant, a sample of parts is produced. The sample is then examined by means of a frequency-distribution analysis.

The conclusions of this analysis may be compared and consolidated with two or three similar studies on the same machine. The final results may be phrased as follows: "Machine 112 has an operation accuracy of ± 0.004 inch on a cutoff operation, on XB5 brass, using as tooling..." With this knowledge, the planner can route metalworking jobs to those machines which are best suited for handling them.

QUESTION 6: IS STATISTICS THE ONLY QUALITY-CONTROL TECHNICAL METHOD?

Statistics is, as has been discussed above, an important technical method. But *X* Company will also require many other technical methods to support a complete program of the quality-control jobs. Here are some examples:

A New-Design-Control Method. Production conditions may result in operators' "taking all the tolerance" that is permitted by parts drawings. Difficulties may develop in assembling these parts which had not been visualized when the product was on the drafting board. *Tolerance analysis* is a basic quality-control method, because it establishes an organized means for determining tolerance build-ups while the product is being designed and developed.

An Incoming-Material-Control Method. Variations of one ten-thousandth of an inch among manufactured parts may lead to premature failure of the product while operating in the field. Similarly, close measurements may be required for the approval of critical purchased materials. *Precision-gaging* techniques and equipment are a valuable quality-control aid, since they assure the accuracy of measurements of these major characteristics.

A Product-Control Method. Machine tools, processing equipments, jigs, and fixtures will inevitably wear under constant use. The resulting loose bearings and worn pins may cause poor-quality products. A program of *preventive maintenance* may be an important quality-control method, since it enables a regularly scheduled examination of processing facilities before they break down.

A host of other quality-control technical methods could be noted. Among these methods are those useful for product planning and merchandizing, in the establishment of guarantees and specifications, in the trouble shooting of factory rejects and field complaints, and in the control of tools and gages.

QUESTION 7: WHAT IS THE ORGANIZATION FOR QUALITY CONTROL?

With statistics as well as many other methods available for use in the four quality-control jobs, the importance of adequate organization of the quality-control program is obvious. The objective of such an organization for X Company is the establishment and maintenance of these quality-control activities.

The wide scope of the quality-control organization required becomes apparent from the many phases of the production process affected by these activities. With so many scattered threads to gather together, it is easy to understand why the basic pattern of a successful quality-control organization for X Company must be coordination of the quality efforts of various plant groups — engineering, manufacturing, sales, inspection. The type of organization indicated by this pattern in those companies large enough to require it is a staff group reporting directly to X Company top management and supervised by a quality-control head.

This direct line of authority is very important. Without it, the task of coordination, control, and the sometimes necessary education of the plant organization would be extremely difficult.

It is not the responsibility of the full-time members of the X Company quality-control staff to carry on the various details of the quality-control activities. The men best qualified for this work are those in already existing line and functional groups.

It is the quality-control staff responsibility to assist in administering the overall program for X company and to coordinate the various product-quality projects. One way of accomplishing this coordination is through a quality-control committee, headed by the chief of the quality-control staff and composed of representatives from each of the important groups which enter into the production cycle.

This approach makes it possible to obtain the benefits of quality-control organization with a minimum of full-time expense personnel. X Company, with a fifty-million-dollar annual output and a large weekly payroll, can operate its quality-control organization with one quality-control head and two full-time assistants.

The actual details of X Company's quality-control organization will naturally differ from that of other companies owing to variations in products, company size, personalities, and product-quality history. The program may be assigned to a quality-control engineer, a quality manager, a quality-control coordinator, or a quality-appraisal supervisor. Organization of effort may be gained through working committees or through individual activity. The program may be highly technical and complex in some companies and extremely simple in others.

The common denominator through all these variations, however, is that coordination and control are the basic pattern and that the four quality-control jobs are the functions carried on.

QUESTION 8: HOW SHOULD A MODERN QUALITY-CONTROL PROGRAM BE INTRODUCED?

Without the proper attitudes among *X* Company's factory personnel, even adequate methods and sound organization cannot assure any degree of success to its quality-control program. These attitudes must be primarily represented by the very intangible but very important spirit of quality-mindedness extending from top management right through to the men and women at the bench.

Whatever is new about the quality-control program must gradually be sold to the entire plant so as to obtain its willing acceptance and cooperation. The statement is sometimes made by quality-control personnel that their factory organization is "not quality-conscious"—that it is not "going along with the quality-control program." This may be largely an admission by the quality-control people that, in introducing their program, they took into proper account only mechanical and not human factors.

Without complete top-management support for quality control, of course, no degree of "selling" can be genuinely effective. The quality-control program which receives only lukewarm support from management is foredoomed to a hard road and very likely, to failure.

Experience seems to indicate that a program such as *X* Company's should be allowed to develop gradually within the factory. This approach both aids in the selling activity and also permits tailoring of the general routines to the particular needs of the various shops. It is often found wise to select two or three troublesome quality problems, to obtain successful results by attacking them, and to allow the four quality-control jobs to grow step-by-step in this fashion.

QUESTION 9: WHAT BENEFITS MAY BE OBTAINED FROM MODERN QUALITY CONTROL?

When a quality-control program has attained its full growth within a factory, it should be in a position to carry on, for the entire factory organization, all four of the quality-control jobs. A typical overall quality-control application of this sort is one for the *X* Company electric snapper that was discussed above. A brief resume of the control on this device, broken down by the four quality-control jobs which are carried on, is as follows:

New-Design Control. While the snapper was being designed and planned, special tests and pilot runs located sources of possible manufacturing troubles, and these troubles were eliminated by design and method changes.

Incoming-Material Control. Critical dimensions were determined, and very careful checks were made of the first lots of parts purchased from vendors. From these, the degree of sampling that could be done was ascertained. Quality contacts with vendors were established and maintained.

Product Control. Charts were set up on production lines showing how many and what percentage of each part were rejects, so that the factory supervisors could get immediate information as to the presence of quality troubles. Careful attention was paid such factors as preventive maintenance and operator education.

Special Process Studies. If the factory supervision was unable to solve a quality problem, the quality-control organization supplied help from the person or persons who were in a position to be helpful—whether Engineering, Planning, Inspection, Laboratory, or others.

Compared with the previous model of the snapper on which no such program had been carried out, this overall quality control aided in obtaining a considerable improvement of product quality, a reduction of 35 percent in manufacturing losses, and another 35 percent in inspection and testing costs.

The benefits that management may gain from a Modern Quality Control program are represented in this electric-snapper example. Expressed in more general terms, they are

1. Improvement in product quality.
2. Improvement in product design.
3. Reduction in operating costs.
4. Reduction in operating losses.
5. Reduction of production-line bottlenecks.
6. Improvement in employee morale.

Conclusion

From the foregoing discussion, it is readily apparent that Modern Quality Control is not a new cure-all which overnight will gain for management its product-quality objectives. Nor is it a substitute for the good manufacturing and engineering practices that have been successful over the years.

It is, however, an increasingly necessary management method to be used in conjunction with these time-honored procedures. It is necessary because existing, uncoordinated, individual quality-control techniques are not able to cope with customers' demands for greater precision and the diffusion of quality responsibility—the two modern factors which have developed to affect industrial product quality. Modern Quality Control attacks these two factors directly—through improved organization for attaining quality objectives and through more effective use of technical methods.

Properly understood, properly staffed, and above all properly organized, Modern Quality Control is industrial management's tool for pursuing one of its most important objectives: to manufacture products into which quality is built and maintained at the most economical costs which yield full customer satisfaction.

TOTAL QUALITY CONTROL

ARMAND V. FEIGENBAUM

To design, process, and sell products competitively in the 1956 market place, American businessmen must take full account of these crucial trends.

Customers—both industrial and consumer—have been increasing their quality requirements very sharply in recent years. This tendency is likely to be greatly amplified by the intense competition that seems inevitable in the near future.

For example, the electrical relay that could command the lion's share of the 1950 industrial market is no longer acceptable for 1956 operating needs. Consumers are progressively more minute in their examination of the finish of appliances, or in their judgment of the tone of a radio or television set. Even for military products on which quality has always been the major consideration—e.g., jet engines, airborne electronics, and ordnance—specifications are continually being made more rigorous.

As a result of this increased customer demand for higher quality products, present in-plant quality practices and techniques are now, or soon will be, outmoded.

Thus, the machined part that could once be checked with a pocket scale or a pair of micrometers must now be carefully measured with an air gage; and material that could once be visually accepted if it were "reddish brown and shiny" must now be carefully analyzed both chemically and physically to assure that it is beryllium copper instead of phosphor bronze. At the same time, automation, in which rapid quality evaluation is a pivotal point, has magnified the need for mechanization of inspection and test equipment—much of which is now in the hand-tool stage. Indeed, the quality control content of the manufacturing equipment investment dollar may well double in the next decade to purchase the benefit of this mechanization.

Quality costs have become very high. For many companies they may be much too high if these companies are to maintain and improve their competitive position over the long run.

"Total Quality Control," *Harvard Business Review* 34:6 (1956): 93–101. Reprinted with permission from *Harvard Business Review*.

In fact, quality costs (inspection, testing, laboratory checks, scrap, rework, customer complaints, and similar expenses) have crept up to become a multimillion-dollar item. For many businesses they are comparable in degree with total direct labor dollars, with distribution dollars, or with purchased material dollars! While I can find no documented research on the subject, evidence points strongly to the fact that many businesses have quality-cost expenditures representing 7 percent, 8 percent, 10 percent, and even more of their cost of sales!

Taken together, these three trends spell out the twin quality objective that 1956 competitive conditions present to American business management:

> *a. considerable improvement in the quality of many products and many quality practices, and, at the same time,*
> *b. substantial reductions in the overall costs of maintaining quality.*

Under these conditions, if quality must be not only maintained but upgraded, the wave of the future looks like an expensive one to ride. How many of the frailer business craft will be able to avoid getting swamped?

BROAD SCOPE

Fortunately, there is a way out of the dilemma imposed on businessmen by increasingly demanding customers and by ever-spiraling costs of quality. This "way out" seems to lie in a new kind of quality control, which might be called "total quality control."

The underlying principle of this total quality view—and its basic difference from all other concepts—is that, to provide genuine effectiveness, control must start with the design of the product and end only when the product has been placed in the hands of a customer who remains satisfied.

The reason for this breadth of scope is that the quality of any product is affected at many stages of the industrial cycle:

1. Marketing evaluates the level of quality which customers want and for which they are willing to pay.
2. Engineering reduces this marketing evaluation to exact specifications.
3. Purchasing chooses, contracts with, and retains vendors for parts and materials.
4. Manufacturing engineering selects the jigs, tools, and processes for relay production.
5. Manufacturing supervision and shop operators exert a major quality influence during parts making, subassembly, and final assembly.
6. Mechanical inspection and functional test check conformance to specifications.

7. Shipping influences the caliber of the packaging and transportation.

In other words, the determination both of quality and of quality cost actually takes place throughout the entire industrial cycle. This is the reason why real quality control cannot be accomplished by concentrating on inspection alone, or design alone, or reject troubleshooting alone, or operator education alone, or statistical analysis alone—important as each of these individual elements is.

The breadth of the job makes quality control a new and important business management function. Just as the theme of the historical inspection activity was "they (i.e., bad parts) shall not pass," the theme of this new approach is "make them right the first time." Emphasis is on defect prevention so that routine inspection will not be needed to as large an extent. The burden of quality proof rests, not with inspection, but with the makers of the part—machinist, assembly foreman, vendor, as the case may be.

Like traditional inspection, the quality control function in this total quality view is still responsible for assurance of the quality of products shipped, but its broader scope places a major addition on this responsibility. Quality control becomes responsible for quality assurance *at optimum quality costs*.

The total quality view sees the prototype quality control man, not as an inspector, but as a quality control engineer—with an adequate background of the applicable product technology and with training in statistical methods, in inspection techniques, and in other useful tools for improving and controlling product quality.

COMPARED WITH OTHER VIEWS

It may serve further to clarify the character of the total quality view if we compare it with other quality control concepts. Actually, there have been and are today a great many different concepts both of the meaning of the term "quality control" and of what the principal elements of the quality control activity are. The two most widely accepted of these concepts may be described as the "modern inspection view" and the "statistical view."

Historically, quality control meant nothing more than the activity of traditional factory inspection, which was intended to protect the customer by screening bad material from good prior to shipment. In the *modern inspection view*, quality control means this traditional inspection function updated and made more efficient by the use of certain statistical methods and work-in-process inspection routines. Thus:

- Statistically verified sampling plans assure the quality of outgoing lots better and more economically than do the older 100 percent inspection or hit-or-miss spot check procedures.

- In-process sampling inspections detect quality errors before too many bad parts have been produced, and are consequently more effective than concentration on final inspection with its risk of producing a large number of bad parts.

An impressive weight of dollars-and-cents evidence demonstrates that such techniques represent a great improvement over oldfashioned practices. Probably most systems of quality control in American business today are examples of this modern inspection point of view. That is, they see the prototype quality control man as a well-grounded inspection specialist who has had training in useful statistical methods.

The *statistical view*, in turn, reflects the major and increasing contributions which probability methods are making to the improvement of industrial decision making. It is a view that predominates both in the literature of quality control and in professional meetings on the subject. It sees the prototype quality control man as an industrial statistician, who works on problems ranging from the design of laboratory experiments, through the establishment of control charts for production processes, on to the analysis of manufacturing rejects. It sees him, in other words, as capable of making contributions in fields not directly connected with product quality, such as time study and safety.

These modern inspection and statistical concepts of quality control have been and are highly useful in the areas of product quality which they cover. But, compared with total quality control, their scope is much too limited; they are able to provide only a partial grasp of the overall quality problem that faces American businessmen. They simply are not geared to the fact that quality considerations are involved in every phase of industrial activity, and are not equipped to keep overall costs of quality at a minimum.

EFFECT OF COST ACCOUNTING

If the burden and sharp upward trend of these quality costs—and the need for genuinely broad quality control effort—are only now becoming recognized in some businesses, part of the reason must be ascribed to traditional industrial cost accounting practices. Cost accounting methods often have not identified and grouped quality costs in a form suitable for the development of adequate controls. The magnitude of the quality cost sum has tended to be obscured by the piecemeal identification of certain individual quality cost elements: for example, scrap and spoilage, or field complaint expense. Most often, quality cost has been conceived as the cost of the company inspection activity—actually just a fraction of overall quality cost—and controls have been established on this fragmentary basis.

Regardless of the source of the fault, the only clear answer to the quality cost problem seems to lie in the new concept of total quality control.

OPERATION OF THE FUNCTION

The work of this total quality control function may be classified into four broad categories, as follows (see Exhibit 1 for elaboration):

1. New design control, or the planning of controls for new or modified products prior to the start of production.
2. Incoming material control, or the control of incoming purchased parts and materials.
3. Product control, or the shop floor control of materials, parts, and batches from machines, processes, and assembly lines.
4. Special process studies, or the conducting of special analyses of factory and processing problems.

EXHIBIT 1   QUALITY CONTROL IN THE QUALITY ACTIVITY CYCLE

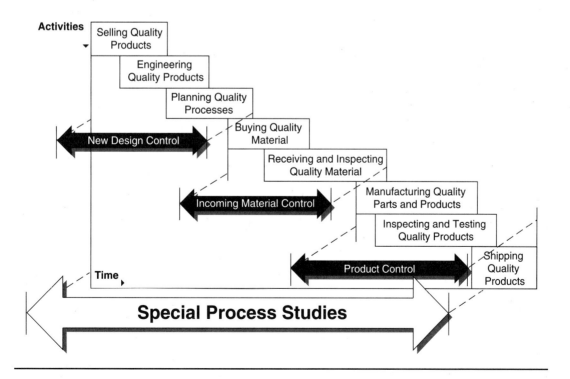

In this work, the two basic responsibilities of the quality control function are:

1. to provide quality assurance for the company's product—i.e., simply, to be sure that the products shipped are right; and
2. to assist in assuring optimum quality costs for those products.

It fulfills these responsibilities through its subfunctions: *quality control engineering, inspection,* and *test,* which operate a continuous feedback cycle:

1. Quality control engineering does *quality planning;* this establishes the basic framework of the quality control system for the firm's products.
2. Inspection and test do *quality measuring;* this determines, in accordance with the quality plan, the conformance and performance of parts and products with engineering specifications.
3. There is rapid feedback to quality control engineering for *quality analysis,* which results in new quality planning, thus completing the cycle. (This analysis also fosters corrective action for product quality deviations.)

ENGINEERING COMPONENT

The true nerve center of the total quality control function is the engineering component. Its activities in each of the four broad quality control jobs deserve examination in some detail.

NEW DESIGN CONTROL

In this area, quality control engineering provides three main activities:

1. *Preproduction service to design engineering and manufacturing engineering in analyzing the quality-ability of new products and production processes, and in debugging quality problems*—This assures a product which will be as defect-free as possible *prior* to the start of production. Among the new technical tools which the quality control engineer brings to this effort are process quality capability studies, tolerance analysis technique, pilot run practice, and a wide variety of statistical methods.

2. *Planning of inspections and tests to be carried on when production is under way on the new product*—This is to establish continuous control of in-process quality. It involves determining the following:

- Dimensions and characteristics of the parts to be checked.
- Degree to which they are to be checked.

- In-process and final production points at which checks are required.
- Methods and procedures to be used—including statistical sampling plans, control charts, and so on.
- Personnel who will make the checks—that is, production operators or people from the inspection and test subfunctions.

3. *Design of genuinely modern inspection and testing equipment, which, to the fullest possible extent, is physically integrated with manufacturing equipment to permit the machine to check its own work*—The aim of this activity is economical investment expenditures, maximum equipment utilization, and fullest practical mechanization and automation both of operations and of quality control paper work.

INCOMING MATERIAL CONTROL

In this area, quality control engineering must assist in the establishment of good quality relationships with suppliers. It contributes to this objective in the following ways:

- By planning the periodic rating of the quality performance of present suppliers, it provides facts which assist the purchasing function in quickly bringing satisfactory or unsatisfactory quality performance to the attention of vendors.
- By evaluating the quality capability of potential suppliers, it provides facts which assist purchasing to select good quality vendors.
- By working with the vendors, it assists them in understanding the quality control requirements of the purchase contracts they have won.
- By establishing quality certification programs, it places the burden of quality proof on the vendor rather than on an extensive, expensive in-plant incoming inspection effort.

PRODUCT CONTROL

In this area, quality control engineering carries on the cost measurement and quality cost reduction project activity required for overall quality cost control and reduction, and it works closely with the inspection and test subfunctions which perform the actual measuring work. It also performs process quality capability studies to determine the quality limits within which a machine or process may be expected to operate. The aim is to make sure that parts will be routed to equipment which is capable of economically maintaining engineering specifications.

SPECIAL PROCESS STUDIES

In this area, the job of quality control engineering is to analyze complex, in-process quality problems which have been fed back to it by inspection and test. These studies are directed both to the elimination of defects and to the development of possible improvements in present quality levels.

SPECIALIZED ACTIVITY

Certain elements of this quality control engineering work have previously been performed on a sporadic or divided basis. But the quality control engineer himself is something new under the sun. For quality control engineering is not merely a new label for the inspection planning package, nor a fresh designation for the test equipment engineer, nor yet a technologically flavored title for the industrial statistician. It is, instead, a specialized activity with a character all its own, calling for a unique combination of skills.

Quality control engineering work is the product of the crossfertilization of modern developments in several fields—in statistical methodology, in fast-response high-precision inspection and testing equipment, in management understanding of the nature of the control function in modern business. Altogether, it has the attributes of a genuinely new sector of the engineering profession.

In experience, education, aptitude, and attitude, the man entering quality control engineering work today is, in fact, not very different from the man entering other longer established major technical fields as, for example, product engineering or manufacturing engineering. He must possess, or have the capacity to acquire, the necessary product and process background. He must have the personal characteristics to work effectively in a dynamic atmosphere with people of diverse interests. He must possess the technical background which will enable him to acquire, if he does not already have it, a growing body of quality control engineering knowledge. Finally, he needs the analytical ability to use this knowledge in solving new and different quality problems.

INSPECTION AND TEST

The planning and analysis work of the quality control engineer makes a new, more positive type of inspection and test both possible and necessary in the modern quality control function. Instead of policing the manufacturing process, this type of inspection and test becomes a direct *part* of that process by assisting in the production of good quality products.

Thus, during incoming material control and product control, the inspection and test subfunctions are responsible not only for fully establishing that the materials received and the products in-process and shipped are of the specified quality, but also for thoroughly and promptly feeding back facts for preventing the purchase and production of poor quality material in the future.

This positive quality measuring requires only a very minimum of routine hand-sorting inspection and test. In product control, for example, this result is made possible through a continuous sequence of engineering work to assure that with the facilities provided production operators can make parts right the first time, know that they can, and have the necessary equipment and gauges to check their own work. On this basis, then, inspection and test can provide genuine assistance in the production of the right quality by:

- Becoming auditors of the good quality practices that have been established.
- Providing as much as possible on-the-spot, shop floor analysis of defects.
- Feeding back facts about these defects for corrective analysis and action elsewhere.

Such quality assurance effort has been termed *control-audit* inspection and test. Inevitably it means the upgrading of traditional inspection and test; it requires considerably fewer but much more highly qualified and more specialized personnel—those who have genuine ability to be helpful in making the right quality. An instance in point is the arc-welding inspector who now not only knows whether or not weld penetration on a part is satisfactory but also, in the case of defective welds, may be able to counsel the shop on the reasons why the penetration has been unsatisfactory.

ORGANIZATIONAL PROBLEM

In organizing a modern quality control function, the first principle to recognize is *that quality is everybody's job.*

In defiance of this principle, there have been many business experiments over the years which have attempted to make the quality activity cycle less of a decentralized, Tinkers-to-Evers-to-Chance sequence. Often these attempts have taken the form of centralizing all quality responsibility by organizing a component whose job was handsomely described as "responsibility for all factors affecting product quality."

These experiments have had a life span of as long as six months—when the job incumbent had the advantage of a strong stomach, a rhinoceros hide, and a well-spent and sober boyhood. Others not similarly endowed did not last even that long.

The simple fact of the matter is that the marketing man is in the best position to evaluate adequately customer's quality preferences; the design engineer is the only man who can effectively establish specification quality levels; the shop supervisor is the individual who can best concentrate on the building of quality. Total quality control programs therefore require, as a first step, top management's re-emphasis on the responsibility and accountability of *all* company employees in new design control, incoming material control, product control, and special process studies.

The second principle of total quality control organization is a corollary to the first one. It is *that because quality is everybody's job, it may become nobody's job.* Thus the second major step required in total quality programs becomes clear. Top management must recognize that the many individual responsibilities for quality will be exercised most effectively when they are buttressed and serviced by a well-organized, genuinely modern management function whose only area of specialization is product quality, and whose only area of operation is in the quality control job.

LOCATION OF THE FUNCTION

In view of these two organizational principles, where should the quality control function be placed in the larger structure of company organization? Should it be part of marketing, or engineering, or manufacturing? Should it report direct to general management?

While these are crucial questions, they are not susceptible to categorical answers. Certainly, quality control in any company should report high enough so that it can implement its responsibilities for quality assurance at optimum costs. Certainly, also, it should be close enough to the firing line so that it will be able to fulfill its technological role. However, companies vary widely in their objectives, their character, their philosophy of organization structure, and their technology. The answer to the question of where to locate quality control will necessarily vary also.

It may be worthwhile, however, to report one firm's approach to this issue. In the General Electric Company's product departments, each of which operates as a decentralized business with profit and loss accountability reposing with the department general manager, the cycle of basic quality responsibility is as follows:

> The marketing component is responsible for evaluating customers' quality preferences and determining the prices these customers are willing to pay for the various quality levels.

The engineering component is responsible for translating marketing's requirements into exact drawings and specifications.

The manufacturing component is responsible for building products to these drawings, and for knowing that it has done so.

Within this structure of responsibility, quality control clearly emerges as a *manufacturing* function. Thus, in the General Electric product department, the quality control manager reports to the chief manufacturing executive in that department—the manufacturing manager—and operates at the same organization level as the production superintendents, the managers of materials, and the managers of manufacturing engineering.

THE RESULTS

Experience in an increasing number of companies shows that operation of a total quality control program has paid off in six ways:

1. Improved product quality.
2. Reduced scrap, complaint, inspection, and other quality costs.
3. Better product design.
4. Elimination of many production bottlenecks.
5. Improved processing methods.
6. Development of a greater spirit of quality-mindedness on the production shop floor.

Certainly our experience with this program has been highly satisfactory in the General Electric Company, where we have been developing the concept and procedure for some years.

Total quality control has thus, in actual practice, been successful in meeting the dual objective of better quality at lower quality costs. The reason for the satisfactory better-quality result is fairly clear from the very nature of the prevention-centered, step-by-step, technically thorough program. But the explanation may not be nearly so obvious for the accompanying by-product of lower overall quality cost. This needs to be spelled out, especially since it includes, in the long run, lower expenses for the quality control activities themselves as compared with the costs of traditional inspection and test.

COSTS OF QUALITY

The reason for the favorable cost result of total quality control is that it cuts the two *major* cost segments of quality (which might be called failure and appraisal costs) by means of much smaller increases in the third and *smallest* segment (prevention costs). Why this is possible can be seen as soon as the character of these three categories is considered:

1. Failure costs are caused by defective materials and products that do not meet company quality specifications. They include such loss elements as scrap, spoilage, rework, field complaints, etc.
2. Appraisal costs include the expenses for maintaining company quality levels by means of formal evaluations of product quality. This involves such cost elements as inspection, test, quality audits, laboratory acceptance examinations, and outside endorsements.
3. Prevention costs are for the purpose of keeping defects from occurring in the first place. Included here are such costs as quality control engineering, employee quality training, and the quality maintenance of patterns and tools.

In the absence of formal nationwide studies of quality costs in various businesses, it is impossible to generalize with any authority about the relative magnitude of these three elements of quality cost. However, I believe it would not be far wrong to assert that failure costs may represent from one-half to three-quarters of total quality costs, while appraisal costs probably range in the neighborhood of one-quarter of this total. Prevention costs, on the other hand, probably do not exceed one-tenth of the quality cost total in most businesses. Out of this 10 percent, usually 8 percent–9 percent are directed into such traditional channels as pattern and tool maintenance and the specification-changing or interpreting work of product engineering. This leaves only 1 percent or 2 percent that is spent for elements of quality control engineering work.

It is a significant fact that, historically, under the traditional inspection function, failure and appraisal costs have tended to move upward together, and it has been difficult to pull them down once they have started to rise. The reason for this relationship is that:

As defects increase—thus pushing up failure costs—the number of inspectors has been increased to maintain the "they shall not pass" screen to protect the customer. This, in turn, has pushed up appraisal costs.

For the reasons mentioned earlier in this article, screening inspection does not have much effect in eliminating the defects, nor can it completely prevent some of the defective products from leaving the plant and going into the hands of complaining customers.

Appraisal costs thus stay up as long as failure costs remain high. In fact, the higher these failure and appraisal costs go, the higher they are likely to go without successful preventive activity.

Once these two main elements of quality cost have started to rise—as they seem to have throughout industry generally today—the one best hope for pulling them to earth again seems to be spending more on the third and smallest element, namely, prevention cost. The 10 percent now spent may well need to be doubled, much of the increase going for quality control engineering as well as for improved methods of inspection and test equipment automation.

At first glance such increases in prevention costs may not seem to be in the interest of quality cost improvement, but this objection is rapidly dispelled as soon as results are considered. Translated into quality cost terms, the operation of total quality control has the following sequence of results:

1. A substantial cut in failure costs—which has the highest cost reduction potential of all quality cost elements—occurs because of the reduced number of defects and the improvements in product quality brought about by modern quality control practice.
2. Fewer defects mean somewhat less need for routine inspection and test, causing a reduction in appraisal costs.
3. Better inspection and test equipment and practices, and the replacement of many routine operators by less numerous but more effective *control audit* inspectors and testers, bring about additional reductions in appraisal costs.
4. Because the new *control-audit* inspection and test is effective in preventing defects, appraisal dollars for the first time begin to exercise a positive downward pull on failure costs.

The ultimate end result is that total quality control brings about a sizable reduction in overall quality costs, and a major alteration in the proportions of the three cost segments. No large, long-term increase in the size of the quality control function is required as a necessary condition for quality cost improvement. Instead, quality control expense, as a proportion of total company expense, will be down in the long run. Improvements of one-third or more in overall quality costs are not unusual.

QUALITY DOLLAR BUDGETING

It is worth noting that this identification and analysis of quality costs permits a major forward step in the business budgeting process. That is, it makes feasible determining the dollars needed for quality control, not on the basis of historical inspection cost experience, but on the basis of current company objectives in product quality and quality costs.

Quality needs and problems differ so much from company to company that it is not realistic to generalize about the specific mix of quality costs that should be budgeted under total quality control. But the direction of budgetary trends may be suggested by an example, which embodies current industrial experience in this area. Exhibit 2 shows how one company expects to cut its quality costs by switching from a mild version of the inspection view to total quality control. The company anticipates that total quality expenses will drop from the current high of 7 percent of sales to 5 percent, with declines achieved both in failure and appraisal costs while prevention costs increase from only 0.70 percent of sales to a still modest 1.25 percent. In this example, the cost savings budgeted are rather moderate, owing to the presence of complicating factors such as the following:

- An anticipated 50 percent increase in sales over the next five years—from $50 million to $75 million.
- Planned additions to a product line that is already highly technical and diversified, hence accompanied by major quality problems.

Such a planned 30 percent improvement in quality cost ratios is feasible, indeed conservative, with a successful total quality control program—even with a 50 percent business expansion and even with counterbalancing quality cost increases brought about by the introduction of new products. While the company in the example may not be typical (probably there is no such thing as a typical business enterprise), it is at least illustrative of the good results that can be achieved even when circumstances pose unusual difficulties.

CONCLUSION

Total quality control thus represents another forward step in management science. Its integration of design-through-shipment control of the many

| EXHIBIT 2 | BUDGETED QUALITY COSTS AND SAVINGS UNDER TOTAL QUALITY CONTROL (ASSUMING SALES INCREASE FROM $50 MILLION TO $75 MILLION) |

QUALITY COST ELEMENT	TOTAL DOLLARS		PERCENT OF SALES		PERCENT OF TOTAL QUALITY COST	
	PRESENT	5-YEAR GOAL	PRESENT	5-YEAR GOAL	PRESENT	5-YEAR GOAL
Failure	$2,275,000	$2,062,500	4.55%	2.75%	65%	55%
Appraisal	875,000	750,000	1.75	1.00	25	20
Prevention	350,000	937,500	0.70	1.25	10	25
Total	$3,500,000	$3,750,000	7.00%	5.00%	100%	100%

elements in the quality picture makes it much more effective than the unlinked fragmentary controls of the past. As a major new business management activity, it provides professional effort in meeting the objective of assured product quality at minimum quality cost.

With this concept, inspection and test have a chance to develop in the direction that conscientious inspectors and testers have always sought; that is, into an activity with a positive role in assisting other members of the manufacturing, engineering, and marketing team toward quality improvement and quality cost control. No longer are inspection and test confined to essentially a negative, fist-shaking role in sorting bad parts from good, a role placing them continually on the defensive and evoking the hostility of other managers.

Further, those tools of statistical methodology that have proved practical and useful can now be brought to their fullest effectiveness. With the quality control engineers as tool builders, and the control-audit inspectors as tool users, statistical techniques can be put to work in a down-to-earth fashion that welds them into regular day-by-day controls. No longer will these techniques be treated—as too often in the past—merely as curiosities, to be employed in special situations on a pinch-hitting basis.

With equipment for inspection and test a direct and major responsibility of the quality control function, more use can be made of equipment specialists who wish to concentrate their skills on the great needs, opportunities, and unique complexities of today's quality control equipment field.

Total quality control thus welds this new technology into a strong yet flexible weapon, capable of successfully coming to grips with the three major quality problems that modern business must face and solve: the upward customer pressure on quality levels, the resulting rapid obsolescence of quality practices, the very high level of quality costs.

While delivery and other factors may sell a product the first time, it is usually quality which keeps the product sold and which keeps the customer coming back a second and a third time. Quality cost—perhaps 8 percent or more of cost of sales—is one of the major elements of product cost that must be made right to permit the setting of the right price to the customer. Helping to assure this right quality at this right quality cost is the way the new *total quality control* can serve its company in the years ahead.

COMPETING ON THE EIGHT DIMENSIONS OF QUALITY

DAVID A. GARVIN

U.S. managers know that they have to improve the quality of their products because, alas, U.S. consumers have told them so. A survey in 1981 reported that nearly 50 percent of U.S. consumers believed that the quality of U.S. products had dropped during the previous five years; more recent surveys have found that a quarter of consumers are "not at all" confident that U.S. industry can be depended on to deliver reliable products. Many companies have tried to upgrade their quality, adopting programs that have been staples of the quality movement for a generation: cost of quality calculations, interfunctional teams, reliability engineering, or statistical quality control. Few companies, however, have learned to *compete* on quality. Why?

Part of the problem, of course, is that until Japanese and European competition intensified, not many companies seriously tried to make quality programs work even as they implemented them. But even if companies *had* implemented the traditional principles of quality control more rigorously, it is doubtful that U.S. consumers would be satisfied today. In my view, most of those principles were narrow in scope; they were designed as purely defensive measures to preempt failures or eliminate "defects." What managers need now is an aggressive strategy to gain and hold markets, with high quality as a competitive linchpin.

QUALITY CONTROL

To get a better grasp of the defensive character of traditional quality control, we should understand what the quality movement in the United States has achieved so far. How much expense on quality was tolerable? How

"Competing on the Eight Dimensions of Quality," *Harvard Business Review* 65:6 (1987): 101–109. Reprinted with permission from *Harvard Business Review*.

much "quality" was enough? In 1951, Joseph Juran tackled these questions in the first edition of his *Quality Control Handbook,* a publication that became the quality movement's bible. Juran observed that quality could be understood in terms of avoidable and unavoidable costs: the former resulted from defects and product failures like scrapped materials or labor hours required for rework, repair, and complaint processing; the latter were associated with prevention, i.e., inspection, sampling, sorting, and other quality control initiatives. Juran regarded failure costs as "gold in the mine" because they could be reduced sharply by investing in quality improvement. He estimated that avoidable quality losses typically ranged from $500 to $1,000 per productive operator per year—big money back in the 1950s.

Reading Juran's book, executives inferred roughly how much to invest in quality improvement: expenditures on prevention were justified if they were lower than the costs of product failure. A corollary principle was that decisions made early in the production chain (e.g., when engineers first sketched out a product's design) have implications for the level of quality costs incurred later, both in the factory and the field.

In 1956, Armand Feigenbaum took Juran's ideas a step further by proposing "total quality control" (TQC). Companies would never make high-quality products, he argued, if the manufacturing department were forced to pursue quality in isolation. TQC called for "interfunctional teams" from marketing, engineering, purchasing, and manufacturing. These teams would share responsibility for all phases of design and manufacturing and would disband only when they had placed a product in the hands of a satisfied customer—who remained satisfied.

Feigenbaum noted that all new products moved through three stages of activity: design control, incoming material control, and product or shop-floor control. This was a step in the right direction. But Feigenbaum did not really consider how quality was first of all a strategic question for any business; how, for instance, quality might govern the development of a design and the choice of features or options. Rather, design control meant for Feigenbaum mainly preproduction assessments of a new design's manufacturability, or that projected manufacturing techniques should be debugged through pilot runs. Materials control included vendor evaluations and incoming inspection procedures.

In TQC, quality was a kind of burden to be shared—no single department shouldered all the responsibility. Top management was ultimately accountable for the effectiveness of the system; Feigenbaum, like Juran, proposed careful reporting of the costs of quality to senior executives in order to ensure their commitment. The two also stressed statistical approaches to quality, including process control charts that set limits to acceptable variations in key variables affecting a product's production. They endorsed sampling procedures that allowed managers to draw inferences about the quality of entire batches of products from the condition of items in a small, randomly selected sample.

Despite their attention to these techniques, Juran, Feigenbaum, and other experts like W. Edwards Deming were trying to get managers to see beyond purely statistical controls on quality. Meanwhile, another branch of the quality movement emerged, relying even more heavily on probability theory and statistics. This was "reliability engineering," which originated in the aerospace and electronics industries.

In 1950, only one-third of the U.S Navy's electronic devices worked properly. A subsequent study by the Rand Corporation estimated that every vacuum tube the military used had to be backed by nine others in warehouses or on order. Reliability engineering addressed these problems by adapting the laws of probability to the challenge of predicting equipment stress.

Reliability engineering measures led to:

Techniques for reducing failure rates while products were still in the design stage.

Failure mode and effect analysis, which systematically reviewed how alternative designs could fail.

Individual component analysis, which computed the failure probability of key components and aimed to eliminate or strengthen the weakest links.

Derating, which required that parts be used below their specified stress levels.

Redundancy, which called for a parallel system to back up an important component or subsystem in case it failed.

Naturally, an effective reliability program required managers to monitor field failures closely to give company engineers the information needed to plan new designs. Effective field failure reporting also demanded the development of systems of data collection, including return of failed parts to the laboratory for testing and analysis.

Now, the proponents of all these approaches to quality control might well have denied that their views of quality were purely defensive. But what else was implied by the solutions they stressed—material controls, outgoing batch inspections, stress tests? Perhaps the best way to see the implications of their logic is in traditional quality control's most extreme form, a program called "Zero Defects." No other program defined quality so stringently as an absence of failures—and no wonder, since it emerged from the defense industries where the product was a missile whose flawless operation was, for obvious reasons, imperative.

In 1961, the Martin Company was building Pershing missiles for the U.S. Army. The design of the missile was sound, but Martin found that it could

"I spoke to my attorney today, Wendell, and I'm thinking of putting you into play."

maintain high quality only through a massive program of inspection. It decided to offer workers incentives to lower the defect rate, and in December 1961, delivered a Pershing missile to Cape Canaveral with "zero discrepancies." Buoyed by this success, Martin's general manager in Orlando, Florida accepted a challenge, issued by the U.S. Army's missile command, to deliver the first field Pershing one month ahead of schedule. But he went even further. He promised that the missile would be perfect, with no hardware problems or document errors, and that all equipment would be fully operational 10 days after delivery (the norm was 90 days or more).

Two months of feverish activity followed; Martin asked all employees to contribute to building the missile exactly right the first time since there would be virtually no time for the usual inspections. Management worked hard to maintain enthusiasm on the plant floor. In February 1962, Martin delivered on time a perfect missile that was fully operational in less than 24 hours.

This experience was eye-opening for both Martin and the rest of the aerospace industry. After careful review, management concluded that, in effect, its own changed attitude has assured the project's success. In the words of one close observer: "The one time management demanded perfection, it happened!"[1] Martin management thereafter told employees that the only acceptable quality standard was "zero defects." It instilled this principle in the work force through training, special events, and by posting quality results. It set goals for workers and put great effort into giving each worker positive criticism. Formal techniques for problem solving, however, remained limited. For the most part, the program focused on motivation—on changing the attitudes of employees.

STRATEGIC QUALITY MANAGEMENT

On the whole, U.S. corporations did not keep pace with quality control innovations the way a number of overseas competitors did. Particularly after World War II, U.S. corporations expanded rapidly and many became complacent. Managers knew that consumers wouldn't drive a VW Beetle, indestructible as it was, if they could afford a fancier car—even if this meant more visits to the repair shop.

But if U.S. car manufacturers *had* gotten their products to outlast Beetles, U.S. quality managers still would not have been prepared for Toyota Corollas, or Sony televisions. Indeed, there was nothing in the principles of quality control to disabuse them of the idea that quality was merely something that could hurt a company if ignored; that added quality was the designer's business—a matter, perhaps, of chrome and push buttons.

The beginnings of strategic quality management cannot be dated precisely because no single book or article marks its inception. But even more than in consumer electronics and cars, the volatile market in semiconductors provides a telling example of change. In March 1980, Richard W. Anderson, general manager of Hewlett-Packard's Data Systems Division, reported that after testing 300,000 16K RAM chips from 3 U.S. and 3 Japanese manufacturers, Hewlett-Packard had discovered wide disparities in quality. At incoming inspection, the Japanese chips had a failure rate of zero; the comparable rate for the 3 U.S. manufacturers was between 11 and 19 failures per 1,000. After 1,000 hours of use, the failure rate of the Japanese chips was between 1 and 2 per 1,000; usable U.S. chips failed up to 27 times per thousand.

Several U.S. semiconductor companies reacted to the news impulsively, complaining that the Japanese were sending only their best components to the all-important U.S. market. Others disputed the basic data. The most perceptive market analysts, however, noted how differences in quality coincided

---

[1] James F. Halpin, *Zero Defects* (New York: McGraw-Hill, 1966), 15.

with the rapid ascendancy of Japanese chip manufacturers. In a few years the Japanese had gone from a standing start to significant market shares in both the 16K and 64K chip markets. Their message—intentional or not—was that quality could be a potent strategic weapon.

U.S. semiconductor manufacturers got the message. In 16K chips the quality gap soon closed. And in industries as diverse as machine tools and radial tires, each of which had seen its position erode in the face of Japanese competition, there has been a new seriousness about quality too. But how to translate seriousness into action? Managers who are now determined to compete on quality have been thrown back on the old questions: How much quality is enough? What does it take to look at quality from the customer's vantage point? These are still hard questions today.

To achieve quality gains, I believe, managers need a new way of thinking, a conceptual bridge to the consumer's vantage point. Obviously, market studies acquire a new importance in this context, as does a careful review of competitors' products. One thing is certain: high quality means pleasing consumers, not just protecting them from annoyances. Product designers, in turn, should shift their attention from prices at the time of purchase to life cycle costs that include expenditures on service and maintenance—the customer's total costs. Even consumer complaints play a new role because they provide a valuable source of product information.

But managers have to take a more preliminary step—a crucial one, however obvious it may appear. They must first develop a clear vocabulary with which to discuss quality as *strategy*. They must break down the word quality into manageable parts. Only then can they define the quality niches in which to compete.

I propose eight critical dimensions or categories of quality that can serve as a framework for strategic analysis: performance, features, reliability, conformance, durability, serviceability, aesthetics, and perceived quality.[2] Some of these are always mutually reinforcing; some are not. A product or service can rank high on one dimension of quality and low on another—indeed, an improvement in one may be achieved only at the expense of another. It is precisely this interplay that makes strategic quality management possible; the challenge to managers is to compete on selected dimensions.

1. PERFORMANCE

Of course, performance refers to a product's primary operating characteristics. For an automobile, performance would include traits like acceleration, handling, cruising speed, and comfort; for a television set, performance

---

[2]This framework first appeared, in a preliminary form, in my article "What Does 'Product Quality' Really Mean?" *Sloan Management Review* (Fall 1984).

means sound and picture clarity, color, and the ability to receive distant stations. In service businesses—say, fast food and airlines—performance often means prompt service.

Because this dimension of quality involves measurable attributes, brands can usually be ranked objectively on individual aspects of performance. Overall performance rankings, however, are more difficult to develop, especially when they involve benefits that not every consumer needs. A power shovel with a capacity of 100 cubic yards per hour will "out-perform" one with a capacity of 10 cubic yards per hour. Suppose, however, that the two shovels possessed the identical capacity—60 cubic yards per hour—but achieved it differently: one with a 1-cubic-yard bucket operating at 60 cycles per hour, the other with a 2-cubic-yard bucket operating at 30 cycles per hour. The capacities of the shovels would then be the same, but the shovel with the larger bucket could handle massive boulders while the shovel with the smaller bucket could perform precision work. The "superior performer" depends entirely on the task.

Some cosmetics wearers judge quality by a product's resistance to smudging; others, with more sensitive skin, assess it by how well it leaves skin irritation-free. A 100-watt light bulb provides greater candlepower than a 60-watt bulb, yet few customers would regard the difference as a measure of quality. The bulbs simply belong to different performance classes. So the question of whether performance differences are quality differences may depend on circumstantial preferences—but preferences based on functional requirements, not taste.

Some performance standards *are* based on subjective preferences, but the preferences are so universal that they have the force of an objective standard. The quietness of an automobile's ride is usually viewed as a direct reflection of its quality. Some people like a dimmer room, but who wants a noisy car?

2. FEATURES

Similar thinking can be applied to features, a second dimension of quality that is often a secondary aspect of performance. Features are the "bells and whistles" of products and services, those characteristics that supplement their basic functioning. Examples include free drinks on a plane, permanent-press cycles on a washing machine, and automatic tuners on a color television set. The line separating primary performance characteristics from secondary features is often difficult to draw. What is crucial, again, is that features involve objective and measurable attributes; objective individual needs, not prejudices, affect their translation into quality differences.

To many customers, of course, superior quality is less a reflection of the availability of particular features than of the total number of options available.

Often, choice is quality: buyers may wish to customize or personalize their purchases. Fidelity Investments and other mutual fund operators have pursued this more "flexible" approach. By offering their clients a wide range of funds covering such diverse fields as health care, technology, and energy—and by then encouraging clients to shift savings among these—they have virtually tailored investment portfolios.

Employing the latest in flexible manufacturing technology, Allen-Bradley customizes starter motors for its buyers without having to price its products prohibitively. Fine furniture stores offer their customers countless variations in fabric and color. Such strategies impose heavy demands on operating managers; they are an aspect of quality likely to grow in importance with the perfection of flexible manufacturing technology.

3. RELIABILITY

This dimension reflects the probability of a product malfunctioning or failing within a specified time period. Among the most common measures of reliability are the mean time to first failure, the mean time between failures, and the failure rate per unit time. Because these measures require a product to be in use for a specified period, they are more relevant to durable goods than to products and services that are consumed instantly.

Reliability normally becomes more important to consumers as downtime and maintenance become more expensive. Farmers, for example, are especially sensitive to downtime during the short harvest season. Reliable equipment can mean the difference between a good year and spoiled crops. But consumers in other markets are more attuned than ever to product reliability too. Computers and copying machines certainly compete on this basis. And recent market research shows that, especially for young women, reliability has become an automobile's most desired attribute. Nor is the government, our biggest single consumer, immune. After seeing its expenditures for major weapons repair jump from $7.4 billion in fiscal year 1980 to $14.9 billion in fiscal year 1985, the Department of Defense has begun cracking down on contractors whose weapons fail frequently in the field.

4. CONFORMANCE

A related dimension of quality is conformance, or the degree to which a product's design and operating characteristics meet established standards. This dimension owes the most to the traditional approaches to quality pioneered by experts like Juran.

All products and services involve specifications of some sort. When new designs or models are developed, dimensions are set for parts and purity standards for materials. These specifications are normally expressed as a target or "center"; deviance from the center is permitted within a specified range. Because this approach to conformance equates good quality with operating inside a tolerance band, there is little interest in whether specifications have been met exactly. For the most part, dispersion within specification limits is ignored.

One drawback of this approach is the problem of "tolerance stack-up": when two or more parts are to be fit together, the size of their tolerances often determines how well they will match. Should one part fall at a lower limit of its specification, and a matching part at its upper limit, a tight fit is unlikely. Even if the parts are rated acceptable initially, the link between them is likely to wear more quickly than one made from parts whose dimensions have been centered more exactly.

To address this problem, a more imaginative approach to conformance has emerged. It is closely associated with Japanese manufacturers and the work of Genichi Taguchi, a prizewinning Japanese statistician. Taguchi begins with the idea of "loss function," a measure of losses from the time a product is shipped. (These losses include warranty costs, nonrepeating customers, and other problems resulting from performance failure.) Taguchi then compares such losses to two alternative approaches to quality: on the one hand, simple conformance to specifications, and on the other, a measure of the degree to which parts or products diverge from the ideal target or center.

He demonstrates that "tolerance stack-up" will be worse—more costly— when the dimensions of parts are more distant from the center than when they cluster around it, even if some parts fall outside the tolerance band entirely. According to Taguchi's approach, production process 1 in the *Exhibit* is better even though some items fall beyond specification limits. Traditional approaches favor production process 2. The challenge for quality managers is obvious.

Incidentally, the two most common measures of failure in conformance—for Taguchi and everyone else—are defect rates in the factory and, once a product is in the hands of the customer, the incidence of service calls. But these measures neglect other deviations from standard, like misspelled labels or shoddy construction, that do not lead to service or repair. In service businesses, measures of conformance normally focus on accuracy and timeliness and include counts of processing errors, unanticipated delays, and other frequent mistakes.

5. Durability

A measure of product life, durability has both economic and technical dimensions. Technically, durability can be defined as the amount of use one gets from a product before it deteriorates. After so many hours of use, the filament of a light bulb burns up and the bulb must be replaced. Repair is impossible.

In the following graphs, shaded areas under the curves indicate items whose measurements meet specifications. White areas indicate items not meeting specifications.

Production process 1

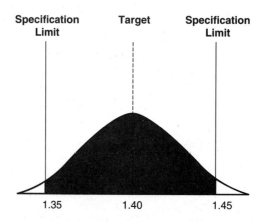

In production process 1 (favored by Taguchi), items distribute closely around the target, although some items fall outside specifications.

Production process 2

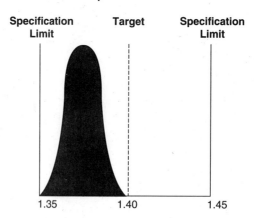

In production process 2 (favored in traditional approaches), items all distribute within specifications, but not tightly around the target.

Source: L. P. Sullivan, "Reducing Variability: A New Approach to Quality," *Quality Progress,* July 1984, p. 16.

Economists call such products "one-hoss shays" (after the carriage in the Oliver Wendell Holmes poem that was designed by the deacon to last a hundred years, and whose parts broke down simultaneously at the end of the century).

In other cases, consumers must weigh the expected cost, in both dollars and personal inconvenience, of future repairs against the investment and operating expenses of a newer, more reliable model. Durability, then, may be defined as the amount of use one gets from a product before it breaks down and replacement is preferable to continued repair.

This approach to durability has two important implications. First, it suggests that durability and reliability are closely linked. A product that often fails is likely to be scrapped earlier than one that is more reliable; repair costs will be correspondingly higher and the purchase of a competitive brand will look that much more desirable. Because of this linkage, companies sometimes try to reassure customers by offering lifetime guarantees on their products, as 3M has done with its videocassettes. Second, this approach implies that durability figures should be interpreted with care. An increase in product life may not be the result of technical improvements or the use of longer-lived materials. Rather, the underlying economic environment simply may have changed.

For example, the expected life of an automobile rose during the last decade—it now averages 14 years—mainly because rising gasoline prices and a weak economy reduced the average number of miles driven per year. Still, durability varies widely among brands. In 1981, estimated product lives for major home appliances ranged from 9.9 years (Westinghouse) to 13.2 years (Frigidaire) for refrigerators, 5.8 years (Gibson) to 18 years (Maytag) for clothes washers, 6.6 years (Montgomery Ward) to 13.5 years (Maytag) for dryers, and 6 years (Sears) to 17 years (Kirby) for vacuum cleaners.[3] This wide dispersion suggests that durability is a potentially fertile area for further quality differentiation.

6. SERVICEABILITY

A sixth dimension of quality is serviceability, or the speed, courtesy, competence, and ease of repair. Consumers are concerned not only about a product breaking down but also about the time before service is restored, the timeliness with which service appointments are kept, the nature of dealings with service personnel, and the frequency with which service calls or repairs fail to correct outstanding problems. In those cases where problems are not immediately resolved and complaints are filed, a company's complaint-handling procedures are also likely to affect customers' ultimate evaluation of product and service quality.

---

[3]Roger B. Yepsen, Jr., ed., *The Durability Factor* (Emmaus, Penn.: Rodale Press, 1982), 190.

Some of these variables reflect differing personal standards of acceptable service. Others can be measured quite objectively. Responsiveness is typically measured by the mean time to repair, while technical competence is reflected in the incidence of multiple service calls required to correct a particular problem. Because most consumers equate rapid repair and reduced downtime with higher quality, these elements of serviceability are less subject to personal interpretation than are those involving evaluations of courtesy or standards of professional behavior.

Even reactions to downtime, however, can be quite complex. In certain environments, rapid response becomes critical only after certain thresholds have been reached. During harvest season, farmers generally accept downtime of one to six hours on harvesting equipment, such as combines, with little resistance. As downtime increases, they become anxious; beyond eight hours of downtime they become frantic and frequently go to great lengths to continue harvesting even if it means purchasing or leasing additional equipment. In markets like this, superior service can be a powerful selling tool. Caterpillar guarantees delivery of repair parts anywhere in the world within 48 hours; a competitor offers the free loan of farm equipment during critical periods should its customers' machines break down.

Customers may remain dissatisfied even after completion of repairs. How these complaints are handled is important to a company's reputation for quality and service. Eventually, profitability is likely to be affected as well. A 1976 consumer survey found that among households that initiated complaints to resolve problems, more than 40 percent were not satisfied with the results. Understandably, the degree of satisfaction with complaint resolution closely correlated with consumers' willingness to repurchase the offending brands.[4]

Companies differ widely in their approaches to complaint handling and in the importance they attach to this element of serviceability. Some do their best to resolve complaints; others use legal gimmicks, the silent treatment, and similar ploys to rebuff dissatisfied customers. Recently, General Electric, Pillsbury, Procter & Gamble, Polaroid, Whirlpool, Johnson & Johnson, and other companies have sought to preempt consumer dissatisfaction by installing toll-free telephone hot lines to their customer relations departments.

7. AESTHETICS

The final two dimensions of quality are the most subjective. Aesthetics— how a product looks, feels, sounds, tastes, or smells—is clearly a matter of

---

[4]TARP, *Consumer Complaint Handling in America: Final Report* (Springfield, Va.: National Technical Information Service, U.S. Department of Commerce, 1979).

personal judgment and a reflection of individual preference. Nevertheless, there appear to be some patterns in consumers' rankings of products on the basis of taste. A recent study of quality in 33 food categories, for example, found that high quality was most often associated with "rich and full flavor, tastes natural, tastes fresh, good aroma, and looks appetizing."[5]

The aesthetics dimension differs from subjective criteria pertaining to "performance"—the quiet car engine, say—in that aesthetic choices are not nearly universal. Not all people prefer "rich and full" flavor or even agree on what it means. Companies therefore have to search for a niche. On this dimension of quality, it is impossible to please everyone.

8. PERCEIVED QUALITY

Consumers do not always have complete information about a product's or service's attributes; indirect measures may be their only basis for comparing brands. A product's durability, for example, can seldom be observed directly; it usually must be inferred from various tangible and intangible aspects of the product. In such circumstances, images, advertising, and brand names—inferences about quality rather than the reality itself—can be critical. For this reason, both Honda—which makes cars in Marysville, Ohio—and Sony—which builds color televisions in San Diego—have been reluctant to publicize that their products are "made in America."

Reputation is the primary stuff of perceived quality. Its power comes from an unstated analogy: that the quality of products today is similar to the quality of products yesterday, or the quality of goods in a new product line is similar to the quality of a company's established products. In the early 1980s, Maytag introduced a new line of dishwashers. Needless to say, salespeople immediately emphasized the product's reliability—not yet proven—because of the reputation of Maytag's clothes washers and dryers.

COMPETING ON QUALITY

This completes the list of the eight dimensions of quality. The most traditional notions—conformance and reliability—remain important, but they are subsumed within a broader strategic framework. A company's first challenge is to use this framework to explore the opportunities it has to distinguish its products from another company's wares.

---

[5]P. Greg Bonner and Richard Nelson, "Product Attributes and Perceived Quality: Foods," in *Perceived Quality*, ed. Jacob Jacoby and Jerry C. Olsen (Lexington, Mass.: Lexington Books, D.C. Heath, 1985), 71.

The quality of an automobile tire may reflect its tread-wear rate, handling, traction in dangerous driving conditions, rolling resistance (i.e., impact on gas mileage), noise levels, resistance to punctures, or appearance. High-quality furniture may be distinguished by its uniform finish, an absence of surface flaws, reinforced frames, comfort, or superior design. Even the quality of a less tangible product like computer software can be evaluated in multiple dimensions. These dimensions include reliability, ease of maintenance, match with users' needs, integrity (the extent to which unauthorized access can be controlled), and portability (the ease with which a program can be transferred from one hardware or software environment to another).

A company need not pursue all eight dimensions simultaneously. In fact, that is seldom possible unless it intends to charge unreasonably high prices. Technological limitations may impose a further constraint. In some cases, a product or service can be improved in one dimension of quality only if it becomes worse in another. Cray Research, a manufacturer of supercomputers, has faced particularly difficult choices of this sort. According to the company's chairman, if a supercomputer doesn't fail every month or so, it probably wasn't built for maximum speed; in pursuit of higher speed, Cray has deliberately sacrificed reliability.

There are other trade-offs. Consider the following:

- In entering U.S. markets, Japanese manufacturers often emphasize their products' reliability and conformance while downplaying options and features. The superior "fits and finishes" and low repair rates of Japanese cars are well known; less often recognized are their poor safety records and low resistance to corrosion.
- Tandem Computers has based its business on superior reliability. For computer users that find downtime intolerable, like telephone companies and utilities, Tandem has devised a fail-safe system: two processors working in parallel and linked by software that shifts responsibility between the two if an important component or subsystem fails. The result, in an industry already well-known for quality products, has been spectacular corporate growth. In 1984, after less than 10 years in business, Tandem's annual sales topped $500 million.
- Not long ago, New York's Chemical Bank upgraded its services for collecting payments for corporations. Managers had first conducted a user survey indicating that what customers wanted most was rapid response to queries about account status. After it installed a computerized system to answer customers' calls, Chemical, which banking consumers had ranked fourth in quality in the industry, jumped to first.
- In the piano business, Steinway & Sons has long been the quality leader. Its instruments are known for their even voicing (the evenness

of character and timbre in each of the 88 notes on the keyboard), the sweetness of their registers, the duration of their tone, their long lives, and even their fine cabinet work. Each piano is built by hand and is distinctive in sound and style. Despite these advantages, Steinway recently has been challenged by Yamaha, a Japanese manufacturer that has built a strong reputation for quality in a relatively short time. Yamaha has done so by emphasizing reliability and conformance, two quality dimensions that are low on Steinway's list.

These examples confirm that companies can pursue a selective quality niche. In fact, they may have no other choice, especially if competitors have established reputations for a certain kind of excellence. Few products rank high on all eight dimensions of quality. Those that do—Cross pens, Rolex watches, Rolls-Royce automobiles—require consumers to pay the cost of skilled workmanship.

STRATEGIC ERRORS

A final word, not about strategic opportunities, but about the worst strategic mistakes. The first is direct confrontation with an industry's leader. As with Yamaha vs. Steinway, it is far preferable to nullify the leader's advantage in a particular niche while avoiding the risk of retaliation. Moreover, a common error is to introduce dimensions of quality that are unimportant to consumers. When deregulation unlocked the market for residential telephones, a number of manufacturers, including AT&T, assumed that customers equated quality with a wide range of expensive features. They were soon proven wrong. Fancy telephones sold poorly while durable, reliable, and easy-to-operate sets gained large market shares.

Shoddy market research often results in neglect of quality dimensions that *are* critical to consumers. Using outdated surveys, car companies overlooked how important reliability and conformance were becoming in the 1970s; ironically, these companies failed consumers on the very dimensions that were key targets of traditional approaches to quality control.

It is often a mistake to stick with old quality measures when the external environment has changed. A major telecommunications company had always evaluated its quality by measuring timeliness—the amount of time it took to provide a dial tone, to connect a call, or to be connected to an operator. On these measures it performed well. More sophisticated market surveys, conducted in anticipation of the industry's deregulation, found that consumers were not really concerned about call connection time; consumers assumed that this would be more or less acceptable. They were more concerned with the clarity of transmission and the degree of static on the line. On these measures, the company found it was well behind its competitors.

In an industry like semiconductor manufacturing equipment, Japanese machines generally require less set-up time; they break down less often and have few problems meeting their specified performance levels. These are precisely the traits desired by most buyers. Still, U.S. equipment can *do* more. As one U.S. plant manager put it: "Our equipment is more advanced, but Japanese equipment is more developed."

Quality measures may be inadequate in less obvious ways. Some measures are too limited; they fail to capture aspects of quality that are important for competitive success. Singapore International Airlines, a carrier with a reputation for excellent service, saw its market share decline in the early 1980s. The company dismissed quality problems as the cause of its difficulties because data on service complaints showed steady improvement during the period. Only later, after SIA solicited consumer responses, did managers see the weakness of their former measures. Relative declines in service had indeed been responsible for the loss of market share. Complaint counts had failed to register problems because the proportion of passengers who wrote complaint letters was small—they were primarily Europeans and U.S. citizens rather than Asians, the largest percentage of SIA passengers. SIA also had failed to capture data about its competitors' service improvements.

The pervasiveness of these errors is difficult to determine. Anecdotal evidence suggests that many U.S. companies lack hard data and are thus more vulnerable than they need be. One survey found that 65 percent of executives thought that consumers could readily name—without help—a good quality brand in a big-ticket category like major home appliances. But when the question was actually posed to consumers, only 16 percent could name a brand for small appliances, and only 23 percent for large appliances.[6] Are U.S. executives that ill-informed about consumers' perceptions? The answer is not likely to be reassuring.

Managers have to stop thinking about quality merely as a narrow effort to gain control of the production process, and start thinking more rigorously about consumers' needs and preferences. Quality is not simply a problem to be solved; it is a competitive opportunity.

---

[6]Consumer Network, Inc., *Brand Quality Perceptions* (Philadelphia: Consumer Network, August 1983), 17 and 50–51.

SELECTED READINGS

AT&T, *SQC Handbook,* Indianapolis, AT&T Technologies, 1956.

Crosby, P. B., *Quality is Free,* New York, McGraw-Hill Book Co., 1979.

Crosby, P. B., *Quality Without Tears,* New York, McGraw-Hill Book Co., 1984.

Deming, W. E., "What Happened in Japan?" *Industrial Quality Control,* v. 24, no. 2 (August 1967), pp. 89–93.

Deming, W. E., "On Some Statistical Aids Toward Economic Production," *Interfaces,* v. 5, no. 5 (August 1975), pp. 1–15.

Deming, W. E., *Out of the Crisis,* Cambridge, MA, MIT Center for Advanced Engineering Study, 1986.

Feigenbaum, A. V., *Total Quality Control: Engineering and Management,* New York, McGraw-Hill, 1961.

Feigenbaum, A. V., "The Internationalization of Quality," *Quality Progress,* v. 12, no. 2 (Feb. 1979), pp. 30–32.

Garvin, D. A., "Quality on the Line," *Harvard Business Review,* v. 61, no. 5, 1983, pp. 65–75.

Garvin, D. A., "What Does Product Quality Really Mean?" *Sloan Management Review,* v. 26, no. 1 (1984), pp. 25–43.

Garvin, D. A., "Quality Problems, Policies, and Attitudes in the United States and Japan: An Exploratory Study," *Academy of Management Journal,* v. 29, no. 4 (1986), pp. 653–673.

Ishikawa, K., *What is Total Quality Control? The Japanese Way,* Englewood Cliffs, NJ, Prentice-Hall, 1985.

Juran, J. M., *Management of Inspection and Quality Control,* New York, Harper, 1945.

Juran, J. M., *Quality Control Handbook,* New York, McGraw-Hill, 1979.

Juran, J. M. and F. Gryrla, *Quality Planning and Analysis,* New York, McGraw-Hill Book Co., 1980.

Juran, J. M., "Product Quality—A Prescription for the West," *Management Review,* (June–July 1981).

Juran, J. M., *Juran On Leadership for Quality,* New York, The Free Press, 1989.

Shingo, S., *Zero Quality Control: Source Inspection and the Poka-yoke System,* trans. A. P. Dillon, Stamford, CT, Productivity Press, 1985.

Taguchi, G. and Y. Wu, *Introduction to Off-Line Quality Control,* Magoya, Japan, Central Japan Quality Control Association, 1980.

Taguchi, G., *Introduction to Quality Engineering,* White Plains, NY, Asian Productivity Organization, UNIPUB, 1986.

Taguchi, G., E. Elsayed, and T. Hsiang, *Quality Engineering in Production Systems,* New York, McGraw-Hill Book Co., 1989.

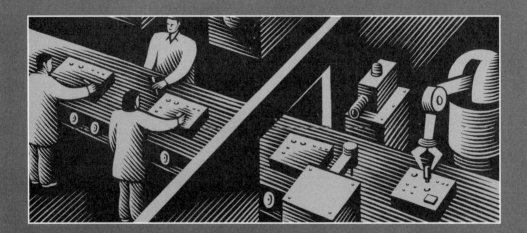

CHAPTER FOUR

PRODUCTIVITY

From the beginning, man has struggled with the issue of productivity. Early man searched for ways to make the hunt more productive. New tools and strategies were the result. Early farmers looked for ways to farm more land in a shorter amount of time. Multirow plows and harvesters resulted.

In industry, the search was for ways to make the worker more productive. Volumes could have been filled on the techniques used by ancient and medieval "business men"—traders and merchants—on how they achieved their productivity.

Today, we trace what is considered "modern" productivity back to the writings of Frederick Taylor. Taylor's early work, which became known as Scientific Management, studied the work habits of employees. He developed tools to measure the amount of work, or productivity, of each worker. New techniques were tried to improve the productivity of the worker. As these new techniques were used, they were measured using Taylor's productivity tools and compared to other techniques. This scientific approach to productivity has remained with us since the turn of the century.

Taylor's "disciples" included Henry Gantt, inventor of the Gantt chart, and Frank and Lillian Gilbreth. The Gilbreths extended Taylor's work in Time and Motion Studies. Much of today's tools and techniques used in time and motion studies were developed by the Gilbreths. (See Chapter Two for articles from Gantt and Frank Gilbreth.)

Taylor's work in productivity was also the basis for the Hawthorne studies at Western Electric. However, the findings of this study, led by Elton Mayo, found that there was a behavioral aspect to productivity that had not been studied previously (although Taylor did touch on this issue with his "first man" concept). The field of behavioral science developed as a result of the Hawthorne studies.

As factories grew, the productivity question shifted from one of improving the productivity of the individual to improving the productivity of the system. Oliver Wight began studying the flow of materials in a factory setting, focusing on when and where the materials were required. His studies resulted in the creation of Material Requirements Planning, or MRP, in the early 1970s. Others who studied the flow of the system include Joseph Orlicky and George Plossl.

In 1979, Oliver Wight expanded on his original studies in material requirements planning (MRP) to include areas outside of "traditional" production, including accounting and procurement. This integrated system he referred to as Manufacturing Resource Planning, or MRP II.

In 1980, the documentary "If Japan Can, Why Can't We?" was shown in the United States. In addition to re-introducing W. Edwards Deming to U.S. manufacturers, it inspired many U.S. companies to look to Japan for ideas on how to increase productivity. One of the first articles to look at Japanese productivity studies was Takeuchi's "Productivity: Learning from the Japanese." Hundreds of articles and dozens of books have been published on how the Japanese have increased their productivity so dramatically, and what American industry can do to achieve the same results.

As the 1980s was a decade of self-review for American industry, so the 1990s will prove a decade of application. U.S. industry has come to the realization that to compete internationally, they must be as productive as possible. Major American companies such as Xerox and Motorola have shown that it is possible for American industry to compete—and win—against its overseas competitors.

The 1980s were a boom time for studies in American productivity. The quality movement, global competitiveness, and the burgeoning American trade deficit left many U.S. companies wondering what they needed to do to increase productivity and once again become internationally competitive. The myriad of solutions offered during the 1980s brought much confusion as well. In 1986, Wickam Skinner wrote "The Productivity Paradox" to address many of the conflicting ideas and theories that had sprung up since 1980. Since 1986, U.S. manufacturers have started looking at why their productivity levels are where they are, rather than looking for a "quick fix" solution. (Hayes and Clark address this issue in the last article in this chapter.)

BASIS FOR ARTICLE SELECTION

Based on the study discussed in Chapter One, the authors associated with productivity studies were rated by the respondents as follows.

AUTHOR	RATING (1–5 WITH 5 BEING BEST)
Taylor	4.45
Skinner	4.24
Gantt	4.06
Gilbreth	3.98
Hayes	3.93
Orlicky	3.79
Wight	3.52
Clark	3.27
Mayo	3.20

A one-way ANOVA was run on these authors and resulted in the following mean and standard error values. The results are displayed in the Venn Diagram in Figure 4-1.

TREATMENT	MEAN	STANDARD ERROR	NO. OF OBSERVATIONS
Clark	3.267	.120888	60
Gantt	4.060	.130892	67
Gilbreth	3.984	.138179	64
Hayes	3.934	.136043	61
Mayo	3.200	.157308	60
Orlicky	3.794	.143397	63
Skinner	4.238	.125406	63
Taylor	4.446	.122142	65
Wight	3.517	.131251	60

The articles of Gantt and Gilbreth are located in Chapter Two, as is one of the articles of Frederick Taylor. Another of Taylor's articles, which focuses more on the productivity issue than the strategy issue, is included in this chapter. In addition, a series of articles written by Frederick Taylor to explain the concept of Scientific Management are included, along with a criticism by Upton Sinclare and a response to the criticism by Taylor. Readers interested in pursuing a further understanding of the productivity issue are encouraged to review the articles and books included in the readings list.

FIGURE 4-1

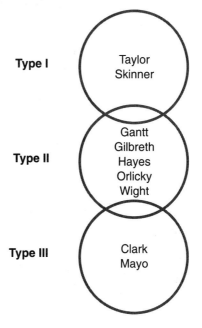

Type I

Taylor
Skinner

Type II

Gantt
Gilbreth
Hayes
Orlicky
Wight

Type III

Clark
Mayo

A Piece-Rate System, Being a Step toward Partial Solution of the Labor Problem

Frederick W. Taylor

Introduction

The ordinary piecework system involves a permanent antagonism between employers and men, and a certainty of punishment for each workman who reaches a high rate of efficiency. The demoralizing effect of this system is most serious. Under it, even the best workmen are forced continually to act the part of hypocrites, to hold their own in the struggle against the encroachments of their employers.

The system introduced by the writer, however, is directly the opposite, both in theory and in its results. It makes each workman's interests the same as that of his employer, pays a premium for high efficiency, and soon convinces each man that it is for his permanent advantage to turn out each day the best quality and maximum quantity of work.

The writer has endeavored in the following pages to describe the system of management introduced by him in the works of the Midvale Steel Company, of Philadelphia, which has been employed by them during the past ten years with the most satisfactory results.

The system consists of three principal elements:

1. An elementary rate-fixing department.
2. The differential rate system of piecework.
3. What he believes to be the best method of managing men who work by the day.

Presented at the Detroit Meeting (June 1895) of the American Society of Mechanical Engineers, and forming part of Volume XVI of the *Transactions*.

Elementary rate-fixing differs from other methods of making piecework prices in that a careful study is made of the time required to do each of the many elementary operations into which the manufacturing of an establishment may be analyzed or divided. These elementary operations are then classified, recorded, and indexed, and when a piecework price is wanted for work, the job is first divided into its elementary operations, the time required to do each elementary operation is found from the records, and the total time for the job is summed up from these data. While this method seems complicated at the first glance, it is, in fact, far simpler and more effective than the old method of recording the time required to do whole jobs of work, and then, after looking over the records of similar jobs, guessing at the time required for any new piece of work.

The differential rate system of piecework consists briefly in offering two different rates for the same job; a high price per piece, in case the work is finished in the shortest possible time and in perfect condition, and a low price, if it takes a longer time to do the job, or if there are any imperfections in the work. (The high rate should be such that the workman can earn more per day than is usually paid in similar establishments.) This is directly the opposite of the ordinary plan of piecework, in which the wages of the workmen are reduced when they increase their productivity.

The system by which the writer proposes managing the men who are on day-work consists in paying *men* and not *positions*. Each man's wages, as far as possible, are fixed according to the skill and energy with which he performs his work, and not according to the position which he fills. Every endeavor is made to stimulate each man's personal ambition. This involves keeping systematic and careful records of the performance of each man, as to his punctuality, attendance, integrity, rapidity, skill, and accuracy, and a readjustment from time to time of the wages paid him, in accordance with this record.

The advantages of this system of management are:

First. That the manufactures are produced cheaper under it, while at the same time the workmen earn higher wages than are usually paid.

Second. Since the rate-fixing is done from accurate knowledge instead of more or less by guesswork, the motive for holding back on work, or "soldiering," and endeavoring to deceive the employers as to the time required to do work, is entirely removed, and with it the greatest cause for hard feelings and war between the management and the men.

Third. Since the basis from which piecework as well as day rates are fixed is that of exact observation, instead of being founded upon accident or deception, as is too frequently the case under ordinary systems, the men are treated with greater uniformity and justice, and respond by doing more and better work.

Fourth. It is for the common interest of both the management and the men to cooperate in every way, so as to turn out each day the maximum quantity and best quality of work.

Fifth. The system is rapid, while other systems are slow, in attaining the maximum productivity of each machine and man; and when this maximum is once reached, it is automatically maintained by the differential rate.

Sixth. It automatically selects and attracts the best men for each class of work, and it develops many first-class men who would otherwise remain slow or inaccurate, while at the same time it discourages and sifts out men who are incurably lazy or inferior.

Finally. One of the chief advantages derived from the above effects of the system is, that it promotes a most friendly feeling between the men and their employers, and so renders labor unions and strikes unnecessary.

There has never been a strike under the differential rate system of piece-work, although it has been in operation for the past ten years in the steel business, which has been during this period more subject to strikes and labor troubles than almost any other industry. In describing the above system of management, the writer has been obliged to refer to other piecework methods, and to indicate briefly what he believes to be their shortcomings.

As but few will care to read the whole paper, the following index to its contents is given.

INDEX

	Paragraph
Need of System and Method in Managing Men	1–9
System of Managing Men Who Are Paid by the Day	
Ordinary system of paying men by the position they occupy instead of by individual merit	10
Bad effects of this system	11, 12
Proper method of handling men working by the day is to study each man and fix his rate of pay according to his individual merit, not to pay them by classes	13–15, 84–87
Necessity for clerk in managing men	14, 15
Defects in even the best-managed day-work	16, 17
Methods of Fixing Piecework Prices or Rates	
Ordinary Plan of Fixing Rates	41, 42
Description of Elementary Rate-Fixing	39–43
Description of the starting and development of the first elementary rate-fixing department	44–48
Illustration of elementary rate-fixing	48
Size and scope of rate-fixing department	69, 70
Indirect benefits of elementary rate-fixing almost as	

great as the direct 74–76

A handbook on the speed with which different kinds
of work can be done badly needed 67, 68

Systems of Piecework in Common Use

Ordinary Piecework System 19

Defects in this system 20–24

Slight improvement in ordinary piecework system 26

"Gain Sharing" Plan 27, 29

"Premium Plan of Paying for Labor" 28, 29

Benefits and defects of these two systems 30

The relation of trades unions to other systems
of management 92

Cooperation or Profit Sharing 31–34

Antagonism of interests of employers and workmen
in all ordinary piecework systems 35

Fundamental basis for harmonious cooperation
between workmen and employers 36, 37, 53–55, 59, 61, 65

Obstacles to be overcome before both sides can
cooperate harmoniously 38, 39, 49

And principles underlying true cooperation 53–55, 59, 61, 65

Description of Differential Rate System of Piecework 50–52

Advantages of this system 53–65

Description of first application of differential rate,
with results attained 71, 79-82

Modification of the differential rate 72, 73

Illustrations of the possibility of increasing the daily
output of men and machines 78, 79

Relative importance of elementary rate-fixing department
and differential rate 66

There have never been any strikes under the differential
rate system of piecework 83

Moral effect of the various piecework systems on the men 20–24

Ordinary systems, differential rate 88

Probable future development of this system 89–91

1. Capital demands fully twice the return for money placed in manufacturing enterprises that it does for real estate or transportation ventures. And
this probably represents the difference in the risk between these classes of
investments.

2. Among the risks of a manufacturing business, by far the greatest is that
of bad management; and of the three managing departments, the commercial, the financing, and the productive, the latter, in most cases, receives the

least attention from those that have invested their money in the business, and contains the greatest elements of risk. This risk arises not so much from the evident mismanagement, which plainly discloses itself through occasional strikes and similar troubles, as from the daily more insidious and fatal failure on the part of the superintendents to secure anything even approaching the maximum work from their men and machines.

3. It is not unusual for the manager of a manufacturing business to go most minutely into every detail of the buying and selling and financing, and arrange every element of these branches in the most systematic manner, and according to principles that have been carefully planned to insure the business against almost any contingency which may arise, while the manufacturing is turned over to a superintendent or foreman, with little or no restrictions as to the principles and methods which he is to pursue, either in the management of his men or the care of the company's plant.

4. Such managers belong distinctly to the old school of manufacturers; and among them are to be found, in spite of their lack of system, many of the best and most successful men of the country. They believe in men, not in methods, in the management of their shops; and what they would call system in the office and sales departments, would be called red tape by them in the factory. Through their keen insight and knowledge of character they are able to select and train good superintendents, who in turn secure good workmen; and frequently the business prospers under this system (or rather, lack of system) for a term of years.

5. The modern manufacturer, however, seeks not only to secure the best superintendents and workmen, but to surround each department of his manufacture with the most carefully woven network of system and method, which should render the business, for a considerable period, at least, independent of the loss of any one man, and frequently of any combination of men.

6. It is the lack of this system and method which, in the judgement of the writer, constitutes the greatest risk in manufacturing; placing, as it frequently does, the success of the business at the hazard of the health or whims of a few employees.

7. Even after fully realizing the importance of adopting the best possible system and methods of management for securing a proper return from employees and as an insurance against strikes and the carelessness and laziness of men, there are difficulties in the problem of selecting methods of management which shall be adequate to the purpose, and yet be free from red tape, and inexpensive.

8. The literature on the subject is meager, especially that which comes from men of practical experience and observation. And the problem is usually solved, after but little investigation, by the adoption of the system with

which the managers are most familiar, or by taking a system which has worked well in similar lines of manufacture.

9. Now, among the methods of management in common use there is certainly a great choice; and before describing the "differential rate" system it is desirable to briefly consider the more important of the other methods

10. The simplest of all systems is the "day-work" plan, in which the employees are divided into certain classes, and a standard rate of wages is paid to each class of men; the laborers all receiving one rate of pay, the machinists all another rate, and the engineers all another, etc. The men are paid according to the position which they fill, and not according to their individual character, energy, skill, and reliability.

11. The effect of this system is distinctly demoralizing and levelling; even the ambitious men soon conclude that since there is no profit to them in working hard, the best thing for them to do is to work just as little as they can and still keep their position. And under these conditions the invariable tendency is to drag them all down even below the level of the medium.

12. The proper and legitimate answer to this herding of men together into classes, regardless of personal character and performance, is the formation of the labor union, and the strike, either to increase the rate of pay and improve conditions of employment, or to resist the lowering of wages and other encroachments on the part of employers.

13. The necessity for the labor union, however, disappears when *men* are paid, and not *positions*; that is, when the employers take pains to study the character and performance of each of their employees and pay them accordingly, when accurate records are kept of each man's attendance, punctuality, the amount and quality of work done by him, and his attitude towards his employers and fellow workmen.

As soon as the men recognize that they have free scope for the exercise of their proper ambition, that as they work harder and better their wages are from time to time increased, and that they are given a better class of work to do—when they recognize this, the best of them have no use for the labor union.

14. Every manufacturer must from necessity employ a certain amount of day-labor which cannot come under the piecework system; and yet how few employers are willing to go to the trouble and expense of the slight organization necessary to handle their men in this way? How few of them realize that, by the employment of an extra clerk and foreman, and a simple system of labor returns, to record the performance and readjust the wages of their men, so as to stimulate their personal ambition, the output of a gang of twenty or thirty men can be readily doubled in many cases, and at a comparatively slight increase of wages per capita!

15. The clerk in the factory is the particular horror of the old-style manufacturer. He realizes the expense each time that he looks at him, and fails to

see any adequate return; yet by the plan here described the clerk becomes one of the most valuable agents of the company.

16. If the plan of grading labor and recording each man's performance is so much superior to the old day-work method of handling men, why is it not all that is required? Because no foreman can watch and study all of his men all of the time, and because any system of laying out and apportioning work, and of returns and records, which is sufficiently elaborate to keep proper account of the performance of each workman, is more complicated than piecework. It is evident that that system is the best which, in attaining the desired result, presents in the long run the course of least resistance.

17. The inherent and most serious defect of even the best managed day-work lies in the fact that there is nothing about the system that is self-sustaining. When once the men are working at a rapid pace, there is nothing but the constant unremitting watchfulness and energy of the management to keep them there; while with every form of piecework each new rate that is fixed ensures a given speed for another section of work, and to that extent relieves the foreman from worry.

18. From the best type of day-work to ordinary piecework the step is a short one. With good day-work the various operations of manufacturing should have been divided into small sections or jobs, in order to properly gage the efficiency of the men; and the quickest time should have been recorded in which each operation has been performed. The change from paying by the hour to paying by the job is then readily accomplished.

19. The theory upon which the ordinary system of piecework operates to the benefit of the manufacturer is exceedingly simple. Each workman, with a definite price for each job before him, contrives a way of doing it in a shorter time, either by working harder or by improving his method; and he thus makes a larger profit. After the job has been repeated a number of times at the more rapid rate, the manufacturer thinks that he should also begin to share in the gain, and therefore reduces the price of the job to a figure at which the workman, although working harder, earns, perhaps, but little more than he originally did when on day-work.

20. The actual working of the system, however, is far different. Even the most stupid man, after receiving two or three piecework "cuts" as a reward for his having worked harder, resents this treatment and seeks a remedy for it in the future. Thus begins a war, generally an amicable war, but none the less a war, between the workmen and the management. The latter endeavors by every means to induce the workmen to increase the out-put, and the men gage the rapidity with which they work, so as never to earn over a certain rate of wages, knowing that if they exceed this amount the piecework price will surely be cut, sooner or later.

21. But the war is by no means restricted to piecework. Every intelligent workman realizes the importance, to his own interest, of starting in on each new job as slowly as possible. There are few foremen or superintendents who have anything but a general idea as to how long it should take to do a piece of work that is new to them. Therefore, before fixing a piecework price, they prefer to have the job done for the first time by the day. They watch the progress of the work as closely as their other duties will permit, and make up their minds how quickly it can be done. It becomes the workman's interest then to go just as slowly as possible, and still convince his foreman that he is working well.

22. The extent to which, even in our largest and best-managed establishments, this plan of holding back on the work—"marking time," or "soldiering," as it is called—is carried by the men, can scarcely be understood by one who has not worked among them. It is by no means uncommon for men to work at the rate of one-third, or even one-quarter, their maximum speed, and still preserve the appearance of working hard. And when a rate has once been fixed on such a false basis, it is easy for the men to nurse successfully "a soft snap" of this sort through a term of years, earning in the meanwhile just as much wages as they think they can without having the rate cut.

23. Thus arises a system of hypocrisy and deceit on the part of the men which is thoroughly demoralizing, and which has led many workmen to regard their employers as their natural enemies, to be opposed in whatever they want, believing that whatever is for the interest of the management must necessarily be to their detriment.

24. The effect of this system of piecework on the character of the men is, in many cases, so serious as to make it doubtful whether, on the whole, well-managed day-work is not preferable.

25. There are several modifications of the ordinary method of piecework which tend to lessen the evils of the system, but I know of none that can eradicate the fundamental causes for war, and enable the managers and the men to heartily cooperate in obtaining the maximum product from the establishment. It is the writer's opinion, however, that the differential rate system of piecework, which will be described later, in most cases entirely harmonizes the interests of both parties.

26. One method of temporarily relieving the strain between workmen and employers consists in reducing the price paid for work, and at the same time guaranteeing the men against further reduction for a definite period. If this period be made sufficiently long, the men are tempted to let themselves out and earn as much money as they can thus "spoiling" their own job by another "cut" in rates when the period has expired.

27. Perhaps the most successful modification of the ordinary system of piecework is the "gain-sharing plan." This was invented by Mr. Henry R.

Towne, in 1886, and has since been extensively and successfully applied by him in the Yale & Towne Manufacturing Co. at Stamford, Conn. It was admirably described in a paper which he read before this Society in 1888. This system of paying men is, however, subject to the serious, and I think fatal, defect that it does not recognize the personal merit of each workman; the tendency being rather to herd men together and promote trades-unionism, than to develop each man's individuality.

28. A still further improvement of this method was made by Mr. F.A. Halsey, and described by him in a paper entitled "The Premium Plan of Paying for Labor," and presented to this Society in 1891. Mr. Halsey's plan allows free scope for each man's personal ambition, which Mr. Towne's does not.

29. Messrs. Towne and Halsey's plans consist briefly in recording the cost of each job as a starting point at a certain time; then, if, through the effort of the workmen in the future, the job is done in a shorter time and at a lower cost, the gain is divided among the workmen and the employer in a definite ratio, the workmen receiving, say, one-half, and the employer one-half.

30. Under this plan, if the employer lives up to his promise, and the workman has confidence in his integrity, there is the proper basis for cooperation to secure sooner or later a large increase in the output of the establishment.

Yet there still remains the temptation for the workman to "soldier" or hold back while on day-work, which is the most difficult thing to overcome. And in this as well as in all the systems heretofore referred to, there is the common defect: that the starting-point from which the first rate is fixed is unequal and unjust. Some of the rates may have resulted from records obtained when a good man was working close to his maximum speed, while others are based on the performance of a medium man at one-third or one-quarter speed. From this follows a great inequality and injustice in the reward even of the same man when at work on different jobs. The result is far from a realization of the ideal condition in which the same return is uniformly received for a given expenditure of brains and energy. Other defects in the gain-sharing plan, and which are corrected by the differential rate system, are:

1. That it is slow and irregular in its operation in reducing costs, being dependent upon the whims of the men working under it.
2. That it fails to especially attract first-class men and discourage inferior men.
3. That it does not automatically ensure the maximum output of the establishment per man and machine.

31. Cooperation, or profit sharing, has entered the mind of every student of the subject as one of the possible and most attractive solutions of

the problem; and there have been certain instances, both in England and France, of at least a partial success of cooperative experiments.

So far as I know, however, these trials have been made either in small towns, remote from the manufacturing centres, or in industries which in many respects are not subject to ordinary manufacturing conditions.

32. Cooperative experiments have failed, and, I think, are generally destined to fail, for several reasons, the first and most important of which is, that no form of cooperation has yet been devised in which each individual is allowed free scope for his personal ambition. This always has been and will remain a more powerful incentive to exertion than a desire for the general welfare. The few misplaced drones, who do the loafing and share equally in the profits with the rest, under cooperation are sure to drag the better men down toward their level.

33. The second and almost equally strong reason for failure lies in the remoteness of the reward. The average workman (I don't say all men) cannot look forward to a profit which is six months or a year away. The nice time which they are sure to have today, if they take things easily, proves more attractive than hard work, with a possible reward to be shared with others six months later.

34. Other and formidable difficulties in the path of cooperation are, the equitable division of the profits, and the fact that, while workmen are always ready to share the profits, they are neither able nor willing to share the losses. Further than this, in many cases, it is neither right nor just that they should share either in the profits or the losses, since these may be due in great part to causes entirely beyond their influence or control, and to which they do not contribute.

35. When we recognize the real antagonism that exists between the interests of the men and their employers, under all of the systems of piecework in common use; and when we remember the apparently irreconcilable conflict implied in the fundamental and perfectly legitimate aims of the two: namely, on the part of the men:

THE UNIVERSAL DESIRE TO RECEIVE THE LARGEST
POSSIBLE WAGES FOR THEIR TIME.

And on the part of the employers:

THE DESIRE TO RECEIVE THE LARGEST POSSIBLE RETURN
FOR THE WAGES PAID.

What wonder that most of us arrive at the conclusion that no system of piecework can be devised which shall enable the two to cooperate without antagonism, and to their mutual benefit.

36. Yet it is the opinion of the writer, that even if a system has not already been found which harmonizes the interests of the two, still the basis for harmonious cooperation lies in the two following facts:

First. That the workmen in nearly* every trade can and will materially increase their present output per day providing they are assured of a permanent and larger return for their time than they have heretofore received.

Second. That the employers can well afford to pay higher wages per piece even permanently, providing each man and machine in the establishment turns out a proportionately larger amount of work.

37. The truth of the latter statement arises from the well-recognized fact that, in most lines of manufacture, the indirect expenses equal or exceed the wages paid directly to the workmen, and that these expenses remain approximately constant, whether the output of the establishment is great or small.

From this it follows that it is always cheaper to pay higher wages to the workmen when the output is proportionately increased; the diminution in the indirect portion of the cost per piece being greater than the increase in wages. Many manufacturers, in considering the cost of production, fail to realize the effect that the *volume of output has on the cost.* They lose sight of the fact that taxes, insurance, depreciation, rent, interest, salaries, office expenses, miscellaneous labor, sales expenses, and frequently the cost of power (which in the aggregate amounts to as much as wages paid to workmen), remain about the same whether the output of the establishment is great or small.

38. In our endeavor to solve the piecework problem by the application of the two fundamental facts above referred to, let us consider the obstacles in the path of harmonious cooperation, and suggest a method for their removal.

39. The most formidable obstacle is the lack of knowledge on the part of both the men and the management (but chiefly the latter) of the quickest time in which each piece of work can be done; or, briefly, the lack of accurate timetables for the work of the place.

40. The remedy for this trouble lies in the establishment in every factory of a proper rate-fixing department; a department which shall have equal dignity and command equal respect with the engineering and managing departments, and which shall be organized and conducted in an equally scientific and practical manner.

41. The rate-fixing, as at present conducted, even in our best-managed establishments, is very similar to the mechanical engineering of fifty or sixty

---

*The writer's knowledge of the speed attained in the manufacture of textile goods is very limited. It is his opinion, however, that owing to the comparative uniformity of this class of work, and the enormous number of machines and men engaged on similar operations, the maximum output per man and machine is more nearly realized in this class of manufactures than in any other. If this is the case, the opportunity for improvement does not exist to the same extent here as in other trades. Some illustrations of the possible increase in the daily output of men and machines are given in paragraphs 78 to 82.

years ago. Mechanical engineering at that time consisted in imitating machines which were in more or less successful use, or in guessing at the dimensions and strength of the parts of a new machine; and as the parts broke down or gave out, in replacing them with stronger ones. Thus, each new machine presented a problem almost independent of former designs, and one which could only be solved by months or years of practical experience and a series of breakdowns.

Modern engineering, however, has become a study, not of individual machines, but of the resistance of materials, the fundamental principles of mechanics, and of the elements of design.

42. On the other hand, the ordinarily rate-fixing (even the best of it), like the old-style engineering, is done by a foreman or superintendent, who, with the aid of a clerk, looks over the record of the time in which a whole job was done as nearly like the new one as can be found, and then guesses at the time required to do the new job. No attempt is made to analyze and time each of the classes of work, or elements of which a job is composed; although it is a far simpler task to resolve each job into its elements, to make a careful study of the quickest time in which each of the elementary operations can be done, and then to properly classify, tabulate, and index this information, and use it when required for rate-fixing, than it is to fix rates, with even an approximation to justice, under the common system of guessing.

43. In fact, it has never occurred to most superintendents that the work of their establishments consists of various combinations of elementary operations which can be timed in this way; and a suggestion that this is a practical way of dealing with the piecework problem usually meets with derision, or, at the best, with the answer that "It might do for some simple business, but my work is entirely too complicated."

44. Yet this elementary system of fixing rates has been in successful operation for the past ten years, on work complicated in its nature, and covering almost as wide a range of variety as any manufacturing that the writer knows of. In 1883, while foreman of the machine shop of the Midvale Steel Company of Philadelphia, it occurred to the writer that it was simpler to time each of the elements of the various kinds of work done in the place, and then find the quickest time in which each job could be done, by summing up the total times of its component parts, than it was to search through the records of former jobs, and guess at the proper price. After practicing this method of rate-fixing himself for about a year, as well as circumstances would permit, it became evident that the system was a success. The writer then established the rate-fixing department; which has given out piecework prices in the place ever since.

45. This department far more than paid for itself from the very start; but it was several years before the full benefits of the system were felt, owing to

the fact that the best methods of making and recording time observations of work done by the men, as well as of determining the maximum capacity of each of the machines in the place, and of making working tables and timetables, were not at first adopted.

46. Before the best results were finally attained in the case of work done by metal-cutting tools, such as lathes, planers, boring mills, etc., a long and expensive series of experiments was made, to determine, formulate, and finally practically apply to each machine the law governing the proper cutting speed of tools; namely, the effect on the cutting speed of altering any one of the following variables: the shape of the tool (that is, lip angle, clearance angle, and the line of the cutting edge), the duration of the cut, the quality or hardness of the metal being cut, the depth of the cut, and the thickness of the feed or shaving.

47. It is the writer's opinion that a more complicated and difficult piece of rate-fixing could not be found than that of determining the proper price for doing all kinds of machine work on miscellaneous steel and iron castings and forging, which vary in their chemical composition from the softest iron to the hardest tool steel. Yet this problem was solved through the rate-fixing department and the "differential rate," with the final result of completely harmonizing the men and the management, in place of the constant war that existed under the old system. At the same time, the quality of the work was improved, and the output of the machinery and the men was doubled, and, in many cases, trebled. At the start there was naturally great opposition to the rate-fixing department, particularly to the man who was taking time observations of the various elements of the work, but when the men found that rates were fixed without regard to the records of the quickest time in which they had actually done each job, and that the knowledge of the department was more accurate than their own, the motive for hanging back or "soldiering" on this work ceased, and with it the greatest cause for antagonism and war between the men and the management.

48. As an illustration of the great variety of work to which elementary rate-fixing has already been successfully applied, the writer would state that, while acting as general manager of two large sulphite pulp mills, he directed the application of piecework to all of the complicated operations of manufacturing throughout one of these mills, by means of elementary rate-fixing, with the result, within eighteen months, of more than doubling, the output of the mill.

The difference between elementary rate-fixing and the ordinary plan can perhaps be best explained by a simple illustration. Suppose the work to be planing a surface on a piece of cast iron. In the ordinary system the rate-fixer would look through his records of work done by the planing machine, until he found a piece of work as nearly as possible similar to the proposed job, and then guess at the time required to do the new piece of work. Under the elementary system, however, some such analysis as the following would be made:

WORK DONE BY MAN	MINUTES
Time to lift piece from floor to planer table	_____
Time to level and set work true on table	_____
Time to put on stops and bolts.	_____
Time to remove stops and bolts	_____
Time to remove piece to floor	_____
Time to clean machine	_____
WORK DONE BY MACHINE	**MINUTES**
Time to rough off cut 1/4 in. thick, 4 ft. long, 2 1/2 in. wide	_____
Time to rough off cut 1/8 in. thick, 3 ft. long, 12 in. wide, etc.	_____
Time to finish cut 4 ft. long, 2 1/2 in. wide etc.	_____
Time to finish cut 3 ft. long, 12 in. wide, etc.	_____
Total	_____
Add _____ percent for unavoidable delays	_____

It is evident that this job consists of a combination of elementary operations, the time required to do each of which can be readily determined by observation.

This exact combination of operations may never occur again, but elementary operations similar to these will be performed in differing combinations almost every day in the same shop.

A man whose business it is to fix rates soon becomes so familiar with the time required to do each kind of elementary work performed by the men, that he can write down the time from memory.

In the case of that part of the work which is done by the machine the rate-fixer refers to tables which are made out for each machine, and from which he takes the time required for any combination of breadth, depth, and length of cut.

49. While, however, the accurate knowledge of the quickest time in which work can be done, obtained by the rate-fixing department and accepted by the men as standard, is the greatest and most important step towards obtaining the maximum output of the establishment, it is one thing to know how much work can be done in a day, and an entirely different matter to get even the best men to work at their fastest speed or anywhere near it.

50. The means which the writer has found to be by far the most effective in obtaining the maximum output of a shop, and which, so far as he can see, satisfies the legitimate requirements, both of the men and the management, is the *differential rate system of piecework.*

This consists briefly in paying a higher price per piece, or per unit, or per job, if the work is done in the shortest possible time, and without imperfections, than is paid if the work takes a longer time or is imperfectly done.

51. To illustrate: Suppose 20 units or pieces to be the largest amount of work of a certain kind that can be done in a day. Under the differential rate system, if a workman finishes 20 pieces per day, and all of these pieces are perfect, he receives, say, 15 cents per piece, making his pay for the day 15 x 20 = $3.00. If, however, he works too slowly and turns out, say, only 19 pieces, then, instead of receiving 15 cents per piece he gets only 12 cents per piece, making his pay for the day 12 x 19 = $2.28, instead of $3.00. per day.

If he succeeds in finishing 20 pieces, some of which are imperfect, then he should receive a still lower rate of pay, say, 10 cents or 5 cents per piece, according to circumstances, making his pay for the day $2, or only $1, instead of $3.

52. It will be observed that this style of piecework is directly the opposite of the ordinary plan. To make the difference between the two methods more clear: Supposing, under the ordinary system of piecework, that the workman has been turning out 16 pieces per day, and has received 15 cents per piece, then his day's wages would be 15 x 16 = $2.40. Through extra exertion he succeeds in increasing his output to 20 pieces per day, and thereby increases his pay to 15 x 20 = $3.00. The employer, under the old system, however, concludes that $3.00 is too much for the man to earn per day, since other men are only getting, from $2.25 to $2.50, and therefore cuts the price from 15 cents per piece to 12 cents, and the man finds himself working at a more rapid pace, and yet earning only the same old wages, 12 x 20 = $2.40 per day. What wonder that men do not care to repeat this performance many times.

53. Whether cooperation, the differential plan, or some other form of piecework be chosen in connection with elementary rate-fixing, as the best method of working, there are certain fundamental facts and principles which must be recognized and incorporated in any system of management, before true and lasting success can be attained; and most of these facts and principles will be found to be not far removed from what the strictest moralists would call justice.

54. The most important of these facts is, that men will not do an extraordinary day's work for an ordinary day's pay; and any attempt on the part of employers to get the best work out of their men and give them the standard wages paid by their neighbors will surely be, and ought to be, doomed to failure.

55. Justice, however, not only demands for the workman an increased reward for a large day's work, but should compel him to suffer an appropriate loss in case his work falls off either in quantity or quality. It is quite as important that the deductions for bad work should be just, and graded in proportion to the shortcomings of the workman, as that the reward should be proportional to the work done.

The fear of being discharged, which is practically the only penalty applied in many establishments, is entirely inadequate to producing the best quantity and quality of work; since the workmen find that they can take many liberties before the management makes up its mind to apply this extreme penalty.

56. It is clear that the differential rate satisfies automatically, as it were, the above conditions of properly graded rewards and deductions. Whenever a workman works for a day (or even a shorter period) at his maximum, he receives under this system unusually high wages; but when he falls off either in quantity or quality from the highest rate of efficiency his pay falls below even the ordinary.

57. The lower differential rate should be fixed at a figure which will allow the workman to earn scarcely an ordinary day's pay when he falls off from his maximum pace, so as to give him every inducement to work hard and well.

58. The exact percentage beyond the usual standard which must be paid to induce men to work to their maximum varies with different trades and with different sections of the country. And there are places in the United States where the men (generally speaking) are so lazy and demoralized that no sufficient inducement can be offered to make them do a full day's work.

59. It is not, however, sufficient that each workman's ambition should be aroused by the prospect of larger pay at the end of even a comparatively short period of time. The stimulus to maximum exertion should be a daily one.

This involves such vigorous and rapid inspection and returns as to enable each workman in most cases to know each day the exact result of his previous day's work—that is, whether he has succeeded in earning his maximum pay, and exactly what his losses are for careless or defective work. Two-thirds of the moral effect, either of a reward or penalty, is lost by even a short postponement.

60. It will again be noted that the differential rate system forces this condition both upon the management and the workmen, since the men, while working under it, are above all anxious to know at the earliest possible minute whether they have earned their high rate or not. And it is equally important for the management to know whether the work has been properly done.

61. As far as possible each man's work should be inspected and measured separately, and his pay and losses should depend upon his individual efforts alone. It is, of course, a necessity that much of the work of manufacturing—such, for instance, as running roll-trains, hammers, or paper machines—should be done by gangs of men who cooperate to turn out a common product, and that each gang of men should be paid a definite price for the work turned out, just as if they were a single man.

In the distribution of the earnings of a gang among its members, the percentage which each man receives should, however, depend not only upon the kind of work which each man performs, but upon the accuracy and energy with which he fills his position.

In this way the personal ambition of each of gang of men may be given its proper scope.

62. Again, we find the differential rate acting as a most powerful lever to force each man in a gang of workmen to do his best; since if, through the carelessness or laziness of any one man, the gang fails to earn its high rate, the drone will surely be obliged by his companions to do his best the next time or else get out.

63. A great advantage of the differential rate system is that it quickly drives away all inferior workmen, and attracts the men best suited to the class of work to which it is applied; since none but really good men can work fast enough and accurately enough to earn the high rate; and the low rate should be made so small as to be unattractive even to an inferior man.

64. If for no other reason than it secures to an establishment a quick and active set of workmen, the differential rate is a valuable aid, since men are largely creatures of habit; and if the pieceworkers of a place are forced to move quickly and work hard the day-workers soon get into the same way, and the whole shop takes on a more rapid pace.

65. The greatest advantage, however, of the differential rate for piece-work, in connection with a proper rate-fixing department, is that together they produce the proper mental attitude on the part of the men and the management toward each other. In place of the indolence and indifference which characterize the workmen of many day-work establishments, and to a considerable extent also their employers; and in place of the constant watchfulness, suspicion, and even antagonism with which too frequently the men and the management regard each other, under the ordinary piecework plan, both sides soon appreciate the fact that with the differential rate it is their common interest to cooperate to the fullest extent, and to devote every energy to turning out daily the largest possible output. This common interest quickly replaces antagonism, and establishes a most friendly feeling.

66. Of the two devices for increasing the output of a shop, the differential rate and the scientific rate-fixing department, the latter is by far the more important. The differential rate is invaluable at the start, as a means of convincing men that the management is in earnest in its intention of paying a premium for hard work; and it at all times furnishes the best means of maintaining the top notch of production; but when, through its application, the men and the management have come to appreciate the mutual benefit of harmonious cooperation and respect for each other's rights, it ceases to be an absolute necessity. On the other hand, the rate-fixing department, for an establishment doing a large variety of work, becomes absolutely indispensable. The longer it is in operation the more necessary it becomes.

67. Practically, the greatest need felt in an establishment wishing to start a rate-fixing department is the lack of data as to the proper rate of speed at which work should be done.

There, are hundreds of operations which are common to most large establishments; yet each concern studies the speed problem for itself, and days of labor are wasted in what should be settled once for all, and recorded in a form which is available to all manufacturers.

68. What is needed is a handbook on the speed with which work can be done, similar to the elementary engineering handbooks. And the writer ventures to predict that such a book will before long be forthcoming. Such a book should describe the best method of making, recording, tabulating, and indexing time observations, since much time and effort are wasted by the adoption of inferior methods.

69. The term "rate-fixing department" has rather a formidable sound. In fact, however, that department should consist in most establishments of one man, who, in many cases, need give only a part of his time to the work.

70. When the manufacturing operations are uniform in character, and repeat themselves day after day—as, for instance, in paper or pulp mills— the whole work of the place can be put upon piecework in a comparatively short time; and when once proper rates are fixed, the rate-fixing department can be dispensed with, at any rate until some new line of manufacture is taken up.

71. The system of differential rates was first applied by the writer to a part of the work in the machine shop of the Midvale Steel Company, in 1884. Its effect in increasing and then maintaining the output of each machine to which it was applied was almost immediate, and so remarkable that it soon came into high favor, with both the men and the management. It was gradually applied to a great part of the work of the establishment, with the result, in combination with the rate-fixing department, of doubling and in many cases trebling the output, and at the same time increasing instead of diminishing the accuracy of the work.

72. In some cases it was applied by the rate-fixing department without an elementary analysis of the time required to do the work; simply offering a higher price per piece providing the maximum output before attained was increased to a given extent. Even this system met with success, although it is by no means correct, since there is no certainty that the reward is in just proportion to the efforts of the workmen.

73. In cases where large and expensive machines are used, such as paper machines, steam hammers, or rolling mills, in which a large output is dependent upon the severe manual labor as well as the skill of the workmen (while the chief cost of production lies in the expense of running the machines rather than in the wages paid), it has been found of great advantage to establish

two or three differential rates, offering a higher and higher price per piece or per ton as the maximum possible output is approached.

74. As before stated, not the least of the benefits of elementary rate-fixing are the indirect results.

The careful study of the capabilities of the machines, and the analysis of the speeds at which they must run, before differential rates can be fixed which will ensure their maximum output, almost invariably result in first indicating and then correcting the defects in their design, and in the method of running and caring for them.

75. In the case of the Midvale Steel Company, to which I have already referred, the machine shop was equiped with standard tools furnished by the best makers, and the study of these machines, such as lathes, planers, boring mills, etc., which was made in fixing rates, developed the fact that they were none of them designed and speeded so as to cut steel to the best advantage. As a result, this company has demanded alterations from the standard in almost every machine which they have bought during the past eight years. They have themselves been obliged to superintend the design of many special tools which would not have been thought of had it not been for elementary rate-fixing.

76. But what is, perhaps, of more importance still, the rate-fixing department has shown the necessity of carefully systematizing all of the small details in the running of each shop; such as the care of belting, the proper shape for cutting tools, and the dressing, grinding, and issuing same, oiling machines, issuing orders for work, obtaining accurate labor and material returns, and a host of other minor methods and processes. These details, which are usually regarded as of comparatively small importance, and many of which are left to the individual judgment of the foreman and workmen, are shown by the rate-fixing department to be of paramount importance in obtaining the maximum output, and to require the most careful and systematic study and attention in order to insure uniformity and a fair and equal chance for each workman. Without this, preliminary study and systematizing of details, it is impossible to apply successfully the differential rate in most establishments.

77. As before stated, the success of this system of piecework depends fundamentally upon the possibility of materially increasing the output per man and per machine, providing the proper man be found for each job, and the proper incentive be offered to him.

78. As an illustration of the difference between what ought to be done by a workman well suited to his job, and what is generally done, I will mention a single class of work, performed in almost every establishment in the country. In shovelling coal from a car over the side on to a pile one man should unload forty tons per day, and keep it up, year in and year out, and thrive under it.

With this knowledge of the possibilities I have never failed to find men who were glad to work at this speed for from four and a half to five cents per ton. The average speed for unloading coal in most places, however, is nearer fifteen than forty tons per day. In securing the above rate of speed it must be clearly understood that the problem is not how to force men to work harder or longer hours than their health will permanently allow; but, rather, first, to select among the laborers which are to be found in every community the men who are physically able to work permanently at that job, and at the speed mentioned, without damage to their health, and who are mentally sufficiently inert to be satisfied with the monotony of the work, and then, to offer them such inducements as will make them happy and contented in doing so.

79. The first case in which a differential rate was applied furnishes a good illustration of what can be accomplished by it.

A standard steel forging, many thousands of which are used each year, had for several years been turned at the rate of from four to five per day under the ordinary system of piecework, fifty cents per piece being the price paid for the work. After analyzing the job and determining the shortest time required to do each, of the elementary operations of which it was composed, and then summing up the total, the writer became convinced that it was possible to turn ten pieces a day. To finish the forging at this rate, however, the machinists were obliged to work at their maximum pace from morning to night, and the lathes were run as fast as the tools would allow, and under a heavy feed.

It will be appreciated that this was a big day's work, both for men and machines, when it is understood that it involved removing, with a single 16-inch lathe, having two saddles, an average of more than 800 pounds of steel chips in ten hours. In place of the 50-cent rate that they had been paid before, they were given 35 cents per piece when they turned them at the speed of 10 per day, and when they produced less than 10, they received only 25 cents per piece.

80. It took considerable trouble to induce the men to turn at this high speed, since they did not at first fully appreciate that it was the intention of the firm to allow them to earn permanently at the rate of $3.50 per day. But from the day they first turned 10 pieces to the present time, a period of more than ten years, the men who understood their work have scarcely failed a single day to turn at this rate. Throughout that time, until the beginning of the recent fall in the scale of wages throughout the country, the rate was not cut.

81. During this whole period the competitors of the company never succeeded in averaging over half of this production per lathe, although they knew and even saw what was being done at Midvale. They, however, did not allow their men to earn over from $2.00 to $2.50 per day, and so never even approached the maximum output.

82. The following table will show the economy of paying high wages under the differential rate in doing the above job:

COST OF PRODUCTION PER LATHE PER DAY

ORDINARY SYSTEM OF PIECEWORK		DIFFERENTIAL RATE SYSTEM	
Man's wages	$2.50	Man's wages	$3.50
Machine cost	3.37	Machine cost	3.37
Total cost per day	$5.87	Total cost per day	$6.87
5 pieces produced		10 piece produced	
Cost per piece	$1.17	Cost per piece	$0.69

The above result was mostly, though not entirely, due to the differential rate. The superior system of managing all of the small details of the shop counted for considerable.

83. There has never been a strike by men working under differential rates, although these rates have been applied at the Midvale Steel Works for the past ten years; and the steel business has proved during this period the most fruitful field for labor organizations and strikes. And this notwithstanding, the Midvale Company has never prevented its men from joining any labor organization. All of the best men in the company saw clearly that the success of a labor organization meant the lowering of their wages, in order that the inferior men might earn more, and, of course, could not be persuaded to join.

84. I attribute a great part of this success in avoiding strikes to the high wages which the best men were able to earn with the differential rates, and to the pleasant feeling fostered by this system; but this is by no means the whole cause. It has for years been the policy of that company to stimulate the personal ambition of every man in their employ, by promoting them either in wages or position whenever they deserve it, and the opportunity came.

A careful record has been kept of each man's good points as well as his shortcomings, and one of the principal duties of each foreman was to make this careful study of his men, so that substantial justice could be done to each. When men, throughout an establishment, are paid varying rates of day-work wages, according to their individual worth, some being above and some below the average, it cannot be for the interest of those receiving high pay to join a union with the cheap men.

85. No system of management, however good, should be applied in a wooden way. The proper personal relations should always be maintained between the employers and men; and even the prejudices of the workmen should be considered in dealing with them.

The employer who goes through his works with kid gloves on, and is never known to dirty his hands or clothes, and who either talks to his men in a condescending or patronizing way, or else not at all, has no chance whatever of ascertaining their real thoughts or feelings.

86. Above all it is desirable that men should be talked to on their own level by those who are over them. Each man should be encouraged to discuss any trouble which he may have, either in the works or outside, with those over him. Men would far rather even be blamed by their bosses, especially if the "tearing out" has a touch of human nature and feeling in it, than to be passed by day after day without a word, and with no more notice than if they were part of the machinery.

The opportunity which each man should have of airing his mind freely, and having it out with his employers, is a safety valve; and if the superintendents are reasonable men, and listen to and treat with respect what their men have to say, there is absolutely no reason for labor unions and strikes.

87. It is not the large charities (however generous they may be) that are needed or appreciated by workmen, such as the founding of libraries and starting workingmen's clubs, so much as small acts of personal kindness and sympathy, which establish a bond of friendly feeling between them and their employers.

88. The moral effect of the writer's system on the men is marked. The feeling that substantial justice is being done them renders them on the whole much more manly, straight-forward, and truthful. They work more cheerfully, and are more obliging to one another and their employers. They are not soured, as under the old system, by brooding over the injustice done them; and their spare minutes are not spent to the same extent in criticizing their employers.

A noted French engineer and steel manufacturer, who recently spent several weeks in the works of the Midvale Company in introducing a new branch of manufacture, stated before leaving that the one thing which had impressed him as most unusual and remarkable about the place was the fact that not only the foremen, but the workmen, were expected to and did in the main tell the truth in case of any blunder or carelessness, even when they had to suffer from it themselves.

89. From what the writer has said he is afraid that many readers may gain the impression that he regards elementary rate-fixing and the differential rate as a sort of panacea for all human ills.

This is, however, far from the case. While he regards the possibilities of these methods as great, he is of the opinion, on the contrary, that this system of management will be adopted by but few establishments, in the near future, at least; since its really successful application not only involves a thorough organization, but requires the machinery and tools throughout the place to be kept in such good repair that it will be possible for the workmen each day to produce their maximum output. But few manufacturers will care to go to this trouble until they are forced to.

90. It is his opinion that the most successful manufacturers, those who are always ready to adopt the best machinery and methods when they see them, will gradually avail themselves of the benefits of scientific rate-fixing; and that competition will compel the others to follow slowly in the same direction.

91. Even if all of the manufacturers in the country who are competing in the same line of business were to adopt these methods, they could still well afford to pay the high rate of wages demanded by the differential rate, and necessary to induce men to work fast, since it is a well-recognized fact the world over that the highest priced labor, providing it is proportionately productive, is the cheapest; and the low cost at which they could produce their goods would enable them to sell in foreign markets and still pay high wages.

92. The writer is far from taking the view held by many manufacturers that labor unions are an almost unmitigated detriment to those who join them, as well as to employers and the general public.

The labor unions—particularly the trades unions of England—have rendered a great service not only to their members, but to the world, in shortening the hours of labor and in modifying the hardships and improving the conditions of wage-workers.

In the writer's judgment the system of treating with labor unions would seem to occupy a middle position among the various methods of adjusting the relations between employers and men.

When employers herd their men together in classes, pay all of each class the same wages, and offer none of them any inducements to work harder or do better than the average, the only remedy for the men lies in combination; and frequently the only possible answer to encroachments on the part of their employers is a strike.

This state of affairs is far from satisfactory to either employers or men, and the writer believes the system of regulating the wages and conditions of employment of whole classes of men by conference and agreement between the leaders, unions, and manufacturers to be vastly inferior, both in its moral effect on the men and on the material interests of both parties, to the plan of stimulating each workman's ambition by paying him according to his individual worth, and without limiting him to the rate of work or pay of the average of his class.

93. The level of the great mass of the world's labor has been, and must continue to be, regulated by causes so many and so complex as to be at best but dimly recognized.

The utmost effect of any system, whether of management, social combination, or legislation, can be but to raise a small ripple or wave of prosperity above the surrounding level, and the greatest hope of the writer is that, here and there, a few workmen, with their employers, may be helped, through this system, toward the crest of the wave.

DISCUSSION

Mr. H.L. Gantt: One cannot read Mr. Taylor's admirable paper on "A Piece-Rate System" without realizing that it contains vastly more than the title suggests. It is really a system by which the employer attempts to do justice to the employee, and in return requires the employee to be honest.

His method of fixing rates by elements eliminates, as nearly as possible, all chance of error, and his differential rates go a long way toward harmonizing interests of employer and employee.

It was my good fortune to work for a year as his assistant in this work, and I fully agree with him as to the effect on the men. They improve under it, both in honesty and efficiency, more than I have ever seen them do elsewhere. Realizing that substantial justice was being done, and that to do their duty was to follow their own interest, it soon became a matter of habit with them.

The greatest obstacle in the way of adopting this system is that the man in charge of the rate-fixing department must be a man of more than ordinary ability, and should have had a very wide experience. To err in fixing a rate has a very bad effect upon the men who should never have reason to think that the element of "guess" occurs in their rate. It is therefore only in a comparatively very large establishment, where a capable man can be employed to give his time to this work, or in a very small one, where the superintendent can give it his personal attention, that the plan is entirely applicable.

His idea of a handbook on the speed with which work can be done, similar to the elementary engineering handbooks, is one which is bound to interest all progressive engineers, and I hope that he will see that his predictions about such a book do not fail.

In paragraph 15 he states that a clerk in the factory is the particular horror of the old-time manufacturer. Why is this? In many cases the manufacturer is a shrewd and successful man, and if so, why has he not seen the advantage of using a clerk in connection with his foreman?

FREDERICK W. TAYLOR—SCIENTIST IN BUSINESS MANAGEMENT

RAY STANNARD BAKER

For three days last November I sat in the court room of the Interstate Commerce Commission at Washington, listening to one of the most remarkable cases ever presented before that distinguished body. On one side were ranged the powerful Eastern railroads, present in the persons of some half a hundred attorneys, and pleading permission from the Government to raise their rates; on the other side were the Eastern shippers, disputing the demands of the railroads. Upon the issue hung vast commercial and financial interests.

The railroads pleaded that they must have more money from the people to meet the "increased cost of living," especially the wages of their employees. The shippers responded by boldly attacking the railroads at the point where they have always felt strongest—that of managerial efficiency. The shippers declared that the railroads were not efficiently managed, and that if they would "look within," they could save more money than they now demanded in increased rates.

To support this bold response Mr. Louis D. Brandeis, the shippers' attorney, placed on the stand eleven witnesses who told of a singular new system or method of securing a marvelous degree of efficiency in all manner of industrial operations. This new system, or philosophy, which they said, frankly, was revolutionary in its aims, they called Scientific Management.

Few of those present had ever even heard of Scientific Management or of Mr. Taylor, its originator, and the testimony, at first, awakened a clearly perceptible incredulity. Nor was such incredulity surprising; for it was asserted that Scientific Management would commonly double or treble the producing capacity of every workman in a given industry, it would raise wages, it would increase profits, it would go far toward solving the labor problem. It was even asserted with confidence by one witness, Mr. Emerson, that, if applied to the railroads, Scientific Management could be counted upon to save at least $1,000,000 a day.

Reprinted from *The American Magazine*, vol. LXXI, March 1911.

To those who heard this testimony there seemed at first something almost magical about the new idea; but as one sober, hard-headed business man after another testified as to what had been actually accomplished in his plant, when it appeared that Scientific Management had been applied with extraordinary results to widely diversified industries, from steel plants to bleacheries and cotton mills, and including railroad repair shops, the spirit of incredulity changed to one of deep interest. Another factor in carrying conviction to the hearers was the extraordinary fervor and enthusiasm expressed by every man who testified. Theirs was the firm faith of apostles: it was a philosophy which worked, and they had the figures to show it.

"This," said Mr. Commissioner Lane to one of the witnesses, "has become a sort of substitute for religion with you."

"Yes, sir," responded Mr. Gilbreth.

Since then I suppose there have been thousands of articles and editorials written for the newspapers regarding Scientific Management, with every view advanced, from that of sarcastic unbelief to that of firm conviction.

Mr. Taylor himself was not present at the hearing, but he was constantly referred to as the originator of the system; and he has since become a man of whom the world wishes to know more. What is this Scientific Management, and who is Mr. Taylor?

With my interest keenly aroused, I went to see Mr. Taylor at his beautiful home at Chestnut Hill, Philadelphia; and I have talked with most of the men who have been prominent in developing the principles of Scientific Management. I have also visited some of the shops and factories where its introduction has produced such extraordinary results.

One day, some thirty-six years ago, a young man named Taylor began work in a Philadelphia machine shop. He swept up the shavings in the morning, handled the materials, and attended the wants of the patternmakers. He was an apprentice. A boyish-looking young man, small of stature, he was as close-knit and wiry as a steel spring, and he had the peculiar light, quick step which goes with superior physical and intellectual energy. Also, he was equipped with a gray eye and a square chin. He had an air of determination.

Emerson has commented somewhere upon the commotion which arises when the Almighty lets loose a thinker upon this planet. This young man Taylor was a thinker. He had come of one of the old Quaker families of Philadelphia. One of his ancestors came over from England in the *Mayflower*, another followed William Penn to the settlements in Pennsylvania. His father's father was a rich East India merchant and his father a lawyer and a Princeton man of the class of 1840. On his mother's side, his grandfather, Isaac Winslow of New Bedford, was so successful as a whale fisher that he was selected by the French Government to introduce the art of whale fishing in France. After making a large fortune at this employment he returned to America and devoted his remaining years to mechanical inventions, obtaining a patent for a process of canning vegetables upon which is founded the modern canning industry. Mr. Taylor's mother, Emily Winslow, was a woman of extraordinary talent and of unusual beauty. When only twenty years old she was one of the group of remarkable women, including Lucretia Mott, who were appointed delegates to the World's Anti-Slavery Convention in London. She was one of the earliest of the defenders of women's rights, and the Taylor home in Church Lane in Philadelphia during young Taylor's boyhood was frequented by the leading spirits in the anti-slavery and reform causes.

The boy was given two years of school in France and Germany and then a year and a half of travel in Italy, Switzerland, Norway, England, France, Germany and Austria—"All of which," he says, "I heartily disapprove of for a young boy." After this he returned to the healthy outdoor life of Germantown, in which sport was the leading idea—"than which there is nothing finer in the world"—then two years of really very hard study, coupled with athletics at Exeter. At that time one half the pupils at Exeter were dropped each year and the discipline was exceedingly severe.

Young Taylor was preparing for Harvard, but after two years at Exeter his eyes failed, and he went home to Philadelphia and began work as an apprentice in a pattern shop, and afterward in a machine shop.

Here he met workingmen for the first time and made the discovery which some young men of his upbringing never make, that the finest kinds of men and women live in all ranks of society and in the smallest and most out-of-the-way places. He made, in short, that democratic discovery without which a man's life in modern America is not worth much. He regards the early years of his apprenticeship as the best training he ever had and the workman under whom he served, who was a man of extraordinary ability, coupled with fine character, as one of the best teachers. He was instinctively democratic and it was not long before the workmen all called him "Fred," as many of them do to this day. For many years, while he served as a laborer, as a machinist, as a boss, as a foreman, and finally as chief engineer of the great steel works of the Midvale Company, his interests and sympathies were strongly enlisted by the human element in industry.

Serving as a workman, he knew the workman's side, and serving as a boss and foreman, he knew the employer's side. He had also gone through the bitter struggle for more education which so many workmen have to meet. He was told that he could not become chief engineer of the Midvale plant without a college degree; accordingly, he set to work at nights and in two years and a half he had passed all the examinations and won the degree of M.E. from Stevens Institute.

From the very first young Taylor, with his early home environment in a reform atmosphere and his natural democratic instincts, was impressed with the deplorable conditions of industry, the bitter warfare between capital and labor, the neglect of the employer, the "soldiering" of the employees; the utter wastefulness, inefficiency, and heartlessness which characterized nearly all industrial operations. It was as natural as sunlight for him to inquire:

"How can I change these things?"

No sooner did he reach a position where he had any authority at all than he began the long series of experiments which have resulted in the remarkable new Science of Management. I shall not here go into these experiments in detail: Mr. Taylor tells the whole story much better than I could in his own articles in this magazine. But this point I wish strongly to make: While the attention of most industrial scientists and inventors has been fixed upon the machine—the material aspects of industry—Mr. Taylor's eye has always been fixed upon the man. It has been his chief ambition, as he says, to make every industry, first of all, a "man-factory." He has invented many useful mechanical devices, and his studies in the art of cutting metals have revolutionized machine-shop practice, but whether he studied belting, or experimented with tool steel, or worked on the problem of the storage of materials, it was always with a clear eye to the effect upon the man in the shops. He would make the machines serve the man, not the man the machines.

There are two varieties of the scientific mind—one the mind that with infinite analytical patience studies minute details and produces the data, the raw material, of science; the other and far rarer type, that which combines the infinite patience of the investigator with the imaginative genius of the generalizer. Taylor belongs to this higher type of the scientist.

When he began he had no idea of a new system of managing industry. He found himself face to face with a practical question which he could not answer:

How can all the forces of industry, the workman on one side and the employer on the other, be made to work harmoniously together?

In seeking to answer that question, he found that he must formulate a vast range of knowledge which had always in the past lain inchoate and unorganized in the brains of workingmen. In short, he had to work out a science of metal-cutting, a science of brick-laying, a science of plastering. His effort was to socialize and render available a vast body of knowledge hitherto possessed only by individuals and passed down from father to son by word of mouth. In doing this he carried on tens of thousands of careful experiments, under the most difficult conditions, for he had to make his work pay as he went along; that is, he had to show results enough to warrant the owners of the plant where he worked in advancing the money for these experiments. Thus he collected a vast amount of data in regard to the human element of industry.

Having this data, he discovered that in order to use the cunning human machine with real efficiency the whole system of management must be changed. No army can advance far while two internal factions are bitterly quarreling. Industry cannot advance by war and waste; it must advance by coöperation and efficiency. Employer and employee must work together. Instead of commanding the workman as in the past, requiring him often to make bricks without straw, the management under Mr. Taylor's system is to use its new scientific information as a basis for teaching and serving the workmen, with the end that not only the product but the rewards of both hand-worker and brain-worker may be largely increased. In short, Mr. Taylor would shift the management of industry from the old military basis to an educational and cooperative basis. Under the new system a man who enters a factory as a workman does not find himself driven to his task and exploited, but discovers that he has entered a great educational institution where the management is eager to train him to his utmost ability, pay him according to his product, and advance him as rapidly as his capabilities permit. When scientifically regarded there is no employment that is not skilled, no employment to which brains will not add a vast increment of improvement.

Upon these great fundamental ideas Mr. Taylor's fame will ultimately rest. But it is a significant fact that until recently, even among engineers, his work in developing Scientific Management has not been as highly regarded as his work in inventing high-speed steel and in improving the art of cutting metals. This is easily explainable: high-speed steel is a mechanical device which can be handled and seen, and its adoption results in immediate profit, while the Science of Management is a philosophy, dealing with intangible human and psychological elements, and, like any great step forward, it requires care in its application and time before it begins to show profits in dollars and cents.

Scientific Management was presented in two papers before the American Society of Mechanical Engineers; the first called "A Piece Rate System" in 1895, and the second, "Shop Management," in 1903. "Shop Management" is one of the great books of recent years, and will in time be so regarded. As Harrington Emerson said of it, in the discussion which followed its presentation:

"I regard the paper presented at this meeting by Mr. Taylor as the most important contribution ever presented to the society, and one of the most important papers ever published in the United States."

It has now been translated into German, French, Russian, Dutch, and Danish, and is known to students all over the world. Dean E.F. Gay, of the Harvard Graduate School of Business Administration, early recognizing the great importance of Mr. Taylor's work, has devoted an entire course to the presentation of the principles of Scientific Management, and Mr. Taylor, Mr. Barth, Mr. Emerson, Mr. Gantt, Mr. Cooke, Mr. Thompson, and other leaders of the movement have lectured before the Harvard classes. The system is now being studied and adopted not only in this country, but in England, France, and Germany, although this country, so far, has a long start.

The other notable work of Mr. Taylor, an offshoot of his studies in Scientific Management, was his paper "On the Art of Cutting Metals," which he delivered as his presidential address in 1900 before the American Society of Mechanical Engineers. It was the first account of his discovery and invention of high-speed steel and of his studies in the forms and sizes of tools for cutting metals. High-speed steel is now used in every well-equipped machine shop in the world, and Mr. Taylor's paper "On the Art of Cutting Metals" is recognized by the highest authorities as being one of the greatest studies in industrial science ever produced.

Professor H. Le Chatelier, member of the French Academy and the foremost French authority on metallurgy, has said:

"Few discoveries in the arts have been the occasion of so many successive surprises as those of Mr. Taylor. At the time of the exhibition in Paris, nobody quite believed in the prodigious result which was claimed by the Bethlehem Works (for tools made of high-speed steel), but we had to accept the evidence of our eyes when we saw enormous chips of steel cut off from a forging at such high speed that the nose of the tool was heated to a dull red color.... We can admire without reserve the scientific method which has controlled this whole work. It is an example unique in the history of the mechanic arts. We have all admired the researches of Sir Lothian Bell on blast furnaces, and those of Sir William Siemens on the regenerative furnace, but in reading their papers neither of them leaves an impression on the mind which can be compared with that of Mr. Taylor's paper."

Other tributes to Mr. Taylor's work are published in the introduction to this article.

Mr. Taylor was also rewarded at the Paris Exposition with a personal gold medal, and the Franklin Institute of Philadelphia has conferred upon him the distinguished honor of the Elliott Cresson gold medal.

His inventions have brought him a considerable fortune, and he lives now at Chestnut Hill, Philadelphia, in one of the most beautiful of homes, a stately house, surrounded by wide-stretching gardens and hedges of box. Since 1901 he has devoted practically his entire time, and wholly with out pay, to spreading the knowledge of his new philosophy of management.

"I can no longer afford to work for money," he says.

He has drawn around him a notable group of associates and assistants. Essentially he is a great teacher, for he possesses not only the ability to impart knowledge, but the genius to inspire his followers with a sort of passion of enthusiasm. All of his associates, being men of unusual ability, have contributed much to the development of his ideas and have borne the brunt of the practical work of introducing the system into shops and factories. Mr. Taylor has recognized the coöperative accomplishment in the true scientific spirit when, in his "On the Art of Cutting Metals," he gave to Mr. White the credit of being "a much more accomplished metallurgist than any of the rest of us," when he said that Mr. Gantt was "a better all-round manager," and Mr. Barth "the best mathematician of the group." He has given credit in similar terms to the work of Mr. Cooke, Mr. Emerson, Mr. Thompson, Mr. Day and others. To himself he gives this credit:

"And the writer of this paper has perhaps the faculty of holding on tighter with his teeth than any of the others."

He has cooperated with Mr. Sanford E. Thompson in conducting a series of studies of other industries, such as cement work, plastering, bricklaying, excavating, and so on. One book, called "Concrete, Plain and Reinforced," under the joint authorship of Taylor and Thompson, has now been issued and is already regarded as the standard work on the subject, having sold upward of ten thousand copies at $5 each, a remarkable circulation for a technical book. In time other books will be issued, on the various building trades, which are expected to be as thorough studies in those subjects as Mr. Taylor's "Art of Cutting Metals" is in that field.

Outside of these notable scientific accomplishments, Mr. Taylor is a man of wide cultivation, of varied interests and of personal charm. He has a lively and progressive mind, seizing eagerly upon the problems of the day. He has always had a keen interest in sport, having in the year 1881 won the national championship at tennis (doubles) in a tournament played at Newport. His inventions of tennis posts and tennis nets are still widely in use. He is also an enthusiastic golf-player.

At present he is gratifying his love of investigation by a series of truly remarkable experiments in grass-growing. He started with the idea of learning how to grow better grass for putting greens, and he has made a number of notable discoveries. The United States Department of Agriculture, recognizing the importance of his results, is now cooperating with him in his further experiments. A rare, high type of American, a public servant in the best sense, the nation surely is not to be despaired of when it affords an atmosphere in which such a man can be developed. It is to the fine scientific habit of mind, with its catholicity of interest, its reverence for facts, its high sense of the value of human life, that the country must look for its salvation. There have been times in recent years when it seemed as though our civilization were being throttled by things, by property, by the very weight of industrial mechanism, and it is no small matter when a man arises who can show us new ways of commanding our environment.

"The genius of mechanism," says Carlyle, "will not always sit like a choking incubus on our soul; but at length, when by a new Magic Word the old spell is broken, become our slave, and as familiar-spirit do all our bidding."

THE GOSPEL OF EFFICIENCY: THE PRINCIPLES OF SCIENTIFIC MANAGEMENT

FREDERICK W. TAYLOR

President Roosevelt, in his address to the Governors at the White House, prophetically remarked that "the conservation of our national resources is only preliminary to the larger question of national efficiency."

The whole country at once recognized the importance of conserving our material resources, and a large movement has been started which will be effective in accomplishing this object. As yet, however, we have but vaguely appreciated the importance of "the larger question of increasing our national efficiency."

We can see our forests vanishing, our water powers going to waste, our soil being carried by floods into the sea; and the end of our coal and our iron is in sight.

We can see and feel the waste of material things. But we cannot see or feel the larger wastes of human effort going on all around us. Awkward, inefficient, or ill-directed movements of men leave nothing visible or tangible behind them. Their appreciation calls for an act of memory, an effort of the imagination. And for this reason, even though our daily loss from this source is greater than from our waste of material things, the one has stirred us deeply, while the other has moved us but little.

The search for better, for more competent men, from the presidents of our great companies down to our household servants, was never more vigorous than it is now. And more than ever before is the demand for competent men in excess of the supply.

What we are all looking for is the ready-made, competent man; the man whom someone else has trained. It is only when we fully realize that our duty, as well as our opportunity, lies in systematically cooperating to train this competent man that we shall be on the road to national efficiency.

In the past the man has been first; in the future the system must be first. This in no sense, however, implies that great men are not needed. On the contrary, the first object of any good system must be that of developing first-class men; and under Scientific Management the best man rises to the top more certainly and more rapidly than ever before.

This article has been written:

First. To point out the great loss which the whole country is suffering through inefficiency in almost all of our daily acts.

Second. To try to convince the reader that the remedy for this inefficiency lies in systematic management, rather than in searching for some unusual or extraordinary man.

Third. To prove that the best management is a true science, resting upon clearly defined laws, rules, and principles, and that these fundamental principles of Scientific Management are applicable to all kinds of human activities, from our simplest individual acts to the work of our great corporations. And that whenever these principles are correctly applied results follow which are truly astounding.

In order to develop the subject of Scientific Management in a logical and orderly manner, the writer will present the problems of industry in exactly the way in which he himself had to meet them. He encountered the difficulties blindly, and the conclusions at which he has arrived are the results of the hard teachings of actual experience.

The writer came into the machine shop of the Midvale Steel Company of Philadelphia in 1878, after having served an apprenticeship as a pattern-maker and as a machinist. This was close to the end of the long period of depression following the panic of 1873 and business was so poor that it was impossible for many mechanics to get work at their trades. For this reason he was obliged to start to work as an unskilled day laborer, instead of working as a mechanic. Fortunately for him, soon after he came into the shop the clerk was found to be stealing. There was no one else available, and so, having more education than the other laborers (since he had been prepared for college), he was advanced to the position of clerk. Shortly after this he was given work as a machinist in running one of the lathes, and as he turned out rather more work than other machinists were doing on similar lathes, after several months he was made gang boss over the lathes.

Almost all of the work of this shop had been done on piecework for several years. As was usual then, and in fact as is still usual in most shops of the country, the shop was really run by the workmen and not by the bosses. The workmen together had carefully planned just how fast each job should be done, and they had set a pace for each machine, which amounted to about one third of a good day's work. Every new workman who came into the shop was told at once by other workmen exactly how fast he was to work on every job, and unless he obeyed these instructions he was sure before long to find himself out of work.

In short, the writer here made, for the first time, an intimate acquaintance with the fundamental principle upon which industry seems now to be run in this country. This principle is that the employer shall pay just as low wages as he can and that the workman shall retaliate by doing just as little work as he can. Industry is thus a warfare, in which both sides, instead of giving out the best that is in them, seem determined to give out the worst that is in them.

The English and American people are the greatest sportsmen in the world. Whenever an American workman plays baseball, or an English workman plays cricket, it is safe to say that he strains every nerve to secure victory for his side. He does his very best to make the largest possible number of runs. The universal sentiment is so strong that any man who fails to give out all there is in him in sport is branded as a "quitter" and treated with contempt by those around him.

When the same workman returns to work on the following day, instead of using every effort to turn out the largest possible amount of work, in a majority of cases this man deliberately plans to turn out far less work than he is well able to do—in many instances he does not more than one third or one half of a proper day's work. And in fact if he were to do his best to turn out his largest possible day's work, he would be abused by his fellow workers for so doing, even more than he would if he had proved himself a "quitter" at sport.

"Soldiering" as it is called in this country, "hanging it out" in England, "ca canny" in Scotland, is thus almost universal in industrial establishments, and prevails also to a large extent in the building trades; and the writer asserts without fear of contradiction that this constitutes the greatest misfortune, one may almost say the greatest evil, with which the working people of both England and America are now afflicted.

When to soldiering is added the natural inefficiency, ignorance, and wastefulness which characterize many if not most of the common operations of industrial establishments, it will be seen in what a deplorable state modern industry finds itself. What other reforms, among those which are being discussed by these two nations, could do more toward promoting prosperity than the introduction of some form of coöperation which should abolish this warfare of industry, which results in so much wastefulness, inefficiency, and soldiering? Is it not the root question of all the questions?

It was not, however, until the writer had been made gang boss over the lathes that he began to see the full iniquity of the system under which he and all his fellow workmen were making their living. As soon as his appointment was known, one after another of the men came to him and talked somewhat as follows:

"Now, Fred, we're very glad to see that you've been made gang boss. You know the game all right, and we're sure that you're not likely to be a piecework hog. You come along with us and everything will be all right, but if you try breaking any of these rates you can be mighty sure that we'll throw you over the fence."

The writer told them plainly that he was now working on the side of the management, and that he proposed to do whatever he could to get a fair day's work out of the lathes. This immediately started a war; in most cases a friendly war, because the men who were under him were his personal friends, but none the less a war, which as time went on grew more and more bitter, the writer using every expedient to make the men do a fair day's work, such as discharging or lowering the wages of the more stubborn men, lowering the piecework price, hiring green men and personally teaching them how to do the work with the promise from them that when they had learned how they would then do a fair day's work, and later, after they had become skilled, having them forced by the public opinion of the shop to do what all the rest were doing. No one who has not had this experience can have an idea of the bitterness which is gradually developed in such a struggle. In a war of this kind, the workmen have one expedient which is usually effective. They use their ingenuity to contrive various ways in which the machines are broken or damaged apparently by accident, or in the regular course of work—and this they lay always at the door of the foreman, who, they assert, is forcing them to drive the machine so hard that it is being ruined. And there are few foremen who are able to stand up against the combined pressure of all of the men in the shop.

The writer had certain advantages, however, which are not possessed by the ordinary foreman. *First,* owing to the fact that he happened not to be of working parents, the owners of the company believed that he had the interest of the works more at heart than the other workmen, and they therefore had more confidence in his word. When the machinists reported to the general superintendent that the machines were being smashed up because of an incompetent foreman, the general superintendent accepted the word of the writer when he said that these men were deliberately breaking their machines as a part of the piecework war.

Second, if the writer had been one of the workmen, and had lived where they lived, they would have brought such social pressure to bear upon him that it would have been impossible to have stood out against them. He would have been called "scab" and other foul names every time he appeared on the street; his wife would have been abused and his children would have been stoned. Once or twice he was begged by some of his friends among the workmen not to walk home about two and a half miles along the lonely path by the side of the railway. He was told that if he continued to do this it would be at the risk of his life. In all such cases, however, a display of timidity is apt to increase rather than diminish the risk so the writer told these men to say to the other men in the shop that he proposed to walk home every night right up that railway track; that he never had carried and never would carry any weapon of any kind, and that they could shoot and be d— [*sic*].

After about three years of this kind of struggling, the output of the machines had been materially increased, in many cases doubled, and as a result the writer had been promoted from one gang boss-ship to another until he became foreman of the shop. For any right-minded man, however, such a success was in no sense a recompense for the bitter relations which he was forced to maintain with all of those around him. Life which is one continuous struggle with other men is hardly worth living. His workmen friends came to him continually and asked him, in a personal, friendly way, whether he would advise them, for their own interest, to turn out more work. And, as a truthful man, he had to tell them that if he were in their place, he would fight against turning out any more work, just as they were doing, because under the piecework system they would be allowed to earn no more wages than they had been earning, and yet they would be made to work harder. That is the meanness of the old system; it is based on hatred and force and greed.

Soon after being made foreman, therefore he decided to try to change in some way the system of management, so that the interests of the workman and the management would be coöperative instead of antagonistic. He began his experiments gropingly, but with the result that three years later he started a new type of management in the Midvale shops which he described later in two papers read before the American Society of Mechanical Engineers and entitled, "A Piece-Rate System," and "Shop Management."

In beginning his studies the writer realized that the greatest obstacle to harmonious coöperation between the workmen and the management lay in the ignorance of the management as to what really constituted a proper day's work for a workman. He therefore obtained the permission of Mr. William Sellers, who was at that time president of the Midvale Steel Company, to spend some money in a careful scientific study of the men and the processes of work in the shops, and particularly the amount of time required to do various kinds of work. Mr. Sellers permitted this more as a reward to the writer for having, to a certain extent, "made good" as foreman of the shop in getting more work out of the men than for any other reason. He stated that he did not believe that any scientific study of this sort would give results of much value.

It was these investigations, however, the minute, pains-taking analysis and study of the movements of men to find their quickest and best motions, which were started in 1881 at the Midvale Steel Works, and which have been carried on in increasing volume ever since, that mark the first steps taken toward Scientific Management. Particular illustrations explaining the methods of making this time study will be given later in this paper.

At the same time that this study of men was started, a similar investigation as to the best tools and implements to be used in each trade was begun.

In the study of the tools and methods which constitute the art of cutting metals alone, and which lasted through a term of twenty-six years, between 30,000 and 50,000 experiments have been carefully recorded and many experiments have been made of which no record was kept. In studying these laws more than 800,000 pounds of steel and iron have been cut up into chips with experimental tools, and it is estimated that from $150,000 to $200,000 has been spent in the investigation.

These were only two of many lines of investigation into which our studies carried us. In addition to this detail study of men and implements, we found that in order to bring about a greater efficiency of the men and better relationship between the management and the men, we had also to study shop arrangement, methods of keeping stores, the routing of materials, the best ways of using belts, etc., and we had to establish standards for all details throughout the works, and finally undertake the scientific planning of the work.

As a result of these studies certain principles of coöperation—which we have called Scientific Management—were discovered. These principles are no mere theories, for they have now been applied practically and profitably for nearly thirty years. During this period the employees of one company after another, including a large range and diversity of industries, have gradually changed from the ordinary to the scientific type of management. At least 50,000 workmen in the United States are now employed under the new system and they are receiving from 33 to 100% higher wages daily than are paid to workmen of similar caliber with whom they are surrounded, while the companies employing them are more prosperous than ever before. In these companies the output per man per machine has on an average been doubled. Under this type of management there has never been during all these years a single strike. In place of the suspicious watchfulness and the more or less open warfare which characterize the ordinary types of management, there is universally friendly coöperation between the management and the men.

THE FINEST TYPE OF ORDINARY MANAGEMENT

Before starting to illustrate the principles of Scientific Management, it seems desirable to outline what the writer believes will be recognized as the best type of management which is in common use. This is done so that the great difference between the best of the ordinary management and Scientific Management may be fully appreciated.

In an industrial establishment which employs, say, from 500 to 1,000 workmen, there will be found in many cases at least twenty to thirty different trades. The workmen in each of these trades have had their knowledge handed down to them by word of mouth, through the many years in which their trade has been developed from the primitive condition to the present state of great subdivision of labor, in which each man specializes upon some comparatively small class of work.

The methods which are now in use may in a broad sense be said to be an evolution representing the survival of the fittest and best of the ideas which have been developed since the starting of each trade. However, while this is true in a broad sense, only those who are intimately acquainted with each of these trades are fully aware of the fact that in hardly any element of any trade is there uniformity in the methods which are used. Instead of having only one way which is generally accepted as a standard there are in daily use, say, fifty or a hundred different ways of doing each element of the work. And a little thought will make it clear that this must inevitably be the case, since our methods have been handed down from man to man by word of mouth, or have, in most cases, been almost unconsciously learned through personal observation. Practically in no instances have they been codified or systematically analyzed or described.

Now, in the best of the ordinary types of management, the managers recognize frankly the fact that the 500 or 1,000 workmen, included in the twenty to thirty trades, who are under them possess this mass of traditional knowledge, a large part of which is not in the possession of the management. The management, of course, including foreman and superintendents, know, better than anyone else, that their own knowledge and personal skill fall far short of the combined knowledge and dexterity of all the workmen under them. The most experienced managers, therefore, frankly place before their workmen the problem of doing the work in the best and most economical way. They recognize the task before them as that of inducing each workman to use his best endeavors, his hardest work, all his traditional knowledge, his skill, his ingenuity and his good will—in a word, his "initiative" so as to yield the largest possible return to his employer. The problem before the management, then, may be briefly said to be that of obtaining the best *initiative* of every workman.

On the other hand, no intelligent manager would hope to obtain in any full measure the initiative of his workmen unless he felt that he was giving them something more than they usually receive from their employers. Only those among the readers of this article who have been managers or who have worked themselves at a trade realize how far the average workman falls short of giving his employer his full initiative. It is well within the mark to state that in nineteen out of twenty industrial establishments the workmen believe it to be directly against their interests to give their employers their best initiative, and that instead of working hard to do the largest possible amount of work and the best quality of work for their employers, they deliberately work as slowly as they dare while they at the same time try to make those over them believe that they are working fast.

This *special incentive* can be given in several different ways, as, for example, the hope of rapid promotion or advancement; higher wages; shorter hours of labor; better surroundings and working conditions than are ordinarily given, etc.; and above all, that personal consideration for, and friendly contact with the workmen which comes only from a genuine and kindly interest in their welfare and their success. It is only by giving a special inducement or "incentive" of this kind that the employer can hope to even approximately get the "initiative" of his workmen. Under the ordinary type of management, the necessity for offering the workman a special inducement has come to be so generally recognized that a large proportion of those most interested in the subject look upon the adoption of some one of the modern schemes for paying men (such as piecework, the premium plan, or the bonus plan, for instance) as practically the whole system of management.*

Broadly speaking, then, the best type of management in ordinary use may be defined as management in which the workmen give their best *initiative* and in return receive some *special incentive* from their employers. This type of management will be referred to as the management of *"initiative and incentive"* in contradistinction to modern scientific management, or task management, with which it is to be compared.

Under the old type of management (the management of "initiative and incentive") success depends almost entirely upon getting the "initiative" of the workmen, and it is indeed a rare case in which this initiative is attained. Under scientific management the "initiative" of the workmen (that is, their hard work, their good will, and their ingenuity) is obtained with absolute uniformity and to a greater extent than is possible under the old system. In addition to this improvement on the part of the men the managers assume new burdens, new duties and responsibilities never dreamed of in the past. The managers assume, for instance, the burden of gathering together all of the traditional knowledge which in the past has been possessed by the workmen and then of classifying, tabulating and reducing this knowledge to rules and formulae which are immensely helpful to the workmen in doing their daily work.

These new duties of the management are grouped under four heads:

FOUR FUNDAMENTAL ELEMENTS

First: They develop a science for each element of a man's work, which replaces the old rule of thumb method.

---

*Under Scientific Management, the particular pay system which is adopted is merely one of the subordinate elements of management.

Second: They scientifically select and train the workman, where in the past he chose his own work and trained himself as best he could.

Third: They heartily cooperate with the men, so as to ensure all of the work being done in accordance with the principles of the science which has been developed.

Fourth: There is an almost equal division of the work and the responsibility between the management and the workmen. The management take over all work for which they are better fitted than the workmen, while in the past almost all of the work and the greater part of the responsibility were thrown upon the men.

It is this combination of the initiative of the workmen coupled with the new types of work done by the management that makes Scientific Management so much more efficient than the old plan. Three of these elements exist in many cases under the management of "initiative and incentive," in a small and rudimentary way, but they are, under this management, of minor importance, whereas under Scientific Management they form the very essence of the whole system.

The writer is fully aware that, to perhaps most of the readers of this paper, the four elements which differentiate the new management from the old, will at first appear to be merely high-sounding phrases; and he would again repeat that he has no idea of convincing the reader of their value merely through announcing their existence. His hope of carrying conviction rests upon demonstrating the tremendous force and effect of these four elements through a series of practical illustrations. It will be shown, first, that they can be applied absolutely to all classes of work, from the most elementary to the most intricate, and second, that when they are applied the results must of necessity be overwhelmingly greater than those which it is possible to attain under the management of initiative and incentive.

The first illustration is that of handling pig iron and this work is chosen because it is typical of perhaps the crudest and most elementary form of labor which is performed by man. This work is done by men with no other implements than their hands. The pig iron handler stoops down, picks up a pig weighing about 92 pounds, walks for a few feet or yards and then drops it on to the ground or upon a pile. This work is so crude and elementary in its nature that the writer firmly believes that it would be possible to train an intelligent gorilla so as to be a more efficient pig-iron handler than any man can be. Yet it will be shown that the science of handling pig iron is so great and amounts to so much that it is impossible for the man who is best suited to this type of work to understand the principles of this science, or even to work in accordance with these principles, without the aid of a man better educated than he is. And further illustrations to be given will make it clear that in almost all of the mechanic arts the science which underlies each workman's act is so great and amounts to so much that the workman who is best suited to actually doing the work is incapable (either through lack of education or through insufficient mental capacity) of understanding this science. This is announced as a general principle, the truth of which will become apparent as one illustration after another is given. After showing these three elements in the handling of pig iron, several illustrations will be given of their application to different kinds of work in the field of the mechanic arts, at intervals in a rising scale beginning with the simplest and ending with the more intricate forms of labor.

One of the first pieces of work undertaken by us, when the writer started to introduce Scientific Management into the Bethlehem Steel Company, was to handle pig iron. The opening of the Spanish war found some 80,000 tons of pig iron piled in small piles in an open field adjoining the works. With the opening of the war, the price rose and the pig iron was sold. This gave us a good opportunity to show the workmen, as well as the owners and managers of the works, on a fairly large scale the advantages of Scientific Management over the old-fashioned day work and piecework system.

The Bethlehem Steel Company had a pig iron gang consisting of about 75 men. They were good, average pig-iron handlers, were under an excellent foreman who himself had been a pig-iron handler, and the work was done, on the whole, about as fast and as cheaply as it was anywhere else at that time.

A railroad switch was run into the field right along the edge of the piles of pig iron. An inclined plank was placed against the side of a car, and each man picked up from his pile a pig of iron weighing about 92 pounds, walked up the inclined plant and dropped it on the end of the car.

This gang was loading on the average about 12½ long tons per man per day. We were surprised to find, after a scientific study of the men at work, that a first-class pig-iron handler ought to handle between 47 and 48 long tons per day, instead of 12½ tons. This task seemed to us so very large that we were obliged to go over our work several times before we were absolutely sure that we were right. Once we were sure, however, that 47 tons was a proper day's work for a first-class pig-iron handler, the task which faced us as managers under the modern scientific plan was clearly before us.

It was our duty to see that the 80,000 tons of pig iron piled on the open lot was loaded on to the cars at the rate of 47 tons per man per day, in place of 12½ tons. And it was further our duty to see that this work was done without bringing on a strike among the men, without any quarrel with the men, and to see that the men were happier and better contented when loading at the new rate of 47 tons than they were when loading at the old rate of 12½ tons.

The first practical step, therefore, was the scientific selection of the workman.

In dealing with workmen under this type of management, it is an inflexible rule to talk to and deal with only one man at a time, since each workman has his own special abilities and limitations, and men vary to such an extent that it is impossible to educate and improve them in masses. What we are trying to do, then, is to develop each individual man to his highest state of efficiency and prosperity. We therefore carefully watched and studied these 75 men for three or four days. We finally picked out four men, looked up their history as far back as we could, and made thorough inquiries as to the character, habits and the ambition of each of them. Finally we selected one as well from among the four as the most likely man to start with. He was a little Pennsylvania Dutchman, who would trot back home for a mile or so after his work in the evening, about as fresh as he was when he came trotting down to work in the morning. We found that upon wages of $1.15 a day he had succeeded in buying a small plot of ground, and that he was engaged in putting up the walls of a little house for himself in the morning before starting to work and at night after leaving. He also had the reputation of being exceedingly "close." As one man whom we talked to about him said, "A penny looks about the size of a cartwheel to him." This man we will call Schmidt.

The task before us, then, narrowed itself down to getting Schmidt to handle 47 tons of pig iron per day and making him glad to do it. Schmidt was called out from among the gang of pig-iron handlers and talked to somewhat in this way:

"Schmidt, are you a high-priced man?"

"Vell, I don't know vat you mean."

"Oh, come now, you answer my questions. What I want to find out is, whether you are a high-priced man or one of these cheap fellows here. What I want to find out is whether you want to earn $1.85 a day or whether you are satisfied with $1.15, just the same as all those cheap fellows are getting."

"Did I vant $1.85 a day? Vas dot a high-priced man? Vell, yes, I vas a high-priced man."

"Oh, you're irritating me. Of course you want $1.85 a day—everyone wants it! You know perfectly well that that has very little to do with your being a high-priced man. Now come over here. You see that pile of pig iron?"

"Yes."

"You see that car?"

"Yes."

"Well, if you are a high-priced man, you will load that pig iron on that car tomorrow for $1.85. Now do wake up and answer my questions. Tell me whether you are a high-priced man or not?"

"Vell—did I get $1.85 for loading dot pig iron on dot car tomorrow?"

"Yes, of course, you do, and you get $1.85 for loading a pile like that every day right through the year."

"Vell, dot's all right. I could load dot pig iron on the car tomorrow for $1.85; and I get it every day, don't I?"

"Certainly you do—certainly you do."

"Vell, den, I vas a high-priced man."

"Now, hold on, hold on. You know just as I do that a high-priced man has to do exactly as he's told from morning till night. You have seen this man here before, haven't you?"

"No, I never saw him."

"Well, if you are a high-priced man, you will do exactly as this man tells you tomorrow, from morning till night. When he tells you to pick up a pig and walk, you pick it up and you walk, and when he tells you to sit down and rest, you sit down. You do that right straight through the day. Now you come on to work here tomorrow morning and I'll know before night whether you are really a high-priced man or not."

This seems to be rather rough talk. And indeed it would be if applied to an educated mechanic, or even an intelligent laborer. With a man of the mental type of Schmidt, it is appropriate and not unkind.

What would Schmidt's answer be if he were talked to in the manner which is usual under the old system of management, that of initiative and incentive, say as follows?

"Now, Schmidt, you are a first-class pig-iron handler and know your business well. You have been handling at the rate of 12½ tons per day. I have given considerable study to handling pig iron, and feel sure that a you could do a much larger day's work than you have here. Now don't you think that if you really tried you could handle 47 tons of pig iron per day, instead of 12½ tons?"

What do you think Schmidt's answer would be to this?

Schmidt started in to work, and all day long, and at regular intervals, was told by the man who stood over him with a watch, "Now, pick up a pig and walk. Now sit down and rest. Now, walk—now, rest," etc. He worked when he was told to work, and rested when he was told to rest, and at half-past five in the afternoon had his 47½ tons loaded on the car. And he practically never failed to work at this pace and do the task that was set him during the three years that the writer was at Bethlehem. And throughout this time he averaged a little more than $1.85 per day, whereas before he had never received over $1.15 per day, which was the ruling rate of wages at that time in Bethlehem. One man after another was picked out and trained to handle pig iron at the rate of 47 ½ tons per day, until all of the pig iron was handled at this rate, and all of this gang were receiving 60% more wages than other workmen around them.

If Schmidt had been allowed to attack the pile of 47 tons of pig iron without the guidance or direction of a man who understood the art, or science, of handling pig iron, in his desire to earn his high wages he would probably have tired himself out by 11 or 12 o'clock in the day. He would have kept so steadily at work that his muscles would not have had the proper periods of rest absolutely needed for recuperation, and he would have been completely exhausted. By having a man, however, who understood this law stand over him and direct his work, day after day, until he acquired the habit of resting at proper intervals, he was able to work at an even gait all day long.

To go into the matter in more detail, however, as to the scientific selection of the men: it is a fact that in this gang of 75 pig-iron handlers, only about 1 man in 8 was physically capable of handling 47½ tons per day. With the very best of intentions, the other 7 out of 8 men were physically unable to work at this pace. Now, the 1 man in 8 who was able to do this work was in no sense superior to the other men who were working on the gang. He merely happened to be a man of the type of the ox—no rare specimen of humanity, difficult to find and therefore very highly prized. On the contrary, he was man so stupid that he was unfitted to do most kinds of laboring work, even. The selection of the man, then, does not involve the finding of some extraordinary individual, but merely the picking out from among very ordinary men the few who are especially suited to this type of work. Although in this particular gang only 1 man in 8 was suited to doing the work, we had not the slightest difficulty in getting all the men who were needed, some of them from inside of the works and others from the neighboring country.

CAN WORKMEN SELECT THEMSELVES?

Under the old forms of management, the attitude of the management is that of "putting the work up to the workmen." What likelihood would there be, then, under the old type of management, of these men properly selecting themselves for pig-iron handling? Would they be likely to get rid of seven out of eight from their own gang, and retain only the eighth man? No. And no expedient could be devised which would make these men properly select themselves. Even if they fully realized the necessity of doing so in order to obtain high wages (and they are not sufficiently intelligent to properly grasp this necessity), the fact that their friends or their brothers who were working right along-side of them would temporarily be thrown out of a job because they were not suited to this kind of work, would entirely prevent them from properly selecting themselves.

The writer has given above a brief description of the practical application of three of the four elements which constitute the essence of Scientific Management: first, the careful selection of the workman, and second and third, the method of first inducing and then training and helping the workman to work according to the scientific method. Nothing has as yet been said about the science of handling pig iron. The writer trusts, however, that before leaving this illustration the reader will be thoroughly convinced that there is a science of handling pig iron, and that this science amounts to so much that the man who is suited to handle pig iron cannot possibly understand it, nor even work in accordance with its laws without the help of those who are over him.

WORK A MAN SHOULD DO IN A DAY

This science was developed as the result of experiments started while the writer was foreman in the Midvale works in 1881 to find some rule, or law, which would enable a foreman to know in advance how much of any kind of heavy laboring work a man who was well suited to his job ought to do in a day. That is, to study the tiring effect of heavy labor upon a first-class man. Our first step was to employ a young college graduate to look up all that had been written on the subject in English, German and French. Two classes of experiments had been made; one by physiologists who were studying the endurance of the human animal, and the other by engineers who wished to determine what fraction of a horse-power a manpower was. These experiments had been made largely upon men who were lifting loads by means of turning the crank of a winch from which weights were suspended. Others, to determine the energy expended in walking, running and lifting weights in various ways. However, the records of these experiments were so meager that no law of any value could be deduced from them. We therefore started a series of experiments of our own.

Two first-class laborers were selected, men who had proved themselves to be physically powerful, and who were also good, steady workers. These men were paid double wages during the experiments, and were told that they must work to the best of their ability at all times, and that we should make certain tests with them from time to time to find whether they were "soldiering" or not, and the moment either one of them started to try to deceive us that he would be discharged.

Now, it must be clearly understood that in these experiments we were *not* trying to find the maximum work that any man could do on a short spurt or for a few days, but that our endeavor was to learn what really constituted a full day's work for a first-class man; the best day's work that a man could properly do, year in and year out, and still thrive under. These men were given all kinds of tasks, which were carried out each day under the close observation of the young college man who was conducting the experiments, and who at the same time noted with a stopwatch the proper time for all of the motions that were made by the men. Useless motions were eliminated, and fast motions substituted for awkward, inefficient movements. Every element in any way connected with the work which we believed could have a bearing on the speed and efficiency was carefully studied and recorded. What we hoped ultimately to determine was what fraction of a horsepower a man was able to exert—that is, how many foot pounds of work a man could do in a day.

After making this series of experiments, therefore, each man's work for each day was translated into foot pounds of energy, and to our surprise we found that there was no apparent relation between the foot pounds of energy which the man exerted during a day and the tiring effect of his work. On some kinds of work the man would be tired out when doing perhaps not more than one eighth of a horse-power, while in others he would be tired to no greater extent by doing half a horse-power of work. We failed, therefore, to find any law which was an accurate guide to the maximum day's work for a first-class workman.

Some years later a second series of experiments was made, similar to the first, but somewhat more thorough. This, however, resulted, as the first experiments, in obtaining valuable information, but not in the development of a law. Again, some years later, a third series of experiments was made, and this time no trouble was spared in our endeavor to make the work thorough. After this data was again translated into foot pounds of energy exerted for each man each day, it became perfectly clear that there is no direct relation between the horse-power which a man exerts (that is, his foot pounds of energy per day), and the tiring effect of the work on the man. The writer, however, was quite as firmly convinced as ever that some definite, clear-cut law existed as to what constitutes a full day's work for a first-class laborer, and our data had been so carefully collected and recorded that he felt sure that the necessary information was included somewhere in the records. The problem of developing this law from our accumulated facts was therefore handed over to Mr. Carl G. Barth, who is a better mathematician than any of the rest of us, and we decided to investigate the problem in a new way, by graphically representing each element of the work through plotting curves, which should give us, as it were, a bird's-eye view of every element. In a comparatively short time Mr. Barth had discovered the law governing the tiring effect of heavy labor on a first-class man. And it is so simple in its nature that it is truly remarkable that it should not have been discovered and dearly understood years before.

The law is confined to that class of work in which the limit of a man's capacity is reached because he is tired out. It is the law of heavy laboring, corresponding to the work of the cart horse, rather than that of the trotter. Practically all such work consists of a heavy pull or a push on the man's arms, that is, the man's strength is exerted by either lifting or pushing something which he grasps in his hands. And the law is, that for each given pull or push on the man's arms it is possible for the workman to be under load for only a definite percentage of the day. For example, when pig iron is being handled (each pig weighing 92 pounds), a first-class workman can be under load only

43 percent of the day. He must be entirely free from load during 57 percent of the day. And as the load becomes lighter, the percentage of the day under which the man can remain under load increases. So that, if the workman is handling a half pig, weighing 46 pounds, he can then be under load 58 percent of the day, and only has to rest during 42 percent. As the load grows lighter the man can remain under load during a larger and larger percentage of the day, until finally a load is reached which he can carry in his hands all day long without being tired out.

When a laborer is carrying a piece of pig iron weighing 92 pounds in his hands, it tires him about as much to stand still under the load as it does to walk with it, since his arm muscles are under the same severe tension whether he is moving or not. A man, however, who stands still under a load is exerting no horse-power whatever, and this accounts for the fact that no constant relation could be traced in various kinds of heavy laboring work between the foot pounds of energy exerted and the tiring effect of the work on the man. It will also be clear that in all work of this kind, it is necessary for the arms of the workman to be completely free from load—that is, for the workman to rest—at frequent intervals. Throughout the time that the man is under heavy load, the tissues of his arm muscles are in process of degeneration, and frequent periods of rest are required in order that the blood may have a chance to restore these tissues to their normal condition.

As to the possibility, under the old type of management, of inducing these pig-iron handlers (after they had been properly selected) to work in accordance with the science of doing heavy laboring, namely, having proper scientifically determined periods of rest in close sequence to periods of work. As has been indicated before, the essential idea of the ordinary types of management is that each workman has become more skilled in his own trade than it is possible for anyone in the management to be, and that, therefore, the details of how the work shall best be done must be left to him. The idea, then, of taking one man after another and training him under a competent teacher into new working habits until he continually and habitually works in accordance with scientific laws, which have been developed by someone else, is directly antagonistic to the old idea that each workman can best regulate his own way of doing the work. And besides this, the man suited to handling pig iron is too stupid to properly train himself. Thus it will be seen that with the ordinary types of management, the development of a science to replace rule of thumb, the scientific selection of the men, and inducing the men to work in accordance with these scientific principles, are entirely out of the question. And this because the philosophy of the old management puts the entire responsibility upon the workmen and uses force to secure results, while the philosophy of the new places a great part of it upon the management and seeks coöperation.

With most readers great sympathy will be aroused because seven out of eight of these pig-iron handlers were thrown out of a job. This sympathy is entirely wasted, because almost all of them were immediately given other jobs with the Bethlehem Steel Company. And indeed it should be understood that the removal of these men from pig-iron handling, for which they were unfit, was really a kindness to themselves, because it was the first step toward finding them work for which they were fitted, and at which, after receiving proper training, they could permanently and legitimately earn higher wages.

THE GOSPEL OF EFFICIENCY II: THE PRINCIPLES OF SCIENTIFIC MANAGEMENT

FREDERICK W. TAYLOR

Although the reader may be convinced that there is a certain science back of the handling of pig iron, still it is more than likely that he is still skeptical as to the existence of a science for doing other kinds of laboring.

For example, the average man would question whether there is much of any science in the work of shoveling. Yet there is but little doubt, if any intelligent reader of this paper were to set out deliberately to find what may be called the foundation of the science of shoveling, that with perhaps fifteen or twenty hours of thought and analysis he would be almost sure to have arrived at the essence of this science. On the other hand, so completely are the rule-of-thumb ideas still dominant that the writer has never met a single shovel contractor to whom it had ever even occurred that there was such a thing as a science of shoveling.

THE SCIENCE OF SHOVELING

For a first-class shoveler there is a given shovel load at which he will do his biggest day's work. What is this shovel load? Will a first-class man do more work per day with a shovel load of five pounds, ten pounds, fifteen pounds, twenty, twenty-five, thirty, or forty pounds? Now, this is a question which can be answered only through carefully made experiments. By first selecting two or three first-class shovelers, paying them extra wages for doing trustworthy work, and then gradually varying the shovel load and having all the conditions accompanying the work carefully observed for several weeks at a time by men who were used to experimenting, it was found that a first-class man would do his biggest day's work with a shovel load of about twenty-one pounds. For instance, that this man would shovel a larger tonnage per day with a twenty-one-pound load than with a twenty-four-pound load or than with an eighteen-pound load on his shovel. It is, of course, evident that no shoveler can always take a load of exactly twenty-one pounds on his shovel, but nevertheless, although his load may vary three or four pounds one way or the other, either below or above the twenty-one pounds, the shoveler will do his biggest day's work when his average for the day is about twenty-one pounds.

The writer does not wish it to be understood that this is the whole of the art or science of shoveling. There are many other elements which, together, go to make up this science. But he wishes to indicate the important effect which this one piece of scientific knowledge has upon the work of shoveling.

TEN DIFFERENT KINDS OF SHOVELS

At the works of the Bethlehem Steel Company, for example, as a result of this law, instead of allowing each shoveler to select and own his own shovel it became necessary to provide some eight or ten different kinds of shovels, each one appropriate to handling a given type of material. A large tool room was built, in which were stored not only shovels but carefully designed and standardized labor implements of all kinds, such as picks, crowbars, etc. This made it possible to issue to each workman a shovel which would hold a load of twenty-one pounds of whatever class of material he was to shovel: a small shovel for ore, say, or a large one for ashes. Iron ore is one of the heavy materials which are handled in a works of this kind, and rice coal, owing to the fact that it is so slippery on the shovel, is one of the lightest materials. And it was found on studying the rule-of-thumb plan at the Bethlehem Steel Company that a workman would frequently go from shoveling ore, with a load of about thirty pounds per shovel, to handling rice coal, with a load on the same shovel of less than four pounds. In the one case, he was so overloaded that it was impossible for him to do a full day's work, and in the other case he was so ridiculously underloaded that it was manifestly impossible even to approximate a day's work.

To illustrate briefly some of the other elements which go to make up the science of shoveling, thousands of stopwatch observations were made to study just how quickly a shoveler, provided in each case with the proper type of shovel, can push his shovel into the pile of materials and then draw it out properly loaded. These observations were made first when pushing the shovel into the body of the pile. Next, when shoveling on a dirt bottom, that is, at the outside edge of the pile, and next with a wooden bottom, and finally with an iron bottom. Again, a similar accurate time study was made of the time required to swing the shovel backward and then throw the load for a given horizontal distance, accompanied by a given height. Time studies were made for various combinations of distance and height. Having data of this sort coupled with the law of endurance described in the case of the pig-iron handlers, it becomes evident that the man who is directing shovelers can first teach them the exact methods which should be employed to use their strength to the very best advantage, and can then assign them daily tasks which are so just that the workman can each day be sure of earning the large bonus which is paid whenever he successfully performs this task.

There were about six hundred shovelers and laborers of this general class in the yard of the Bethlehem Steel Company at this time. These men were scattered in their work over a yard which was, roughly, about two miles long and half a mile wide. In order that each workman should be given his proper implement and his proper instruction for doing each new job, it was necessary to establish a detailed system for directing men in their work, in place of the old plan of handling groups, or gangs, under a few yard foremen. As each workman came into the works in the morning, he took out of his own special pigeonhole, with his number on the outside, two pieces of paper, one of which stated just what implements he was to get from the tool room and where he was to start to work, and the other of which gave the record of his previous day's work and earnings. Many of these men were foreigners and unable to read and write, but they all knew at a glance the essence of this report, because yellow paper showed the man that he had failed to do his full task the day before, and informed him that he had not earned as much as $1.85 a day, and that none but high-priced men would be allowed to stay permanently with this gang. Whenever a man received a white slip he knew that everything was all right.

SAVING THE ENERGIES OF WORKINGMEN

Dealing with every workman as a separate individual in this way involved the building of a labor office for the superintendent and clerks who were in charge of this section of the work. In this office every laborer's work was planned out well in advance, and the workmen were all moved from place to place by the clerks with elaborate diagrams or maps of the yard and lists of the various jobs to be done before them, very much as chess-men are moved on a chess board—a more or less elaborate telephone and messenger system having been installed for this purpose. In this way a large amount of the time lost through having too many men in one place and too few in another and through waiting between jobs, which occurred under the old system, was entirely eliminated. Under the old system, the workmen were kept day after day in comparatively large gangs, each under a single foreman, and the gang was apt to remain of pretty nearly the same size whether there was much or little of any particular kind of work on hand, since each gang had to be kept large enough to handle whatever work in its special line was likely to come along.

When one ceases to deal with men in large gangs or groups, and proceeds to study each workman as an individual, if the workman fails to do his task, some competent teacher is sent to show him exactly how his work can best be done, to guide, help and encourage him, and, at the same time, to study his possibilities as a workman. So that, under the plan which individualizes each workman, instead of brutally discharging the man or lowering his wages for failing to make good at once, he is given the time and the help required to make him proficient at his present job, or he is shifted to another class of work for which he is either mentally or physically better suited.

All of this requires the kindly coöperation of the management, and involves a much more elaborate organization and system than the old-fashioned herding of men in large gangs. This organization consisted, in this case of one set of men who were engaged in the development of the science of laboring through time study; another set of men, mostly skilled laborers themselves, who were teachers, and who helped and guided the men in their work; another set of tool-room men who provided them with the proper implements and kept them in perfect order; and another set of clerks who planned the work well in advance, moved the men with the least loss of time from one place to another, and properly recorded each man's earnings. And this furnishes an elementary illustration of what has been referred to as cooperation between management and the workmen.

The question which naturally presents itself is, whether an elaborate organization of this sort can be made to pay for itself. This question will best be answered by a statement of the results of the third year of working under this plan.

And in computing the low cost of $0.033 per ton, the office and tool-room expenses, wages of all labor superintendents, foremen, clerks, time study, etc., are included.

TABLE		**OLD PLAN**	**NEW PLAN** **TASK WORK**
The number of yard laborers was reduced from between		400 and 600 to about	140
Average number of tons per man per day		16	59
Average earnings per man per day		$1.15	$1.88
Average cost of handling a ton of 2,240 lbs		0.072	0.033

During this year the total saving of the new plan over the old amounted to $36,417.69, and during the six months following, when all of the work of the yard was under scientific management, the saving was at the rate of between $75,000 and $80,000 per year.

HOW THE WORKMEN THEMSELVES ARE AFFECTED

Perhaps the most important of all the results attained was the effect on the workmen themselves. A careful inquiry into the condition of these men developed the fact that out of the 140 workmen only two were said to be drinking men. This does not, of course, imply that many of them did not take an occasional drink. The fact is that a steady drinker would find it almost impossible to keep up with the pace which was set, so that they were practically all sober. Many, if not most, of them were saving money, and they all lived better than they had before. These men constituted the finest body of picked laborers the writer has ever seen together, and they looked upon the men who were over them, their bosses and their teachers, as their very best friends; not as nigger drivers, forcing them to work extra hard for ordinary wages, but as friends who were teaching them and helping them to earn much higher wages than they had ever earned before. It would have been absolutely impossible for anyone to have stirred up strife between these men and their employers. And this presents a very simple though effective illustration of what is meant by the words "prosperity for the employee, coupled with prosperity for the employer," the two principal objects of management. It is evident also that this result was brought about by the application of the four fundamental principles of Scientific Management.

These four underlying principles are of such high importance that they will here be repeated.

First: The development of a science for each element of man's work, replacing the old rule-of-thumb method.

Second: The scientific selection and training of each workman.

Third: The hearty coöperation of the management with the men in order that the work may be done strictly in accordance with the principals of the science which has been developed.

Fourth: An almost equal division of the work and the responsibility between the management and the workmen, where in the past the greater part of the responsibility was left by the management to be shouldered by the workman.

DO MEN WORK WELL IN GANGS?

As another illustration of the value of a scientific study of the motives which influence workmen in their daily work, the writer will show how workmen lose ambition and initiative when they are herded into gangs instead of being treated as separate individuals. A careful analysis had demonstrated the fact that when workmen are herded together in gangs, each man in the gang becomes far less efficient than when his personal ambition is stimulated; that when men work in gangs, their individual efficiency almost invariably falls down to the level of the worst man in the gang. For this reason a general order had been issued in the Bethlehem steel works that not more than four men were to be allowed to work in a labor gang without a special permit, signed by the general superintendent of the works.

After gang work had been broken up, and an unusually fine set of ore shovelers had been developed, each of these men was given a separate car to unload each day, and his wages depended upon his own personal work. The men who unloaded the largest amount of ore were paid the largest wages. Much of this ore came from the Lake Superior region, and the same ore was delivered in Pittsburgh and in Bethlehem in exactly similar cars. There was a shortage of ore handlers in Pittsburgh, and hearing of the fine gang of laborers that had been developed at Bethlehem, one of the Pittsburgh steel works sent an agent to hire the Bethlehem men. The Pittsburgh men offered $4\frac{9}{10}$ cents a ton for unloading exactly the same ore, with the same shovels, from the same cars, that were unloaded in Bethlehem for $3\frac{9}{10}$ cents a ton. After carefully considering this situation, it was decided that it would be unwise to pay more than $3\frac{9}{10}$ cents per ton for unloading the Bethlehem cars, because, at this rate, the Bethlehem laborers were earning a little over $1.85 per man per day, and this price was 60 percent more than the ruling rate of wages around Bethlehem.

After deciding not to raise the wages of our ore handlers, these men were brought into the office one at a time, and talked to somewhat as follows:

"Now, Patrick, you have proved to us that you are a high-priced man. You have been earning every day a little more than $1.85, and you are just the sort of man that we want to have in our ore-shoveling gang. A man has come here from Pittsburgh who is offering $4\frac{9}{10}$ cents per ton. That's considerably more than we are paying you. I think, therefore, that you had better apply to this man for a job. Of course, you know we are very sorry to have you leave us, but you have proved yourself a high-priced man, and we are very glad to see you get this chance of earning more money. Just remember, however, that at any time in the future, when you get out of a job, you can always come right back to us."

A GANG TAKES FLIGHT IN PITTSBURGH

Almost all of the ore handlers took this advice and went to Pittsburgh, but in about six weeks most of them were back in Bethlehem unloading ore at the old rate of 3⁹⁄₁₀ cents a ton. The writer had the following talk with one of these men after he had returned.

"Patrick, what are you doing back here? I thought we had gotten rid of you."

"Well, sir, I'll tell you how it was. When we got out there, Jimmy and I were put onto a car with eight other men. We started to shovel the ore out just the same as we do here. After about half an hour, I saw a little devil alongside of me doing pretty near nothing, so I said to him: 'Why don't you go to work? Unless we get the ore out of this car we won't get any money on pay day.' He turned to me and said, 'Who in——are you?' 'Well,' I said, 'that's none of your business'; and the little devil stood up to me and said: 'You'll be minding your own business, or I'll throw you off this car!' Well, I could have spit on him and drowned him, but the rest of the men put down their shovels and looked as if they were going to back him up; so I went round to Jimmy and said (so that the whole gang could hear it): 'Now, Jimmy, you and I will throw a shovelful whenever this little devil throws one, and not another shovelful.' So we watched him, and only shoveled when he shoveled. When pay day came around, though, we had less money than we got here in Bethlehem. After that Jimmy and I went in to the boss and asked him for a car to ourselves, the same as we got at Bethlehem, but he told us to mind our own business. And when another pay day came around we had less money than we got here at Bethlehem, so Jimmy and I got the gang together and brought them all back here to work again."

When working each man for himself, these men were able to earn higher wages at 3⁹⁄₁₀ cents a ton that they could earn when they were paid 4⁹⁄₁₀ cents a ton on gang work; and this again shows the great gain which results from working according to even the most elementary of scientific principles. But it also shows that in the application of the most elementary principles it is necessary for the management to do their share of the work in cooperating with the workmen. The Pittsburgh managers knew just how the results had been attained at Bethlehem, but they were unwilling to go to the small trouble and expense required to plan ahead and assign a separate car to each shoveler, and then keep an individual record of each man's work and pay him just what he had earned.

HOW BRICKS ARE SCIENTIFICALLY LAID

One further illustration will serve to show the effectiveness of Scientific Management in an occupation far more skilled than carrying pig iron or shoveling.

Bricklaying is, perhaps, the oldest of the mechanic arts. Two thousand years before Christ bricks were laid as they are now laid. The same kind of brick, the same kind of mortar, the same kind of trowel, and the same kind of scaffold are now used as were used at that period. If any trade had reached a point at which motion study would be non-productive, one would therefore expect to find the bricklaying trade in that condition, because 4,000 years of work, with thousands of men working at it throughout the world, should certainly have evolved a good system of bricklaying. Some four years ago Frank B. Gilbreth became interested in the subject of Scientific Management. During his youth, Mr. Gilbreth made a very close and accurate study of bricklaying, and he said to himself that if there was anything in the new idea of motion study it ought to be as useful in bricklaying as it was in anything else.

He therefore made an intensely interesting analysis and time study of each movement of the bricklayer. He placed himself on a scaffold with a pile of bricks on the floor and the mortar board alongside him,—a brick wall being built on the left. The first motion made by a bricklayer was to take a step to the right. Was that step really necessary? Next, after taking the step to the right, the bricklayer stooped down to the floor, disengaged a brick from the pile of bricks, and raised his body up again, either to full height or to partial height. Was it really necessary for the bricklayer to lower his body, weighing from 150 to 240 pounds, to the floor in order to raise an 8-pound brick 2½ feet?

To eliminate these waste motions, Mr. Gilbreth, after a great deal of work, devised an adjustable scaffold upon which the bricks were placed at the same level with the wall. It was a scaffold on which the man stood in one place, while a little table was placed alongside him on which the bricks and mortar rested. It was so very simple an invention that one wonders why it was not thought of 4,000 years ago. The bricks were placed on this supplementary platform at just the right height, so that the bricklayer merely turned round, picked up a brick with a rotary motion of the body and put it on the wall.

Mr. Gilbreth next found that every bricklayer, as he raised the brick up, threw it over in his hand at least once, sometimes twice, sometimes three times. This was done for the purpose of examining the brick so that no chipped or imperfect brick should be placed on the outside of the wall where it would show. Mr. Gilbreth asked: Is this act of throwing up the brick for examination absolutely essential, or is it wholly wasteful? After a great deal of thought he devised the following plan for doing away with all of these motions: As the bricks were unloaded from the car or from the team, a laborer was stationed at a suitable bench, where the bricks were examined by him, and placed right side up, with the proper edge and the proper end on a wooden frame about three feet long, called a packet. This frame held about ninety pounds of bricks, and was so constructed that the bricklayer's hand went right into it and seized the brick without having to disengage it from a tangle on the floor. He took a brick out in the exact position in which it was to be laid in the wall, without any throwing.

Mr. Gilbreth next found that the bricklayer worked with one hand only at a time. Why? Because the brick pile being on the floor and the mortar board some distance from it, they were too far apart for the man to take a dip of the mortar and pick up a brick at the same time; it took two motions. By building the scaffold by the method described, and by placing the bricks and the mortar close together, using a deep mortar box instead of a mortar board, brick-pile and mortar box were brought within the range of the bricklayer's eyes at the same time, so that he picked up a brick with the left hand, took a dip of mortar with the right hand with a single movement and then turned around, spread the mortar, and laid the brick in the wall.

All bricklayers, after they set a brick, tap it down in order to get the joint the right thickness. From his experience in his youth, Mr. Gilbreth knew that if the mortar was properly tempered it was possible to place the brick at the right height with a pressure of the hand. The mortar was therefore carefully tempered, so that the bricklayer could readily bed the brick with pressure from the hand and thus save the time taken in tapping.

Through this minute study of the motions to be made by the bricklayer in laying bricks under all standard conditions, Mr. Gilbreth has reduced his movements from eighteen to a brick to five, and even in one case to as low as two motions per brick. He has given all of the details of this analysis to the profession in the chapter headed "Motion Study," of his book entitled "Bricklaying System."

At this point the question naturally arises: What does the bricklayers' union say about all this? The reduction of the motions from eighteen to five would practically amount to nothing, provided the men's unions said "Nay," and the unions at first always do say "Nay." But Mr. Gilbreth, who happens to be an optimist as well as a man of great pertinacity, bided his time, and finally he had his opportunity with the Bricklayers' Union of Boston. He showed the leaders of the union that bricklaying in America is likely to become a lost art, because reinforced concrete construction is growing at such a pace, and he persuaded the leaders of the union to give him a chance to show what he could do if he were not thwarted. Mr. Gilbreth was erecting a large building in the neighborhood of Boston, and he told the bricklayers, in the first place, that he would not employ any of them at less than $6.50 a day, the ruling price at that time being $4.50 a day. That was a very satisfactory proposition to the workmen; but he also stipulated that any bricklayer who did not do exactly what he was told would be promptly discharged. By the time the building was from a quarter to a half way up he had a full complement of bricklayers laying bricks according to the new method, and each of them getting $6.50 a day. On a twelve-inch wall, with drawn joints on both sides, using two kinds of bricks, which all practical men will know was not an easy way to lay, the average was 350 bricks per man per hour, the record number of bricks which had been laid per man per hour in this type of work previous to the adoption of this new system was 120 bricks.

His bricklayers were taught his new method of bricklaying by their fore-man. Those who failed to profit by their teaching were dropped, and each man, as he became proficient under the new method, received a substantial (not a small) increase in his wages. With a view to individualizing his work-men and stimulating each man to do his best, Mr. Gilbreth also developed an ingenious method for measuring and recording the number of bricks laid by each man, and for telling each workman at frequent intervals how many bricks he had succeeded in laying.

It is highly likely that many times during all of these years individual brick-layers have recognized the possibility of eliminating each of these unneces-sary motions. But even if, in the past, they did invent each one of Mr. Gilbreth's improvements, no bricklayer could alone increase his speed through their adoption, because several bricklayers always work together in a row, and the walls all around a building must grow at the same rate of speed. No one bricklayer, then, can work any faster than the one next to him. Nor has any one workman the authority to make other men cooperate with him to do faster work. It is only through *enforced* standardization of methods, *enforced* adop-tion of the best implements and working conditions, and *enforced* coöperation that this faster work can be assured. And the duty of enforcing the adoption of standards and of enforcing this coöperation rests with the management alone. The management must supply continually one or more teachers to show each new man the new and simpler motions, and the slower men must be con-stantly watched and helped until they have risen to their proper speed.

The management must also recognize the broad fact that workmen will not submit to this more rigid standardization and will not work extra hard, unless for extra pay.

Mr. Gilbreth's method of bricklaying furnishes a simple illustration of true and effective coöperation: where several men in the management (each one in his own way) help each workman individually, not only by studying his needs and his shortcomings and teaching him better methods, but also by seeing that all other workmen with whom he comes in contact help him by doing their part of the work.

The writer has gone thus fully into Mr. Gilbreth's method in order that it may be perfectly clear that this increase in output and this harmony could not have been attained under the management of "initiative and incentive." And that his success has been due to the use of the four elements which consti-tute the essence of Scientific Management.

THE GOSPEL OF EFFICIENCY III: THE PRINCIPLES OF SCIENTIFIC MANAGEMENT

FREDERICK W. TAYLOR

A number of years ago a company employing about three hundred men, which had been manufacturing the same machine for ten or fifteen years, sent for us to report as to whether any gain could be made through the introduction of Scientific Management.

They felt, no doubt, very much as many readers of the writer's paper of last month may have felt, that while it is evident that Scientific Management can be applied with extraordinarily favorable results to the more elementary types of work, such as pig-iron handling, shoveling, and bricklaying, it cannot be used to advantage in the higher mechanic arts. Indeed, we have found this to be the universal objection to our system, that "while it is excellent for some other employer's shop or factory, or for some other kind of work, it will not do for us!"

As a matter of fact, Scientific Management, being a fundamental philosophy of industry, not a mere group of efficiency devices, is applicable to almost every form of human employment. And this is no mere theoretical assertion, for Scientific Management, which was first developed and practised in an important steel plant, has now actually been applied and is being extensively applied to the most highly skilled industries, as of tool-making, optical works, typewriter shops, as well as to a great diversity of other industries, such as machine shops of varied kinds, cotton mills, shoe-manufacturing establishments, printing houses, bleacheries. It is now even being applied in the most important of government work, as in that of the Watertown arsenal. And in all cases it results in better conditions, better pay for the men, a larger product for the employers, and a better relationship between employer and employee, fruits which have been uniformly gratifying.

Accordingly we went with some confidence to investigate the plant of the manufacturing company to which the writer has referred. Their shops had been run for many years under a good superintendent and with excellent foremen and workmen, on piecework. The whole establishment was without doubt, in better physical condition than the average machine shop in this country.

The superintendent was distinctly displeased when told that through the adoption of Scientific Management the output, with the same number of men and machines, could be more than doubled. He said that he believed that any such statement was mere boasting, absolutely false, and, instead of inspiring him with confidence, he was disgusted that anyone should make such an impudent claim. He readily assented, however, to the proposition that he should select any one of the machines whose output he considered as representing the average of the shop, and that we should then demonstrate on this machine that through scientific methods its output could be more than doubled.

A TEST CASE TO SHOW THE VALUE OF SCIENTIFIC MANAGEMENT

The machine selected by him fairly represented the work of the shop. It had been run for ten or twelve years past by a first-class mechanic, who was more than equal in his ability to the average workman in the establishment. In a shop of this sort, in which similar machines are made over and over again, the work is necessarily greatly subdivided, so that no one man works upon more than a comparatively small number of parts during the year. A careful record was therefore made, in the presence of both parties, of the total time required by this workman to finish each piece, as well as the exact speeds and feeds which he took, and a record was kept of the time occupied in setting the work in the machine and removing it. After obtaining in this way a statement of what represented a fair average of the work done in the shop, we applied to this one machine the principles of Scientific Management. By means of four quite elaborate slide rules which we had especially made for the purpose of determining the all-round capacity of metal-cutting machines (reference to which will be made later) a careful analysis was made of every element of this machine in its relation to the work in hand. Its pulling power at its various speeds, its feeding capacity, and its proper speeds were determined by means of the slide rules, and changes were then made in the countershaft and driving pulleys so as to run it at its proper speed. Tools, made of high-speed steel (which was already in use in the shop) and of the proper shapes, were properly dressed, treated, and ground. A large special slide rule was then made, by means of which the exact speeds and feeds were indicated at which each kind of work could be done in the shortest possible time in this particular lathe. One after another, pieces of work were finished in the lathe, corresponding to the work which had been done in our preliminary trials, and the gain in time made through running the machine according to scientific principles ranged from two and one half times the speed in the slowest instance to nine times the speed in the highest.

And it was not more difficult to demonstrate in the whole shop, than with this single machine, how far Scientific Management is superior to the old rule-of-thumb, haphazard methods. In this case the reader must not be misled by the references to slide rules and the changes in the machinery to the conclusion that it is only necessary to adopt such evident and superficial devices. Physical improvements in machinery and motion study with stopwatches are indeed necessary and can be quickly made.

THE CHIEF AND ESSENTIAL FEATURE OF THE NEW SCIENCE

But the chief and essential feature of Scientific Management is the *change in the mental attitude of both employers and employees* toward their common work. Now, the change in the mental attitude and the habits of three hundred or more workmen can be brought about only slowly and through a long series of object lessons, which finally demonstrate to each man the great advantage which he will gain by heartily coöperating in his everyday work with the men in the management. Within three years, however, in this shop, as the principles of Scientific Management were gradually adopted, the output had been more than doubled per man and per machine. The men had been carefully selected and in almost all cases promoted from a lower to a higher order of work, and so instructed by their teachers (the functional foremen) that they were able to earn higher wages than ever before, the average increase in pay which each man received being about thirty-five percent, while, at the same time, the sum total of the wages paid for doing a given amount of work was lower than before.

It seems important to explain fully the reason why, with the aid of a slide rule, and after having studied the art of cutting metals, it was possible for a man who had never before seen these particular jobs, and who had never worked on this machine, to do work from two and one half to nine times as fast as it had been done before by a good mechanic who had spent his whole time for some ten to twelve years in doing this very work upon this particular machine. In a word, this was possible because the art of cutting metals involves a true science of no small magnitude, a science, in fact, so intricate that it is impossible for any ordinary machinist either to understand it or work according to its laws without the help of men who have made this their specialty.

Men who are unfamiliar with machine-shop work are prone to look upon the manufacture of each piece as a special problem, independent of any other kind of machine work. They are apt to think, for instance, that the problems connected with making the parts of an engine require the especial study, one may say almost the life study, of a set of engine-making mechanics, and that these problems are entirely different from those which would be met with in machining lathe or planer parts. In fact, however, a study of those elements which are peculiar either to engine parts or to lathe parts is trifling, compared with the great study of the art, or science, of cutting metals, upon a knowledge of which rests the ability to do really fast machine work of all kinds.

The real problem is how to remove chips fast from a casting or a forging, and how to make the piece smooth and true in the shortest time, and it matters but little whether the piece being worked upon is part, say, of a marine engine, a printing press, or an automobile. For this reason, the man with the slide rule, familiar with the science of cutting metals, who had never before seen this particular work, was able to distance the skilled mechanic who had made the parts of this machine his speciality for years.

WHY COOPERATION IS NECESSARY

It is easy to see why this should be so, because under the old form of management the workman's whole time was each day taken in actually doing the work with his hands, so that, even if he had the necessary education and habits of generalizing in his thought, he lacked the time and the opportunity for developing these laws. Even a simple law involving time-study requires the coöperation of two men, the one doing the work while the other times him with a stop watch, and even if the workman were to develop laws where before existed only rule-of-thumb knowledge, his personal interest would lead him almost inevitably to keep his discoveries secret, so that he could by means of this special knowledge personally do more work than other men and so obtain larger wages.

Under Scientific Management, on the other hand, it becomes the duty and also the pleasure of those who are engaged in the management not only to develop laws to replace rule of thumb, but also to teach impartially all of the workmen who are under them the quickest ways of working. The useful results obtained from these laws are always so great that any company can well afford to pay for the time and the experiments needed to develop them.

THE STORY OF THE NEW ART OF CUTTING METALS

The development of the art or science of cutting metals is an apt illustration of this fact. In the fall of 1880, about the time that the writer started to make the experiments already referred to, to determine what constitutes a day's work for a laborer, he also obtained the permission of Mr. William Sellers, the president of the Midvale Steel Company, to make a series of experiments to determine what angles and shapes of tools were the best for cutting steel. At the time that these experiments were started it was his belief that they would not last longer than six months, and in fact if it had been known that a longer period than this would be required, the permission to spend a considerable sum of money in making them would not have been forthcoming.

A sixty-six-inch-diameter vertical boring mill was the first machine used in making these experiments, and a large locomotive tire, made out of hard steel of uniform quality, was day after day cut up into chips in gradually learning how to make, shape and use the cutting tools so that they would do faster work. At the end of six months sufficient practical information had been obtained to repay far more than the cost of materials and wages which had been expended in experimenting. And yet the comparatively small number of experiments which had been made served principally to make it clear that the actual knowledge attained was but a small fraction of that which still remained to be developed, and which was badly needed by us, in our daily attempt intelligently to direct and help the machinists in their tasks.

OVER THIRTY THOUSAND EXPERIMENTS MADE

Experiments in this field were carried on, with occasional interruptions, through a period of about twenty-six years, in the course of which ten different experimental machines were especially fitted up to do this work. Between thirty thousand and fifty thousand experiments were carefully recorded, and many other experiments were made of which no record was kept. In studying these laws more than eight hundred thousand pounds of steel and iron was cut up into chips with the experimental tools, and it is estimated that from $150,000 to $200,000 was spent in the investigation.

Work of this character is intensely interesting to anyone who has any love for scientific research. For the purpose of this article, however, it should be fully appreciated that the motive power which kept these experiments going through many years, and which supplied the money and the opportunity for their accomplishment, was not the love for abstract search after scientific knowledge, but rather the very practical need to exact information in order to help our machinists to do their work in the best way and in the quickest time. In other words, the experiments had to pay for themselves as we went along.

All of these experiments were made to enable us to answer correctly the two questions which face every machinist each time that he does a piece of work in a metal-cutting machine, such as a lathe, planer, drill-press, or milling machine.

These two questions are:

At what cutting speed shall I run my machine? And What feed shall I use?

PROBLEMS WHICH REQUIRED
TWENTY-SIX YEARS FOR SOLUTION

They sound so simple that they would appear to call for merely the trained judgment of any good mechanic. In fact, however, after working twenty-six years, it has been found that the answer in every case involves the solution of an intricate mathematical problem, in which the effect of twelve independent variables upon the cutting speed must be determined.

(a) The quality of the metal which is to be cut; *i.e.*, its hardness or other qualities which affect the cutting speed.

(b) The chemical composition of the steel from which the tool is made, and the best treatment of the tool.

(c) The thickness of the shaving; or, the thickness of the spiral strip or band of metal which is to be removed by the tool.

(d) The shape or contour of the cutting edge of the tool.

(e) Whether a copious stream of water or other cooling medium is used on the tool.

(f) The depth of the cut.

(g) The duration of the cut; *i.e.*, the time which a tool must last under pressure of the shaving without being reground.

(h) The lip and clearance angles of the tool.

(j) The elasticity of the work and of the tool on account of producing chatter.

(k) The diameter of the casting or forging which is being cut.

(l) The pressure of the chip or shaving upon the cutting surface of the tool.

(m) The pulling power and the speed and feed changes of the machine.

It may seem preposterous to many people that it should have required a period of twenty-six years to investigate the effect of these twelve variables upon the cutting speed of metals. To those, however, who have had personal experience as experimenters, it will be appreciated that the great difficulty of the problem lies in the fact that it contains so many variable elements. And in fact the great length of time consumed in making each single experiment was caused by the difficulty of holding eleven variables constant and uniform throughout the experiment while the effect of the twelfth variable was being investigated. Holding the eleven variables constant was far more difficult than the investigation of the twelfth variable.

As, one after another, the effect upon the cutting speed of each of these variables was investigated, in order that practical use could be made of this knowledge, it was necessary to find a mathematical formula which expressed in concise form the laws which had been obtained.

After these laws had been investigated and the various formulae which mathematically expressed them had been determined, there still remained the difficult task of how to solve one of these complicated mathematical problems quickly enough to make this knowledge available for everyday use. If a good mathematician who had these various formulae before him were to attempt to get the proper answer (i.e., to get the correct cutting speed and feed by working in the ordinary way) it would take him from two to six hours, say, to solve a single problem; far longer to solve the mathematical problem than would be taken in most cases by the workman in doing the whole job on his machine. Thus a task of considerable magnitude which faced us was that of finding a quick solution of this mathematical problem with its twelve variables. And as we made progress in its solution, the whole problem was presented by the writer to one after another of the noted mathematicians in this country. They were offered any reasonable fee for a rapid, practical solution. Some of these men merely glanced at the problem; others, for the sake of being courteous, kept it before them for some two or three weeks. They all gave us practically the same answer: that in many cases it was possible to solve mathematical problems which contained four variables, and in some cases problems with five or six variables, but that it was manifestly impossible to solve a problem containing twelve variables in any other way than by the slow process of "trial and error."

CALLING IN THE MATHEMATICIANS

A quick solution was, however, so much of a necessity in our everyday work of running machine shops that, in spite of the small encouragement received from the mathematicians, we continued at irregular periods, through a term of fifteen years, to give a large amount of time in searching for a solution. Four or five men at various periods gave practically their whole time to this work, and finally,'while we were at the Bethlehem Steel Company, the slide rule was developed which is illustrated on Folder No. II of the writer's paper "On the Art of Cutting Metals," and is described in detail in the paper presented by Mr. Carl G. Barth to the American Society of Mechanical Engineers, entitled "Slide Rules for the Machine Shop, as a Part of the Taylor System of Management" (Vol. XXV of the "Transactions of the American Society of Mechanical Engineers"). By means of this slide rule, one of these intricate problems can be solved in less than half a minute by any good mechanic, whether he understands anything about mathematics or not, thus making available for everyday, practical use the years of experimenting on the art of cutting metals.

This is a good illustration of the fact that some way can always be found of making practical use of complicated scientific data which appears to be beyond the experience and the range of the mental training of ordinary practical men. These slide rules have been for years in constant daily use by machinists having no knowledge of mathematics.

To return to the case of the machinist who had been working for ten to twelve years in machining the same pieces over and over again, there was but a remote chance in any of the various kinds of work which this man did that he should hit upon the one best method of doing each piece of work out of the hundreds of possible methods which lay before him. Moreover, in the machine shops systematized by us, we have found that there is not one machine in a hundred which is speeded by its makers at anywhere near the correct cutting speed. So that, in order to compete with the science of cutting metals the machinist, before he could use proper speeds, would first have to put new pulleys on the countershaft of his machine and also make in most cases changes in the shapes and treatment of his tools. Many of these changes are matters entirely beyond his control, even if he knows what ought to be done.

WHY "RULE OF THUMB" CANNOT COMPETE WITH SCIENCE

If the reason is clear to the reader why the rule-of-thumb knowledge obtained by the machinist who is engaged on "repeat work" cannot possibly compete with the true science of cutting metals, it should be even more apparent why the high-class mechanic who is called upon to do a great variety of work from day to day is even less able to compete with this science. The high-class mechanic who does a different kind of work each day, in order to do each job in the quickest time would need, in addition to a thorough knowledge of the art of cutting metals, a vast knowledge and experience in the quickest way of doing each kind of work. And this knowledge, under Scientific Management, is ready at hand, and teachers are present to convey it.

The development of a science sounds like a formidable undertaking, and in fact anything like a thorough study of a science such as that of cutting metals necessarily involves many years of work. Yet even in this very intricate science, within a few months after starting, enough knowledge had been obtained to much more than pay for the work of experimenting. This holds true in the case of practically all scientific development in the mechanic arts. The first laws for cutting metals which were developed were crude, yet this imperfect knowledge was vastly better than the utter lack of exact knowledge or the chaotic rule of thumb which existed before, and enabled the workmen, with the help of the management, to do far quicker and better work.

For example, a very short time was needed to discover one or two types of tools which, though imperfect as compared with the shapes developed years afterward, were superior to all other shapes and kinds in common use. These tools were adopted as standard and made possible an immediate increase in the speed of every machinist who used them.

There is another type of scientific investigation referred to several times in this paper which should receive special attention, namely, the accurate study of the motives which influence men. At first it may appear that this is not a proper subject for exact scientific experiments. Owing to the fact that a very complex organism—the human animal—is being experimented with, it is true that any law which is deduced is subject to a large number of exceptions. And yet laws which apply to a large majority of men unquestionably exist. In developing these laws, accurate, carefully planned and executed experiments, extending through a term of years, have been made, similar in a general way to the experiments upon various other elements of industrial operations.

SETTING A TASK FOR WORKINGMEN

Perhaps the most important law belonging to this class, in its relation to Scientific Management, is the effect which the task idea has upon the efficiency of the workman. This, in fact, has become such an important element of the mechanism of Scientific Management that by a great number of people Scientific Management has come to be known as "task management."

There is absolutely nothing new in the task idea. Each one of us will remember that this idea was applied with good results in his schoolboy days. No efficient teacher would think of giving a class of students an indefinite lesson to learn. Each day a definite, clear-cut task is set by the teacher before each scholar, stating that he must learn just so much of the subject; and it is only by this means that proper, systematic progress can be made by the students. The average boy would go very slowly if, instead of being given a task, he were told to do as much as he could. All of us are grown-up children, and it is equally true that the average workman will work with the greatest satisfaction, both to himself and to his employer, when he is given each day a definite task which he is to perform in a given time, and which constitutes a proper day's work for a good workman. This furnishes the workman with a clear-cut standard, by which he can throughout the day measure his own progress, and the accomplishment of which affords him the greatest satisfaction.

HOW THE WORKMAN'S WAGE IS INCREASED

It is absolutely necessary, also, when workmen are daily given a task which calls for a high rate of speed on their part, that they should be insured the necessary high rate of pay whenever they are successful. This involves not only fixing for each man his daily task, but also paying him a large bonus, or premium, each time that he succeeds in doing his task in the given time. The workman must also be fully assured that this increase in pay beyond the average is to be permanent. It is difficult to appreciate in full measure the help which the proper use of these two elements is to the workman in elevating him to the highest standard of efficiency and speed in his trade, and then keeping him there, unless one has seen first the old plan and afterward the new tried upon the same workman. The remarkable and almost uniformly good results from the *correct* application of the task and the bonus must have been seen to be appreciated.

These two elements, the task and the bonus, constitute two of the most important elements of the mechanism of Scientific Management. They are especially important from the fact that they are, as it were, a climax, demanding before they can be used almost all of the other elements of the mechanism: such as a planning department, accurate time study, standardization of methods and implements, a routing system, the training of functional foremen or teachers, and in many cases instruction cards, slide rules, etc.

The necessity for systematically teaching workmen how to work to the best advantage has been several times referred to. It seems desirable, therefore, to explain in rather more detail how this teaching is done. In the case of a machine shop which is managed under the modern system, detailed written instructions as to the best way of doing each piece of work are prepared in advance by men in the planning department. These instructions represent the combined work of several men in the planning room, each of whom has his own specialty, or function. One of them, for instance, is a specialist on the proper speeds and cutting tools to be used. He uses the slide rules which have been already described as an aid, to guide him in obtaining proper speeds, etc. Another man analyzes the best and quickest motions to be made in setting the work up in the machine and removing it, etc. Still a third, through the time-study records which have been accumulated, makes out a timetable giving the proper speed for doing each element of the work. The directions of all of these men, however, are written on a single instruction card, or sheet.

These men of necessity spend most of their time in the planning department, because they must be close to the records and data which they continually use in their work, and because this work requires the use of a desk and freedom from interruption. Human nature is such, however, that many of the workmen, if left to themselves, would pay but little attention to their written instructions. It is necessary, therefore, to provide teachers (called functional foremen) to see that the workmen both understand and carry out these written instructions.

How Every Shop Becomes a School

Under functional management, the old-fashioned single foreman is superseded by eight different men, each one of whom has his own special duties, and these men, acting as the agents for the planning department, are the expert teachers, who are at all times in the shop, helping and directing the workmen. Being each one chosen for his knowledge and personal skill in his specialty, they are able not only to tell the workman what he should do, but in case of necessity they do the work themselves in the presence of the workman, so as to show him not only the best but also the quickest methods.

One of these teachers (called the inspector) sees to it that he understands the drawings and instructions for doing the work. He teaches him how to do work of the right quality; how to make it fine and exact where it should be fine and rough and quick where accuracy is not required—the one being just as important for success as the other. The second teacher (the gang boss) shows him how to set up the job in his machine, and teaches him to make all of his personal motions in the quickest and best way. The third (the speed boss) sees that the machine is run at the best speed and that the proper tool is used in the particular way which will enable the machine to finish its product in the shortest possible time. In addition to the assistance given by these teachers, the workmen receive orders and help from four other men: from the repair boss as to the adjustment, cleanliness and general care of his machine, belting, etc.; from the time clerk, as to everything relating to his pay and to proper written reports and returns; from the route clerk, as to the order in which he does his work and as to the movement of the work from one part of the shop to another; and, in case a workman gets into any trouble with any of his various bosses, the disciplinarian interviews him.

It must be understood, of course, that all workmen engaged on the same kind of work do not require the same amount of individual teaching and attention from the functional foremen. The men who are new at a given operation naturally require far more teaching and watching than those who have been a long time at the same kind of jobs.

DOES SCIENTIFIC MANAGEMENT DESTROY INITIATIVE?

Now, when through all of this teaching and this minute instruction the work is apparently made so smooth and easy for the workman, the first impression is that this all tends to make him a mere automaton, a wooden man. As the workmen frequently say when they first come under this system:

"Why, I am not allowed to think or move without someone interfering or doing it for me!"

The same criticism and objection, however, can be raised against all other modern subdivision of labor. It does not follow, for example, that the modern surgeon is any more narrow or wooden a man than the early settler of this country. The frontiersman, however, had to be not only a surgeon, but an architect, housebuilder, lumberman, farmer, soldier, and he had to settle his law cases with a gun. You would hardly say that the life of the modern surgeon is any more narrowing, or that he is more of a wooden man than the frontiersman. The many problems to be met and solved by the surgeon are just as intricate and difficult and as developing and broadening in their way as were those of the frontiersman.

And it should be remembered that the training of the surgeon has been almost identical in type with the teaching and training which is given to the workman under Scientific Management. The surgeon, all through his early years, is under the closest supervision of more experienced men, who show him in the minutest way how each element of his work is best done. They provide him with the finest implements, each one of which has been the subject of special study and development, and then insist upon his using those implements in the very best way. All of this teaching, however, in no way narrows the surgeon. On the contrary, he is quickly given the very best knowledge of his predecessors; and, provided as he is, right from the start, with standard implements and methods which represent the best knowledge of the world up to date, he starts at the very top of his profession, as it were, and is able to use his own originality and ingenuity to make real additions to the world's knowledge, instead of reinventing things which are old. In a similar way, the workman who is coöperating with his many teachers under Scientific Management has an opportunity to develop which is always as good and generally far better than that which he had when the whole problem was up to him and he did his work entirely unaided.

If it were true that the workman would develop into a larger and finer man without all of this teaching, and without the help of the laws which have been formulated for doing his particular job, then it would follow that the young man who now comes to college to have the help of a teacher in mathematics, physics, chemistry, Latin, Greek, etc., would do better to study these things unaided and by himself. The only difference in the two cases is that students come to their teachers, while from the nature of the work done by the mechanic under Scientific Management the teachers must go to him. What really happens is that, with the aid of the science which is invariably developed and through the instructions from his teachers, each workman of a given intellectual capacity is enabled to do a much higher more interesting and finally a more developing and more profitable kind of work than he was before able to do. The laborer who before was unable to do anything beyond, perhaps, shoveling and wheeling dirt from place to place, or carrying the work from one place to another in the shop, is in many cases taught to do the more elementary machinist's work, accompanied by the agreeable surroundings and the interesting variety and higher wages which go with the machinist's trade. The cheap machinist or helper, who before was able to run perhaps merely a drill press, is taught to do the more interesting and higher-priced lathe and planer work, while the highly skilled and more intelligent machinists become functional foremen and teachers. And so on, right up the line.

It may seem that with Scientific Management there is not the same incentive for the workman to use his ingenuity in devising new and better methods of doing the work, as well as in improving his implements, that there is with the old type of management. It is true that with Scientific Management the workman is not allowed to use whatever implements and methods he sees fit in the daily practice of his work. Every encouragement, however, should be given to him to suggest improvements, both in methods and in implements. And whenever a workman suggests an improvement, it should be the policy of the management to make a careful analysis of the new method, and if it is found to be markedly superior to the old, it should be adopted as the standard for the whole establishment. The workman should be given the full credit for the improvement, and should be paid a cash premium for the use of his ingenuity. In this way the true initiative of the workman can be better attained under Scientific Management than under the old individual plan.

A WORD OF WARNING

The history of the development of Scientific Management up to date, however, calls for a word of warning The mechanism of management must not be mistaken for the essence, or underlying philosophy, of management. The same mechanism which will produce the finest results when made to serve the underlying principles of Scientific Management will lead to failure and disaster if accompanied by the wrong spirit in those who are using it. Messrs. Gantt, Barth, and the writer have presented papers to the American Society of Mechanical Engineers on the subject of Scientific Management. In these papers, the mechanism which is used in Scientific Management has been described at some length. When, however, the elements of this mechanism, such as time-study, functional foremanship, the bonus system, etc., are used without being accompanied by the true philosophy of management, the results are in many cases disastrous.

The really great problem involved in a change from the management of "initiative and incentive" to Scientific Management consists in a complete revolution in the mental attitude and in the habits of all those engaged in the management, as well as of the workmen. And this change can only be brought about gradually and through the presentation of many object lessons to the workman, which, together with the teaching which he receives, thoroughly convince him of the superiority of the new over the old way of doing the work. This change in the mental attitude of the workman imperatively demands time. It is impossible to hurry it beyond a certain speed. The writer has over and over again warned those who contemplated making this change that it was a matter, even in a simple establishment, of from two to three years, and that in some cases it extends to from four to five years.

The first few changes which affect the workmen should be made exceedingly slowly, and only one workman at a time should be dealt with at the start. Until this single man has been thoroughly convinced that a great gain has come to him from the new method, no further change should be made. Then one man after another should be tactfully changed over. After passing the point at which from one fourth to one third of the men in the employ of the company have been changed from the old to the new, very rapid progress can be made, because at about this point there is, generally, a complete revolution in the public opinion of the whole establishment, and practically all of the workmen who are working under the old system become desirous to share in the benefits which they see have been received by those working under the new plan.

Inasmuch as the writer has personally retired from the business of introducing this system of management (that is from all work done in return for any money compensation), he does not hesitate again to emphasize the fact that those companies are indeed fortunate who can secure the services of experts who have had the necessary practical experience in introducing Scientific Management, and who have made a special study of its principles. It is not enough that a man should have been a manager in an establishment which is run under this type of management. The man who undertakes to direct the steps which are to be taken in changing from the old to the new (particularly in any establishment doing elaborate work) must have had personal experience in overcoming the especial difficulties which are peculiar to this period of transition. It is for this reason that the writer expects to devote the rest of his life chiefly to trying to help those who wish to take up this work as their profession, and to advising the managers and owners of companies in general as to the steps which they should take in making this change.

A FAILURE CAUSED BY HASTE

As a warning to those who contemplate adopting Scientific Management, the following instance is given. Several men who lacked the necessary experience attempted to increase rapidly the output in quite an elaborate establishment, employing between three and four thousand men. Those who undertook to make this change were men of unusual ability, and were at the same time enthusiastic, and had the interests of the workmen truly at heart. They were, however, warned by the writer before starting that they must go exceedingly slow, and that the work of making the change in this establishment could not be done in less than from three to five years. This warning they entirely disregarded. They evidently believed that, by using much of the mechanism of Scientific Management, they could do, in a year or two, what had been proved in the past to require at least double this time. The knowledge obtained from accurate time-study, for example, is a powerful implement, and can be used, in one case to promote harmony between the workmen and the management, by gradually leading, educating, and training the work-men into new and better methods of doing the work; or, in the other case, it may be used more or less as a club to drive the workmen into doing a larger day's work for approximately the same pay that they received in the past. Unfortunately, the men who had charge of this work did not take the time and the trouble required to train functional foremen, or teachers, who were fitted to lead and educate the workmen gradually. They attempted, through the old-style foreman, armed with his new weapon (accurate time-study), to drive the workmen, against their wishes and without much increase in pay, to work much harder, instead of gradually teaching and leading them toward new methods and convincing them through object lessons that task man-agement means for them somewhat harder work, but also far greater pros-perity. The result of all this disregard of fundamental principles was a series of strikes, followed by the downfall of the men who attempted to make the change, and by a return to conditions throughout the establishment far worse than those which existed before the effort was made.

NEVER A STRIKE AMONG WORKMEN

In this connection, however, it is proper to state again that during the thirty years that we have been engaged in introducing Scientific Management there has not been a single strike among men working in accordance with its principles, even during the critical time when the change was being made from the old to the new. If proper methods are used by men who have had experience in this work, there is absolutely no danger from strikes or labor troubles.

The writer would also insist that in no case should the managers of an establishment, the work of which is elaborate, undertake to change from the old to the new type unless the directors of the company fully understand and believe in the fundamental principles of Scientific Management and unless they appreciate all that is involved in making this change, particularly the time required.

It will doubtless be claimed that in all that has been said no new fact has been brought to light that was not known to someone in the past. Very likely that is true. Scientific Management does not necessarily involve any great invention, nor the discovery of new or startling facts. It does, however, involve a certain *combination* of elements which have not existed in the past.

It is no single element, but rather this whole combination, that constitutes Scientific Management, which may be summarized as:

Science, not rule of thumb.

Harmony, not discord.

Cooperation, not individualism.

Maximum output, in place of restricted output.

The development of each man to his greatest efficiency and prosperity.

WHERE THE VALUE COMES IN

Let us now examine the good which would follow the general adoption of these principles.

The principal profit would come to the whole world at large.

The general adoption of Scientific Management would readily in the future double the productivity of the average man engaged in industrial work. Think of what this means to the whole country! Think of the increase, both in the necessities and luxuries of life, which becomes available for the whole country, of the possibility of shortening the hours of work when this is desirable, and of the increased opportunities for education, culture, and recreation which this implies!

But while the whole world would profit by this increase in production, the manufacturer and the workman will be far more interested in the especial local gain that comes to them and to the people immediately around them. Scientific Management will mean, for the employers and the workmen who adopt it—and particularly for those who adopt it first—the elimination of almost all causes for dispute and disagreement between them. What constitutes a fair day's work will be a question for scientific investigation, instead of a subject to be bargained and haggled over. Soldiering will cease, because the object for soldiering no longer exists. The large increase in wages which accompanies this type of management will largely eliminate the wage question as a source of dispute. But more than all other causes, the close, intimate coöperation, the constant personal contact between the two sides, will tend to diminish friction and discontent. It is difficult for two people whose interests are the same, and who work side by side in accomplishing the same object all day long, to keep up a quarrel.

The low cost of production which accompanies a doubling of the output will enable the companies who adopt this management particularly those who adopt it first, to compete far better than they were able to before, and this will so enlarge their markets that their men will have almost constant work even in dull times, and that they will earn larger profits at all times.

As one of the elements incident to this great gain in output, each workman has been systematically trained to his highest state of efficiency, and has been taught to do a higher class of work than he was able to do under the old types of management; and at the same time, he has acquired a friendly mental attitude toward his employers and his whole working conditions, whereas before a considerable part of his time was spent in criticism, suspicious watchfulness, and sometimes in open warfare. This direct gain to all of those working under the system is without doubt the most important single element in the whole problem.

Is not the realization of results such as these of far more importance than the solution of most of the problems which are now agitating both the English and American peoples? And is it not our duty to exert ourselves to make the whole community realize their importance?

The Principles of Scientific Management

A criticism by Upton Sinclair and an answer by Frederick W. Taylor

A Letter by Upton Sinclair

February 24, 1911.

Editor, The American Magazine: I have been reading with a great deal of interest the first installment of Mr. Frederick W. Taylor's account of "Scientific Management." He tells us how workingmen were loading twelve and a half tons of pig iron and he induced them to load forty-seven tons instead. They had formerly been getting $1.15; he paid them $1.85. Thus it appears that he gave about 61 percent increase in wages, and got 362 percent increase in work. I shall not soon forget the picture which he gave us of the poor old laborer who was trying to build his pitiful little home after hours, and who was induced to give 362 percent more service for 61 percent more pay. I wonder how Mr. Taylor and his colleagues arrived at the latter figure. He tells us just how by scientific figuring he learned that the man could lift forty-seven pound of pig iron, but he does not tell us by what scientific figuring he arrived at the conclusion that he should receive $1.85 for the work, instead of, let us say, $2.85. Can it by any chance be that he figured upon this basis?—The workingmen of the steel plant are at present producing $1,000 worth of value and getting $168; therefore, if we can induce them to produce 362 percent more, they would then receive 16.8 percent of the additional increase. I believe that those members of the working class who read *The American Magazine* would be interested to know just what proportion they get of the value they produce under the old system, and what proportion they are to get under the new "scientific" system.

Also, I want to put a few more questions in elementary political economy to Mr. Taylor. He tells us we have no need to worry because seven men out of eight are turned out of their jobs by the new system, because there are plenty of jobs for them in other parts of the plant. Is that really so? And is it so everywhere? If so, then the phenomenon of overproduction is just a delusion of our captains of industry, and there is no real reason for panics. Our scientific managers will increase the total product of the country's machinery 362 percent; they will have 362 times as many products to market—where will they find the markets for the additional products? When they have taught one fourth of the workingmen to do the work of all the workingmen, is it their plan to organize the remaining three fourths into armies, and send them out to conquer new foreign markets? Or will they find a new world for them to build up?

I, as you may perhaps know, am one of those Utopian persons who do not believe that the working class of America will forever consent to produce $1,000 worth of value and get $168 in return. I believe that the time will come when they will take possession of the instruments and means of production, in order that when they produce $1,000 in value they may receive $1,000 in wages. Let me suggest to Mr. Taylor and his other experts, whose pictures you publish, what is the really great problem of Scientific Management in our time. Let them set themselves down to figure how the ninety million people residing in the United States of America, and being in full communal ownership and democratic control of the instruments and means of production and distribution, can so organize and administer these instruments and means as to produce the greatest quantity of necessary wealth with the least possible expenditure of labor. Let some one of them write another great work, setting forth just how they would arrange for industries, just how much labor they would have to perform, and just how many hours per day would be necessary, to produce a standard income of, say, $5,000 a year for each family. And when they have written this book, let them publish it, not at five dollars per volume, but at fifty cents per volume, and I can guarantee them that they will sell, not ten thousand copies, but one or two million.

UPTON SINCLAIR

AN ANSWER TO THE CRITICISM BY FREDERICK W. TAYLOR

Doubtless some of those who, like Mr. Upton Sinclair, are especially interested in workingmen will complain because under Scientific Management the workman when he is shown how to do twice as much work as he formerly did is not paid twice his former wages, while others who are more interested in the dividends than the workmen will complain that under this system the men receive much higher wages than they did before.

It does seem grossly unjust when the bare statement is made that the competent pig-iron handler, for instance, who has been so trained that he piles three and six tenths times as much iron as the incompetent man formerly did, should receive an increase of only 60 percent in his wages.

It is not fair, however, to form any final judgment until all of the elements in the case have been considered. Mr. Sinclair sees but one man—the workman. He refuses to see that the great increase in output under Scientific Management is the result not only of the workman's effort but quite as much also of the study of pig-iron handling by the management and of the coöperation of teachers who help him and the organization which plans and measures his daily tasks, etc., and that all of this extra work on the part of the management, as well as the proper profit of the latter, must be paid for out of the increase in output. At the first glance most of us, in fact, will see only two parties to the transaction, the workmen and their employers. We overlook the third great party—the whole people—the consumers, who buy the product of the first two and who ultimately pay both the wages of the workmen and the profits of the employers.

The rights of the people are therefore greater than those of either employer or employee. And this third great party should be given its proper share of any gain. In fact, a glance at industrial history shows that in the end the whole people receive the greater part of the benefit coming from all industrial improvements. In the past hundred years, for example, the greatest factor tending toward increasing the output, and thereby the prosperity, of the civilized world has been the introduction of machinery to replace hand labor. And without doubt the greatest gain through this change has come to the whole people—the consumer.

Through short periods, especially in the case of patented apparatus, the dividends of those who have introduced new machinery have been greatly increased, and in most cases, though unfortunately not universally, the employees have obtained materially higher wages, shorter hours, and better working conditions. But in the end the major part of the gain has gone to the whole people.

And this result will follow the introduction of Scientific Management just as surely as it has the introduction of machinery.

To return to the case of the pig-iron handler. We must assume then that the larger part of the gain which has come from his great increase in output will in the end go to the people in the form of cheaper pig iron. And before deciding upon how the balance is to be divided between the workman and the employer—namely, as to what is just and fair compensation for the man who does the piling and what should be left for the company as profit—we must look at the matter from all sides.

First: As we have before stated, the pig-iron handler is not an extraordinary man difficult to find; he is merely a man more or less of the type of the ox, heavy both mentally and physically.

Second: The work which this man does tires him no more than any healthy normal laborer is tired by a proper day's work. (If this man is overtired by his work, then the task has been wrongly set, and this is as far as possible from the object of Scientific Management.)

Third: It was not due to this man's initiative or originality that he did his big day's work, but to the knowledge of pig-iron handling developed and taught him by some one else.

Fourth: It is just and fair that men of the same general grade (when their all-round capacities are considered) should be paid about the same wages when they are all working to the best of their abilities. (It would be grossly unjust to other laborers, for instance, to pay this man three and six tenths as high wages as other men of his general grade receive for an honest full day's work.)

Fifth: A long series of experiments, coupled with close observation, has demonstrated the fact that when workmen of the caliber of the pig-iron handler are given a carefully measured task, which calls for a big day's work on their part, and that when in return for this extra effort they are paid wages up to 60 percent beyond the wages usually paid, that this increase in wages tends to make them not only more thrifty but better men in every way; that they live rather better, begin to save money, become more sober, and work more steadily. When, on the other hand they receive much more than a 60 percent increase in wages, many of them will work irregularly and tend to become more or less shiftless, extravagant and dissipated. Our experiments showed, in other words, that for their own best interest it does not do for most men to get rich too fast.

Thus we see that the pig-iron handler with his 60 percent increase in wages is not an object for pity, but rather a subject for congratulation.

After all, however, facts are in many cases more convincing than opinions or theories and it is a significant fact that those workmen who have come under Scientific Management during the past thirty years have invariably been satisfied with the increase in pay which they have received, while their employers have been equally pleased with their increase in dividends.

The writer is one of those who believes that more and more will the third party (the whole people), as it becomes acquainted with the true facts, insist that justice shall be done to all three parties. First, it will demand the largest efficiency from both employers and employees. It will no longer tolerate the type of employer who has his eye on dividends alone, who refuses to do his full share of the work, and who merely cracks his whip over the heads of his workmen and attempts to drive them into harder work for low pay. No more will it tolerate tyranny on the part of labor which demands one increase after another in pay and shorter hours while at the same time it becomes less instead of more efficient.

And the means which the writer firmly believes will be adopted to bring about, first, efficiency both in employer and employee and then an equitable division of the profits of their joint efforts, will be Scientific Management, which has for its sole aim the attainment of justice for all three parties through impartial scientific investigation of all the elements of the problem. For a time both sides will rebel against this advance. The workers will resent any interference with their old rule-of-thumb methods, and the management will resent being asked to take on new duties and burdens; but in the end the people, through enlightened public opinion, will force the new order of things upon both employer and employee.

Those who, like Mr. Sinclair, are afraid that a large increase in the productivity of each workman will throw other men out of work, should realize that the one element more than any other which differentiates civilized from uncivilized countries—prosperous from poverty-stricken peoples—is that the average man in the one is five or six times as productive as in the other. It is also a fact that the chief cause for the large percentage of the unemployed in England (perhaps the most virile nation in the world) is that the workmen of England, more than in any other civilized country, are deliberately restricting their output because they are possessed by the fallacy that it is against their best interest for each man to work as hard as he can.

FREDERICK W. TAYLOR

STRUCTURING THE BILL OF MATERIAL FOR MRP

JOSEPH A. ORLICKY, GEORGE W. PLOSSL,
OLIVER W. WIGHT

INTRODUCTION

An important distinction between Order Point systems and Material Requirements Planning systems lies in the fact that the order point/order quantity approach is *part based* whereas MRP is *product oriented*. Order Point views each inventory item independently of all the others, whereas MRP looks at the product and the relationships of its components, using bills of material as the basis for planning.

MRP puts the bill of material to a whole new use. Under MRP, the bill acquires a new function, in addition to serving as part of the product specs. It becomes a framework on which the whole planning system hangs.

Often, however, the bill of material furnished by the engineering department is not necessarily *usable* for material requirements planning. As a key input to an MRP system, the bill of material must be accurate and up-to-date if MRP outputs are to be valid. But in addition it must be unambiguous and so structured as to *lend* itself to MRP. The mere existence of a bill of material is no guarantee that MRP will actually work.

To understand the reason for this, we must remember that the bill of material is basically an engineering document. Historically, the function of the bill of material has been to define the product from the design point of view and from the design point of view only. But now, because we want to use the bill of material for purposes of material planning, we must redefine the product from the manufacturing and planning point of view. Proper product definition is crucial to a planning system such as MRP, which directly depends on it, *unlike* an order point system.

Reprinted by permission from *Production and Inventory Management*, 13:4 (1972): 19–42.

People usually think of bills of material, and of MRP as being applicable only in hard goods manufacturing. But businesses that *mix* component materials, *sew* them together, *package* them, etc., can also use material requirements planning to advantage. Companies in the garment industry, pharmaceutical houses, batch chemical manufacturers, and others, all have bills of material except they call them by different names—material lists, formulations, specifications, etc.

With MRP, the prime input to the whole system is the master production schedule. The product must be defined in such a way as to make it possible to put a valid master schedule together in terms of bill of material numbers; i.e., assembly numbers. If the overall plan of production—and that is what the master schedule is—cannot be stated in terms of bills of material, it is not possible to do material requirements planning successfully.

The master schedule and the structure of the bill of material must be thought of together, when an MRP system is being developed. The bills of material and the master schedule must *fit together* like lock and key. If these are not compatible, nothing turns. Neither is there any guarantee that an MRP system can function properly just because the bill may already have been organized and loaded onto a computer file under a Bill of Material Processor program. This type of software will load practically anything onto a disk file, including straight engineering parts lists, which are not much good for purposes of material requirements planning. The functions of a bill processor are merely to organize, maintain, and retrieve bill of material data. A Bill of Material Processor is not designed to *structure* the bill. It assumes that the bill is already properly structured to serve the user's needs.

The intent of the discussion that follows is to clarify the subject of bill of material *structuring*, so that it will not be confused with bill of material *file organization* under a bill processor.

In most instances, companies planning to implement MRP will be wise to review their bills of material, to determine whether certain changes in the structure of this file data may have to be made, and of what kind. In reviewing the bill for this purpose, the following seven-point checklist will help in spotting its structural deficiencies.

1. *The bill should lend itself to the forecasting of optional product features.* This capability is essential for purposes of material requirements planning.
2. *The bill should permit the master schedule to be stated in the fewest possible number of end items.* These end items will be products or major assemblies, as the case may be, but in either case they must be stated in terms of bill of material numbers.
3. *The bill should lend itself to the planning of subassembly priorities.* Orders for subassemblies have to be released at the right time, and with valid due dates.

4. *The bill should permit easy order entry.* It should be possible to take a customer order that describes the product either in terms of a model number, or as a configuration of optional features, and translate it into the language that the MRP system understands: bill of material numbers.
5. *The bill should be usable for purposes of final assembly scheduling.* Apart from MRP, the final assembly scheduling system needs to know, specifically, which assemblies (assembly numbers) are required to build individual units of the end product.
6. *The bill should provide the basis for product costing.*
7. *The bill should lend itself to efficient computer file storage and file maintenance.*

When, in a given case, these yardsticks are applied to the existing bill of material, it will usually be found that some, but not all, of the above requirements can be satisfied. If that is the case, changes in bill of material structure are called for. This can and should be done. While the bill still must serve its primary purpose of providing product specifications, it should not be regarded as a sacrosanct document that must not be tampered with. The bill may have to be modified, or *restructured*, as required for purposes of material requirements planning. This can be done without affecting the integrity of the specs.

The severity of the bill of material structure problem varies from company to company, depending on the complexity of product and nature of the business. The term "bill of material structuring" covers a variety of *types* of changes to the bill, and several different techniques for effecting these changes.

The topics that make up the subject of bill of material structuring, as reviewed in this article, can be categorized as follows:

1. *Assignment of identities*
   a. Elimination of ambiguity
   b. Levels of manufacture
2. *Modular bill of material*
   a. Disentangling product option combinations
   b. Segregating common from unique parts.
3. *Pseudo-bills of material*

IDENTIFICATION OF MATERIALS AND THEIR RELATIONSHIPS

There are several principles involved here. First, the requirement that each individual item of inventory covered by the MRP system be uniquely identified. This includes raw materials and subassemblies.

The assignment of subassembly identities tends to be somewhat arbitrary. Among the design engineer, the industrial engineer, the cost accountant, and the inventory planner, each might prefer to assign them differently. The question is: When do unique subassembly numbers have to be assigned? In reality, it is not the design of the product but the way it is being manufactured; i.e., assembled, that dictates the assignment of subassembly identities.

The unit of work, or task, is the key here. If a number of components are assembled at a bench and then are forwarded as a completed task, to storage or to another bench for further assembly, a subassembly number is required so that orders for these subassemblies can be generated and their priorities planned. An MRP system will do this, but only for items with individual identities.

Some engineering departments are stingy in assigning new part numbers, and we often see the classic example of this in a raw casting that has the same part number as the finished casting. This may suit the engineer, but it is difficult to see how an automated inventory system such as MRP is supposed to distinguish between the two types of items that must be planned and controlled separately.

The second requirement is that an identifying number define the *contents* of the item uniquely, unambiguously. Thus the same subassembly number must not be used to define two or more different sets of components. This sometimes happens when the original design of a product subsequently becomes subject to variation. Instead of creating a new bill with its own unique identity, the old one is specified with instructions to substitute, remove, and add certain components. This shortcut method, called "add and delete," represents a vulnerable procedure, undesirable for MRP. We will come back to it in a later example.

The third requirement is that the bill of material should reflect the way material flows in and out of stock. "Stock" here does not necessarily mean "stockroom" but rather a *state of completion*. Thus when a piecepart is finished or a subassembly is completed, it is considered to be "on hand"; i.e., in stock, until withdrawn and associated with an order for a higher level item as its component. An MRP system is constructed in such a way that it assumes that each inventory item flows into and out of stock at its respective level in the product structure. MRP also assumes that the bill of material accurately reflects this flow.

Thus the bill of material is expected to specify not only the *composition* of a product but also the *process stages* in that product's manufacture. The bill must define the product structure, in terms of so-called *levels of manufacture*, each of which represents the completion of a step in the buildup of the product.

A schematic representation of product structure is shown in Figure 1. The structure defines the relationship among the various items that make up

FIGURE 1

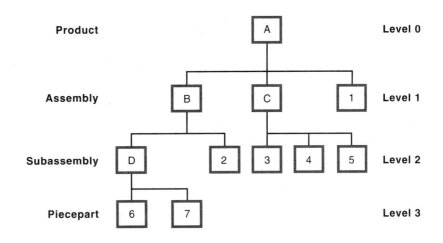

the product in terms of levels, as well as the parent item/component item relationships. These things are vital for material requirements planning because they establish, in conjunction with lead times, the precise *timing* of requirements, order releases, and order priorities.

The product represented by Figure 1 has four levels of manufacture. The end product is designated, by convention, as being at level zero, its immediate components as being at level one, etc. The parent/component relationships depicted in the example indicate that "A" is the parent of component "C" (also of "B" and "1"). Item "C," in turn, is the parent of component "3," etc. Thus "A" is the only item that is not also a component. Items "B," "C," and "D" are both parents (of their components at the next lower level) and components (of their parent items at the next higher level). Items "1" through "7" are components but never parents.

This would be true if all of the pieceparts were purchased. If item "6," however, is manufactured from raw material "X," then it becomes a parent in relationship to this component material. Thus the distinction between parent item and component item appears not only in assembly but also in the conversion of material for a single part from one stage of manufacture to another.

This also applies to semi-finished items that are stocked (in the sense described earlier) and that are to be controlled by the MRP system. The raw material, the semi-finished item, and the finished item must be uniquely identified; i.e., must have different part numbers.

People are sometimes reluctant to assign different identities to semi-finished and finished items, where the conversion to the finished stage is of minor nature. A good example is a die casting that is machined and then painted one of four different colors, as shown in Figure 2. The four varieties of painted casting will have to be assigned separate identities if they are to be ordered, and their order priorities planned, by the MRP system.

This is an example of a situation where item identity (of the painted casting) would normally not exist, but would have to be established prerequisite to MRP, because otherwise such items would fall outside the scope of the system and loss of control would result.

Another example of an item identity problem that is almost the opposite is the transient subassembly, sometimes called a "blow-through" or "phantom." Assemblies of this type never see a stockroom, because they are immediately consumed in the assembly of their parent items. An example of this is a subassembly built on a feeder line that flows directly into the main assembly line. Here the subassembly normally carries a separate identity. Because it is recognized in the bill of material, the MRP system would treat it the same as any other subassembly.

This may be undesirable, because if this kind of item is to be planned under an MRP system, we must remember that the logic of MRP assumes that each component item goes in and out of stock. That is the way the basic time-phased record is designed and updated. So the question arises as to how to handle such subassemblies within an MRP system. MRP users have worked out techniques to deal with this situation. People often wonder whether this type of assembly should be identified in the bill at all.

FIGURE 2

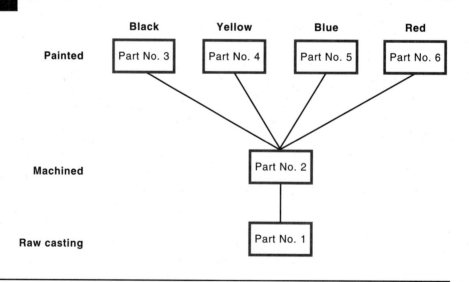

The phantom does not require separate identity in the bill of material, provided there is never

1. An overrun,
2. A service part demand,
3. A customer return.

Otherwise, it must be separately identified in the bill and item records (stock status) must be maintained. This is so because overruns, service demand, and returns create a need to stock material, and to control it. But then the MRP user would have to report all transactions for the phantom subassemblies, so that the system can post these and keep the records up-to-date. This seems like unnecessary effort and paperwork in the case of order releases and order completions.

Fortunately, there is no need to do this. A technique called the "phantom bill" eliminates the need for posting such transactions for these items. (This technique is used, for instance, by the Black & Decker Manufacturing Company, a skilled MRP user.) Using this technique, it is possible to have your cake and eat it too. While transactions of the type mentioned do not have to be reported and posted, the MRP system will pick up and use any phantom items that may happen to be on hand. Service part requirements can also be centered into the record and will be correctly handled by the system. But otherwise MRP will, in effect, bypass the phantom item's record and go from its parent item to its components directly.

To describe the application of this technique, let's assume that assembly "A" has a transient subassembly "B" as one of its components, and part "C" is a component of "B." Thus, for purposes of illustration, item "B," the phantom, is envisioned as being sandwiched between "A," its parent, and "C," its component.

To implement this technique, the phantom item is treated as follows:

1. Lead time is specified as zero.
2. Lot sizing is discrete (lot for lot).
3. The bill of material (or the item record) is coded, so that the system can recognize that it is a phantom and apply special treatment.

The special treatment referred to above means departing from regular procedure, or record update logic, when processing the phantom record. The difference between the procedures can best be described through examples.

In Figure 3, inventory status data for items "A" (top), "B" (middle), and "C" (bottom) are shown. Note that the zero lead time offset on the item in

FIGURE 3

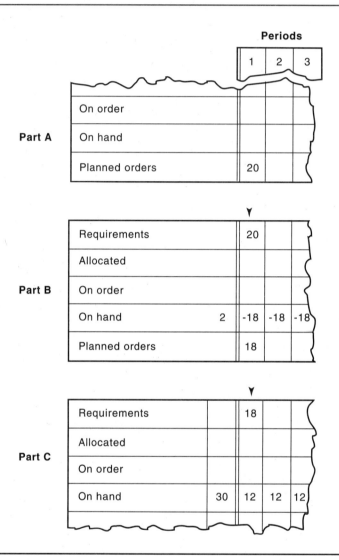

the middle places the planned order release for 18 pieces in the same period as the net requirement. This, in turn, corresponds to the requirement for 18 "C"s in the same period.

Following the release of the planned order for "A," the update procedure for item record "B" will vary, depending on whether it is coded as a phantom. In the absence of such a code, regular logic applies. The regularly updated records of "A" and "B" are shown in Figure 4. Record "C" continues unchanged. Following the release of the planned order for "B," item record "C" is updated, as shown in Figure 5.

Had item "B" been coded as a phantom, all three records would have been updated in one step, as shown in Figure 6, as a result of the planned order release of item "A." Note that the release of planned order "A," which normally would reduce only the corresponding requirement "B" (as in Figure 4), in this case reduces also the requirement for "C," *as though "C" were a direct component of "A."*

Note also that the two pieces of "B" in stock (perhaps a return from a previous overrun) are applied to the requirement for "A," and that the allocation has been *distributed* between "B" and "C." Upon closer examination

---

FIGURE 4

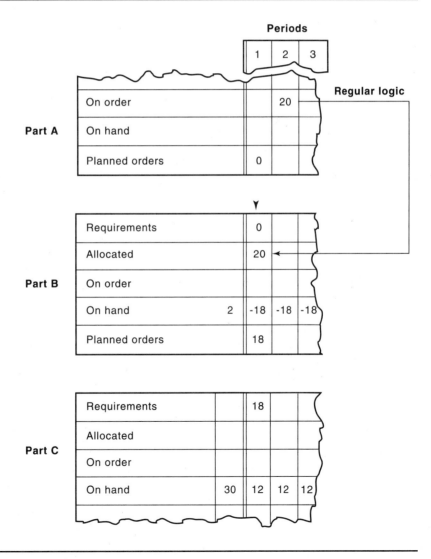

FIGURE 5

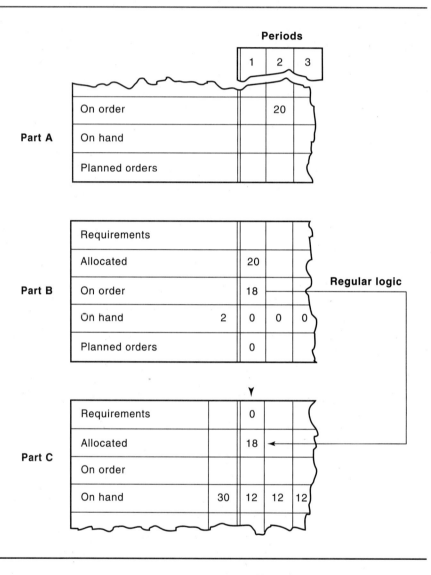

of these examples it will be seen that the phantom logic is nothing more than a different treatment of *allocation.* (Zero lead time and discrete lot sizing are assumed. These can, however, be specified for non-phantom subassemblies also.) Once this step is carried out, regular logic applies, causing the records to be updated and their data aligned, in the correct manner.

The objective of not having to post phantom transactions still remains, however, and it can be achieved by, again, setting lead time to zero, specifying discrete lot sizing, and coding the phantom item so that notices for planned order releases are either suppressed or flagged to be disregarded. The MRP system will function correctly.

The problem then becomes one of component requisitioning (for the phantom parent order) and it must be solved by modifying the requisition generating procedure. When some phantom items are on hand, *two* requisitions will have to be generated:

1. One for the quantity of the phantom on hand.
2. One for the balance of the order; for the phantom's components.

In the Figure 6 example, these quantities are 2 and 18, respectively.

MODULAR BILLS OF MATERIAL

The term "bill of material structuring" is most commonly used in reference to modularizing the bill of material file. The process of modularizing consists of *breaking down* the bills of high-level items (products, end items) and *reorganizing* them into product modules. There are two, somewhat different, objectives in modularizing the bill:

1. To disentangle combinations of optional product features.
2. To segregate common from unique, or peculiar, parts.

The first is required to facilitate forecasting, or, in some cases, to make it possible at all under the MRP approach. The second has as its goal to minimize inventory investment in components common to optional units which must be forecast and thus make it necessary to carry safety stock. We will deal separately with each of these two objectives, and the techniques used to achieve them.

The question probably most frequently asked by people interested in MRP is what to do with the bill of material to handle product variations. Under MRP, these product variations, or optional features, must be forecast at the master schedule level, that is to say, we must be able to forecast end items rather than their individual components, as we do under Order Point. If a product has many optional features, their combinations can be astronomical and forecasting them becomes impossible. Furthermore, if separate bills of material were to be set up for each of the unique end products that it is possible to build, the file would be enormous—too costly to store and maintain. Not only that. A valid master schedule could not even be put together, using such bills, for the MRP system to explode.

The solution to this problem is the modular bill of material. Instead of maintaining bills for individual end products, under this approach the bill of

FIGURE 6

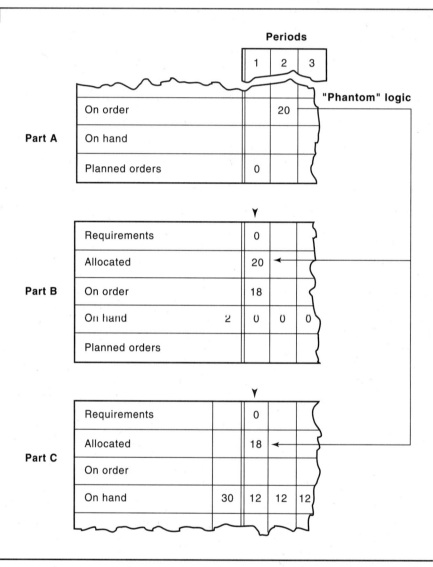

material is restated in terms of the building blocks, or modules, from which the final product is put together. The problem, and its solution, can best be demonstrated on an example. Figure 7 represents a familiar product, a hoist that is used to handle material in a factory.

The hoist manufacturer offers his customers a number of options, in this case 10 motors, 30 drums, 4 gear boxes, and 2 pendants (the hook assembly is standard), from which a customer configurates the specific hoist he wants. Figure 8 shows the schematic product structure of this family of hoists. By

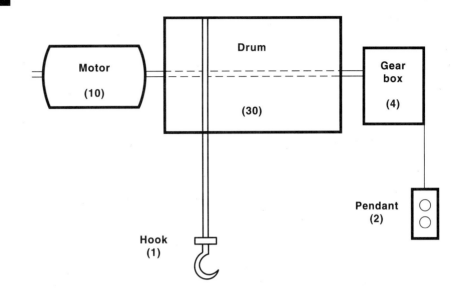

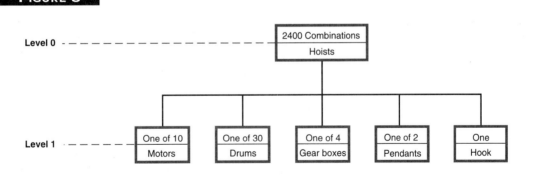

assembling the optional features in various combinations, it is possible to build 2,400 models; i.e., 2,400 unique configurations.

Assuming we manufacture this product and wish to implement MRP, the question is what to do with the bill of material. We can see clearly how to write a bill of material for each of the 2,400 molds, but we certainly would not want to carry all those bills. Consider this: There is only one variety of hook on this product, but the engineers are probably working on that. If they introduce just one more option, a choice between two hooks, the number of possible configurations will *double* from 2,400 to 4,800, and another 2,400 bills would have to be added to the file.

That is one reason we do not want to set up bills for the end products themselves. But aside from this consideration, with all those bills we would not know how to develop a master schedule showing a quantity of each model needed in specific time periods.

Suppose we produce 100 hoists per month. Which 100 out of 2,400 should we select as a forecast for a particular month? This is clearly an impossible situation. Note that *volume* is part of the problem here. A product family with 100 models is a problem if volume is 20 per month. If volume were 10,000 per month, the forecasting problem would not be nearly as serious.

The solution here is to forecast each of the highest-level *components* (i.e., major assembly units) separately, and not to try to forecast the end products at all. That way, we would forecast each of the ten different motor variations, the thirty drum sizes, the four types of gear box, and the two types of pendant.

Specifically, since we only have one hook assembly and want to make 100 hoists during a month, we will need 100 hooks. This quantity would appear in the master schedule, and a bill of material for this "module" would be required to match the schedule. But we have two types of pendant. From previous sales of this product we know that, let us say, 75 percent of the orders call for type "A" and 25 percent for type "B." Applying these percentages to the pendant option, we could schedule 75 "As" and 25 "Bs." But here we would probably want some safety stock, because the batch of 100 customer orders in any one month is unlikely to break down exactly 75 percent and 25 percent.

The proper way to handle safety stock under material requirements planning is to plan it at the master schedule level. Thus, instead of scheduling 75 percent and 25 percent of the pendants we would deliberately overplan and put, let us say, 90 and 30 into the master schedule. (This would not be done in every period; the unused safety stock is rolled forward.) The same approach would be followed for the motor option, the drum option, and the gear box option.

Each of the options, or *modules*, would have to have a bill of material, for use by the MRP system. Under this approach, the total number of bills of materials—and the things to forecast—would be as follows:

Motors	10
Pendants	2
Drums	30
Hook	1
Gear Boxes	4
Total	47

This total of 47 compares with 2,400 if each product model had a bill of its own. If the engineers add a second variety of hook, this would only add one more bill to the 47, instead of doubling the file.

At this point, the reader may be wondering how this type of problem is being handled in a real life situation, if the manufacturer *does not* have the bills set up in modular form. Chances are that there would be several bills, for *some* of the 2,400 configurations, and they would be used for everything by adding and subtracting optional components. Quite a few companies use this "add-and-delete" technique as a solution to the problem we have discussed.

This technique solves some but not all of the problems. Its main disadvantages are vulnerability to human error, slowing down Order Entry, but mainly, failure to establish the proper historical data for option forecasting purposes. Under this approach, the company would most likely use order points and safety stock on the "add-and-delete" components. That would be highly undesirable because it would deprive the user of some important benefits of an MRP system.

But suppose we *have* a certain number of bills for end products, and we want to restructure them in a modular fashion, so we can get away from adding and deleting. How do we go about such restructuring, specifically? We will demonstrate this on the next example. For this purpose, we have to scale down the previous example somewhat, so the solution can be seen clearly. Let us assume that the product has only *two* optional features, the motor and the drum, each with only two choices. The customer can then select between motor #1 and motor #2, and between drum "A" and drum "B."

Figure 9 represents the four bills of material: the first combines motor #1 with drum "A," the second one, motor #1 with drum "B," etc. In the product structure, the end product (model) numbers, 12-4010 etc., are considered to be on level zero. The level-one components, A13, C41, etc., may represent assemblies, but their components are not shown on the chart, so as not to make it too busy.

To restructure these bills into modules, we break them down, analyze and compare the use of level-1 items, and group them by use. For example, we see that the first component in the first bill, A13, is common to all products, and assign it to the *Common* group. The next item, C41, is found in #1-A and #1B combinations but not in #2-A and #2-B, which indicates that it is *unique to motor option #1*. The item that follows, L40, is *used only with drum option "A."* The remaining component items are similarly examined and assigned to groups. The result is shown in Figure 10.

Note, in Figure 10, that the last level-1 component item, D14, does not fit into any of the groupings. When all of the bills are broken down this way and their level-1 components are grouped by option, items D14, H23, J39, and N44 in our example remain unassigned, because each of them is used only with one or the other of the option *combinations*. Here we must carry the process one step further; i.e., break down these items, as shown in Figure 11, and assign *their* (level-2) components to the groupings by option.

FIGURE 9

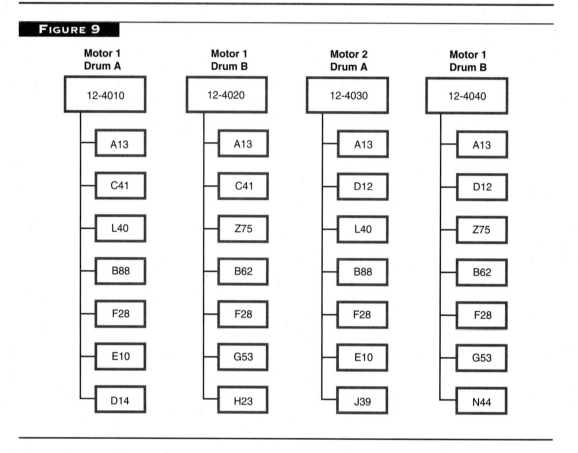

The final result is represented by Figure 12, where all of the items involved in our example are grouped into the respective modules.

In our case, we solved the entire problem through the technique of breakdown and group assignment. But if items D14, H23, etc. had not been subassemblies but pieceparts, we would not have been able to break them down. In a case like that, the part that is used only with a certain combination of options should, if possible, be redesigned, particularly if it is an expensive item.

Low-cost items of this type need not be reengineered, because we can afford to overplan them and carry some excess inventory. In the modularizing process, such parts can simply be assigned to more than one grouping. For example, item D14 (Figure 9) could be duplicated in both #1 and "A" modules (Figure 12), ensuring that it would never be planned short. Another solution, of course, is to forecast (and overforecast) the option combinations for purposes of ordering this type of component.

Let us recap what we have done with the example under discussion, up to this point. We have *abolished* the end product numbers and we have done away

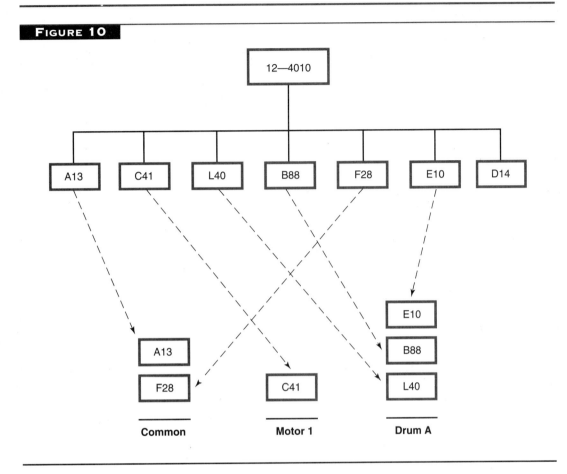

FIGURE 10

with their bills of material as unnecessary for purposes of MRP. Where the final product formerly served as the end item in the bill of material, we have now *promoted* level-1 items (and in one case, level-2 items) to end item status.

This procedure established a new, modular *planning bill* suitable for forecasting, master scheduling, and material requirements planning. The job of restructuring is not finished, however. The former level-1 items, D14, H23, etc., that are excluded from the planning bill cannot simply be abolished. These items will eventually have to be assembled, and the production control system has to be able to place orders for these items, schedule them, and requisition their components. These bills must therefore be retained for the purposes just mentioned.

This represents another technique of bill of material structuring: the establishment of *manufacturing bills,* or *M-bills,* which together constitute the M-bill file. These bills are coded to distinguish them from planning bills, so

FIGURE 11

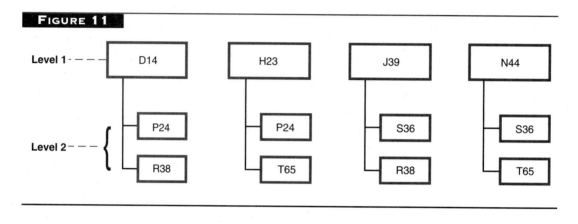

FIGURE 12

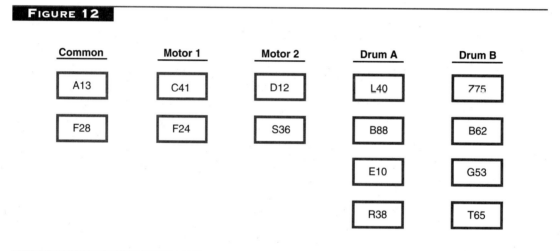

that the MRP system will, in effect, bypass them. M-bills are not involved in the process of component requirements planning. They are used for purposes of assembly only. M-items are built against the final assembly schedule, usually to customer order (or warehouse order), using the components planned through MRP.

The principle involved here is that in modularizing the bill of material at whatever level, *end product bills (level-0) can be abolished entirely but not any bills formerly on level-1 or lower*. These must be segregated in the M-bill file and retained for purposes of ordering, scheduling, costing, etc. Specifying options in Order Entry (or in scheduling a warehouse order) will call out and reconstruct the proper bills for individual end products, but not for lower level assemblies that have been removed from the planning bill file.

In the example we have been using, the total bill of material file would consist of:

1. *The planning bill file* comprising bills shown in Figure 12.
2. *The M-bill file* comprising bills for D14, H23, J39, and N44.

The Production and Inventory Control Handbook* contains an example of bill of material restructuring that illustrates another technique. Namely, *reassigning* components from one bill to another. It is in chapter 17, and the reader is referred to the detailed discussion and illustrations contained there. The example used involves an engine, transmission, intake manifold, carburetor, and flywheel housing. This technique is really another version of modularizing. The difference is that the items being broken out, like the manifold, are *not* being promoted to level-1 status but are reassigned as components of another level-1 item, such as the carburetor.

This will get the right components planned but, because the manifold, for instance, does not *really* get assembled with the carburetor, certain new problems will be created. For example, stock requisitions or service parts orders for the carburetor should not call out manifolds, the cost buildup of the carburetor must not include the manifold, etc. Special procedures would have to be established within the system to handle this. Two bills would have to be maintained for the carburetor. One, a planning bill, with the manifold and another one, an M-bill, without it. But in this case, it would not otherwise be necessary to set up two carburetor bills if the illegitimate components were not assigned to it.

This technique of reassigning components is unnecessarily complicated and vulnerable. The straight modularization technique demonstrated on the previous example is cleaner and gets the job done in a simpler fashion. We mentioned earlier that one reason for modularizing is to disentangle option combinations, for purposes of forecasting and master scheduling. In our example of the hoist, this has been accomplished by establishing the modular planning bill shown in Figure 12. The other objective of modularization, segregating common from unique (optional) parts for purposes of inventory minimization, has not been fully met, however.

In modularizing the bills, we assigned level-1 items to groups, by option. But those items were *assemblies*, and they may contain common components. For example, a subassembly that is only used for motor #1 could have some common parts with another subassembly used for motor #2. Requirements for such common parts will be overstated, if they are included in the safety

---

* *Production & Inventory Control Handbook*, McGraw-Hill, 1970.

stock for *both* options. If we want to get at these common parts, we would have to tear the bills apart even further. In some cases it is desirable to do that, but if this technique is carried to its extreme, we might finally end up with a planning bill that has only pieceparts in it and no subassemblies. The ultimate module of the product is really the piecepart.

The question is this: When we do modularize, how far down the product structure should we go? What we are really doing when we modularize is determining the right level in the bill of material at which to forecast. Whether we should forecast the subassembly itself or just its components—and that is the question here—depends on *when* we need to assemble it.

We have two choices. Either we assemble it as a function of executing the master schedule, through MRP. This means assembling to stock, or *pre-assembling*, before the end product itself is scheduled to be built, which is probably after receipt of a customer order. Or we defer putting this sub-assembly together until such time when we build the end product. The making of the subassembly then becomes a function of executing the final assembly schedule. The decision between these two alternatives is pretty much dictated by the nature of the product in question, and by the nature of the business. Lead times and the economics of subassembly operations will determine, in each case, whether the item should be preassembled or whether it can wait until final product assembly.

Let us take the pendant on the hoist as an example. We can wait and assemble the pendant, and *its* subassemblies, when we built the final hoist to customer or warehouse order. But, on the other hand, we may want to have the pendants in stock when the order comes in, so as not to have to assemble them one at a time. If this is the case, we would have to leave the respective bills alone, even though some common parts will consequently be tied up in the pendant assemblies. The master schedule would then contain pendant bill numbers rather than their component numbers.

In trying to arrive at the answer to the question we are examining here it is helpful to distinguish between the

1. master production schedule and
2. final assembly schedule.

The master schedule represents a *procurement and fabrication schedule*. The final assembly schedule, created later in time, must stay within the constraints of component availability provided by the master schedule through the MRP system. (These schedules may coincide where the product either contains no options, or is small and simple, etc.) Different subassemblies are under the control of these two schedules, and in modularizing bills of material we are, in effect, assigning a given subassembly to either one of these schedules:

1. To the master schedule, by retaining it in the planning bill.
2. To the final assembly schedule, by breaking down its bill (i.e., transforming it into an M-bill).

Thus the question of how far down the product structure one should go in modularizing tends to answer itself when the bill for a particular product is analyzed, and when we look at the nature of the various subassemblies in a particular business environment.

To conclude the discussion of modular bills of material, it may be proper to reflect on the objectives of modularization. Besides the specific objectives brought out earlier, there is a broader, more fundamental reason. And that is to maintain flexibility of production with a minimum investment in materials inventory. We want to offer a wide choice of products and to give maximum service to customers, and at the same time keep component inventories down. Modular bills of material are intended to help us do just that.

PSEUDO-BILLS OF MATERIAL

There is one more problem that is related to the modular bill of material. When the bill is broken down in the process of modularizing, various assemblies are promoted and become end items; i.e., highest level items with no parent. This tends to create a large number of end items. Because it is the end items that will have to be forecast, and because the master schedule has to be stated in terms of these end items, we could end up with hundreds (or thousands) of end items, too many to work with.

Fortunately, there is a simple solution to this. We certainly want the smallest possible number of things to forecast, and the smallest possible number of end items shown on the master schedule. To accomplish this, we can use the technique of creating "pseudo-bills of material." If we go back to Figure 12, where the newly created end items are grouped by option, there is nothing to stop us from taking any group of such items and creating a pseudo-bill to cover all of them. We have done so in Figure 13, where an artificial parent has been assigned to each group, and a new series of (pseudo) bills has been created.

These new bills, sometimes called *super-bills* or *S-bills*, are an example of *nonengineering part numbers* being introduced into a restructured bill of material. An S-number, such as S-101 in Figure 13, identifies an artificial bill of material for an imaginary item that, in reality, will never be built. The only purpose of the S-number is to facilitate planning. With the S-bills set up, when we forecast drum size, for instance, we forecast S-104 and S-105 only. These pseudo-bill numbers will also represent these options in the master

FIGURE 13

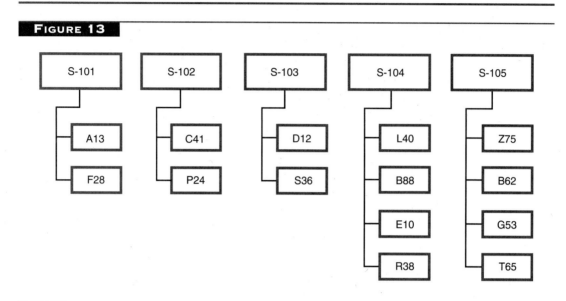

FIGURE 14

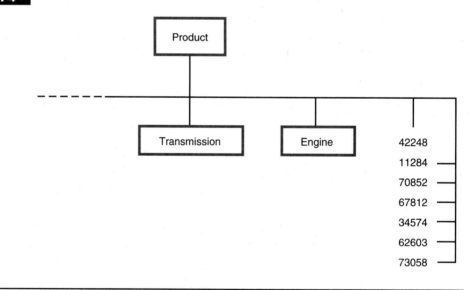

schedule. The MRP system will explode the requirements automatically from this point on, using the S-bills in the bill of material file.

A total of 47 S-bills (one for each option plus one for common items including the hook) would cover the original (nonsimplified) example of the hoist represented in Figures 7 and 8. The 47 compares with 2,400 end product bills, or with several hundred end item (level-1) bills.

In this article, the terms "S-bills," "S-number," and others, are being used for lack of standard terms. The terminology in this whole area is unfortunately entirely nonstandard, as the subject has been almost totally neglected in literature. One of very few exceptions is the article by Dave Garwood* in which he described the results of restructuring the bills of material at Fisher Controls Co. In his article, the term "partial parts list" (PPL) corresponds to the S-bill, and the term "Item" to an option or option grouping.

Another pseudo-bill term in current use is the "Kit number" or "K-number." This technique is used by some companies that have a lot of small loose parts on level one in the product structure, as in the example in Figure 14. These are often the fasteners, nuts, and bolts, used to assemble the major assemblies together. If you do not want to deal with all these parts individually—and you certainly do not under an MRP system—you can put them into an imaginary bag, as depicted in Figure 15. You can then assign a part number to this bag of parts and treat it, in effect, as an assembly. This means setting up a bill of material for such a kit number (also shown in Figure 15).

The principle is the same as in the case of the S-bill—assigning a single new identity code to individually coded items that constitute a logical grouping, and employing the format of a bill of material to relate the items together for system purposes. The K-bill is another nonengineering part number created in the process of structuring the bill of material. These artificial identity codes have little to do with the design of the product and are not part of the product specs, but are created for more convenient planning, forecasting, and master scheduling.

These newly created bills, along with the M-bills we discussed earlier are sometimes collectively called the *superstructure*. The superstructure, once established, must then be maintained along with the rest of the bill of material file. This is a new job, which means that the cost of file maintenance will normally go up.

CONCLUSION

In the previous sections of this article we have reviewed modularization which does away with end product bills and creates separate planning bills and manufacturing bills. We have seen how artificial bills are created in the process of restructuring, and for what purpose. We have also touched on

---

*"Stop: Before You Use the Bill Processor," by D. Garwood, *Production & Inventory Management*, Second Quarter 1970.

FIGURE 15

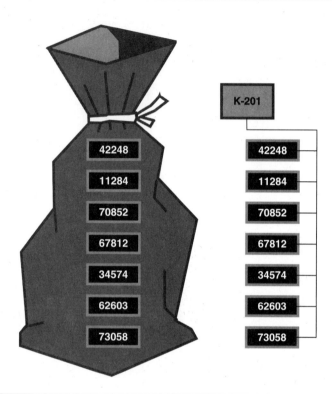

the relationship of item identities to material requirements planning, and on the treatment of "phantom" assemblies. All of this goes to show that by making these kinds of changes, we can put the bill to new uses.

There are still other uses that can be assigned to the bill of material. An interesting example of modifying and using the bill of material in a new way is to expand the traditional concept of the bill to include other materials which may not actually be part of the product, but which are consumed in its making. For example, a ball bearing manufacturer has added special grinding wheels to bills of material for ball bearings. In effect, they are saying that a "part" made of a portion of the grinding wheel goes into each bearing assembly. The "quantity per" is the fraction of wheel life to make one bearing. Adding this item to bills of material makes it possible for this company to project requirements for expensive grinding wheels and thus minimize investment in this inventory, as well as to reduce the possibility of a shortage of grinding wheels.

An electrical machinery manufacturer has added electrical specification numbers for power transformers to bills of material. The assembly orders generated from these bills then show not only the parts that go into the assembly but also the proper specifications for final inspection and test.

In conclusion, we want to indicate who does and who does not need to restructure the bill of material, as a precondition to successful MRP system operation. Where the product line consists of a finite, limited number of items (models), modularizing the bill, or any other changes for the sake of bill of material structure may be unnecessary. For example, a company making power tools—a highly successful user of MRP—did not have to restructure bills of material. In their business the bill simply is no problem, because they manufacture only so many varieties of power drill, power saw, etc., in large quantities. Furthermore, the product is relatively simple and small, in terms of the number of different components used per unit of end product. With a product line like that, it is feasible to maintain complete bills for each product model, and forecast and plan by model.

On the other hand, bill of material restructuring is called for where the product line consists of a virtually infinite number of end products, due to complexity of design and wide choice of optional features. Modular bills of material make material requirements planning possible for such diverse products as highway truck trailers, mining machines, gasoline station pumps, cranes, elevators, office machinery, farm machinery, computers, machine tools, instruments, industrial tractors, and a multitude of others, who have the common problem of an almost endless product variety that makes it otherwise impossible to develop valid master schedules.

The study of how bills of material should be constructed is therefore a vital part of the work of designing and implementing an MRP system. Structuring the bill of material requires some real cooperation from the engineering department, and sometimes this can be a problem. After the bill is restructured, it can no longer "belong" to the engineers exclusively, and that can sometimes be a problem also.

The bill of material can and should be more than just part of product specs. It should also be viewed and used as a *tool for planning*. The resistance by some engineering departments to change in bill of material format, structure, maintenance, etc., cannot really be justified. After all, the engineers create the bill so that, by definition, somebody other than the designer can make the product. The bill of material is, therefore, really made for others, in the first place. And it would seem to follow that it should be structured for the *user's*, not the designer's, convenience.

An ex-engineer friend of ours put it this way: "When I worked as an engineer, I saw the creation of the bill of material as the *last step in the process of design*. But when I later moved into production and inventory control, I began to see it as a *first step in the process of planning*."

EFFECTIVE COMPANY OPERATION AS NEVER BEFORE!

OLIVER W. WIGHT

Manufacturing Resource Planning is, without question, the most significant development in the management of manufacturing companies of this decade. In the few companies where it is working, you can see for the first time ever, the full value of the computer as a management tool. Why do I say for the first time ever? Because never before has the computer had in its memory so complete and accurate a picture of what is happening in the manufacturing operations—the heart and soul of a manufacturing company. This makes it possible to plan the resources of the *entire company* with an unprecedented level of confidence.

Further, this exceptionally detailed, timely, and accurate information—which was only until recently the exclusive property of the production and inventory control people—is made easily accessible to people in every function and at all management levels. And they can get what they need in their own "language," their own terminology, and their own context.

Top management can get profit-and-loss projections in a format they are used to, but with an accuracy and precision that cannot be achieved any other way. Financial people can get inventory level data, expressed in dollars, with unprecedented accuracy. Marketing can get cost information so reliable that they can work out pricing strategies with complete confidence, not only with the knowledge that their pricing will produce profit, but also how much profit will be produced.

These are but samples of what really amounts to a new way of life for manufacturing company managers. And the new way of life extends right down to the factory floor. Foremen become true managers who can plan their own budgets—labor, material, overhead, capacity—and be fairly held accountable for them. A foreman can predict his labor requirements, months into the future, with an accuracy within one percent!

Reprinted by permission from *Modern Materials Handling,* September, 1979.

MRP II—A TOOL FOR BETTER PLANNING THROUGHOUT THE COMPANY

Management
Planning information that is realistic as never before; ability to deal with changes in planning; ability to monitor operations against the plan; ability to predict shipment, labor, inventory, investment, and profits well into the future.

Manufacturing
Ability to work to plans agreed to in advance by other functions; ability to build what will contribute most to profit; a new understanding in management and finance of what it takes to manufacture a product.

Factory Supervison
Ability for foremen to become professional managers since 60 to 80 percent of their time no longer is devoted to compensating for problems created by unreal plans and schedules.

Research & Development
Ability to cost out new products or improvements down to the finest detail when preparing data for management's planning.

Production & Inventory Control
Ability to create firm schedules that are workable and are agreed to by all involved in advance; ability to make schedule changes without creating problems of overtime, capacity, use or customer service.

The Heart of it- A Common Data Base
In the central computer, the data created by Manufacturing's MRP program, expressed in standard units and quantities by time period, becomes available to all functions in dollars or other terms they can understand and make sense of.

Finance
Ability to monitor costs of company operations on a dynamic basis with numbers that are realistic; ability to project inventory and other items accurately by time period, rather than projecting from historical data.

Marketing
Ability to focus selling efforts accurately on those products which will generate the most profit and the least backlog; ability to improve customer service without creating problems for other functions.

Engineering
Ability to create plans that are executed as conceived; ability to present proposal justifications in terms understandable by management and with numbers that a post-audit will confirm as true; ability to submit engineering changes when most economical.

Purchasing
Ability to make the most of vendor capacity; ability to eliminate most expediting; better understanding of what carrying costs really are; ability to make "buys" that really contribute to profit.

It's a new way of life for people in most functions. Because the plans and schedules are built on real facts and figures, everyone does less "fire-fighting" and more of what he ideally should do. The MRP system at the heart summarizes manufacturing operations with accurate data, updated continuously as things change. Plans can be made with input from all involved, using the same data. Operations can be accurately monitored against the plan. Alternatives can be considered with full understanding of consequences. And projections and predictions can be accurate as never before.

How is all this possible? Two things are essential: first, a material requirements planning system—one that is a true "closed loop" system where nothing happens until the plan is proved correct, and where schedules are not only valid but are followed and work as they are supposed to.

This is vital. The materials requirements planning (MRP) system must generate information that truly represents what is happening in the manufacturing operations, without fudge factors, assumptions, or guesswork. Otherwise, going to the second step is a tragic waste of time and effort.

The second essential step in Manufacturing Resource Planning is to tie the MRP system to the financial system. This is a job for the data processing people. They must use the information generated by the MRP system, which is usually expressed in standard units and quantities, by time period, to build a common data base in the computer. They must make it possible to reduce the MRP data to common denominator elements. An inventory, expressed in standard units, for example, becomes expressible also in dollars.

When the common data base is created, remarkable things begin to happen. The functions find that they can work together. One quick example: marketing historically has tended to sell what is built because that's what they have, or they generate orders without knowing whether or not the factory can produce the products at a profit. With Manufacturing Resource Planning, and that data base, marketing can ask, "Should we put our sales effort into Product *A*? Can it be built at a profit?" And they get accurate feedback. They find out quickly to what extent manufacturing can deliver what they need, or when they should change their plans to accommodate what the factory *can* deliver.

A key word to describe what takes place is "accountability." Just as the foremen can be made accountable, so, too, can people in all functions. There is no longer any justification for charging ahead without caring who takes the lumps. Every course of action can be agreed to, in advance, by all concerned. The consequences are known and predictable for every alternative.

Manufacturing Resource Planning has been called a "company-operating system" and a "total business plan." It's also been called a "computer model of the business." These are all true. And if that last one suggests that you can simulate the business, or any part of it, to test the impact of any course of action in advance, that's true, too. It's probably the best way to find profitable trade-offs ever devised.

Best of all, you needn't be a corporate giant to develop Manufacturing Resource Planning. In fact, it may be easier for a smaller company than a larger one!

WHAT MRP II CAN DO

Let's look at the potential in a little greater detail. There are six basic reports generated by MRP. Let's see what can be obtained, once those reports have been costed out and summarized in the common data base.

Production plans. The data from these make it possible to create a company business plan, and coordinate all functions with it. Records of sales, production, and inventory become control reports. Comparing them against the production plan shows the financial impact of production changes on the business plan.

Master production schedules.   These give you accurate "transfers to inventory" or "shipping budgets" depending on whether you make to stock or build to order.

Management can review projected shipping budgets to make sure that the objective of shipping to budget is properly reconciled with the need to ship the right order to the right customer.

Material requirements plans.   With these summarized by product groups, you can get on-hand inventory by product group, in dollars. You can see how much material in dollars is needed to support a production plan. You can predict inventory balances, in dollars and product groups, for months ahead. You'll know what must be built to support the production plan, in dollars, and you can convert this to labor dollars. You can compare what actually happens against what was planned, and see that the business plan is met at the detailed level.

Capacity requirement plans.   You can get standard hours by work center and by time period that are needed to satisfy the master production schedule and production plans. You can convert these to labor dollars by labor grade, by time period, or by product group.

Dispatch lists.   You can get your current work-in-process expressed in dollars and, since labor reporting is usually tied in with dispatching, you also can get the basis for labor-efficiency reports.

Vendor schedules.   You can see how much purchased material is due to be shipped by each vendor by time period to support the plan.

WHY THE FUNCTIONS LIKE IT

Top management, of course, is not the only function that benefits from Manufacturing Resource Planning. Nearly every function finds that it can do its work more effectively. Let's look at the experience of those who have seen what it can be like, so far.

Marketing.   It's a new opportunity to improve customer service. This results from better planning and a clearer understanding of what it means to work effectively with manufacturing. It also creates a greater ability to contribute to profit by concentrating on activities that generate income rather than those that merely increase backlogs.

Engineering.   It eliminates the frustration of creating plans that are never executed as conceived. Engineering becomes a part of the team because the business plan deals with facts and works with reality.

Manufacturing.   It means plans that will work, because they are agreed to, in advance, by all concerned; and because they are based on knowledge on the part of management, and marketing, of what it will take to deliver what is planned.

Production supervision.   Foremen become professional managers since they must no longer spend 60 percent to 80 percent of their time looking for parts, expediting, or attending shortage meetings.

Purchasing.   Time becomes available to get out and negotiate with vendors and to help engineering work effectively with vendors, because nearly 90 percent of all expediting is eliminated.

Production and inventory control.   An ability to plan schedules on the basis of reality, knowing in advance that they can and will be followed, and that changes can be coped with on a routine basis without panics.

Data processing.   The opportunity to work within a single overall system, rather than having to resolve the conflicts of many separate systems, and time to work out ways to make the system easier to use.

Personnel.   Once the company is hitting its shipping budget 100 percent, customer service is close to 100 percent, and profit objectives are being exceeded, job satisfaction throughout the company is high. The personnel manager is able to work from a base of positive attitudes without spending most of his time fighting psychological fires.

The list of benefits goes on and on.

THE PRODUCTIVITY PARADOX

WICKHAM SKINNER

American manufacturers' near heroic efforts to regain a competitive edge through productivity improvements have been disappointing. Worse, the results of these efforts have been paradoxical. The harder these companies pursue productivity, the more elusive it becomes.

In the late 1970s, after facing a severe loss of market share in dozens of industries, U.S. producers aggressively mounted programs to revitalize their manufacturing functions. This effort to restore the productivity gains that had regularly been achieved for over 75 years has been extraordinary. (Productivity is defined by the Bureau of Labor Statistics as the value of goods manufactured divided by the amount of labor input. In this article "productivity" is used in the same sense, that is, as a measure of manufacturing employees' performance.) Few companies have failed to measure and analyze productivity or to set about to raise output/input ratios. But the results overall have been dismal.

From 1978 through 1982 U.S. manufacturing productivity was essentially flat. Although results during the past three years of business upturn have been better, they ran 25 percent lower than productivity improvements during earlier, postwar upturns.

Consider, for example, the XYZ Corporation, which I visited recently. The company operates a large manufacturing plant, where a well-organized productivity program, marshaling its best manufacturing talent, has been under way for three years. Its objective was to boost productivity so as to remove a 30 percent competitive cost disadvantage.

The program has included: appointing a corporate productivity manager; establishing departmental productivity committees; raising the number of industrial engineering professionals by 50 percent; carrying out operation-by-operation analyses to improve efficiency levels, avoid waste, and simplify jobs; retraining employees to work "smarter not harder"; streamlining work flow and materials movement; replacing out-of-date equipment; retooling

---

Reprinted by permission of *Harvard Business Review* 64:4 (1986): 55–59.

operations to cut operator time; tightening standards; installing a computerized production control system; training foremen in work simplification; emphasizing good housekeeping and cleanliness; and installing a computer-based, measured-day work plan, which allows for daily performance reports on every operation, worker, and department.

For all this effort—and all the boost it gave to production managers' morale—little good has come of the program. Productivity has crept up by about 7 percent over three years, but profits remain negligible and market share continues to fall. As one executive said, "It's been great finally getting management support and the resources needed to get this plant cleaned up and efficient. But it is extremely discouraging to have worked so hard and, after three years, to be in worse competitive shape than when we started. I don't know how long we can keep trying harder when it doesn't seem to be getting us anywhere."

Unfortunately, XYZ's frustration with a full-out effort that achieves only insignificant competitive results is typical of what has been going on in much of American industry. Why so little competitive return—even a negative return—on so much effort? Is it the high value of the dollar, which cheapens imports? Is the cost gap just too great for us to overcome? Or are we going at the problems in the wrong way? What is going wrong? Why this apparent paradox?

THE WRONG APPROACH

With these questions in mind, I have visited some 25 manufacturing companies during the last two years. Never have I seen so much energetic attention to productivity starting from the top and ricocheting all the way through organizations. This is American hustle and determination at its best. Productivity committees, productivity czars, productivity seminars, and productivity campaigns abound.

But the harder these companies work to improve productivity, the less they sharpen the competitive edge that *should* be improved by better productivity. Elusive gains and vanishing market share point not to a lack of effort but to a central flaw in how that effort is conceived. The very way managers define productivity improvement and the tools they use to achieve it push their goal further out of reach.

Resolutely chipping away at waste and inefficiency—the heart of most productivity programs—is not enough to restore competitive health. Indeed, a focus on cost reductions (that is, on raising labor output while holding the amount of labor constant or, better, reducing it) is proving harmful.

Let me repeat: not only is the productivity approach to manufacturing management not enough (companies cannot cut costs deeply enough to restore competitive vitality); it actually hurts as much as it helps. It is an instinctive response that absorbs managers' minds and diverts them from more effective manufacturing approaches.

Chipping away at productivity:

is mostly concerned with direct labor efficiency, although direct labor costs exceed 10 percent of sales in only a few industries. Thus, even an immense jump in productivity—say 20 percent—would not reverse the fortunes of import-damaged industries like autos, consumer electronics, textile machinery, shoes, or textiles.

focuses excessively on the efficiency of factory workers. By trying to squeeze out better efficiency from improved attitudes and tighter discipline on a person-by-person and department-by-department basis, the approach detracts attention from the structure of the production system itself.

Production experience regularly observes a "40 40 20" rule. Roughly 40 percent of any manufacturing-based competitive advantage derives from long-term changes in manufacturing structure (decisions, for example, concerning the number, size, location, and capacity of facilities) and basic approaches in materials and work force management. Another 40 percent comes from major changes in equipment and process technology. The final 20 percent—no more—rests on conventional approaches to productivity improvement.

What this rule says is that the least powerful way to bolster competitive advantage is to focus on conventional productivity and cost-cutting approaches. Far more powerful are changes in manufacturing structure and technology. The rule docs not, of course, say "Don't try to improve productivity." These well-known tools are easy to use and do help to remove unnecessary fat. But they quickly reach the limits of what they can contribute. Productivity is the wrong tree to bark up.

ignores other ways to compete that use manufacturing as a strategic resource. Quality, reliable delivery, short lead times, customer service, rapid product introduction, flexible capacity, and efficient capital deployment—these, not cost reduction, are the primary operational sources of advantage in today's competitive environment.

fails to provide or support a coherent manufacturing strategy. By assuming that manufacturing's essential task is to make a company the low-cost producer in its industry, this approach rashly rules out other strategies.

Most of the productivity-focused programs I have seen blithely assume that competitive position lost on grounds of higher cost is best recovered by installing cost-reduction programs. This logic is tempting but wrong. These programs cannot succeed. They have the wrong targets and misconstrue the nature of the competitive challenge they are supposed to address. Worse, they incur huge opportunity costs. By tying managers at all levels to short-term considerations, they short-circuit the development of an aggressive manufacturing strategy.

But they also do harm. These programs can, for example, hinder innovation. As William Abernathy's study of auto manufacturers has shown, an industry can easily become the prisoner of its own massive investments in low-cost production and in the organizational systems that support it.[1] When process costs and constraints drive both product and corporate strategy, flexibility gets lost, as does the ability to rapidly introduce product changes or develop new products.

Even more is at stake than getting locked into the wrong equipment. Managers under relentless pressure to maximize productivity resist innovation.

"Well, just go and tell Comrade Gorbachev you can't 'intensify' the economy around here without breaking a few eggs!"

[1]William J. Abernathy and Kenneth Wayne, "Limits of the Learning Curve," *Harvard Business Review* September–October 1974, p. 109.

Preoccupied as they are with this week's cost performance, they know well that changes in processes or systems will wreak havoc with the results on which they are measured. Consequently, innovations that lead to, say, better service or shorter lead times for product changeovers are certain to suffer.

Innovation is not, however, all that suffers. A full-out concentration on productivity frequently creates an environment that alienates the work force. Pressure for output and efficiency are the staples of factory life as hourly workers experience it. Engineers and supervisors tell them what to do, how to do it, and how long they may take. Theirs is an often unhappy, quota-measured culture—and has been for more than 150 years. In such an environment, even the most reasonable requests are resented.

Recent admirers of the Japanese argue that low cost and high quality can go hand in hand. Indeed, in the right setting managers need not trade one for the other. But in an efficiency-driven operation, this logic can be a trap. When low cost is the goal, quality often gets lost. But when quality is the goal, lower costs do usually follow.

The will to make large investments in radically new process technology gets lost too. The slow adoption of such manufacturing technologies as CAD/CAM, robotics, and flexible machining centers reflects managers' wise assumptions that these investments would initially drive productivity down.

Fears that several years of debugging and learning to use the new gear would hurt productivity have already cost many companies valuable time in mastering these process technologies. Even more troubling, the companies have failed to acquire a strategic resource that could help them restore their competitive position. A productivity focus inevitably forces managers into a short-term, operational mind-set. When productivity is driving, experimentation takes a backseat.

The emphasis on direct costs, which attends the productivity focus, leads a company to use management controls that focus on the wrong targets. Inevitably, these controls key on direct labor: overhead is allocated by direct labor; variances from standards are calculated from direct labor. Performance in customer service, delivery, lead times, quality, and asset turns are secondary. The reward system based on such controls drives behavior toward simplistic goals that represent only a small fraction of total costs while the real costs lie in overhead and purchased materials.

Why has this gone on year after year even as the cost mix has steadily moved away from direct labor? By now our accounting and control systems are pathetically old-fashioned and ineffective. But nothing changes. Our continuing obsession with productivity as the be-all measure of factory performance is to blame, not the stubbornness of accountants.

When managers grow up in this atmosphere, their skills and vision never fully develop. They instinctively seize on inefficiencies and waste while missing broad opportunities to compete through manufacturing. The harsh fact is that generations of production managers have been stunted by this efficiency-driven mentality. Theirs is the oldest management function, yet today it is often the most backward. Unable to join finance, marketing, and general management in thinking strategically about their businesses, they are cut off from corporate leadership. As my recent study of 66 "comers" in production management shows, 10 or 15 years' immersion in a productivity-directed organization creates severe limitations of vision.[2] These limitations, in time, form a long-term mind-set that only a few can shake. Today the production function is seldom the place to find managers who can design competitive manufacturing structures.

Indeed, ever since Fredrick Winslow Taylor, our obsession with productivity and efficiency has spoiled the atmosphere of the factory. "Factory" is a bad word. Production managers first came into existence not as architects of competitive systems but as custodians of large, capital-intensive assets. Their job was to control and coordinate all factors of production so as to minimize costs and maximize output. This single dimension of performance is deeply ingrained in the profession and until recently has sufficed as a basis of evaluation.

Not surprisingly, it created a negative, penny-pinching, mechanistic culture in most factories—a culture that has driven out and kept away creative people at all levels. Who among our young today wishes to work in an environment where one is told what to do, how to do it, when to do it, is measured in minutes and sometimes seconds, is supervised closely to prevent any inefficiencies, and is paced by assembly lines or machines to produce at a rapid and relentless pace?

Today's problems in making the factory into a more attractive place to work are not new. They are the direct outcome of the 150-year history of an institution based on productivity. As long as cost and efficiency are the primary measurements of factory success, the manufacturing plant will continue to repel many able, creative people.

BREAKING OUT

Faced with this paradox—efforts to improve productivity driving competitive success further out of reach—a number of companies have broken out of the bind with extraordinary success. Their experience suggests, however, that breaking loose from so long-established a mind-set is not easy. It requires

---

[2]Wickham Skinner, "The Taming of Lions: How Manufacturing Leadership Evolved, 1780–1984," in *The Uneasy Alliance,* ed. Kim B. Clark, Robert H. Hayes, and Christopher Lorenz (Boston: Harvard Business School Press, 1985), 63.

a change in culture, habits, instincts, and ways of thinking and reasoning. And it means modifying a set of values that current reward systems and day-to-day operational demands reinforce. This is a tall order.

Every company I know that has freed itself from the paradox has done so, in part, by:

Recognizing that its approach to productivity was not working well enough to make the company cost competitive.   This recognition allowed managers to seek strategic objectives for manufacturing other than those determined primarily by cost.

About 12 years ago, a key division of American Standard adopted a "become the low-cost producer" strategy. Its productivity-driven focus did little to reduce costs but had an immediate negative effect on quality, delivery, and market share. What Standard needed was a totally new manufacturing strategy—one that allowed different areas of the factory to specialize in different markets and quality levels. When this approach replaced the low-cost strategy, the division regained its strong competitive position within three years.

Accepting the fact that its manufacturing was in trouble and needed to be run differently.   In the mid-1970s officers of the Copeland Corporation, a large producer of refrigeration compressors, decided that their industry was fast becoming mature. An analysis of their nearly obsolete production facilities and equipment made it clear that manufacturing had become a corporate millstone. Without a major change in the number, size, location, and focus of these facilities, long-term survival would be impossible. Copeland made these changes. The results (described later) were remarkable.

Developing and implementing a manufacturing strategy (see the insert). When production managers actively seek to understand (and, in some cases, to help develop) the competitive strategy of relevant business units, they are better able to work out the objectives for their own function that will turn it into a competitive weapon. The requirements of such a manufacturing strategy will then determine needed changes in the manufacturing system's structure and infrastructure.

At Copeland, this approach led to order-of-magnitude improvements in quality, shortened delivery cycles, lower inventory investments, and much greater flexibility in product and volume changes.

Adopting new process technology.   Changes in equipment and process technology are powerful engines of change. Bringing such technology on line helps force adjustments in work flow, key skills, and information systems as

MANUFACTURING STRATEGY

A manufacturing strategy describes the competitive leverage required of—and made possible by—the production function. It analyzes the entire manufacturing function relative to its ability to provide such leverage, on which task it then focuses each element of manufacturing structure. It also allows the structure to be managed, not just the short-term, operational details of cost, quality, and delivery. And it spells out an internally consistent set of structural decisions designed to forge manufacturing into a strategic weapon. These structural decisions include:

- What to make and what to buy.
- The capacity levels to be provided.
- The number and sizes of plants.
- The location of plants.
- Choices of equipment and process technology.
- The production and inventory control systems.
- The quality control system.
- The cost and other information systems.
- Work force management policies.
- Organizational structure.

---

well as in systems for inventory control, materials management, and human resource management. There are few more effective means of loosening up old ways of organizing production.

General Electric and Deere & Company have made wholesale process changes at their dishwasher and locomotive (GE) and tractor (Deere) plants—changes that boosted product quality and reliability. Timken and Cooper Industries have each made large investments in radical new technologies that speeded up their ability to deliver new products and customer specials.

Making major changes in the selection, development, assignments, and reward systems for manufacturing managers. The successful companies I looked at decided they needed a new breed of production leader—managers able to focus on a wider set of objectives than efficiency and cost. It was, however, no simple matter to find or train this new breed.

Some, in fact, turned up in unexpected places: marketing, sales, engineering, research, general management. As a group, they were good team builders and problem solvers and had broad enough experience to hold their own in top corporate councils. Their companies considered them among the most promising, high-potential "comers" for future leadership at the highest levels.

Only when manufacturers were willing to try such novel approaches to the competitive challenges facing them have they broken loose from the productivity paradox and transformed their production function into a strategic weapon. There is hope for manufacturing in America, but it rests on a different way of managing in this oldest of managerial professions.

As we have seen, our pursuit of productivity is paradoxical: the more we pursue it, the more elusive it becomes. An obsession with cost reduction produces a narrowness of vision and an organizational backlash that work against its underlying purpose. To boost productivity in its fullest sense—that is to unleash a powerful team of people supported by the right technology— we must first let go of old-fashioned productivity as a primary goal. In its place we must set a new, simple but powerful objective for manufacturing: to be competitive.

Labor intensive

That people love their work, who work a drill
Or run a lathe, sounds alien to some
Who see in them "the robots they've become":
Automatons bent to assembly's will.

And some are that, who welcome programmed steel
Greet automation heralded as Change—
But others feel an intimate exchange,
The tiniest components but a field

As varied as a single breed of snail,
With textures, contours hidden from all eyes
Save those communing daily half their lives
With parts they know like totems. They have nailed

That one philosophy, have made the grade
Who see in work their lives, and love their trade.

Elissa Malcohn

Elissa Malcohn has published her poetry, fiction, and commentary in various magazines. She works on the staff of the Harvard Business School News and Information Bureau.

WHY SOME FACTORIES ARE MORE PRODUCTIVE THAN OTHERS

ROBERT H. HAYES AND KIM B. CLARK

The battle for attention is over. The time for banging drums is long past. Everyone now understands that manufacturing provides an essential source of competitive leverage. No longer does anyone seriously think that domestic producers can outdo their competitors by clever marketing only—"selling the sizzle" while cheating on quality or letting deliveries slip. It is now time for concrete action on a practical level: action to change facilities, update processing technologies, adjust work-force practices, and perfect information and management systems.

But when managers turn to these tasks, they quickly run up against a stumbling block. Namely, they do not have adequate measures for judging factory-level performance or for comparing overall performance from one facility to the next. Of course, they can use the traditional cost-accounting figures, but these figures often do not tell them what they really need to know. Worse, even the best numbers do not sufficiently reflect the important contributions that managers can make by reducing confusion in the system and promoting organizational learning.

Consider the experience of a U.S. auto manufacturer that discovered itself with a big cost disadvantage. The company put together a group to study its principal competitor's manufacturing operations. The study generated reams of data, but the senior executive in charge of the activity still felt uneasy. He feared that the group was getting mired in details and that things other than managerial practices—like the age of facilities and their location—might be the primary drivers of performance. How to tell?

Similarly, a vice president of manufacturing for a specialty chemical producer had misgivings about the emphasis his company's system for evaluating plant managers placed on variances from standard costs. Differences in these standards made comparisons across plants difficult. What was more troubling,

Reprinted by permission of *Harvard Business Review* 64:5 (1986) 66–73.

the system did not easily capture the trade-offs among factors of production or consider the role played by capital equipment or materials. What to do?

Another manufacturer—this time of paper products—found quite different patterns of learning in the same departments of five of its plants scattered across the United States. Although each department made much the same products using similar equipment and materials, they varied widely in performance over a period of years. Why such differences?

Our point is simple: before managers can pinpoint what's needed to boost manufacturing performance, they must have a reliable way of ascertaining why some factories are more productive than others. They also need a dependable metric for identifying and measuring such differences and a framework for thinking about how to improve their performance—and keep it improving. This is no easy order.

These issues led us to embark on a continuing, multiyear study of 12 factories in 3 companies (see the appendix for details on research methodology). The study's purpose is to clarify the variables that influence productivity growth at the microlevel.

The first company we looked at, which employs a highly connected and automated manufacturing process, we refer to as the Process Company. Another, which employs a batch approach based on a disconnected line-flow organization of work, we refer to as the Fab (fabrication-assembly) Company. The third, which uses several different batch processes to make components for sophisticated electronic systems, is characterized by very rapid changes in both product and process. We refer to it as the Hi-Tech Company. All five factories of the Process Company and three of the four factories of the Fab Company are in the United States (the fourth is just across the border in Canada). Of the three factories belonging to the Hi-Tech Company, one is in the United States, one in Europe, and one in Asia.

In none of these companies did the usual profit-and-loss statements—or the familiar monthly operating reports—provide adequate, up-to-date information about factory performance. Certainly, managers routinely evaluated such performance, but the metrics they used made their task like that of watching a distant activity through a thick, fogged window. Indeed, the measurement systems in place at many factories obscure and even alter the details of their performance.

A FOGGED WINDOW

Every plant we studied employed a traditional standard cost system: the controller collected and reported data each month on the actual costs incurred during the period for labor, materials, energy, and depreciation, as well as on the costs that would have been incurred had workers and equipment performed at predetermined "standard" levels. The variances from these standard costs became the basis for problem identification and performance evaluation. Other departments in the plants kept track of head counts, work-in-process inventory, engineering changes, the value of newly installed equipment, reject rates, and so forth.

In theory, this kind of measurement system should take a diverse range of activities and summarize them in a way that clarifies what is going on. It should act like a lens that brings a blurry picture into sharp focus. Yet, time and again, we found that these systems often masked critical developments in the factories and, worse, often distorted management's perspective.

Each month, most of the managers we worked with received a blizzard of variance reports but no overall measure of efficiency. Yet this measure is not hard to calculate. In our study, we took the same data generated by plant managers and combined them into a measure of the total factor productivity (TFP)—the ratio of total output to total input (see the appendix for more details on TFP).

This approach helps dissipate some of the fog—especially because our TFP data are presented in constant dollars instead of the usual current dollars. Doing so cuts through the distortions produced by periods of high inflation. Consider the situation at Fab's Plant 1, where from 1974 to 1982 output fluctuated between $45 million and $70 million—in nominal (current dollar) terms. In real terms, however, there was a steep and significant decline in unit output. Several executives initially expressed disbelief at the magnitude of this decline because they had come to think of the plant as a "$50 million plant." Their traditional accounting measures had masked the fundamental changes taking place.

Another advantage of the TFP approach is that it integrates the contributions of all the factors of production into a single measure of total input. Traditional systems offer no such integration. Moreover, they often overlook important factors. One of the plant managers at the Process Company gaged performance in a key department by improvements in labor hours and wage costs. Our data showed that these "improvements" came largely from the substitution of capital for labor. Conscientious efforts to prune labor content by installing equipment—without developing the management skills and systems needed to realize its full potential—proved shortsighted. The plant's TFP (which, remember, takes into account both labor and capital costs) improved very little.

This preoccupation with labor costs, particularly direct labor costs, is quite common—even though direct labor now accounts for less than 15 percent of total costs in most manufacturing companies. The managers we studied focused heavily on these costs; indeed, their systems for measuring direct labor were generally more detailed and extensive than those for measuring other inputs that were several times more costly. Using sophisticated bar-code scanners, Hi-Tech's managers tracked line operators by the minute but had difficulty identifying the number of manufacturing engineers in the same department. Yet these engineers accounted for 20 percent to 25 percent of total cost, as compared with 5 percent for line operators.

Just as surprising, the companies we studied paid little attention to the effect of materials consumption or productivity. Early on, we asked managers at one of the Fab plants for data on materials consumed in production during each of a series of months. Using these data to estimate materials productivity gave us highly erratic values.

Investigation showed that this plant, like many others, kept careful records of materials purchased but not of the direct or indirect materials actually consumed in a month. (The latter, which includes things like paper forms, showed up only in a catchall manufacturing overhead account.) Further, most of the factories recorded materials transactions only in dollar, rather than in physical, terms and did not readily adjust their standard costs figures when inflation or substitution altered materials prices.

What managers at Fab plants called "materials consumed" was simply an estimate derived by multiplying a product's standard materials cost—which itself assumes a constant usage of materials—by its unit output and adding an adjustment based on the current variation from standard materials prices. Every year or half year, managers would reconcile this estimated consumption with actual materials usage, based on a physical count. As a result, data on actual materials consumption in any one period were lost.

Finally, the TFP approach makes clear the difference between the data that managers see and what those data actually measure. In one plant, the controller argued that our numbers on engineering changes were way off base. "We don't have anything like this level of changes," he claimed. "My office signs off on all changes that go through this place, and I can tell you that the number you have here is wrong." After a brief silence, the engineering manager spoke up. He said that the controller reviewed only very large (in dollar terms) engineering changes and that our data were quite accurate. He was right. The plant had been tracking all engineering changes, not just the major changes reported to the controller.

A CLEAR VIEW

With the foglike distortions of poor measurement systems cleared away, we were able to identify the real levers for improving factory performance. Some, of course, were structural—that is, they involve things like plant location or plant size, which lie outside the control of a plant's managers. But a handful of managerial policies and practices consistently turned up as significant. Across industries, companies, and plants, they regularly exerted a powerful influence on productivity. In short, these are the managerial actions that make a difference.

INVEST CAPITAL

Our data show unequivocally that capital investment in new equipment is essential to sustaining growth in TFP over a long time (that is, a decade or more). But they also show that capital investment all too often reduces TFP for up to a year. Simply investing money in new technology or systems guarantees nothing. What matters is how their introduction is managed, as well as the extent to which they support and reinforce continual improvement throughout a factory. Managed right, new investment supports cumulative, long-term productivity improvement and process understanding—what we refer to as "learning."

The Process Company committed itself to providing new, internally designed equipment to meet the needs of a rapidly growing product. Over time, as the company's engineers and operating managers gained experience, they made many small changes in product design, machinery, and operating practices. These incremental adjustments added up to major growth in TFP.

Seeking new business, the Fab Company redesigned an established product and purchased the equipment needed to make it. This new equipment was similar to the plant's existing machinery, but its introduction allowed for TFP-enhancing changes in work flows. Plant managers discovered how the new configuration could accommodate expanded production without a proportional increase in the work force. These benefits spilled over: even the older machinery was made to run more efficiently.

In both cases, the real boost in TFP came not just from the equipment itself but also from the opportunities it provided to search for and apply new knowledge to the overall production process. Again, managed right, investment unfreezes old assumptions, generates more efficient concepts and designs for a production system, and expands a factory's skills and capabilities.

Exhibit 1 shows the importance of such learning for long-term TFP growth at one of Fab's plants between 1973 and 1982. TFP rose by 96 percent. Part of this increase, of course, reflected changes in utilization rates and the introduction of new technology. Even so, roughly two-thirds (65 percent) of TFP growth was learning-based, and fully three-fourths of that learning effect (or 49 percent of TFP growth) was related to capital investment. Without capital investment, TFP would have increased, but at a much slower rate.

Such long-term benefits incur costs; in fact, the indirect costs associated with introducing new equipment can be staggering. In Fab's Plant 1, for example, a $1 million investment in new equipment imposed *$1.75 million* of

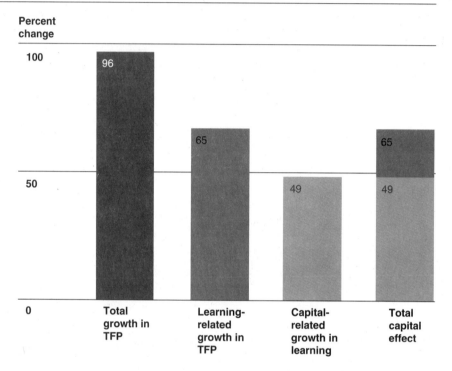

EXHIBIT 1   CAPITAL INVESTMENT, LEARNING, AND PRODUCTIVITY GROWTH IN FAB
COMPANY'S PLANT 2, 1973–1982

**Percent
change**

100	96
50	

- Total growth in TFP — 96
- Learning-related growth in TFP — 65
- Capital-related growth in learning — 49
- Total capital effect — 65 / 49

These estimates are based on a regression analysis of TFP growth. We estimated learning-related changes by using both a time trend and cumulative output. The capital-related learning effect represents the difference between the total learning effect and the effect that remained once capital was introduced into the regression. The total capital effect is composed of a learning component and a component reflecting technical advance.

additional costs on the plant during its first year of operation! Had the plant cut these indirect costs by half, TFP would have grown an additional 5 percent during that year.

Everyone knows that putting in new equipment usually causes problems. Everyone expects a temporary drop in efficiency as equipment is installed and workers learn to use it. But managers often underestimate the costly ripple effects of new equipment on inventory, quality, equipment utilization, reject rates, downtime, and material waste. Indeed, these indirect costs often exceed the direct cost of the new equipment and can persist for more than a year after the equipment is installed.

Here, then, is the paradox of capital investment. It is essential to long-term productivity growth, yet in the short run, if poorly managed, it can play havoc with TFP. It is risky indeed for a company to try to "invest its way" out of a productivity problem. Putting in new equipment is just as likely to create confusion and make things worse for a number of months. Unless the investment is made with a commitment to continual learning—and unless performance measures are chosen carefully—the benefits that finally emerge will be small and slow in coming. Still, many companies today are trying to meet their competitive problems by throwing money at them—new equipment and new plants. Our findings suggest that there are other things they ought to do first, things that take less time to show results and are much less expensive.

REDUCE WASTE

We were not surprised to find a negative correlation between waste rates (or the percentage of rejects) and TFP, but we were amazed by its magnitude. In the Process plants, changes in the waste rate (measured by the ratio of waste material to total cost, expressed as a percentage) led to dramatic operating improvements. As Exhibit 2 shows, reducing the percentage of waste in Plant 4's Department C by only one-tenth led to a 3 percent improvement in TFP, conservatively estimated.

The strength of this relationship is more surprising when we remember that a decision to boost the production throughput rate (which ought to raise TFP because of the large fixed components in labor and capital costs) also causes waste ratios to increase. In theory, therefore, TFP and waste percent should increase together. The fact that they do not indicates the truly powerful impact that waste reduction has on productivity.

GET WIP OUT

The positive effect on TFP of cutting work-in-process (WIP) inventories for a given level of output was much greater than we could explain by

EXHIBIT 2	IMPACT OF WASTE ON TFP IN PROCESS COMPANY PLANTS		
PLANT/ DEPARTMENT	**AVERAGE WASTE RATE**	**EFFECT ON TFP OF A 10 PERCENT REDUCTION IN WASTE RATE**	**DEGREE OF UNCERTAINTY***
1-C	11.2%	+1.2%	.009
2-C	12.4	+1.8	.000
3-C	12.7	+2.0	.000
4-C	9.3	+3.1	.002
5-C	8.2	+0.8	.006

*The probability that waste rate reductions have a zero or negative impact on TFP.

EXHIBIT 3	IMPACT OF WORK-IN-PROCESS REDUCTIONS ON TFP		
COMPANY	**PLANT/ DEPARTMENT**	**EFFECT ON TFP A 10 PERCENT REDUCTION IN WIP**	**DEGREE OF UNCERTAINTY***
Hi-Tech	1-A	+1.15%	.238
	1-B	+1.18	.306
	1-C	+3.73	.103
	1-D	+9.11	.003
Process	1-H	+1.63%	.001
	2-H	+4.01	.000
	3-H	+4.65	.000
	4-H	+3.52	.000
	5-H	+3.84	.000
Fab	1	+2.86%	.000
	2	+1.14	.000
	3	+3.59	.002

*The probability that work-in-process reductions have a zero or negative impact on TFP.

reductions in working capital. Exhibit 3 documents the relationship between WIP reductions and TFP in the three companies. Although there are important plant-to-plant variations, all reductions in WIP are associated with increases in TFP. In some plants, the effect is quite powerful; in Department D of Hi-Tech's Plant 1, reducing WIP by one-tenth produced a 9 percent rise in TFP.

These data support the growing body of empirical evidence about the benefits of reducing WIP. From studies of both Japanese and American companies, we know that cutting WIP leads to faster, more reliable delivery times, lowers reject rates (faster production cycle times reduce inventory obsolescence and make possible rapid feedback when a process starts to misfunction), and cuts overhead costs. We now know it also drives up TFP.

The trouble is, simply pulling work-in-process inventory out of a factory will not, by itself, lead to such improvements. More likely, it will lead to disaster. WIP is there for a reason, usually for many reasons; it is a symptom, not the disease itself. A long-term program for reducing WIP must attack the reasons for its being there in the first place: erratic process yields, unreliable equipment, long production change-over and set-up times, ever-changing production schedules, and suppliers who do not deliver on time. Without a cure for these deeper problems, a factory's cushion of WIP is often all that stands between it and chaos.

REDUCING CONFUSION

Defective products, mismanaged equipment, and excess work-in-process inventory are not only problems in themselves. They are also sources of confusion. Many things that managers do can confuse or disrupt a factory's operation: erratically varying the rate of production, changing a production schedule at the last minute, overriding the schedule by expediting orders, changing the crews (or the workers on a specific crew) assigned to a given machine, haphazardly adding new products, altering the specifications of an existing product through an engineering change order (ECO), or monkeying with the process itself by adding to or altering the equipment used.

Managers may be tempted to ask, "Doesn't what you call confusion—changing production schedules, expediting orders, shifting work crews, adding or overhauling equipment and changing product specifications—reflect what companies inevitably have to do to respond to changing customer demands and technological opportunities?"

Our answer to this question is an emphatic, No! Responding to new demands and new opportunities requires change, but it does not require the confusion it usually creates. Much of our evidence on confusion comes from factories that belong to the same company and face the same external pressures. Some plant managers are better than others at keeping these pressures at bay. The good ones limit the number of changes introduced at any one time and carefully handle their implementation. Less able managers always seem caught by surprise, operate haphazardly, and leap-frog from one crisis to the next. Much of the confusion in their plants is internally generated.

While confusion is not the same thing as complexity, complexity in a factory's operation usually produces confusion. In general, a factory's mission becomes more complex—and its focus looser—as it becomes larger, as it adds different technologies and products, and as the number and variety of production orders it must accommodate grow. Although the evidence suggests that complexity harms performance, each company's factories were too similar for us to analyze the effects of complexity on TFP. But we could see that what managers did to mitigate or fuel confusion within factories at a given level of complexity had a profound impact on TFP.

Of the sources of confusion we examined, none better illustrated this relationship with TFP than engineering change orders. ECOs require a change in the materials used to make a product, the manufacturing process employed, or the specifications of the product itself. We expected ECOs to lower productivity in the short run but lead to higher TFP over time. Exhibit 4, which presents data on ECO activity in three Fab plants, shows its effects to be sizable. In Plant 2, for

EXHIBIT 4	IMPACT OF ENGINEERING CHANGE ORDERS ON TFP IN THREE FAB COMPANY PLANTS			
PLANT	**MEAN LEVEL OF ECOS PER MONTH**	**NUMBER OF ECOS IN LOWEST MONTH**	**NUMBER OF ECOS IN HIGHEST MONTH**	**EFFECT ON TFP OF INCREASING NUMBER OF ECOS FROM 5 TO 15 PER MONTH**
1	16.5	1	41	- 2.8%
2	12.2	2	43	- 4.6
3	7.0	1	19	-16.6

example, increasing ECOs by just 10 per month reduced TFP by almost 5 percent. Moreover, the debilitating effects of ECOs persisted for up to a year.

Our data suggest that the average level of ECOs implemented in a given month, as well as the variation in this level, is detrimental to TFP. Many companies would therefore be wise to reduce the number of ECOs to which their plants must respond. This notion suggests, in turn, that more pressure should be placed on engineering and marketing departments to focus attention on only the most important changes—as well as to design things right the first time.

Essential ECOs should be released in a controlled, steady fashion rather than in bunches. In the one plant that divided ECOs into categories reflecting their cost, low-cost ECOs were most harmful to TFP. More expensive ECOs actually had a positive effect. The reason: plant managers usually had warning of major changes and, recognizing that they were potentially disruptive, carefully prepared the ground by warning supervisors, training workers, and bringing in engineers. By contrast, minor ECOs were simply dumped on the factory out of the blue.

VALUE OF LEARNING

If setting up adequate measures of performance is the first step toward getting full competitive leverage out of manufacturing, identifying factory-level goals like waste or WIP reduction is the second. But without making a commitment to ongoing learning, a factory will gain no more from these first two steps than a one-time boost in performance. To sustain the leverage of plant-level operations, managers must pay close attention to—and actively plan for—learning.

We are convinced that a factory's learning rate—the rate at which its managers and operators learn to make it run better—is at least of equal importance as its current level of productivity. A factory whose TFP is lower than another's, but whose rate of learning is higher, will eventually surpass the leader. Confusion, as we have seen, is especially harmful to TFP. Thus the two essential tasks of factory management are to create clarity and order (that is, to prevent confusion) and to facilitate learning.

But doesn't learning always involve a good deal of experimentation and confusion? Isn't there an inherent conflict between creating clarity and order and facilitating learning? Not at all.

Confusion, like noise or static in an audio system, makes it hard to pick up the underlying message or figure out the source of the problem. It impedes learning, which requires controlled experimentation, good data, and careful analysis. It chews up time, resources, and energy in efforts to deal with issues whose solution adds little to a factory's performance. Worse, engineers, supervisors, operators, and managers easily become discouraged by the futility of piecemeal efforts. In such environments, TFP lags or falls.

Reducing confusion and enhancing learning do not conflict. They make for a powerful combination—and a powerful lever on competitiveness. A factory that manages change poorly, that does not have its processes under control, and that is distracted by the noise in its systems learns too slowly, if at all, or learns the wrong things.

In such a factory, new equipment will only create more confusion, not more productivity. Equally troubling, both managers and workers in such a factory will be slow to believe reports that a sister plant—or a competitor's plant—can do things better than they can. If the evidence is overwhelming, they will simply argue, "It can't work here. We're different." Indeed they are—and less productive too.

'WHERE THE MONEY IS'

Many companies have tried to solve their data-processing problems by bringing in computers. They soon learned that computerizing a poorly organized and error-ridden information system simply creates more problems: garbage in, garbage out. That lesson, learned so long ago, has been largely forgotten by today's managers, who are trying to improve manufacturing performance by bringing in sophisticated new equipment without first reducing the complexity and confusion of their operations.

Spending big money on hardware fixes will not help if managers have not taken the time to simplify and clarify their factories' operations, eliminate sources of error and confusion, and boost the rate of learning. Of course, advanced technology is important, often essential. But there are many things that managers must do first to prepare their organizations for these new technologies.

When plant managers are stuck with poor measures of how they are doing and when a rigid, by-the-book emphasis on standards, budgets, and exception reports discourages the kind of experimentation that leads to learning, the real levers on factory performance remain hidden. No amount of capital investment can buy heightened competitiveness. There is no way around the importance of building clarity into the system, eliminating unnecessary disruptions and distractions, ensuring careful process control, and nurturing in-depth technical competence. The reason for understanding why some factories perform better than others is the same reason that Willie Sutton robbed banks: "That's where the money is."

Research Methods

There are three basic approaches for identifying the effects of management actions and policies on factory-level productivity: first, a longitudinal analysis, which looks at a single factory over a long time; second, a cross-sectional analysis, which compares the performance (at the same time) of two or more factories that make similar products and have similar manufacturing processes; and third, a combined approach, which collects several years' worth of data for factories having a variety of structural characteristics and uses statistical analysis to identify the effects of what managers do. We have used all three methods.

For each factory, we gathered data on a monthly basis for at least one-and-a-half years and usually for more than five. In several cases, we were able to track performance over a nine-year period; in more than half the cases, our data go back to the factory's start-up. To our knowledge, this is the first attempt to explore in such depth the sources of productivity growth at the factory level in the United States, and our data base is the most comprehensive yet compiled.

We developed our central performance measure, total factor productivity, by first calculating each factory's monthly partial factor productivities—that is, by dividing its output in turn by labor, materials, capital, and energy (for both outputs and inputs, we used 1982 dollars to eliminate the impact of inflation). To calculate a factory's total monthly output, we multiplied the quantity of each of the products it made in any month by that product's 1982 standard cost. To estimate labor input, we relied on total hours of work in each major employee classification (direct labor, indirect labor, and so forth) to estimate capital input, we used the book value of assets adjusted for inflation; and to estimate materials input, we deflated the dollar values of materials consumption by a materials price index based on 1982 dollars.

We then combined these partial measures into an index of overall total factor productivity (TFP). Because of the large fixed component in capital as well as labor cost, each factory's TFP is quite sensitive to changes in production volume and to the timing of major capital investments. To separate the movements in TFP linked to changes in production capacity from those linked to changes in operating efficiency, we included an estimate of capacity utilization in all regression analyses.

The Figure shows the quite different productivity experience at the Process Company's five plants. Hi-Tech's plants enjoyed rapid growth in output and productivity, but some of the Process and Fab plants had declining productivity and (in one case) declining output. All the Hi-Tech plants learned at a very high rate, although productivity growth in the early months was anything but fast or smooth, and some plants seemed to learn faster than others. Moderate growth and

PRODUCTIVITY AT PROCESS COMPANY PLANTS

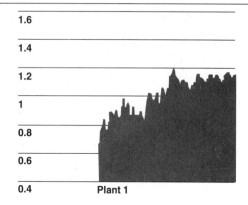

Plant 1

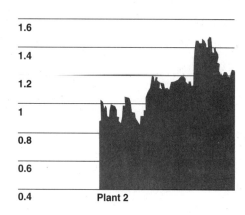

Plant 2

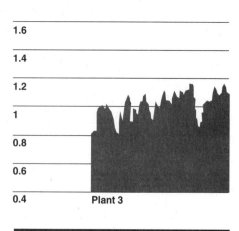

Plant 3

Months

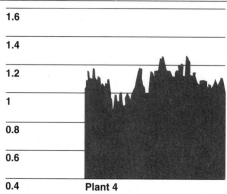

Plant 4

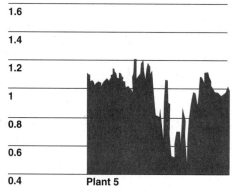

Plant 5

Months

learning characterized the Fab Company's plants 2, 3, and 4; at Plant 1, however, volume declined, and TFP growth was flat or negative during much of the time we studied it.

This disparity in performance is not limited to comparisons across companies. Even within a company, productivity growth differed significantly across plants—even where each produced identical products and faced the same market and technological conditions. We cannot explain these differences by reference to technology, product variety, or market demands—they have to do with management.

Once we developed the data on TFP, we discussed each factory's results with its management. Some of the anomalies we found resulted from errors in the data provided us; others were caused by certain events (the advent of the deer-hunting season, for example, or a year-end peak in purchased materials). We made no attempt to relate monthly TFP figures to managerial variables until each factory's managers understood our method of calculating TFP and agreed that the patterns we found fairly represented their factory's behavior.

After developing credible TFP estimates, we had to identify and measure those managerial policies that might have an impact on TFP. The Table lists these policies and describes the measures we used to capture them.

Using multiple linear regression analysis, we first examined the effect of these policy variables on TFP in the same factory over time. Early findings, coupled with discussions with a number of managers, suggested that the simple ratios and averages we were using did not adequately capture the phenomena we were trying to understand. Actions like overhauling older equipment, training workers, and implementing an engineering change order are similar in nature to investments—that is, they will likely cause short-term inefficiencies. To test the long-term effects of such actions, we included lagged variables, which allowed us to estimate the effect on TFP of management actions taken in previous months.

Other management activities may have little effect on productivity unless they are held at a certain level for several months. Boosting the amount spent on maintaining equipment, for example, does not do much if sustained for only one month. In these cases, we looked at the relationship between TFP and a five-month moving average of relevant management variables. For still other activities—a profound change, say, in production rates—it matters greatly if the change is highly unusual or is part of a pattern of widely fluctuating rates. For each of these variables, we examined the relationship between TFP and the variable's average absolute deviation (using the five-month moving average as the estimated mean value for the variable).

A last, brief note about the importance of combining statistical analysis with ongoing field research. We found immense value in discussing our findings with the managers involved. We expected, for example, that equipment maintenance and workforce training would share a positive relationship to productivity growth. Our plant data, however, revealed a consistently negative relationship:

MANAGERIAL POLICIES

POLICY CATAGORY	INDICATORS
Equipment	Average age of equipment
	Average maintenance expense as a percentage of equipment book value
Quality	Process waste; yield as a percentage of total input materials
	Intermediate and final reject rates
	Customer return rates
Inventory	Work-in-process as a percentage of total materials or production cost
Work Force	Average age and education of workers
	Hours of overtime per week
	Absenteeism rate
	Hiring and layoff rates
	Average hours of training per employee
Policies affecting confusion	Fluctuations in production volume
	Number of product types produced
	Number of production orders scheduled
	Number of schedule changes as a percentage of number of production orders scheduled
	Number and type of engineering change orders
	Introduction of new processing equipment

---

high expenditures on maintenance and training, even in lagged forms, generally were associated with *low* TFP. When we talked about this with plant managers in all three companies, we discovered that they used maintenance and training as *corrective* measures. That is they boosted maintenance in response to equipment problems; when the problems were solved, they reduced it. By themselves, the data would not allow us to separate corrective from preventive maintenance, or even from the costs of modifying or rebuilding equipment.

SELECTED READINGS

Abernathy, W., and K. Wayne. "Limits of the Learning Curve." *Harvard Business Review* 52:5 (1973): 109–119.

Abernathy, W.J. "The Limits of the Learning Curve." *Harvard Business Review,* September–October 1974, pp. 109–119.

Andress, F. J. "The Learning Curve as a Production Tool." *Harvard Business Review* 32:1 (1954): 1–11.

Chase, R., and David Garvin, "The Service Factory." *Harvard Business Review,* July–August 1989, pp. 61–69.

Chew, W.B. "No-Nonsense Guide to Measuring Productivity." *Harvard Business Review* 66:1 (1988): 110-118.

Hall, R. W. *Zero Inventories* New York: Dow Jones-Irwin, 1983.

Hayes, R., and W. Abernathy. "Managing Our Way to Economic Decline." *Harvard Business Review* 58:4 (1980): 67–77.

Mayo, Elton. *The Human Problems of an Industrial Civilization,* Boston: Harvard Business School, 1946.

Nakane, J., and R. Hall. "Manufacturing Specs for Stockless Production." *Harvard Business Review* 61:3 (1983): 84–91.

Orlicky, J. *Materials Requirement Planning.* New York: McGraw–Hill, 1975.

Pennock, George A. "Industrial Research at Hawthorne." *Personnel Journal* 8 (February, 1930): 296–313.

Takeuchi, H. "Productivity: Learning from the Japanese." *California Management Review* 23:4 (1981): 5–19.

Vollman, Thomas. "Capacity Planning: The Missing Link." *Production and Inventory Management.* (First Quarter, 1973): 61–73.

Wagnor and Whitin. "A Dynamic Version of the ELS Model." *Management Science* 5:1 (1958): 89–96.

CHAPTER FIVE

SERVICE OPERATIONS MANAGEMENT

T
hroughout the latter part of the Twentieth Century, the American economy has been based more and more on the service industry rather than manufacturing. This has been especially true during the 1980s. In 1992, the service sector accounted for roughly 80 percent of the U.S. economy. In spite of this growth, however, studies on the operations of a service industry have been relatively slow in coming.

The field of service operations management is not yet old enough to have established "classic" articles, however, this area does need to be mentioned. As such, the editors reviewed the list of authors produced by the first study for articles relating to the service sector. Richard Chase has produced works relating to the service sector as early as 1978. One of his articles is reproduced here. Several other articles were reviewed by the editors but were not cited by the respondents of the survey. These articles have been included in the readings list.

As the field of service operations develops, more articles will be generated. And, as further study of the area occurs, a framework will be developed and classics defined. The editors hope that future questionnaires will result in the definition of this framework and identification of classics in the field of service operations.

WHERE DOES THE CUSTOMER FIT IN A SERVICE OPERATION?

RICHARD B. CHASE

With the recently legislated increase in the minimum wage law in the United States and the current economic downswing in Europe, service system managers in Western economies can look forward to continued pressure to run their operations more efficiently. While most managers are aware of the success stories of companies in a few industries (notably fast foods), there is little in the way of theory to help them decide how far they should go in altering their products, technologies, work forces, and work methods in attempting to achieve the nebulous goal of an efficient production system for services.

To appreciate the nature of the problem, consider the following stereotypical comment from the operations vice president of a finance company:

"I just don't understand it—the branch managers of our company never seem to run their offices in an efficient fashion. They rarely have the right match between lending personnel and clients demanding their services; they need more typists and clerks to do essentially the same amount of clerical duties that we perform in the home office. In my opinion, what we need is more work out of our methods department to get these branches as efficient as my home office operations. After all, we are in the same company providing the same general service to our customers."

Much has been written about improving service company operations, and many useful distinctions have been drawn among different kinds of service operations. In this article, I wish to propose still another way of looking at service organizations, a method of analysis that can be very helpful to managers. The essential features of this method are a classification scheme for service systems and a list of leading questions to be used in developing a production policy for the service system at hand.

Reprinted by permission of *Harvard Business Review,* 56:6 (1978): 137–42.

EXTENT OF CONTACT

Service systems are generally classified according to the service they provide, as delineated in the Standard Industrial Classification (SIC) code. This classification, though useful in presenting aggregate economic data for comparative purposes, does not deal with the production activities through which the service is carried out. What the manager needs, it would seem, is a service classification system that indicates with greater precision the nature of the demands on his or her particular service system in terms of its operating requirements. In manufacturing, by contrast, there are fairly evocative terms to classify production activities (e.g., unit, batch, and mass production), which, when applied to a manufacturing setting, readily convey the essence of the process.

It is possible, of course, to describe certain service systems using manufacturing terms, but such terms, as in the case of the SIC code, are insufficient for diagnosing and thinking about how to improve the systems without one additional item of information. That item—which I believe operationally distinguishes one service system from another in terms of what they can and cannot achieve in the way of efficiency—is the extent of customer contact in the creation of the service.

To elaborate, *customer contact* refers to the physical presence of the customer in the system, and *creation of the service* refers to the work process that is entailed in providing the service itself. *Extent* of contact here may be roughly defined as the percentage of time the customer must be in the system relative to the total time it takes to serve him. Obviously, the greater the percentage of contact time between the service system and the customer, the greater the degree of interaction between the two during the production process.

From this conceptualization, it follows that service systems with high customer contact are more difficult to control and more difficult to rationalize than those with low customer contact. In high-contact systems, such as those listed in Exhibit 1, the customer can affect the time of demand, the exact nature of the service, and the quality of service since he tends to become involved in the process itself. In low-contact systems, by definition, customer interaction with the system is infrequent or of short duration and hence has little impact on the system during the production process.

TECHNICAL CORE

One way to conceive of high- versus low-contact business is that the low-contact system has the capability of decoupling operations and sealing off the "techni-

[1]James D. Thompson, *Organizations in Action* (New York: McGraw-Hill, 1967), 20.

EXHIBIT 1	CLASSIFICATION OF SERVICE SYSTEMS BY EXTENT OF REQUIRED CUSTOMER CONTACT IN CREATION OF THE SERVICE

High contact	**Pure service** Health centers Hotels Public transportation Restaurants Schools Personal services	Increasing freedom in designing efficient production procedures
	Mixed service Branch offices of: Banks Computer companies Real estate Post offices Funeral homes	
	Quasimanufacturing Home offices of: Banks Computer companies Government administration Wholesale houses Post offices	
	Manufacturing Factories producing durable goods Food processors Mining companies	
Low contact	Chemical plants	

cal core" from the environment, while the high-contact system does not. As one researcher has pointed out, "The technical core must be able to operate as if the market will absorb the single kind of product at a continuous rate, and as if inputs flowed continuously at a steady rate with specified quality."[1] Indeed, decoupling production from outside influences (for example, via inventory buffers) is a common objective in designing manufacturing systems.

Several industries provide examples of shifts in customer contact through two or more of the stages given in Exhibit 1:

- Automatic banking tellers, with their 24-hour availability and their location for easy access, illustrate pure service; branch offices, with their provision of drive-in tellers, coordinated waiting lines, and often visible back offices, illustrate mixed service; and home offices, designed for efficient receipt, processing, and shipping of bank paper, illustrate quasimanufacturing.

- Airlines exhibit mixed service characteristics at their terminals (high-contact ticket counters and low-contact baggage handling), pure service characteristics within the planes, and quasimanufacturing characteristics in their billing and airplane maintenance operations.
- Blood collection stations provide an obvious example of pure service—they are (or should be) operated with the psychological and physiological needs of the donor in mind and, in fact, often take the "service" to the donor by using bloodmobiles. The blood itself is processed at specialized facilities (blood banks) following "manufacturing" procedures common to batch processing.
- Many consulting firms switch back and forth between pure service and quasimanufacturing. Pure service takes place when data are gathered at the client's facility, while quasimanufacturing takes place when data are analyzed and reports are prepared at the firm's home offices. Other firms, of course, have facilities designed for mixed service operations; their client waiting areas are planned in detail to convey a particular image, and back offices are arranged for efficient noncontact work.

EFFECT ON OPERATIONS

Of course, the reason it is important to determine how much customer contact is required to provide a service is that it has an effect on every decision that production managers must make. Exhibit 2 is a list of some of the more interesting decisions relating to system design. The points made in this exhibit lead to four generalizations about the two classes of service systems.

First, high-contact systems have more uncertainty about their day-to-day operations since the customer can always make an input to (or cause a disruption in) the production process. Even in those high-contact systems that have relatively highly specified products and processes, the customer can "have it his way." Burger King will fill special orders, TWA will (on occasion) delay a takeoff for a late arrival, a hospital operating room schedule will be disrupted for emergency surgery, and so on.

Second, unless the system operates on an appointments-only basis, it is only by happenstance that the capacity of a high-contact system will match the demand on that system at any given time.[2] The manager of a supermarket, branch bank, or entertainment facility can predict only statistically the number of people that will be in line demanding service at, say, two o'clock on Tuesday afternoon. Hence, employing the correct number of servers (neither too many nor too few) must also depend on probability.

---

[2]For a detailed discussion of capacity planning in services, see W. Earl Sasser, "Match Supply and Demand in Service Industries," *Harvard Business Review*, November–December 1976, 132.

EXHIBIT 2	MAJOR DESIGN CONSIDERATIONS IN HIGH- AND LOW-CONTACT SYSTEMS	
DECISION	**HIGH-CONTACT SYSTEM**	**LOW-CONTACT SYSTEM**
Facility location	Operations must be near the customer.	Operatings may be placed near supply, transportation, or labor.
Facility layout	Facility should accommodate the customer's physical and psychological needs and expectations.	Facility should enhance production.
Product design	Environment as well as the physical product define the nature of the service.	Customer is not in the service environment so the product can be defined by fewer attributes.
Process design	Stages of production process have a direct immediate effect on the customer.	Customer is not involved in the majority of the processing steps.
Scheduling	Customer is in the production schedule and must be accommodated.	Customer is concerned mainly with completion dates.
Production planning	Orders cannot be stored, so smoothing production flow will result in loss of business.	Both backlogging and production smoothing are possible.
Worker skills	Direct work force comprises a major part of the service product and so must be able to interact well with the public.	Direct work force need only have technical skills.
Quality control	Quality standards are often in the eye of the beholder and hence variable.	Quality standards are generally measurable and hence fixed.
Time standards	Service time depends on customer needs, and therefore time standards are inherently loose.	Work is performed on customer surrogates (e.g., forms), and time standards can be tight.
Wage payment	Variable output requires time-based wage systems.	"Fixable" output permits output-based wage systems.
Capacity planning	To avoid lost sales, capacity must be set to match peak demand.	Storable output permits setting capacity at some average demand level.
Forecasting	Forecasts are short term, time-oriented.	Forecasts are long term, output-oriented.

Low-contact systems, on the other hand, have the potential to exactly match supply and demand for their services since the work to be done (e.g., forms to be completed, credit ratings analyzed, or household goods shipped) can be carried out following a resource-oriented schedule permitting a direct equivalency between producer and product.

Third, by definition, the required skills of the work force in high-contact systems are characterized by a significant public relations component. Any interaction with the customer makes the direct worker in fact part of the product and therefore his attitude can affect the customer's view of the service provided.

Finally, high-contact systems are at the mercy of time far more than low-contact systems. Batching of orders for purposes of efficient production scheduling is rarely possible in high-contact operations since a few minutes' delay or a violation of the law of the queue (first come, first served) has an immediate effect on the customer. Indeed, "unfair" preferential treatment in a line at a box office often gives rise to some of the darker human emotions, which are rarely evoked by the same unfair preferential treatment that is employed by a distant ticket agency whose machinations go unobserved by the customer.

IMPLICATIONS FOR MANAGEMENT

Several implications may be drawn from the foregoing discussion of differences between high-contact and low-contact systems.

To start with, rationalizing the operations of a high-contact system can be carried only so far. While technological devices can be substituted for some jobs performed by direct-contact workers, the worker's attitude, the environment of the facility, and the attitude of the customer will determine the ultimate quality of the service experience.

Another point to keep in mind is that the often-drawn distinction between for-profit and not-for-profit services has little, if any, meaning from a production management standpoint. A not-for-profit home office can be operated as efficiently as a for-profit home office, and conversely, a high-contact for-profit branch is subject to the same inherent limitations on its efficiency as its not-for-profit counterpart.

Clearly, wherever possible, a distinction should be made between the high-contact and low-contact elements of a service system. This can be done by a separation of functions: all high-contact activities should be performed by one group of people, all low-contact activities by another. Such an adjustment minimizes the influence of the customer on the production process and provides opportunities to achieve efficiency where it is actually possible to do so.

Finally, it follows that separation of functions enhances the development of two contrasting classes of worker skills and orientations—public relations and interpersonal attributes for high-contact purposes and technical and analytical attributes for low-contact purposes. While some writers have urged mixing of duties under the general rubric of job enrichment, a careful analysis before doing so seems warranted when one recognizes the considerable differences in the skills required between high- and low-contact systems.

POLICY DEVELOPMENT

Applying the foregoing concepts for developing a production policy for services entails answering several questions:

What kind of operating system do you have? Is it a pure service, mixed service, or quasimanufacturing? What percentage of your business activity in terms of labor hours is devoted to direct customer contact?

A good indication of where a production system falls along the contact continuum can be obtained by using the industrial engineering technique of work sampling. This approach involves taking a statistically determined random sample of work activities to find how much time is being spent in customer-contact work. The Pacific Finance Company has regularly used this method to determine if a branch office is properly staffed and if some of its paperwork activities should be shifted to the home office. Another industrial engineering technique, process charting, has been used successfully to help specify the proper balance between front-office and back-office capacity in the mixed services operations of the Arizona Auto Licensing Bureau.

Are your operating procedures geared to your present structure?   Specifically, have you matched your compensation system to the nature of the service system—for example, high-contact systems based on time and low-contact systems on output? Are you appropriately allocating contact and no-contact tasks? Are you using cost or profit centers where these two measures are subject to control by the on-site manager?

Obviously, paying service workers according to the number of customers served tends to speed up service in the high-contact system. However, with the exception of extremely simple standardized operations, such as toll booths, mailing a package from a post office, and supermarket checkouts, speed of processing is not the most important element of service to the customer. Indeed, if the customer feels rushed in a hospital, bank, or restaurant, he is likely to be dissatisfied with the organization.

Further, it makes little sense for a seller of any service that can be at all customized to measure system effectiveness in terms of total number of customers served when in fact one should be giving more leisurely attention to a smaller number of "big spenders." (The reader may verify this point by comparing the attention accorded the casino bettor at the $2 blackjack table with the amenities observed at the $25 table.)

Can you realign your operations to reduce unnecessary direct customer service? Can tasks performed in the presence of the customer be shifted to the back office? Can you divide your labor force into high-contact and no-contact areas? Can you set up plants within plants to permit development of unique organizational structures for a narrower set of tasks for each subunit of the service organization?[3]

---

[3]See Wickham Skinner, "The Focused Factory," *Harvard Business Review,* May–June 1974, 113.

The idea of shifting operations to the back office has recently become popular among tax preparation companies that now take a client's tax records and prepare a computer-processed return in his absence. Likewise, word-processing centers prepare documents in the absence of the customer, who provides original copy.

Managers have long recognized the desirability of having "attractive" personnel greet the public in such job classifications as receptionist, restaurant hostess, and stewardess, while being more concerned with technical skills on the part of those individuals removed from customer contact, such as typists, cooks, and those in maintenance positions. Plants-within-plants are typical in hospitals (e.g., labs, food service, and laundry), in insurance companies (e.g., underwriters, pool typists, and records), and in restaurants (e.g., cooking, table service, and bar).

Can you take advantage of the efficiencies offered by low-contact operations?   In particular, can you apply the production management concepts of batch scheduling, forecasting, inventory control, work measurement, and simplification to back-office operations? Can you now use the latest technologies in assembling, packaging, cooking, testing, and so on, to support front-office operations?

The production management literature offers numerous applications of the foregoing concepts to low-contact systems. One interesting example concerns the improvement of the forecasting procedure used to determine manpower requirements at the Chemical Bank of New York.[4] Daily volume of transit checks (checks drawn on other banks and cashed at Chemical Bank) averages $2 billion a day, often with a $1 billion variation from day to day. The new forecasting method employs a two-stage approach using multiple regression followed by exponential smoothing to forecast daily loads in pounds of checks per day. This approach yields significant improvement in forecast accuracy over the previous intuitive methods and thereby provides a basis for effective production planning.

Can you enhance the customer contact you do provide?   With all nonessential customer-contact duties shifted, can you speed up operations, by adding part-time, more narrowly skilled workers at peak hours, keep longer business hours, or add personal touches to the contacts you do have?

The key to employing this step lies in recognizing the implications of Sasser's and Pettway's observation: "Although bank tellers, chambermaids,

---

[4]Kevin Boyd and Vincent A. Mabert, "Two Stage Forecasting Approach at Chemical Bank of New York for Check Processing," *Journal of Bank Research,* Summer 1977, 101.

and short-order cooks may have little in common, they are all at the forefront of their employers' public images."[5] If the low-contact portion of a worker's job can be shifted to a different work force, then the opportunity exists to focus that worker's efforts on critical interpersonal relations aspects.

For example, store sales personnel are frequently called on to engage in stock clerk activities, which often must take precedence over waiting on customers. However, since the salesperson's central function is as a company representative within the store, it may be better to hire more stock clerks and free the salesperson to fulfill that personal function.

Can you relocate parts of your service operations to lower your facility costs? Can you shift back-room operations to lower rent districts, limit your contact facilities to small drop-off facilities (à la Fotomat), or get out of the contact facilities business entirely through the use of jobbers or vending machines?

Unless it is an essential feature of the service package, or an absolute necessity for coordination purposes, managers should carefully scrutinize back-office operations before appending them to customer-contact facilities. As advocated throughout this article, high- and low-contact operations are inherently different and should be located and staffed to maximize their individual as well as joint contribution to the organization. The notion of decentralizing service depots as indicated by my examples is, of course, a well-understood marketing strategy, but it deserves additional consideration as an alternative use of service "production" capacity.

APPLYING THE CONCEPT

Going through the process of answering these policy questions should trigger other questions about the service organization's operation and mission. In particular, it should lead management to question whether its strength lies in high contact or low contact, and it should encourage reflection on what constitutes an optimal balance between the two types of operations relative to resource allocation and market emphasis.

Also, the process should lead to an analysis of the organization structure that is required to effectively administer the individual departments as well as the overall organization of the service business. For example, it is quite probable that separate managements and internally differentiated structures

---

[5]W. Earl Sasser and Samuel H. Pettway, "Case of Big Mac's Pay Plans," *Harvard Business Review,* July–August 1971, 30.

will be in order if tight coordination between high-contact and low-contact units is not necessary. Where tight coordination is necessary, particular attention must be paid to boundary-spanning activities of both labor and management to assure a smooth exchange of material and information among departments.

SELECTED READINGS

E. Sasser, "Matching Supply and Demand in Service Industries." *Harvard Business Review* 54:6 (1976): 133–40.

D. R. Thomas, "Strategy is Different in Service Business." *Harvard Business Review* 56:4 (1978): 158–65.

T. Leavitt, "The Industrialization of Service." *Harvard Business Review* 54:5 (1976): 63–74.

INDEX

Abernathy, William J.,

Abernathy, William J., 7, 8, 9, 463–464, 487
  "Managing Our Way to Economic Decline," 129–149

Accountability, MRP and, 457

Acquisitions, 146. *See also* Mergers

Aesthetics, of products, 334–335

Aggregate planning, research in, 159

Aggregation-disaggregation, research on, 155

Allocation, 438

American National Standards Institute, product quality and, 264

American Printed Circuit Company (APC), 102–103

American Productivity Center, 144

American Society of Mechanical Engineers, The, 69
  scientific management and, 417–418

Anderson, Richard W., 327

Andress, F.J., 487

ANOVA, one-way, 342

Assemblies, 447

Auto industry
  backward integration in, 141
  productivity and, 463–464
  scale and JIT in, 181

Automobile, expected life of, 333

Ayers, Leonard, 54

Babbage, Charles, 49, 151

Backward integration, 140–141

Baker, Ray Stannard, "Frederick W. Taylor—Scientist in Business Management," 369–375

Bancroft, John Sellers, 41

Barnes, Ralph, 152

Barth, Carl George Lange, 37–38

Behrens, N.W. III, 163n

Bell Laboratories, quality and, 187. *See also* Shewhart, Walter A.

Bennett, Roger, 137n

Bethlehem Steel Company, scientific management and, 33–36

Better Business Bureau, company performance rating by, 262

Bills of material, 427–453
  modular, 439–449

Bonner, P. Greg, 335n

Bonus, 13
  specifications for, 21

Bosses, as servants and teachers, 15–16

Boyd, Kevin, 496n

Brandeis, Louis, 49, 269

Bricklaying, scientific process of, 401–402

Budget, quality control, 117–118

Buffa, Elwood, 8, 9
  "Research in Operations Management," 151–163

Business, success in, 149

Capacity
  corporate strategy and, 120
  expansion of, 119

Capacity planning, research in, 162

Capacity requirement plans, MRP II and, 458

Capital equipment-to-labor ratio, decline of, 133

Capital investment, and productivity, 475–477

Cash management, mergers and, 145–146

Caveat emptor, consumerism and, 251–252

Chase, Richard, 487, 489
  "Where Does the Customer Fit in a Service Operation?," 491–500

Chatelier, H., 374

Chemical Bank, 337

Chew, W.B., 487

Chronocyclegraphs, 75–76

Clark, Kim B., 466n, 471–487

Classic contributors
  ratings of, 4
  survey of, 1–5

Classifications, of service systems, 490

Clearinghouse, company performance and, 262

Comparative advantage, 168

Compensation system, matched with service system type, 497

"Competing on the Eight Dimensions of Quality" (Garvin), 323–339

Competition
American manufacturers and, 461
costs and, 103–104
global production and operations strategy for, 165–175
management productivity assessment and, 471–472
manufacturing and, 85
in quality, 284–287

Competitive advantage, innovation and, 173

Competitiveness
decline of U.S., 129–149
divestitures and, 146
increasing, 139–142
innovation and, 138–140

Computer model, MRP as, 457

Computers
proper use of, 481–482
systems design, programming, and, 95–96

Conformance, of products, 330–331, 332

Confusion, reducing, 479–480

Consistency, in manufacturing, 106–107

Consumerism
government regulation and, 270–275
independent laboratory marks and, 264–266
industry as leader in, 259–263
lack of satisfaction and, 256–259
mandatory mark and, 266–270
misrepresentation of quality and, 251–252
product failures and, 252–256
quality and, 307

"Consumerism and Product Quality" (Juran), 249–275

Contact
degree of, and effect on operations, 494–496
degree of customer, in service business, 492–496

Contributors. See Classic contributors

Control
advantages of, 202–205
defined, 194–195
nature of, 193–194
program for, 212–214
for quality, 191–205. See also Quality control
scientific basis for, 195–201
statistical, 201–202, 208–210, 217–229

Conway, William E., 233–235, 237

Cooper, Robert, 137n

Cooperation
for efficiency, 67–68
scientific management and, 65–74, 408
in task and bonus system, 19–20
Taylor on, 353–354
training in, 11–22

Corporate portfolio management, 137

Corporate presidents, professional origins of, 143

Corporate strategy
capacity expansion, 119
conceptual framework for, 119–122
equipment purchase and, 117
implementing, 121–128
labor negotiations, 118
in manufacturing decisions, 115–128
operating decisions and, 124
quality control budget and, 117–118

Cost accounting, total quality control and, 310–311

Costs
manufacturing strategy and, 126
piecework and, 353
productivity and, 465
of quality, 307–308, 317–320
quality correlation with, 235
reducing, 233–235
reduction of inspection, 202–203
scientific management and, 28

Cost system, standard, 472–473

Cotton industry, Taylor on, 25–26

Cray Research, quality competition by, 336

Crosby, Phillip B., 187

Customer contact, 492
enhancing existing, 498–499
extent of, 492–496
Customer orientation, 137–138
Customers, world-class manufacturing and, 179–180. *See also* Consumerism
Customer service
independent laboratory guarantees of, 265
reducing unnecessary, 497–498
Cyclegraphs, 75–76

Daeves, K.H., 193n
Damon, 75n
Daniels, John D., 175
Dannenbring, David G., 175
Data processing, MRP II and, 459
Davison, J. Hugh, 139
Day labor, piecework system and, 350–351
Day rates, 344–345
Day work, 19
Decision making
European process, 147
in manufacturing, 96–98
Dedicated plants, 181
Defense Department, product reliability and, 330
Demand, market, 105
Deming, W. Edwards, 187, 315, 341
14 points of, 238–246
"Improvement of Quality and Productivity through Action by Management," 231–247
Deming Prize, 188
Departments, eliminating barriers between, 244–245
Dependability
manufacturing strategy and, 126
as performance criterion, 121
Dependent product structure systems, research in, 160
Design
control in, 213
trade-offs in, 91–93, 94–95
Design of experiments (DOE), 188
Development, control in, 212–213
Differential rate system, of piecework, 344–368

Dispatch lists, MRP II and, 458
Divestitures, 146
DOE. *See* Design of experiments
Domestic enterprise, vs. global enterprise, 170, 171
Dun & Bradstreet, company performance ratings by, 262
Durability, of products, 331–333
Dyer, James S., 151n

Earnings, distribution of, 360–361
Economic Control of Manufactured Product (Shewhart), 187, 191–214
Economic decline, management and, 129–149
Economics, waste and, 81–82
Economic value, 148–149
Economies, change as life cycle factor, 167
Economies of scope, 173
"Economy of Machinery and Manufacture," 49
Economy of scale, 115
Education, technical or industrial, 14. *See also* Training
"Effective Company Operation as Never Before!" (Wight), 455–459
Efficiency, 462–463
cooperation of management and outside efforts for, 67–68
Gilbreth, Frank, on, 47–48
manufacturing and, 93–95
as performance criterion, 121
science and, 52–53
in service operations, 498
standardization and, 56–61, 69–70
surveys for, 54–56
Taylor on, 345, 377–394
waste and, 81–82
Energy, research in, 162
Enforcement, of standardization quality, 267
Engineering
MRP II and, 459
quality control, 312–315
Ethics, as management standard, 51–52
Europe, competitive success in, 146–148
Expansion, capacity, 119

Expert knowledge, 17
Exploratory research, 1–3
Exports, European vs. U.S., 147

Fab (fabrication-assembly)
  Company, 472
Facilities, corporate strategy and, 120
Facility costs, service operations and,
  499
Factories
  approaches to identifying manage-
  ment effect on, 483–486
  productivity in, 101–114, 471–487.
  See also Industry; Scientific management
  scientific management in, 408–417
  Taylor and, 466
  variables affecting productivity in,
  472–484
Factor productivity, 473
Fast food industry, 491. *See also* Service
  operations management
Fatigue study, 70, 76–80
Features, of products, 329–330
Feigenbaum, Armand V., 187
  *Quality Control—Principles, Practice,
  and Administration* (excerpts),
  289–306
  total quality control (TQC) of,
  324–325
  "Total Quality Control," 307–321
Fidelity Investments, features of, 330
Finance, quality and, 280
Financial control, profit centers for, 367
Financial portfolio mangement, 137
Fisher Controls Co., 451
Flexibility
  manufacturing strategy and, 126
  as performance criterion, 121
FMS (Flexible Manufacturing Systems),
  173–174
Focused factory, 8
  key characteristics of, 104–105
  steps to achieving, 110–113
"Focused Factory, The," 101–114
Follow-up research, 3–5
Ford Company, JIT and, 181
Forecasting, 62–65
Fourteen step quality program
  (Crosby), 188
Fourteen points, for top management

(Deming), 238–246
Frequency distribution, quality control
  and, 300–301

Gain-sharing plan, 350–351
Gangs
  boss of, 15
  workers in, 399–402
Gantt, Henry, 7, 9, 11–22, 341
  commentary on Taylor, 368
  "Training Workmen in Habits of
  Industry and Cooperation," 11
Gantt chart, 341
Garvin, David A., 187, 487
  "Competing on the Eight Dimen-
  sions of Quality," 313–339
Garwood, Dave, 451
Gay, E.F., 373
Gilbreth, Frank B., 6, 9, 341
  "Science in Management for the One
  Best Way to Do Work," 47–84
Gilbreth, Lillian, 7, 341
Global production
  defined, 166–167
  life cycle in, 167–168
  network models for, 168–170
  new tech, production theory, and
  management principles, 173–175
  suppliers for, 173
"Global Production and Operations
  Strategy" (Starr), 165–175
Goal setting, quality and, 285
"Gospel of Efficiency, The. The Princi-
  ples of Scientific Management" (Tay-
  lor), 377–393
"Gospel of Efficiency II, The. The Prin-
  ciples of Scientific Management"
  (Taylor), 395–402
"Gospel of Efficiency III, The. The
  Principles of Scientific Management"
  (Taylor), 405–421
Government, organization, waste, and,
  81–82
Grayson, C. Jackson, 144
Gresham's law of service, 257
Growth, world-class manufacturing and,
  179
Guarantees, service and, 256

Habits, of work and thought, 14

Hall, R.W., 487
Halpin, James F., 327n
Halsey, F.A., 353
Handicapped, scientific management and, 64–65
Happiness, as measurement unit, 52
Hawthorne studies, 341
Hayes, Robert H., 8, 9, 466n, 487
    and Kim B. Clark, "Why Some Factories Are More Productive Than Others," 471–487
    "Managing Our Way to Economic Decline," 129–149
Hewlett-Packard, 327
High-contact systems, 492–496
    design considerations in, 495
Hippel, Eric von, 142n
Hi-Tech Company, 472

IBM, global strategy of, 166
"If Japan Can, Why Can't We?," 341
Imitation, innovation and, 138–140
"Improvement of Quality and Productivity through Action by Management" (Deming), 231–247
Incoming material control
    for quality control, 302, 305
    total quality control and, 311, 313
Independent laboratory, as product quality guarantor, 264–266
Individuals, workers as, 400. See also Scientific management
Industrial education, 14
Industrial innovation, studies of, 142
Industry
    constraints in, 99
    decade of application in, 342
    habits of, 11
    as leaders in consumerism movement, 259–263
    Taylor and, 372–373, 377–394
Industry concentrations, as global life cycle factor, 167–168
Inflation, research in, 162
Infrastructure
    corporate strategy and, 120
    quality and, 285
Initiative, scientific management and, 416–417
Innovation

vs. imitation, 138–140
    industrial, 142
"Inquiry into the Nature and Cause of the Wealth of Nations, An" (Smith), 49
Inspection, quality control and, 312
Instructor, 13
Integration
    backward, 140–141
    vertical, 120
International operations, 8
Interstate Commerce Commission
    scientific management and, 49
    Taylor on, 369
Inventory
    control, MRP II and, 459
    work-in-process (WIP), 477–478
Investment, in process development, 141–142

Jacoby, Jacob, 335n
Jain, Subhash C., 175
Japan
    Deming and, 188
    JIT auto manufacturing in, 181
    management in, 146, 148, 168
    product conformance and, 331
    production in, 236
    productivity and, 341–342, 465
    quality in revitalized industry, 187
    quality process in, 283
Japanese Manufacturing Techniques: Nine Hidden Lessons in Simplicity (Schonberger), 178
JIT (just-in-time) production, 168, 178
    small size and, 181
Job design, manufacturing research and, 158
Job shop, world-class manufacturing and, 179
Journal of Operations Management, 155
Juran, Joseph M., 187, 324
    "Consumerism and Product Quality," 249–275, "Quality Trilogy, The," 277–287
Just-in-time production. See JIT production

Kanban (cards), for production scheduling, 168

Kayanagi, Kenichi, 188
King, Williford, 51n
Kit (K) number, 451

Labor. *See also* Scientific management
   efficiency of, 463
   growth in productivity of, 132, 133
   and management, 80–81
   negotiations and, 118
   in productivity of U.S., 101–102
   role of European, 147
"Labor intensive" (Malcohn), 469
Labor strikes. *See* Strikes
Labor unions, 348
Laws of motion study, in Stone Age, 53,
   55
Leaders
   dominant companies as, 263
   industry association as, 263
Learning, value of, 480–481
Leavitt, T., 500
Leonardo da Vinci, 49
Letter files, tool study laws and, 60–61
Life cycle, global, 167–168
Limits to Growth, The (study), 163
Line management, corporate strategy
   implementation and, 124–128
Location, manufacturing research and,
   158
Lorenz, Christopher, 466n
Low-contact systems, 492–496
   design considerations in, 495

Mabert, Vincent A., 496n
Machines
   productivity of, 358
   quality and, 235–236
Machinists. *See* Scientific management
Mailings, costs of, 61
Malcohn, Elissa, "Labor intensive," 469
Malkiel, Burton G., 132–133
Management. *See also* Line management;
   Scientific management; Staff
   American ideal of, 142–146
   conservation function and. *See* Effi-
   ciency
   differential piecework system and, 350
   economic decline and, 129–149
   European example of, 146–148
   failure of American, 130–136

financial control and, 136
forecasting and planning function of,
   62–65
global effects of new principles,
   173–175
as global life cycle factor, 168
high- and low-contact systems and,
   496
history of, 49–50
inefficiencies in, 26–27
labor and, 80–81
manufacturing focus and, 109–113
merger mania and, 145–146
new (scientific), 384–389
new orthodoxy of, 136–138
ordinary, 382–384
organizational function of, 56–61
portfolio, 137
productivity and policies of, 483–486
professional origins of, 143
quality improvement by, 237–247
relation to existing activities, 65–80
scientific, 23–46, 47–84. *See also* Scientific management
strategic quality, 327–335
strategy, purpose of, 6
structure for quality in, 245–246
units for judging, 50–51
view of manufacturing, 87–89
visualizing problem in, 64–65
Management Science (journal), 152
"Managing Our Way to Economic
   Decline" (Hayes and Abernathy),
   129–149
Mandatory mark, as quality guarantor,
   266–270
Manufactured product, economic control of quality in, 191–214
Manufacturers
   service by, 257–259
   size and, 181
Manufacturing
   competitive, 85, 466–469
   consistent policies in, 106–107
   corporate strategy and, 115–126
   decision making in, 96–98
   focused, 8, 101–114
   management failures in, 88–89
   measuring performance in, 104
   as millstone, 85–88

MRP II and, 459
operating decisions and, 124
policy determination process, 96–98
priorities in, 127–128
quality control as function of, 317
service systems and, 493
shortsighted view of, 87–88
support of corporate strategy by, 119–122
technical dominance in, 93–96
tools of, 105
top-down, 7
trade-offs in, 91–93, 94–95
U.S. competitiveness and, 461
world-class, 177–181
Manufacturing (M) bills, 445–446
Manufacturing focus, 109–113
"Manufacturing—Missing Link in Corporate Strategy," 85–100
Manufacturing processes, investing in new, 141–142
Manufacturing resource planning (MRP II), 341, 455–459
Manufacturing systems
research in operations planning and control, 159–160
research in strategic planning decisions, 156–158
Manufacturing task, 7
Marey, Jules Etienne, 66
Market analysis, need for, 137–138
Market demands, 105
Market-driven behavior, 137–138
Marketing
MRP II and, 458–459
strategies, 89–90
Martin Company, 325–327
Mass production
Ford and, 181
quality control for, 300
Master production schedules, 430
MRP II and, 458
Material(s). See also Bills of material
MRP system and, 431–439
pseudo-bills of, 449–451
Material requirements planning,
Materials requirements planning (MRP)
system, 341, 429–453, 456–459
MRP II and, 458
product orientation of, 429

Mathematicians, metal cutting and, 411–412
Mathematics. See Statistical control
Mayo, Elton, 341, 487
McDonald's, global strategy of, 165–166
Meadows, D.H., 163n
Meadows, D.L., 163n
Measurement
presented as knowledge, 225–229
standard, 473
Mental work
and shop work, 69
tool study and, 60–61
Mergers, 145–146
Metal cutting, Taylor, scientific management, and, 408–412
Midvale Steel Company, 345, 354, 363, 381, 390
scientific management and, 39–41
Miller, Jeffrey G., 151n
Millstone, manufacturing as, 85–88
Mixed service, 493, 494
Modern inspection view, of quality control, 309–310
Modern Quality Control
Feigenbaum on, 290–306. See also Quality control
statistics and, 300–302
Modular bills of material, 439–449
Modules, 442
Moral training, 21–22
Motion study, 53, 55, 70
chronocyclegraphs and, 75–76
development of, 72–73
fatigue study and, 76–80
origins of, 73–74
tools and, 59
Motor vehicles, failures of, 254
MRP. See Material Requirements Planning
MRP II. See Manufacturing Resource Planning
MS/OR, 152–153, 154

Nakane, J., 487
National Commission on Productivity, 101
Nelson, Richard, 335n
Nelson, Rosser T., 151n, 152n
Network models, global, 168–170

New design control
  for quality control, 302, 305
  total quality control and, 311,
    312–313
New York City Consumer Protection
  Act (1969), 257–258

Obeying orders, 15
Olsen, Jerry C., 335n
OM. *See* Operations management
Ombudsman, 263
One Best Way to do work. *See* Scientific
  management
One-way ANOVA, 342
"On the Art of Cutting Metals" (Taylor), 374
Operating characteristics, quality of,
  328–329
Operating system
  present structure and, 497
  service production policy and,
    496–497
Operations, degree of service and,
  494–496
Operations management (OM),
  166–167
  MS/OR in, 152–153
  production management as, 166
  production systems and, 152–154
  research, 151–163
  subject areas in, 157
Operations Management Newsletter, The,
  155
Operations planning and control,
  research in, 159–160
Operations strategy, 6–181
  global production and, 165–175
Order point systems, and material
  requirements planning (MRP), 429
Orders, obeying, 15
Organizational problem, quality as,
  315–317
Orlicky, Joseph A., 341, 487
  George W. Plossl, Oliver W. Wight,
  and, "Structuring the Bill of Material
  for MRP," 429–453
Output
  increase in, 26
  measurement of, 51

scientific rate vs. scientific rate-fixing,
  361
volume and costs, 355

Pareto Principle, 271
Part orientation, order point systems
  and, 429
Pearson, E.S., 222n
Pennock, George A., 487
Perceived quality, of products, 335
Performance
  criteria for, 121
  manufacturing, 104
  quality process ratings, 281–282
  ratings of company, 262
  strategic quality management and,
    328–329
  work habits and, 14–15
Pershing missiles, 325–327
Personnel
  MRP II and, 459
  research in, 159–160
Pettway, Samuel H., 499n
"Piece-Rate System, A, Being a Step
  Toward Partial Solution of the Labor
  Problem" (Taylor), 345–368
Piecework system, 19, 26, 345–368
  advantages of differential rate system,
    344–368
  shortcomings of some types, 347–346
  Taylor and, 345–368, 373, 381
Planned obsolescence, 255
Planning, 62–65
  manufacturing resource, 455–459
  materials requirements (MRP), 341,
    429–453, 456–459
Plossl, George W., 341, 429–453
Pokayoke concept (Shingo), 188
Policy
  development, for services, 496–499
  in manufacturing, 96–98
POM. *See* Production/operations man-
  agement
POM discipline, determining classic
  readings in, 1–5
Porter, Michael F., 175
Portfolio management, 137
Positioning strategy, research in, 161
Pre-assembly, 448

"Principles of Scientific Management," criticism of, 423–427. *See also* Taylor, Frederick W.

Process
configurations as global life cycle factor, 168
corporate strategy and, 120

Process Company, 472
plants, productivity at, 484

Process control, statistical evidence of, 239–243

Process development, 141–142

Process studies, 311, 314

Process technologies, 105, 465

Procurement and fabrication schedule, 448–449

Product control
for quality control, 302, 305
total quality control and, 311, 313

Product design
innovation vs. imitation in, 138–140
trade-offs in, 139

Product failures, consumerism and, 252–256

Production. *See also* Manufacturing
control in, 213
costs and, 103–104
global, 165–175
need for, 68
standardization in tools, 56–61
strategic implications of, 89–91

Production and inventory control, MRP II and, 459

Production and Inventory Control Handbook, The, 447

Production and Operations Society, 1

Production/operations management (POM), 187

Production plans, MRP II and, 457–458

Production policy, for service operations management, 491

Production schedules
as global life cycle factor, 168
MRP and, 430
MRP II and, 458

Production supervision, MRP II and, 459

Production systems

background of, 152–154
conflicting manufacturing tasks in, 112

Production techniques, as global life cycle factor, 168

Productivity, 341–343. *See also* Scientific Management; Taylor, Frederick W.; *See also* Time and Motion Studies
application of, 342
assessing, 472
behavioral aspect of, 341
bills of material and, 427–453
capital investment and, 475–477
computer uses for, 481–482
confusion reduction and, 479–480
differential piecework rate system for, 344–368
learning and, 480–481
management ideal and, 144
as measure of success, 105–109
MRP and, 429–453
quality and, 231–247
reasons for, 471–487
research in, 162–163
studies in, 342
in U.S., 461–462
waste reduction and, 477

"Productivity: Learning from the Japanese," 341

Productivity growth
of labor, 132, 133
slowdown in American, 132–136

"Productivity Paradox, The" (Skinner), 342, 461–469

Product life
as global life cycle factor, 168
for major appliances, 333

Product orientation, of MRP, 429

Product quality
consumerism and, 249–275
cost of service and, 255
government regulation and, 270–275
independent laboratory mark for, 264–266
industry leadership in, 259–263

Products
aesthetics of, 334–335
conformance of, 330–331, 332
durability of, 331–333

economic control of quality for, 191–214
features of, 329–330
perceived quality of, 335
proliferation of, 108–109
reliability of, 330
serviceability of, 333–334
Product volumes, 105
Professionalism, in factory, 107–108
Profit centers, dependence on, 136
Profits, scientific management and, 8
Profit sharing, 353–354
Programming, manufacturing and, 95–96
Pseudo-bills of material, 449–451
Pseudo-professionalism, 144–145
Psychologist, cooperation with, 66
Punishments, 360
Purchasing, MRP II and, 459
Pure service, 493, 494

Quality, 187–339
basic processes of, 281
classic contributors to, 187–190
competing on eight dimensions of, 323–339
consumerism and product, 249–275
control in, 191–205
cost correlation with, 235
costs and, 465
defined, 205–207
Deming on, 231–247. See also Deming, W. Edwards
detection of lack of control in, 211–212
and finance, 280
government regulation and, 270–275
guarantees of, 264–270
Japan and, 187
levels of, 105
manufacturing strategy and, 126
misrepresentation of, 251–252
as performance criterion, 121
strategic errors in, 337–338
uniform, 204–205
Quality circles, 168
Quality control, 278, 279, 281
applications of, 300
benefits of modern, 304–305
budget for, 117–118
defined, 295–297
Garvin on, 323–327
introducing program of, 304
organization for, 303–304
origins of interest in, 294–295
research in, 162
in service industries, 236–237
statistics and, 300–302
technical methods for, 302
TQC and, 168
Quality control engineering, 312
inspection and test for, 315
Quality Control Handbook (Juran), 188, 324
Quality Control Principles, Practice, and Administration (Feigenbaum), 188, 289–306
Quality control program, defined, 297–299
Quality improvement, 278, 279, 281
Quality is Free (Crosby), 188
Quality planning, 278, 279, 281
Quality process, priorities for, 282
Quality Progress (Juran), 188
"Quality Trilogy, The" (Juran), 277–287
Quantity
benefits from, 203–204
and quality, in work, 14
Quasimanufacturing, service systems as, 493, 494

Railroads, applying Scientific Management to, 369–375
Randers, J., 163n
Rate fixing, Taylor on, 355–358, 362–363
Rates, piecework and, 344–345
Raw material, control in purchase of, 213–214
"Reflecting Corporate Strategy in Manufacturing Decisions," 115–128
Regulation, quality and, 270–275
Rejections, reductions of costs, 203
Reliability, of products, 330
Reliability engineering, 325
Repetitive motion, 77–78
Research. See also Classic contributors

control in, 212–213
exploratory, 1–3
follow-up, 3–5
in manufacturing systems, 156–160
projects for, 155–156
in service systems, 160–162
Research and development (R&D)
expenditures on, 132, 134, 135
global views of, 174
"Research in Operations Management"
(Buffa), 151–163
Resources, quality and, 286
Return on investment (ROI)
for performance evaluation, 136
short-term increases in, 140
Rewards, 354, 359–360
Ricardo, 168
ROI. *See* Return on investment
ROI-oriented control system, 139
Russell Sage Foundation, 54

Sampling tables, quality control and,
301
Sarin, Rakesh, 151n
Sasser, W. Earl, 494n, 499n, 500
Schedule, procurement and fabrication,
448–449
Schonberger, Richard J., 8
"Vital Elements of World-Class
Manufacturing, The," 177–181
School, shop as, 415
Schumpeter, Joseph, innovation and,
139
Science
efficiency units and, 52–53
and ethics, 51–52
"Science in Management for the One
Best Way to Do Work" (Gilbreth),
47–84
Scientific management
application of, 82–83
compared with previous techniques,
29–30
criticism of, 423–424
defined, 28
examples of application, 32–46
four principles of, 30–32
Gilbreth on, 47–83
haste and failures, 419
and initiative, 416–417
lack of strikes and, 419–420
principles of, 377–394
Taylor and, 23–46, 369–375,
405–421
value of, 420–421
Self-regulation, of industry, 262
Sellers, William, scientific management
and, 39–41
Semiconductor industry, U.S. vs.
Japanese chips in, 327–328
Service, creation of, 492
Serviceability, of products, 333–334
Service industries, 257–259
quality control in, 236–237
Service operations, facility costs and,
499
Service operations management,
488–500
Chase on, 491–500
high- vs. low-contact business in,
492–496
policy development for, 496–499
technical core of, 492–494
Service quality
government regulation and, 270–275
industry leadership in, 259–263
satisfaction and, 256–259
Service systems, research in, 160–162
Setting, task, 16–17
Shewhart, Walter A., 187
*Economic Control of Quality of Manu-
factured Product* (excerpt), 191–214
*Statistical Method from the Viewpoint
of Quality Control* (excerpt), 215–229
Shift scheduling, research in, 159–160
Shingo, Shigeo, 187
Shipping, global vs. domestic, 171–172
"Shop Management" (Taylor), 373, 381
Shops, as schools, 415
Shop work, mental work and, 69. *See
also* Tool studies
Shoveling, Taylor on, 395–397
SIC. *See* Standard Industrial Classifica-
tion (SIC) code
Sinclair, Upton, 343
criticism of Taylor, 423–424
Single-minute exchange of die (SMED),
188

Skill
  study of, 70–71
  transference of, 74
Skinner, Wickham, 7–8, 9, 115, 342,
  497n
  "Focused Factory, The," 101–114
  "Manufacturing—Missing Link in
  Corporate Strategy," 85–100
  "Productivity Paradox, The,"
  461–469
SMED. *See* Single-minute exchange of die
Smith, Adam, 49, 151
Society of Industrial Engineers, 69
SOM. *See* Strategic operations manage-
  ment
Sourcing, global, 169
Soviet Union, standardization in, 268
Special process studies, total quality con-
  trol and, 311, 314
Sprague, Linda, 155n
Springer, Julius, 192n
Staff, for implementing corporate strat-
  egy, 122–124
Standard Industrial Classification (SIC)
  code, service systems and, 492
Standardization, 17–18
  necessity of, 69–70
  quality and, 267
  tool studies and, 56–61
Standard knowledge, 17
Standards, for work, 54–56
Starr, Chauncey, 253n
Starr, Martin K., 8, 9, 175
  "Global Production and Operations
  Strategy," 165–175
Statistical control, 208–210
  evidence of process control and,
  239–243
  as operation, 222–225
  Shewhart on, 217–229
  state of, 221–222
*Statistical Method from the Viewpoint of
  Quality Control* (Deming), 187–188
*Statistical Method from the Viewpoint of
  Quality Control* (Shewhart), 215–229
Statistical theory, control and, 201–202
Statistics, and quality control, 300–302,
  309, 310
Status quo, reinforcing, 140–141

Steelcraft Division, of American Standard, 177
Steinway & Sons, 336
Stereochronocylegraph, 75
Stopwatch, time study and, 16–17
Strategic operations management
  (SOM), origins of, 7
Strategic planning, for manufacturing
  systems, 156–159
Strategic quality management, 327–335
  aesthetics and, 334–335
  conformance and, 331–333
  perceived quality and, 335
  performance and, 328–329
  product features and, 329–330
  reliability and, 330
  serviceability and, 333–334
Strategy
  for competitive manufacturing,
  466–469
  in manufacturing decisions, 115–128
  operations, 6–181
  production operations and, 89–91
Strikes, scientific management and,
  419–420. *See also* Labor unions
"Structuring the Bill of Material for
  MRP" (Orlicky, Plossl, Wight),
  429–453
Super (S) bills, 449
Superstructure, bills of material as, 451
Supervision, improving, 243
Suppliers
  global, 173
  relationships with, 148
Supply, research in, 163
Surveys
  for efficiency, 54–56
  fatigue, 76–77
Suzuki, Ryohei, 131n
Systematic management, age and origin
  of, 49–50. *See also* Scientific manage-
  ment
Systems design, in manufacturing, 91,
  95–96

Taguchi, Genichi, 188, 331
Takeuchi, H., 341, 487
Tandem Computers, 336
Task(s), 13

introducing, 21
manufacturing, 7
setting for, 16–17
standardization and, 17–18
Task and bonus system, 13–22
cooperation in, 19–20
day work, piecework, and, 19
helps in, 18–19
obstacles to, 18
Task work, Gantt on, 12
Taxation, waste and, 82
Taylor, Frederick W., 7, 9, 12, 49,
72–73, 151, 341, 466. *See also* Productivity
answer to criticism by, 424–427
criticized by Sinclair, 423–424
family background of, 370–372
"Gospel of Efficiency, The. The Prin-
ciples of Scientific Management,"
377–421
"Gospel of Efficiency II, The. The
Principles of Scientific Management,"
395–402
"Gospel of Efficiency III, The. The
Principles of Scientific Management,"
405–421
"Piece-Rate System, A, Being a Step
Toward Partial Solution of the Labor
Problem," 345–368
"Principles of Scientific Management,
The," 23–46
"Taylor, Frederick W.—Scientist in Busi-
ness Management" (Baker), 369–375
Taylor Society, 69
Technical dominance, 93–96
Technical education, 14
Technology
change as global life cycle factor, 168
decline of American growth, 132–136
European and Japanese management
and, 147, 148
global effects of, 173–175
investments in, 465
management and, 144–145
manufacturing research and, 156–158
process, 105
shifts in, 140
Testing, quality control and, 312
Textile industry, speed in, 355

Thomas, D.R., 500
Thompson, James D., 490n
Thompson, Sanford E., 375
Thought, habits of, 14
Thurston, Robert H., 12
Time and Motion Studies, 341
Time study. *See also* Motion study; Time
and Motion Studies; Tool studies
chronocyclegraphs and, 75–76
development of, 72–73
fatigue study and, 76–80
and motion studies, 53, 55
secret, 73
Time Study man, 16
Tolerance, reduction in limits, 205
Tools, of manufacturing, 105
Tool studies, 56–61
Top-down manufacturing, 7
Total factor productivity (TFP)
approach, 473–474. *See also* Produc-
tivity
research methods and, 483–486
Total quality control (TQC), 168,
307–321, 324–325
cost accounting and, 310–311
Feigenbaum and, 188
function placement, 316–317
modern inspection view and,
309–310
results of, 317–321
statistical view and, 309, 310
world-class manufacturing and, 181
"Total Quality Control" (Feigenbaum),
188, 307–321
*Total Quality Control: Engineering and
Management* (Feigenbaum), 189
Towne, Henry R., 352–353
Toyota, 180
TQC. *See* Total quality control
Trade-offs
corporate strategy and, 120–121
in design and manufacturing, 91–93,
94–95
quality and, 336–337
Trades. *See* Scientific management
Training
improving, 243
as management function, 20
moral, 21–22

in new skills, 245
scientific management and, 44–45
in statistical methods, 245
task, instructor, and bonus method
of, 13
"Training Workmen in Habits of Industry and Cooperation" (Gantt), 11–22
Transference, of skill, 74
Transportation, global model of,
171–172
Transshipment, global model of,
171–172
Tsuda, Yoshikasu, 232
Tucker, Louis R., Jr., 175

Underwriters Laboratories (UL), product standards and, 264
United States. *See also* Japan
loss of leadership by, 129–149
management ideal in, 142–146
production in, 236
semiconductor chip industry in,
327–328

Value, economic, 148–149
Vendor schedules, MRP II and, 458
Venn Diagram, 342, 343
Vertical integration, corporate strategy
and, 120
"Vital Elements of World-Class Manu-
facturing, The" (Schonberger)
177–181
Vollman, Thomas, 487

Wages, increase in workers', 414–415
Wagnor, 487
Walsh, C.M., 206n
Waste
lack of cooperation and, 66
productivity and, 462–463
reducing, 232, 477
responsibility for, 81–82
Taylor on, 377
Wayne, Kenneth, 462n, 487
WCM. *See* World-class manufacturing
Western Electric. *See* Hawthorne studies
Wheelwright, Steven C., 8, 9
"Reflecting Corporate Strategy in
Manufacturing Decisions," 115–128

"Where Does the Customer Fit in a Service Operation?" (Chase), 491–500
Whitin, 487
"Why Some Factories Are More Productive Than Others" (Hayes and
Clark), 471–487, 471–487
Wight, Oliver W., 341, 429–453
"Effective Company Operation as
Never Before!," 455–459
WIP. *See* Work-in-process
Work
standards of, 245
systematizing and organizing, 54–56
Workers. *See also* Motion study; Productivity; Scientific management; Time
study
delays and, 78
fatigue and, 76–80
in gangs, 399–402
impact of productivity on, 399
motivating, 260
saving energies of, 397–399
self-selection of, 388–389
suitability to jobs, 390–393
task allotment to, 413
Work-in-process (WIP), 174
inventories, cutting, 477–478
Workmen, training of, 11–22
World-class manufacturing (WCM), 177
World War II, quality needs in, 187

Yale & Towne Manufacturing Co., 353

Zero defects, 245
at Martin Company, 325
Zero Defects Program (Crosby), 188
Zero quality control, 188
*Zero Quality Control: Source Inspection
and the Poka-yoke System* (Shingo),
188